Christopher B. Ansberry
Be Wise, My Son, and Make My Heart Glad

Beihefte zur Zeitschrift für die alttestamentliche Wissenschaft

Herausgegeben von
John Barton · Reinhard G. Kratz
Choon-Leong Seow · Markus Witte

Band 422

De Gruyter

Christopher B. Ansberry

Be Wise, My Son, and Make My Heart Glad

An Exploration of the Courtly Nature of the Book of Proverbs

De Gruyter

ISBN 978-3-11-024790-9

e-ISBN 978-3-11-024791-6

ISSN 0934-2575

Library of Congress Cataloging-in-Publication Data

Ansberry, Christopher B.
    Be wise, my son, and make my heart glad : an exploration of the courtly
nature of the book of Proverbs / Christopher B. Ansberry.
        p. cm. — (Beihefte zur Zeitschrift für die alttestamentliche Wissen-
schaft, ISSN 0934-2575 ; Bd. 422)
    Includes bibliographical references (p.   ) and indexes.
    ISBN 978-3-11-024790-9 (hardcover 23 × 15,5 : alk. paper)
    1. Bible. O.T. Proverbs — Criticism, interpretation, etc.   I. Title.
    BS1465.52.A57   2010
    223'.7066 — dc22

                                                            2010036858

Bibliographic information published by the Deutsche Nationalbibliothek

The Deutsche Nationalbibliothek lists this publication in the Deutsche
Nationalbibliografie; detailed bibliographic data are available in the Internet
at http://dnb.d-nb.de.

To Carolyn, my אֵשֶׁת־חַיִל

Forward

For many readers of Scripture the book of Proverbs is the favorite Old Testament book, in part because it offers short pithy counsel for every conceivable circumstance in life. However, for many the book is also a riddle, raising a host of questions concerning its addressee, purpose, structure and style. Readers can readily follow the flow of thought in the beginning (chapters 1-9) and at the end (chapters 30-31), but the heart of the book (chapters 10-29) appears on first sight to be a hodge-podge collection of short sayings, randomly arranged, and going nowhere. I used to imagine that under the sponsorship of the Israelite court scribes were sent throughout the land to listen to the people, to hear how they express themselves, particularly on lessons on life from everyday experience. Equipped with quill and sherds of pottery (ostraca) they would record the aphoristic wisdom they heard, drop the documents into a bag or bucket, and bring them to a central location, presumably in Jerusalem, where they were stored. At some point the ostraca in the containers from all over the country were dumped into one large container and then removed and read one by one, while a scribe recorded them serially. Admittedly we can see some stylistic structure in the book, which might suggest that when scribes read an emblematic (25:11-26:23), antithetical (28:1-29:27), or prohibitive (24:15-21, 28-29) proverb they set the sherd aside in a separate pile, later to be recorded as a group. Apart from these and a few other sequences of coherent proverbs, the collections seem frustratingly random. Since scholarly investigations of Proverbs have tended to focus on the literary disjunctions within the book, the riddles involving the book's nature, cohesion, and trajectory have not often been addressed.

When investigating the wide range of literature that makes up our sacred Scriptures (the Hebrew Bible and the New Testament) interpreters must answer three questions: (1) The text-critical question: What does the text say? (2) The hermeneutical question: What did the text mean to the first readers (the original horizon)? (3) The practical question: What does/should the text mean to me (the contemporary horizon)? However, there is a fourth that is equally critical in the interpretive enterprise, namely the literary and rhetorical question: Why does it say it like that? With regard to Proverbs, the answers to the last question may derive from the conceptual and literary world out of which the book emerged and to which it spoke, from distinctive Israelite literary conventions, or from the agenda that biblical authors have set for themselves.

In this volume Christopher Ansberry has paid particular attention to the last question. With skill and care he has explored the sapiential world of the ancient Near East and has recognized—as have many before him—that Proverbs fits into that intellectual environment. However, the particular value of his work will be seen in his exploration of how the book works as a coherent whole. Building on the work of predecessors, he acknowledges the disjunctions within the book and the distinctive characteristics of each part. Nevertheless, he argues convincingly that the respective parts are intentionally shaped and arranged to reflect the pedagogical agenda of preparing a noble youth of the court for responsible leadership within the community. However, the focus is not on the youth's administrative duties, nor on giving him the skills needed for administration, but to create for him a moral vision grounded in the fear of YHWH and governed by righteousness.

In addition to arguing convincingly for the literary coherence of the book of Proverbs, perhaps the author's most significant contribution is his demonstration that the moral vision of wisdom in ancient Israel is part and parcel of the theological conceptual world of the Old Testament, and that we need no longer view Israelite wisdom as outside the main stream of biblical theology. As the author declares in his concluding sentence, "The book of Proverbs presents a portrait of concrete Israelite piety; it plays a vital role in describing what the fear of YHWH and practical righteousness look like, especially in the lives of those who govern the people of YHWH." While this conclusion will no doubt provoke a good deal of scholarly and lay discussion, many will thank him for giving them back the *book* of Proverbs. We should not be surprised that as a wisdom composition, the whole actually makes sense.

Daniel I. Block, D.Phil.
Gunther H. Knoedler Professor of Old Testament
Wheaton College

Table of Contents

Acknowledgement

This study represents a revised version of my 2009 Wheaton College dissertation. The work could not have been accomplished without the support of many. To begin, I would like to thank the Taylor Fellowship Providers, whose financial patronage facilitated the preparation of this thesis and supplied the means to study at Wheaton. I cannot adequately express the great debt of gratitude that I owe for their kindness and generosity. I would also like to thank the editors of BZAW for accepting the manuscript and providing invaluable feedback on the original version of the thesis; their comments have strengthened the present work and sharpened the fundamental argument of the piece. Among the staff at Walter de Gruyter, I am grateful for the assistance of Dr. Albrecht Döhnert. Dr. Döhnert guided me through the publication process, provided extensive assistance in formatting the text, and supervised the production of the monograph.

The practical assistance of the faculty in the Department of Biblical and Theological Studies at Wheaton College also deserves acknowledgement; their passion for scholarship and excellence has shaped my understanding of the scriptures and equipped me with the skills necessary for the study of ancient texts. In particular, I am grateful to Dr. C. Hassell Bullock, who introduced me to the treasures of the wisdom literature and inspired my interest in Israel's sapiential tradition. Dr. James K. Hoffmeier's (Trinity Evangelical Divinity School) instruction in hieroglyphs and special attention to Egyptian matters related to my research was also of particular significance. In addition, my external examiner, Rev. Dr. Knut M. Heim, provided invaluable advice concerning the content and argumentation of an earlier draft. His wisdom and perceptive comments have contributed significantly to the present work.

Together with the faculty of Wheaton College, I wish to thank my colleagues for their support in this enterprise. Their partnership and camaraderie provided a respite from the mundane demands of study as well as a fresh perspective on my idiosyncratic ideas.

However, among those who have influenced my intellectual and spiritual life, I owe a special debt of gratitude to my *Doktorvater*, Daniel I. Block. Professor Block's practical suggestions and constructive criticism concerning the direction of the thesis were of inestimable value. His expressions of encouragement and prudent guidance enabled me to complete this study, and his selfless leadership provided me with a model of an exemplary scholar, teacher, and husband. Though Dr. Block is not responsible for the opinions that I have expressed, or for any errors that I have made, the present project is the result of his devoted supervision.

Above all, my dear wife, Carolyn, deserves whatever merit this study may claim. Over the course of the last few years, she managed the basic details of our life, created innumerable opportunities for me to focus on this project, and endured a husband whose mind was often preoccupied with the intricacies of this thesis. She served as my muse, a source of inspiration and a gracious participant in this enterprise. Her ardent support, consistent encouragement, and sacrificial service proved invaluable. Without her partnership the completion of this work would not have been possible.

Christopher Ansberry
August 2010

Abbreviations

AB	Anchor Bible
ABD	*Anchor Bible Dictionary*
ABRL	Anchor Bible Reference Library
AEL	*Ancient Egyptian Literature: A Book of Readings.* M. Lichtheim. 3 vols. Berkeley: University of California, 1973–80. Repr., 2006
ÄgAbh	Ägyptologische Abhandlungen
AnBib	Analecta biblica
AOAT	Alter Orient und Altes Testament
ArBib	The Aramaic Bible
ATA	Alttestamentliche Abhandlungen
ATD	Das Alte Testament Deutsch
AzTh	Arbeiten zur Theologie
BA	*Biblical Archaeologist*
BASOR	*Bulletin of the American Schools of Oriental Research*
BBET	Beiträge zur biblischen Exegese und Theologie
b. B. Qam.	*Babylonian (Talmud) Baba Qamma*
b. Hul.	*Babylonian (Talmud) Hullin*
BETL	Bibliotheca ephemeridum theologicarum lovaniensium
BHQ	*Biblia Hebraica Quinta.* Edited by A. Schenker, Y. A. P. Goldman, A. van der Kooij, G. J. Norton, S. Pisano, J. de Waard, and R. D. Weis. Stuttgart, 2008. *Proverbs* prepared by Jan de Waard
BHS	*Biblia Hebraica Stuttgartensia.* Edited by K. Elliger and W. Rudoph. Stuttgart, 1983. *Proverbia* prepared by J. Fichtner
BHT	Beiträge zur historischen Theologie
Bib	*Biblica*
BiBh	*Bible Bhashyam*
BKAT	Biblischer Kommentar: Altes Testament
BSac	*Bibliotheca sacra*
BTB	*Biblical Theology Bulletin*
BWANT	Beiträge zur Wissenschaft vom Alten und Neuen Testament
BWL	*Babylonian Wisdom Literature.* W. G. Lambert. Oxford: Oxford University Press, 1960. Repr., Winona Lake: Eisenbrauns, 1996
BZAW	Beihefte zur Zeitschrift für die alttestamentliche Wissenschaft

CANE   *Civilizations of the Ancient Near East.* Edited by J. Sasson. 4 vols.
                New York: Charles Scribner's Sons. Repr., 2 vols. Peabody:
                Hendrickson, 2006
CBQ   *Catholic Biblical Quarterly*
CBQMS   Catholic Biblical Quarterly Monograph Series
ConBOT   Coniectanea biblica: Old Testament Series
COS   *The Context of Scripture.* Edited by W. W. Hallo. 3 vols. Leiden:
                Brill, 2003
ExpTim   *Expository Times*
FAT   Forschungen zum Alten Testament
FB   Forschung zur Bibel
FOTL   Forms of the Old Testament Literature
Gen. Rab.   *Genesis Rabbah*
GKC   *Gesenius' Hebrew Grammar.* Edited by E. Kautzsch. Translated
                by A. E. Cowley. 2nd ed. Oxford: Clarendon, 1910
HALOT   Koehler, L., W. Baumgartner, and J. J. Stamm, *The Hebrew and
                Aramaic Lexicon of the Old Testament.* Translated and edited
                under the supervision of M. E. J. Richardson. 4 vols. Leiden:
                Brill, 1994–1999
HAT   Handbuch zum Alten Testament
HS   *Hebrew Studies*
HSM   Harvard Semitic Monographs
HTR   *Harvard Theological Review*
HUCA   *Hebrew Union College Annual*
IBC   Interpretation: A Bible Commentary for Teaching and
                Preaching.
Int   *Interpretation*
JAAR   *Journal of the American Academy of Religion*
JANES   *Journal of the Ancient Near Eastern Society of Columbia University*
JARCE   *Journal of the American Research Center in Egypt*
JAOS   *Journal of the American Oriental Society*
JBL   *Journal of Biblical Literature*
JEA   *Journal of Egyptian Archaeology*
JETS   *Journal of the Evangelical Theological Society*
JHNES   Johns Hopkins Near Eastern Studies
JNES   *Journal of Near Eastern Studies*
JNSL   *Journal of Northwest Semitic Languages*
JQR   *Jewish Quarterly Review*
JSOT   *Journal for the Study of the Old Testament*
JSOTSup   Journal for the Study of the Old Testament: Supplement Series
LÄ   *Lexikon der Ägyptologie.* Edited by W. Helck, E. Otto, and W.
                Westendorf. Wiesbaden, 1972

LAE	*Literature of Ancient Egypt.* W. K. Simpson. New Haven: Yale University Press, 2003
LD	Lectio divina
LUÅ	Lunds universitets årsskrift
LXX	Septuagint
MT	Masoretic Text
NAC	New American Commentary
NASB	New American Standard Bible
NCB	New Century Bible
NIB	*The New Interpreter's Bible*
NICOT	New International Commentary on the Old Testament
NIDOTTE	*New International Dictionary of Old Testament Theology and Exegesis.* Edited by W. A. VanGemeren. 5 vols. Grand Rapids: Zondervan, 1997
NIV	New International Version
NIVAC	The NIV Application Commentary
OBO	Orbis biblicus et orientalis
Or	*Orientalia (NS)*
OrAnt	*Oriens antiquus*
OTL	Old Testament Library
OTP	*Old Testament Pseudepigrapha.* Edited by J. H. Charlesworth. 2 vols. New Haven, 2007
OTS	Old Testament Studies
OtSt	Oudtestamentische Studiën
QR	*Quarterly Review*
RevistB	*Revista bíblica*
RB	*Revue biblique*
RIME	The Royal Inscriptions of Mesopotamia: Early Periods
SAA	State Archives of Assyria
SAAB	*State Archives of Assyria Bulletin*
SANT	Studien zum Alten und Neuen Testaments
SAOC	Studies in Ancient Oriental Civilizations
SB	Sources bibliques
SBLDS	Society of Biblical Literature Dissertation Series
SBLSymS	Society of Biblical Literature Symposium Series
SBLWAW	Society of Biblical Literature Writings from the Ancient World
SBS	Stuttgarter Bibelstudien
SBT	Studies in Biblical Theology
SJOT	*Scandinavian Journal of the Old Testament*
SJT	*Scottish Journal of Theology*
SOTSMS	Society for Old Testament Studies Monograph Series
SPAW	*Sitzungsberichte der preussischen Akademie der Wissenschaften zu Berlin*

Sym.	Symmachus
Syr.	Syriac Version (Peshitta)
Targ.	*The Targum of Proverbs.* Translated by J. F. Healey. The Aramaic Bible 15. Edinburgh: T&T Clark, 1991
TB	Theologische Bücherei: Neudrucke und Berichte aus dem 20. Jahrhundert
TDOT	*Theological Dictionary of the Old Testament.* Edited by G. J. Botterweck and H. Ringgren. Translated by J. T. Willis, G. W. Bromiley, and D. E. Green. 12 vols. Grand Rapids: Eerdmans, 1974–2001.
TLOT	*Theological Lexicon of the Old Testament.* Edited by E. Jenni, with assistance from C. Westermann. Translated by M. E. Biddle. 3 vols. Peabody: Hendrickson, 1997
TLZ	*Theologische Literaturzeitung*
TWOT	*Theological Wordbook of the Old Testament.* Edited by R. L. Harris, G. L. Archer Jr. 2 vols. Chicago, 1980
TynBul	*Tyndale Bulletin*
UF	*Ugarit-Forschungen*
USQR	*Union Seminary Quarterly Review*
VT	*Vetus Testamentum*
VTSup	Supplements to Vetus Testamentum
Vulg.	Vulgate
WBC	Word Biblical Commentary
WMANT	Wissenschaftliche Monographien zum Alten und Neuen Testament
WO	*Die Welt des Orients*
ZA	*Zeitschrift für Assyriologie*
ZAH	*Zeitschrift für Althebräistik*
ZÄS	*Zeitschrift für ägyptische Sprache und Altertumskunde*
ZAW	*Zeitschrift für die alttestamentliche Wissenschaft*
ZBK	Zürcher Bibelkommentare

Chapter 1

Introduction

Any attempt to provide some social and historical background
to Proverbs is fraught with peril.
—L. G. Perdue, "Wisdom Theology and Social History"

The social and intellectual context of the material in the book of Proverbs
continues to be debated by Old Testament scholars. Investigations devoted to the
multifaceted character of the sapiential material have given rise to several
proposals concerning the nature of the constituent compendia within the
document as well as the function of the discourse as a whole. In general, the book
of Proverbs represents a collection of Israel's sapiential lore, produced by distinct
social groups in various locations and then assembled, augmented, and edited by
a group of scribes to provide a complex compendium of wisdom. This notion is
confirmed by the formal and thematic features of the piece. On the one hand, the
book includes popular themes that belong to everyday life and promotes an
ethical vision that reflects the ethos of the people. On the other hand, the
collections contain aristocratic elements that seem to "speak not only *about* kings
and courtiers, but also *to* them and *for* them."[1] Moreover, in contrast to the
traditional sayings that punctuate the constitutional, narratival, and prophetic
texts of the Old Testament, the paronomastic structure, refined form, and
consistent terminology of the aphorisms in the work evince a degree of literary
sophistication. In view of the diverse nature of the sapiential material, scholars
have offered several proposals concerning the social setting of the work, ranging
the world of the simple, rural folk to formal schools or guilds associated with the
royal court. These distinct settings address the compositional history of the

---

1   M. V. Fox, "The Social Location of the Book of Proverbs," in *Texts, Temples, and Traditions: A
    Tribute to Menahem Haran* (ed. M. V. Fox et al.; Winona Lake: Eisenbrauns, 1996), 235, emphasis
    original. Also see H. Duesberg and I. Franzen, *Les scribes inspirés* (2nd ed; Paris: Maredsous, 1966),
    99–176; H.-J. Hermisson, *Studien zur israelitischen Spruchweisheit* (WMANT 28; Neukirchen-Vluyn:
    Neukirchener Verlag, 1968), 97–136; G. von Rad, *Weisheit in Israel* (Neukirchen-Vluyn:
    Neukirchener Verlag, 1970), 28–29; ET, *Wisdom in Israel* (trans. J. D. Martin; London: SCM
    Press, 1972), 15.

material, the variegated concerns that pervade the piece, and the formal texture of the collections. In so doing, these studies highlight the intrinsic difficulties involved in any exploration of the nature and function of the book of Proverbs.

The character of the book of Proverbs poses a problem for an investigation of the nature and function of the work. In essence, proverbs are situationally oriented, open-ended sayings that cut across social barriers and remain relevant to a wide variety of people.[2] The original context of a saying or discourse unit within a collection is usually irrecoverable, and the content of the material cannot provide an absolute indication of its origin.[3] The setting of the sapiential material is made clear only when it is explored within a performance context, that is, in a particular social or dialogical situation that creates a framework through which to identify the function and significance of the discourse.[4] Performance analysis is most problematic in the book of Proverbs, however, for the material has been removed from its original context(s) of use and assembled into an anthology. This loss of a live cultural context has produced a hermeneutical lacuna that has been filled by comparative and thematic analyses in order to determine the nature and function of the work.

1.1 Modern Proposals Concerning the Nature and Function of the Book of Proverbs

In general, comparative studies have identified two distinct settings within the book of Proverbs. The first is among schools or guilds associated with the royal

---

2   R. E. Murphy, "Form Criticism and Wisdom Literature," *CBQ* 31 (1969): 483; W. P. Brown, *Character in Crisis: A Fresh Approach to the Wisdom Literature of the Old Testament* (Grand Rapids: Eerdmans, 1996), 14.

3   C. R. Fontaine, *Traditional Sayings in the Old Testament* (Bible and Literature Series 5; Sheffield: Almond Press, 1982), 12–13; idem, "Proverb Performance in the Hebrew Bible," *JSOT* 32 (1985): 94; K. F. D. Römheld, *Die Weisheitlehre im Alten Orient: Elemente einer Formgeschichte* (Biblische Notizen-Beiheft 4; München: Manfred Görg, 1989), 3; R. E. Murphy, *The Tree of Life: An Exploration of Biblical Wisdom Literature* (3rd ed.; Grand Rapids: Eerdmans, 2002), 4.

4   For folkloric and biblical studies devoted to "proverb performance," see R. Firth, "Proverbs in Native Life, with Particular Reference to Those of the Maori," *Folk-Lore* 37 (1926): 134; P. Seitel, "Proverbs: A Social Use of Metaphor," in *Folklore Genres* (ed. D. Ben-Amos; Austin: University of Texas Press, 1976), 125–43; B. Kirshenblatt-Gimblett, "Toward a Theory of Proverb Meaning," *Proverbium* 22 (1973): 821–27; repr. in *The Wisdom of Many: Essays on the Proverb* (ed. W. Mieder and A. Dundes; New York: Garland, 1981), 111–21; Fontaine, *Traditional Sayings*, 55, *et passim*; idem, "Proverb Performance in the Hebrew Bible," 87–103; idem, *Smooth Words: Women, Proverbs and Performance in Biblical Wisdom* (JSOTSup 356; Sheffield: Sheffield Academic Press, 2002); M. V. Fox, "Wisdom and the Self-Presentation of Wisdom Literature," in *Reading from Right to Left: Essays on the Hebrew Bible in Honour of David J. A. Clines* (Sheffield: Sheffield Academic, 2003), 153–72.

court. In view of the formal and thematic similarities between ancient oriental instructional texts and the book of Proverbs, many situate the material within the international tradition of wisdom literature. That is, they incorporate Near Eastern didactic works to illuminate the nature and function of the material in Proverbs. This has produced a virtual consensus that Proverbs was a standard "textbook" composed by a professional group of "wise men" within administrative circles to meet the educational needs of the bureaucracy.[5] However, in spite of the international flavor of Proverbs, these "assured results" have been reexamined and challenged.[6] Though formal schools existed in ancient Egypt and Mesopotamia to inculcate traditional values and prepare future generations for scribal or bureaucratic service,[7] biblical and epigraphic evidence

---

5　A. Klostermann, "Schulwesen im alten Israel," in *Theologische Studien, Theodor Zahn* (ed. N. Bonwetsch; Leipzig: Deichert, 1908), 193–232; H. Gressmann, "Die neugefundene Lehre des Amenemope und die vorexilische Spruchdichtung Israels," *ZAW* 42 (1924): 272–96; L. B. Dürr, *Das Erziehungswesen im Alten Testament und im antiken Orient* (Leipzig: J. C. Hinrichs, 1932); G. von Rad, "Der Anfang der Geschichtsschreibung im alten Israel," in *Gesammelte Studien zum Alten Testament* (TB 8; München: Chr. Kaiser, 1958), 187–88; idem, *Weisheit in Israel*, 28–32; U. Skladny, *Die ältesten Spruchsammlungen in Israel* (Göttingen: Vandenhoeck & Ruprecht, 1962), 45–61; W. Richter, *Recht und Ethos: Versuch einer Ortung des weisheitlichen Mahnspruches* (SANT 15; München: Kösel, 1966); 183; H.-J. Hermisson, *Studien zur israelitischen Spruchweisheit*, 36, 188; W. McKane, *Proverbs: A New Approach* (OTL; Philadelphia: Westminster, 1970), 8–9; T. N. D. Mettinger, *Solomonic State Officials: A Study of the Civil Government Officials of the Israelite Monarchy* (ConBOT 5; Lund: Gleerup, 1971); J. P. J. Olivier, "Schools and Wisdom Literature," *JNES* 4 (1975): 49–60; B. Lang, *Wie wird man Prophet in Israel? Aufsätze* (Düsseldorf: Patmos, 1980), 104–19; idem, *Wisdom and the Book of Proverbs: A Hebrew Goddess Redefined* (New York: The Pilgrim Press, 1986), 10; M. Fishbane, *Biblical Interpretation in Ancient Israel* (Oxford: Clarendon, 1985), 24–33; N. Shupak, "The 'Sitz Im Leben' of the Book of Proverbs in the Light of a Comparison of Biblical and Egyptian Wisdom Literature," *RB* 94 (1987): 98–119; idem, *Where Can Wisdom Be Found? The Sage's Language in the Bible and in Ancient Egyptian Literature* (OBO 130; Göttingen: Vandenhoeck & Ruprecht, 1993), 339–40; A. Lemaire, "The Sage in School and Temple," in *The Sage in Israel and the Ancient Near East* (ed. J. G. Gammie and L. G. Perdue; Winona Lake: Eisenbrauns, 1990), 165–81; R. J. Clifford, "The Community of the Book of Proverbs," in *Constituting the Community: Studies on the Polity of Ancient Israel in Honor of S. Dean McBride Jr.* (ed. J. T. Strong and S. S. Tuell; Winona Lake: Eisenbrauns, 2005), 281–93.

6　See S. Weeks, *Early Israelite Wisdom* (Oxford Monograph Series; Oxford: Oxford University Press, 1994).

7　C. J. Gadd, *Teachers and Students in the Oldest Schools* (London: University of London, 1956); S. N. Kramer, *The Sumerians: Their History, Culture, and Character* (Chicago: The University of Chicago Press, 1971), 224–45; Å. W. Sjöberg, "The Old Babylonian Eduba," in *Sumerological Studies in Honor of Thorkild Jacobsen on His Seventieth Birthday* (ed. S. J. Lieberman; Chicago: The University of Chicago Press, 1976), 159–79; P. Michalowski, "Charisma and Control: On Continuity and Change in Early Mesopotamian Bureaucratic Systems," in *The Organization of Power: Aspects of Bureaucracy in the Ancient Near East* (ed. M. Gibson and R. D. Biggs; Chicago: The Oriental Institute of the University of Chicago, 1987), 55–68; E. F. Wente, "The Scribes of Ancient Egypt," *CANE* 4:2211–21; J. L. Crenshaw, *Education in Ancient Israel: Across the Deadening Silence* (ABRL; New York: Doubleday, 1998); J. Assmann, *The Mind of Egypt: History and Meaning in the*

for a professional class of wise men and a formal, integrated school system within ancient Israel remains inferential.[8] Moreover, the book's limited concern with the specific responsibilities of the royal institution, coupled with the general, conventional themes that pervade the work, seems to suggest that Proverbs represents a haphazard repository of traditional banalities that are accessible to a large sociological range of individuals. While the book expresses interest in matters pertaining to the royal establishment and contains editorial designations that associate particular compilations with the court (25:1), these features do not provide sufficient evidence for the composition or redaction of the material in or for the royal court.[9] The book of Proverbs bears witness to Israel's intellectual involvement in the international phenomenon of wisdom literature; however, strict social analogies cannot be drawn between Near Eastern works and the book of Proverbs to illuminate the nature and function of the work.[10]

In contrast to the court/school setting, social and anthropological studies situate the production of the sapiential material within a plebeian context, that is, as the oral creation of the simple folk.[11] These studies assume the material arose

---

  Time of the Pharaohs (trans. A. Jenkins; New York: Holt, 2002), 123–27; D. M. Carr, *Writing on the Tablet of the Heart: Origins of Scripture and Literature* (Oxford: Oxford University Press, 2005), 17–109.

8 R. E. Murphy, "Assumptions and Problems in Old Testament Wisdom Research," *CBQ* 29 (1967): 101–12; B. W. Kovacs, "Is There a Class-Ethic in Proverbs?" in *Essays in Old Testament Ethics* (ed. J. L. Crenshaw and J. T. Willis; New York: Ktav, 1974), 179–87; R. N. Whybray, *The Intellectual Tradition in the Old Testament* (BZAW 135; Berlin: de Gruyter, 1974), 15–31; Weeks, *Early Israelite Wisdom*, 74–91, 132–56. The general consensus among these scholars is that there is no reference to a professional class of wise men in ancient Israel and that education took place either in the domestic unit or within an apprentice model at the home of the master/teacher, who may not have been the biological parent of the student. For further discussion, see below pp. 36–45.

9 Weeks, *Early Israelite Wisdom*, 55–56.

10 Weeks, *Early Israelite Wisdom*, 18–19.

11 See O. Eissfeldt, *Der Maschal im Alten Testament* (BZAW 24; Giessen: Töpelmann, 1913); Scott, R. B. Y. "Folk Proverbs of the Ancient Near East," *Transactions of the Royal Society of Canada* 55 (1961): 47–56; C. Westermann, "Weisheit im Sprichwort," in *Schalom. Studien zu Glaube und Geschichte Israels. Alfred Jepsen zum 70. Geburtstag* (ed. K.-H. Bernhardt; Stuttgart: Calwer Verlag, 1971), 73–85; idem, *Roots of Wisdom: The Oldest Proverbs of Israel and Other Peoples* (trans. J. D. Charles; Louisville: Westminster John Knox, 1995), 2, *et passim*; L. Naré, *Proverbes salomoniens et proverbes mossi: etude comparative á partir d'une nouvelle analyse de Pr. 25–29* (Publications Universitaires Européennes 23; Frankfurt am Main: Peter Lang, 1986); R. N. Whybray, *Wealth and Poverty in the Book of Proverbs* (JSOTSup 99; Sheffield: JSOT, 1990), 73; F. W. Golka, *The Leopard's Spots: Biblical and African Wisdom in Proverbs* (Edinburgh: T&T Clark, 1993), 14–15, *et passim*; H. C. Washington, *Wealth and Poverty in the Instruction of Amenemope and the Hebrew Proverbs* (SBLDS 142; Atlanta: Scholars Press, 1994), 179; Dell, *The Book of Proverbs in Social and Theological Context* (Cambridge: Cambridge University Press, 2006), 63–64; L. P. Kimilike, *Poverty in the Book of Proverbs: An African Transformational Hermeneutic of Proverbs on Poverty* (Bible and Theology in Africa 7; New York: Peter Lang, 2008), 26, *et passim*.

in oral form within a pre-literate society before its modification and incorporation into the book of Proverbs. Several features within the book reinforce this conclusion. The constituent collections in Proverbs include various sayings that assume a rural, familial, or agricultural background. Moreover, several aphorisms address topics or themes that resemble the proverbial lore of primitive tribal cultures. Similar to those who postulate a court or school setting, anthropological investigations situate the formation of Israel's sapiential lore within a specific context, viz., a pre-literate stage of social development common to many societies. In light of the general character of the collections, it seems reasonable to assume a popular background for some of the material. However, this social setting does not account for the diverse nature of the material as a whole. As noted above, the paronomastic structure and refined form of the aphorisms in the book of Proverbs seems to oppose the notion that the material arose in a popular, folk setting.[12] In addition, while proverbs from primitive tribal cultures address subjects and themes that are comparable to the sayings in the book of Proverbs, these materials bear little formal resemblance to Israelite aphorisms.[13] The comparative material provides an important distinction between the oral and written stages of production; it serves as a heuristic framework within which to investigate the nature of aphoristic speech and the formal development of the material. Nonetheless, the folk setting does not necessarily establish the origin of a proverb or provide an adequate context for the sapiential material as a whole.

In view of the limitations associated with the court/school and family/folk settings, many scholars have moved to a thematic analysis of the material to identify the nature and function of the constituent compendia within the book. These investigations focus on the formal characteristics, thematic emphases, and distinct concerns of each compilation. Similar to comparative explorations, this form of analysis has produced various conclusions, each of which coincides with the social settings delineated above. On the one hand, several studies suggest that the formal and thematic features of certain collections strongly intimate a courtly context. This is apparent in the prologue (1:8–9:18),[14] the latter half of the first

---

12 See Kovacs, "Is There a Class-Ethic in Proverbs?," 177; L. Boström, *The God of the Sages: The Portrayal of God in the Book of Proverbs* (ConBOT 29; Stockholm: Almqvist & Wiksell International, 1990), 7.

13 Fox, "The Social Location of the Book of Proverbs," 233–37; J. A. Loader, "Wisdom by (the) People for (the) People," *ZAW* 111 (1999): 213–22; T. J. Sandoval, *The Discourse of Wealth and Poverty in the Book of Proverbs* (Biblical Interpretation Series 77; Leiden: Brill, 2006), 37.

14 Whybray, *Wealth and Poverty in the Book of Proverbs*, 114; idem, "City Life in Proverbs 1–9," in *"Jedes Ding hat seine Zeit...": Studien zur israelitischen und altorientalischen Weisheit* (ed. O. Kaiser; New York: Walter de Gruyter, 1996), 243–50; J. L. Crenshaw, "The Sage in Proverbs," in *The Sage in Israel and the Ancient Near East* (ed. J. G. Gammie and L. G. Perdue; Winona Lake: Eisenbrauns, 1990), 211–12; idem, "The Contemplative Life in the Ancient Near East," in *Civilizations of the Ancient Near East* (ed. J. M. Sasson; Peabody: Hendrickson, 2006), 2450; C. R. Yoder, *Wisdom as a*

Solomonic collection (16:1–22:16),[15] the reputed Amenemope section (22:17–24:34),[16] the second Solomonic collection (25:1–29:27),[17] the royal instruction (31:1–9), and the heroic panegyric (31:10–31).[18] On the other hand, some scholars maintain that the constituent collections within the book contain a pastiche of traditional concerns that express the views of simple, rustic farmers.[19] Together, these thematic analyses reveal a fundamental tension in the sapiential material. The book of Proverbs constitutes a mosaic of Israel's sapiential lore; it

---

Woman of Substance: A Socioeconomic Reading of Proverbs 1–9 and 31:10–31 (BZAW 304; Berlin: Walter de Gruyter, 2001), 103; K. J. Dell, *The Book of Proverbs*, 195.

15   Skladny, *Die ältesten Spruchsammlungen in Israel*, 44–46; W. L. Humphreys, "The Motif of the Wise Courtier in the Book of Proverbs," in *Israelite Wisdom: Theological and Literary Essays in Honor of Samuel Terrien* (ed. W. A. Brueggemann et al.; Missoula: Scholars Press, 1978), 183; A. Lemaire, *Les écoles et la formation de la Bible dans l'ancien Israël* (OBO 39; Göttingen: Vandenhoeck & Ruprecht, 1981), 42; L. G. Perdue, *Wisdom Literature: A Theological History* (Louisville: Westminster John Knox, 2007), 44–45.

16   G. E. Bryce, *A Legacy of Wisdom: The Egyptian Contribution to the Wisdom of Israel* (Lewisburg: Bucknell University Press, 1979), 153; Whybray, *Wealth and Poverty in the Book of Proverbs*, 114; Dell, *The Book of Proverbs*, 195.

17   Humphreys, "The Motif of the Wise Courtier in the Book of Proverbs," 185; G. E. Bryce, "Another Wisdom-'Book' in Proverbs," *JBL* 91 (1972): 145–57; idem, *A Legacy of Wisdom*, 145–49; Lemaire, *Les écoles et la formation de la Bible dans l'ancien Israël*, 42; L. Alonso Schökel and J. Vilchez, *Proverbios* (Nueva Biblia Española. Sapienciales I; Madrid: Ediciones Cristiandad, 1984), 482; B. V. Malchow, "A Manual for Future Monarchs: Proverbs 27:23–29:27," *CBQ* 47 (1985): 238–45; repr. in *Learning from the Sages: Selected Studies on the Book of Proverbs* (ed. R. B. Zuck; Grand Rapids: Baker, 1995), 352–60; R. C. Van Leeuwen, *Context and Meaning in Proverbs 25–27* (SBLDS 96; Atlanta: Scholars Press, 1988), 72, *et passim*; A. Meinhold, *Die Sprüche, Teil 2: Sprüche Kapitel 16–31* (ZBK 16.2; Zürich: Theologischer Verlag, 1991), 415; J. Blenkinsopp, *Sage, Priest, Prophet: Religious and Intellectual Leadership in Ancient Israel* (Library of Ancient Israel; Louisville: Westminster John Knox, 1995), 33–36; D. Bergant, *Israel's Wisdom Literature: A Liberation-Critical Reading* (Minneapolis: Fortress, 1997), 101; Murphy, *The Tree of Life*, 22; Perdue, *Wisdom Literature: A Theological History*, 44–45; R. Tavares, *Eine königliche Weisheitslehre? Exegetische Analyse von Sprüche 28–29 und Vergleich mit den ägyptischen Lehren Merikaras und Amenemhats* (OBO 234; Göttingen: Vandenhoeck & Ruprecht, 2007).

18   A. Wolters, "Proverbs XXXI 10–31 as Heroic Hymn: A Form-Critical Analysis," *VT* 4 (1988): 446–57; repr. in *The Song of the Valiant Woman: Studies in the Interpretation of Proverbs 31:10–31* (Carlisle: Paternoster, 2001), 3–14; B. K. Waltke, "The Role of the 'Valiant Wife' in the Marketplace," *Crux* 35 (1999): 25; M. Beth Szlos, "A Portrait of Power: A Literary-Critical Study of the Depiction of the Woman in Proverbs 31:10–31," *USQR* 54 (2000): 103; Yoder, *Wisdom as a Woman of Substance*, 103.

19   In the main, these conclusions pertain to the material in the sentence literature (10:1–22:16; 25:1–29:27). For this proposal, see Skladny, *Die ältesten Spruchsammlungen in Israel*, 23, 56–57; R. N. Whybray, "The Social World of the Wisdom Writers," in *The World of Ancient Israel: Sociological, Anthropological and Political Perspectives* (ed. R. E. Clements; Cambridge: Cambridge University Press, 1989; repr., 1993), 234–35; idem, *Wealth and Poverty in the Book of Proverbs*, 114; idem, *The Composition of the Book of Proverbs* (JSOTSup 168; Sheffield: Sheffield Academic Press, 1994), 62. Also see Weeks, *Early Israelite Wisdom*, 41–56.

incorporates both popular and aristocratic concerns to form an inclusive moral vision that betrays both a strict court/school and family/folk setting. In conjunction with comparative analyses, thematic approaches have illuminated the multifaceted nature of the sapiential material. However, these investigations remain theoretical, for content alone cannot provide an absolute indication of origin.[20] Rather than drawing strict analogies with other Near Eastern societies or searching for the oral/literary origin of the material to determine its character, the discourse setting of the book of Proverbs may provide a more reliable indication of its nature and function. This form of analysis is significant, for discourse settings are comparable to proverb performance.[21] Similar to proverb performance, the discourse setting of Proverbs delineates the social and dialogical context in which the material is conveyed; it provides a concrete context through which to view the various components of the discourse as well as the discourse as a whole. The discourse setting of the book of Proverbs situates the material in a particular context and provides a grid through which to determine the nature and function of the work.

1.2 Proposal and Method

In view of the hermeneutical importance of the document's discourse setting, it is necessary to investigate the character of Proverbs within its distinct, literary context. This study examines the nature and function of the material in Proverbs within its new performance context, viz., the discursive context, the *Sitz im Buch*. The investigation seeks to explore the discourse setting of the book of Proverbs as well as the formal and thematic features of the individual collections. More specifically, the study attempts to highlight the fundamental features of the book's discursive context, the relationship between the various compendia, the thematic development of the material, and the aristocratic elements within the collections to ascertain the degree to which the book of Proverbs may be considered a courtly piece.

This form of analysis has at least three advantages. First, in contrast to several works devoted to the social and intellectual context of Proverbs, this study moves beyond an investigation of the constituent compendia as independent, isolated entities and explores the nature and function of these

---

20   Fontaine, *Traditional Sayings*, 12–13; idem, "Proverb Performance in the Hebrew Bible," 94; Römheld, *Die Weisheitlehre im Alten Orient: Elemente einer Formgeschichte*, 3; Murphy, *The Tree of Life*, 4.

21   Fox, "Wisdom and the Self-Presentation of Wisdom Literature," 153–54.

compositions within the larger moral discourse of the book of Proverbs. Though these collections may have been formulated as discrete compositions, they have been incorporated into a larger literary discourse that evinces a reasonable degree of homogeneity in literary character, presuppositions, and perspective.[22] The history of sapiential interpretation is punctuated by studies that explore the courtly features of specific collections.[23] However, the paucity of full-scale research on the role of the individual collections and the aristocratic character of the document as a whole is surprising.

Second, the investigation attempts to present the multifaceted concerns of the individual compilations. Rather than restricting the discussion to the ostensive *Königssprüche* within the collections or the aristocratic features of the material, the exploration seeks to account for the kaleidoscopic ethos of the compendia and the variegated themes within the constituent collections.

Third, the study attempts to identify the discourse setting in which the material is conveyed; that is, it seeks to delineate the social and dialogical context in which the sapiential material is cast to provide a hermeneutical framework within which to view the various components of the discourse as well as the discourse as a whole. The discourse setting of the book will play a fundamental role in the investigation, for it provides a concrete context within which to explore the nature and function of the material. It serves as a heuristic framework through which to assess the integral elements of the sapiential mosaic and the purpose of the book as a literary whole.

In order to investigate the nature and function of the book of Proverbs, this study will explore the courtly character of the document in two parts. The first will examine the discursive, thematic, and conceptual features of ancient oriental instructional texts. The formal, generic similarities between ancient Near Eastern didactic texts and the book of Proverbs are striking. Since the book of Proverbs was not produced in a literary or cultural vacuum and should be read within the literary and cultural context from which it emerged, the nature and function of the sapiential literature from the ancient Near East is essential to the investigation. The fundamental purpose of the initial chapter is to present the discourse setting, subject matter, and function of these didactic works in order to determine the degree to which they may be considered courtly pieces. The investigation does not attempt to form an ideational foundation from which to construct a pedestrian reading of the book of Proverbs; rather it seeks to

---

22   M. V. Fox, "The Social Location of the Book of Proverbs," 227; K. J. Dell, "How Much Wisdom Literature Has Its Roots in the Pre-Exilic Period?", in *In Search of Pre-Exilic Israel: Proceedings of the Oxford Old Testament* (ed. J. Day; London: T&T Clark International, 2004), 259.

23   For example, see Skladny, *Die ältesten Spruchsammlungen in Israel*, 41–46; Bryce, "Another Wisdom-'Book' in Proverbs," 145–57; Humphreys, "The Motif of the Wise Courtier in the Book of Proverbs," 177–90; Van Leeuwen, *Context and Meaning in Proverbs 25–27*, 60–86, *et passim*.

highlight the formal, generic features of ancient oriental instructional texts in order to produce a heuristic framework through which to read and assess the materials in the book of Proverbs.

In light of the generic features of ancient oriental instructional texts, the second part of the investigation focuses on the formal features, thematic emphases, and aristocratic elements of the individual collections within the book of Proverbs. In general, the study assumes the traditional divisions of the material. The investigation does not attempt to order the collections chronologically; rather it seeks to identify the nature and function of the individual compositions within their final, editorial *Gestalt*. The book of Proverbs consists of several distinct parts. For the purpose of our investigation, we will divide the work into nine primary subsections with the following designations:[24]

Section	Verses	Designation
1	1:1–9:18	Prologue
2	10:1–15:33	Solomon 1A
3	16:1–22:16	Solomon 1B
4	22:17–24:22	Sayings of the Wise 1
5	24:23–34	Sayings of the Wise 2
6	25:1–27:27	Solomon 2A
7	28:1–29:27	Solomon 2B
8	30:1–33	The Words of Agur
9	31:1–31	The Words of Lemuel

Table 1.1: Designations for the Constituent Compendia within Proverbs

The second part of the study explores the character of these collections and their role within the book of Proverbs. Our investigation consists of four distinct chapters.

The initial chapter (chapter 3) examines the discourse setting of the material and the aristocratic elements within the introductory lectures and interludes. In so doing, it seeks to identify the social and dialogical context in which the material is conveyed and assess the degree to which the speaker correlates the discourse with the interests, aspirations, and temptations of the addressee. The remaining chapters (chapters 4–6) focus on the formal features, thematic emphases, and aristocratic elements of the constituent collections in Proverbs 10–31. In the main, these chapters seek to identify the fundamental characteristics of the

---

24 The designations attributed to "Solomon" do not indicate that Solomon was the "author" of these constituent compendia; rather these designations serve as shorthand for the collections that bear his name. For a discussion of the concept of "authorship" in Proverbs, see 3.2.2 below.

sapiential worldview and the thematic development of the material. They give particular expression to the ethical vision of the individual collections and explore the function of these compositions within the book of Proverbs.

In view of these features, the concluding chapter synthesizes the results of the exploration. In the final analysis, I will attempt to determine the nature and function of the book of Proverbs. More specifically, I will consider whether the document represents a courtly piece and reflect on its functional significance. The hope is that the investigation will enhance our understanding of the character of the sapiential material as well as the purpose of the book of Proverbs.

Chapter 2

The Nature of Ancient Near Eastern Instructional Texts

The book of Proverbs is something of a literary anomaly in the Old Testament. In general, the work exhibits two distinctive features. On the one hand, the aphorisms presented in the sentence literature appear to arise from a variety of social settings and periods, with no apparent concern for topical or logical organization. In the main, traditional sayings within the Old Testament are cast in a performance context, that is, in a particular social or dialogical situation that creates a framework through which to identify the function and significance of the saying. However, the book of Proverbs incorporates sayings that are divorced from their performance contexts, leaving the reader to determine the meaning and pragmatic significance of the individual aphorisms. On the other hand, the aesthetic form of the sapiential material distinguishes the aphorisms from the traditional sayings that punctuate the literary compositions of the Old Testament. Though the materials in the book of Proverbs share several formal and thematic similarities with conventional Israelite aphorisms, the paronomastic structure, refined form, and consistent terminology of the sayings differentiate the material from its traditional counterparts. Together, these features highlight the interpretive difficulties that confront the reader of this enigmatic work. The atomistic character of the sentence literature and the artistic form of the material suggests that the book of Proverbs is *sui generis*, a rather haphazard collection of "Words, words, words."[1]

However, within the wider cognitive environment of the ancient Near East, we may identify several literary counterparts to the book of Proverbs. Egypt and Mesopotamia have left documents that have liberated the book of Proverbs from its generic isolation and revealed its international literary character. Since the book of Proverbs was not produced in a literary or cultural vacuum and should be read within the literary and cultural context from which it emerged, it is necessary to explore the sapiential literature from the ancient Near East to assess the nature and function of these literary traditions within their respective social environments. To accomplish this goal, this chapter will examine the instructional

---

1   *Hamlet*, 2.2.192.

literature from Egypt, Mesopotamia and Syria, highlighting the constituent features of the genre and the function of these documents within their respective social contexts. The discourse setting, subject matter, and conceptual world of ancient Near Eastern instructional works provide a framework within which to analyze the nature and function of these literary pieces within their specific social environments. Through an analysis of these features, we will attempt to determine the degree to which these texts may be considered courtly documents. We will begin with Egyptian instructions and then examine the discursive, thematic, and conceptual elements of Mesopotamian and Syrian instructional works.

2.1 Egyptian Instructional Literature

The sapiential imagination of ancient Egypt is manifested in a variety of literary works, ranging from psalms, poems, and panegyrics to tomb biographies and instructions. Among these literary forms, the instructions (*sb3.yt*) are significant, for they give particular expression to the teaching of the sages and the sapiential vision of ancient Egypt. While there is a virtual consensus that Egyptian instructional texts are the product of the aristocracy,[2] the authenticity of their authorial attributions has been vigorously discussed. In principle, these investigations are a worthy enterprise, for they account for the historical dimension of the sapiential writings. However, in light of the difficulties involved in the investigation of these authorial attributions, an examination of the discourse setting of the materials may provide a more reliable indication of their nature and function. Since discursive texts are self-referential, identifying their author and addressee within the setting of the text itself, these compositions can be assessed only through the literatures' social setting and subject matter.[3]

---

2   See R. Gordis, "The Social Background of Wisdom Literature," *HUCA* 18 (1944): 91; H. Brunner, *Altägyptische Erziehung* (Wiesbaden: Harrassowitz, 1957), 66; Bryce, *A Legacy of Wisdom*, 149–50; C. Eyre, "The Semna Stelae: Quotation, Genre, and Functions of Literature," in *Studies in Egyptology Presented to Miriam Lichtheim* (2 vols.; ed. S. Israelit-Groll; Jerusalem: Magnes, 1990), 1:151; S. Weeks, *Early Israelite Wisdom* (Oxford Monograph Series; Oxford: Oxford University Press, 1994), 157.

3   R. B. Parkinson, "Teachings, Discourses and Tales from the Middle Kingdom," in *Middle Kingdom Studies* (ed. S. Quirke; New Malden: SIA Publishing, 1991), 93; idem, "Individual and Society in Middle Kingdom Literature," in *Ancient Egyptian Literature: History and Forms* (Probleme der Ägyptologie 10; Leiden: Brill, 1996), 132–44.

Whether these settings are historical or fictional, they are anchored in reality and establish a mutual solidarity between the author and reader.[4]

2.1.1 The Discourse Setting of Egyptian Instructional Literature

Egyptian instructional texts identify three principal discursive features: the speaker, addressee, and context of the work. These features play a formative role in the sapiential tradition; they represent the fundamental building blocks of the document's discourse setting and provide a lens through which to explore the meaning and pragmatic significance of the material within its wider textual environment. In general, the ostensive authors and addressees of Egyptian instructional texts range from the king and vizier to middle class officials, who represent the functional extension of the pharaonic institution. In contrast to other literary works produced in the ancient oriental world, instructional pieces typically name the author and addressee.[5] Though there are certain exceptions,[6] instructional literary pieces seem to share a common setting and display an unbroken documentary history from the Old Kingdom through the Late Period.[7]

---

4   J. Assmann, "Weisheit, Schrift und Literatur in alten Ägypten," in *Weisheit* (ed. A. Assmann; Münich: Fink, 1991), 475–500; A. Loprieno, "Defining Egyptian Literature: Ancient Texts and Modern Literary Theory," in *The Study of the Ancient Near East in the Twenty-First Century* (ed. J. S. Cooper and G. M. Schwartz; Winona Lake: Eisenbrauns, 1996), 214–17.

5   M. Lichtheim, ed., *Ancient Egyptian Literature: A Book of Readings* (3 vols.; Berkeley: University of California, 1973–80; repr., 2006), 1:6.

6   For example, the Loyalist Instruction, the Teaching of a Man for his Son, and the Oxford Wisdom Text do not name an explicit author or addressee. These texts are either fragmentary or attributed to an anonymous individual. However, the anonymity of the loyalistic literature does not necessarily indicate that these works are more popular in character. Rather, this anonymity seems to allow the writers to voice the opinion of the aristocracy vis-à-vis the state and encourage the reception of their work by neutralizing the critical aspects of the text. See G. Posener, *Littérature et politique dans l'Égypte de la XII Dynastie* (Bibliothéque de l'École des Hautes Études 307; Paris: Librairie Honoré Champion, 1969), 126–27; A. Loprieno, "Loyalistic Instructions," in *Ancient Egyptian Literature: History and Forms* (Probleme der Ägyptologie 10; Leiden: Brill, 1996), 405–06.

7   This chapter is not concerned with the theoretical origin of didactic literature or its relationship with other literary compositions within ancient Egypt. For some recent proposals, see J. Assmann, "Schrift, Tod und Identität: das Grab als Vorschule der Literatur im alten Ägypten," in *Schrift und Gedächtnis: Beiträge zur Archäologie der literarischen Kommunikation* (ed. J. Assmann et al., München: Fink, 1983), 64–93; A. Loprieno, *Topos und Mimesis: zum Ausländer in der ägyptischen Literatur* (ÄgAbh 48; Wiesbaden: Harrasowitz, 1988), 1–21; D. M. Doxey, *Egyptian Non-Royal Epithets in the Middle Kingdom: A Social and Historical Analysis* (Probleme der Ägyptologie 12; Leiden: Brill, 1998), 5.

In view of this continuity, the discursive setting of these didactic works deserves specific comment.

The Instructions of Hardjedef, Kagemni and Ptahhotep are the oldest known instructional texts from ancient Egypt. These compositions were produced during the golden era of Egyptian history, an era in which the empire reached its cultural apex. Though copies of these texts date from the Middle Kingdom and may have been artificially archaized in order to establish a sense of continuity with and confidence in the past, they are cast in the style of Old Kingdom writings and embody the virtues and values of the Old Kingdom.[8] In contrast to Ptahhotep, the instructions of Hardjedef and Kagemni are incomplete. Nevertheless, their discourse setting remains clear. In the former, Hardjedef, the son of Pharaoh Cheops, addresses his son Au-ib-re, who apparently did not become crown prince.[9] In the latter, an unnamed vizier, perhaps Kairsu, assembles his "children" and exhorts them to obey all that he has written.[10] Here the teaching proper is followed by a brief narrative account that describes the ascension of Pharaoh Snefru and the installation of Kagemni as vizier to the king. In each case, the discourse is cast within the courtly context. The speaker is either a king or an eminent member of the ruling elite, who transfers advice either to a member of the royal family or to the next generation of bureaucratic officials.

As the oldest complete exemplar of the instructional genre, the Instruction of Ptahhotep seems to reflect the courtly discourse setting of its instructional counterparts.[11] However, in contrast to Hardjedef and Kagemni, the Instruction of Ptahhotep is arranged within a dual setting.[12] The prologue provides the

---

8   See H. Brunner, *Die Weisheitsbücher der Ägypter: Lehren für das Leben* (2nd ed.; München: Artemis Verlag, 1991), 101, 106, 133; J. Baines, "Society, Morality, and Religious Practice," in *Religion in Ancient Egypt: Gods, Myths, and Personal Practice* (ed. B. E. Shafer; Ithaca: Cornell University Press, 1991), 160; E. Eichler, "Zur Datierung und Interpretation der Lehre des Ptahhotep," *ZÄS* 128 (2001): 97–107; F. Junge, *Die Lehre Ptahhoteps und die Tugenden der ägyptischen Welt* (OBO 193; Göttingen: Vandenhoeck & Ruprecht, 2003), 154.

9   For the text, see W. Helck, *Die Lehre des Djedefhor und Die Lehre eines Vaters an seinen Sohn* (Kleine Ägyptische Texte 8; Wiesbaden: Harrassowitz, 1986); "Die Lehre des Prinzen Djedefhor" (Brunner, *Die Weisheitsbücher der Ägypter*, 101–03); "The Instruction of Hardedef" (*LAE* 127–28); S. Quirke, *Egyptian Literature 1800 BC: Questions and Readings* (Egyptology 2; London: Golden House, 2004), 171–72; "The Instruction of Prince Hardjedef" (*AEL* 1:58–59).

10   For the text, see "Die Lehre für Kagemni" (Brunner, *Die Weisheitsbücher der Ägypter*, 133–36); "The Teaching for the Vizier Kagemni" (*LAE* 149–51); Quirke, *Egyptian Literature*, 178; "The Instruction Addressed to Kagemni" (*AEL* 1:59–61).

11   For the text, see Z. Zybnek, *Les Maximes de Ptahhotep* (Prague: Editions de l'Académie Tchécoslovaque des Sciences, 1956); "Die Lehre des Ptahhotep" (Brunner, *Die Weisheitsbücher der Ägypter*, 104–32); "The Maxims of Ptahhotep" (*LAE* 129–48); Quirke, *Egyptian Literature*, 90–101; "The Instruction of Ptahhotep" (*AEL* 1:61–80).

12   J. Bergman, "Discourse d'adieu—Testament—Discours Posthume: Testaments juifs et enseignements égyptiens," in *Sagesse et Religion* (Paris: Presses Universitaires de France, 1979), 34–37.

external setting of the text, which consists of a dialogue between the aged vizier and King Isesi. Here Ptahhotep describes the debilitating effects of old age and seeks permission to instruct his son and designate successor. When the king approves the appointment, the text shifts to an interior setting, according to which Ptahhotep transmits the "ways of the ancestors" to those who are willing to hear in general and to his son and successor in particular. Though Ptahhotep issues a general invitation to the ignorant, he does not direct his teachings toward listeners or readers of the document; rather, he directs his instructions toward his son, who seems to represent both listeners and readers of the text.[13] While the instructions catalog a series of general virtues that are accessible to a large sociological range of individuals, these principles are directed specifically toward Ptahhotep's son and successor.[14] The discursive context suggests the document represents a series of instructions delivered by the aged vizier to his aristocratic son within a courtly context.

The Instruction Addressed to King Merikare represents a transitional work in Egyptian instructional literature.[15] On the one hand, the document continues the instructional tradition that emerged in the Old Kingdom. Similar to the Instruction of Ptahhotep, the work is cast in the form of an instruction spoken by an aged protagonist, who prepares to hand over his office to his son and successor. On the other hand, the document represents a treatise on kingship that takes the form of a royal testament. Whether or not the text represents a posthumous discourse inspired by Merikare at the debut of his reign to justify his political policies,[16] the discourse setting of the instruction is clear. The work purports to be a royal instruction delivered by the aged king to his son and successor, Merikare, during the political instability of the First Intermediate Period.

The Instruction of King Amenemhet I for his Son Sesostris I is comparable to Merikare, for the composition emulates the tone and topos of a royal

---

13   Junge, *Lehre Ptahhoteps*, 11.

14   See K. F. D. Römheld, *Die Weisheitlehre im alten Orient: Elemente einer Formgeschichte* (Biblische Notizen-Beiheft 4; München: Manfred Görg, 1989), 20–21.

15   For the text, see W. Helck, *Die Lehre für König Merikare* (Kleine Ägyptische Texte 5; Wiesbaden: Harrassowitz, 1977); "Die Lehre für König Merikare" (Brunner, *Die Weisheitsbücher der Ägypter*, 137–54); "The Teaching for King Merikare" (*LAE* 152–65); Quirke, *Egyptian Literature*, 112–20; "The Instruction Addressed to King Merikare" (*AEL* 1:97–109).

16   For a discussion of the nature and function of the document, see E. Blumenthal, "Die Lehre für König Merikare," *ZÄS* 107 (1980): 5–41; G. Posener, "Lehre für Merikare," *LÄ* 3:386–89; R. Gundlach, "Äyptische Weisheit in der politischen 'Lebenslehre' König Amenhemet I," in *"Jedes Ding hat seine Zeit...": Studien zur israelitischen und altorientalischen Weisheit* (ed. A. A. Diesel et al., Berlin: Walter de Gruyter, 1996), 92; H. Goedicke, "Merikare^c E 106–115," *ZÄS* 129 (2002): 115–21; "The Instruction Addressed to King Merikare" (*AEL* 1:97). If the text is the product of court propagandists, then it may have been directed toward the official class, who would carry out the political directives delineated in the instructions. In this case, the real audience would be members of the bureaucracy, who function as the practical extension of the royal institution.

testament.[17] The work is set in the Twelfth Dynasty, and presented as an address to Sesostris I, given by Amenemhet I, who either succumbed to or survived an attempted *coup d'état*. This coup has precipitated several questions regarding the circumstances that gave rise to the production of the work.[18] On the one hand, if Khety produced the work, as P. Chester Beatty IV assumes, then it would appear to be a piece of royal propaganda that seeks to bolster Sesostris' right to the throne. On the other hand, Amenhemet may have created the text in order to justify the institution of coregency, which was never integrated into the official royal ideology. Whether the work serves as a propagandistic piece or functions to legitimize the institution of coregency, the implied author and implied addressee are comparable to the real author and the real addressee: eminent officials and members of the royal house. While the assassination attempt addressed in the instructions is the hinge upon which an understanding of the real author and real addressee turns, the writer portrays King Amenemhet I and the crown prince, Sesostris I, as the implied author and implied addressee, respectively.[19] This discursive setting situates the composition firmly within the court, that is, in the context of the prince's ascension to the throne.

The Instruction of Dua-Khety,[20] or the Satire on the Trades, exhibits a different tone than its instructional predecessors. However, the work incorporates a narrative framework that places it within the stream of

---

17   For the text, see W. Helck, *Der Text der "Lehre Amenemhets I. für seinen Sohn"* (Kleine Ägyptische Texte 1; Wiesbaden: Harrassowitz, 1969); "Die Lehre des Königs Amenemhet I" (Brunner, *Die Weisheitsbücher der Ägypter*, 169–77); "The Teaching of King Amenemhet I for His Son Senwosret" (*LAE* 166–71); Quirke, *Egyptian Literature*, 127–29; "The Instruction of King Amenhemet I for His Son Sesostris I" (*AEL* 1:135–39).

18   For a discussion of the coup, see Posener, *Littérature et politique*, 66–75; E. Blumenthal, "Lehre Amenhemets I," *LÄ* 3:968–71; idem, "Die Lehre des Königs Amenemhet (Teil II)," *ZÄS* 112 (1985): 104–15; J. L. Foster, "The Conclusion to *The Testament of Ammenemes, King of Egypt*," *JEA* 67 (1981): 36–47; J. Baines, "Kingship, Definition of Culture, and Legitimation," in *Ancient Egyptian Kingship* (ed. D. O'Connor and D. P. Silverman; Leiden: Brill, 1995), 21; Gundlach, "Äyptische Weisheit," 93–101; G. Burkard "'Als Gott erschienen spricht er' Die Lehre des Amenemhet als postumes Vermächtnis," in *Literatur und Politik im pharaonischen und ptolemäischen Ägypten: Vorträge der Tagung zum Gedenken an Georges Posener 5.–10. September 1996 in Leipzig* (ed. J. Assmann and E. Blumenthal; Cairo: Institut Français d'Archéologie Orientale, 1999), 153–73; R. B. Parkinson, *Poetry and Culture in Middle Kingdom Egypt: A Dark Side to Perfection* (London: Continuum, 2002), 5–10, 241–48.

19   Although the text contains an injunction to humanity in general, the remainder of the material is directed toward an individual addressee. For a literal reading of the document, see, H. Goedicke, *Studies in 'The Instruction of King Amenhemet I for His Son'* (Varia Aegyptiaca Supplement 2; San Antonio: van Siclen Books, 1988), 5; C. A. Thériault, "The Instruction of Amenemhet as Propaganda," *JARCE* 30 (1993): 151–60.

20   For the reading of the name, see P. Seibert, *Die Charakteristik: Untersuchung zu einer altägyptischen Sprechsitte und ihren Ausprägungen in Folklore und Literatur* (ÄgAbh 17; Wiesbaden: Harrassowitz, 1967), 103–09.

instructional tradition.[21] Similar to its generic antecedents, the Instruction of Dua-Khety is cast in the form of an address from a father to his son within a liminal situation, that is, at a juncture where the addressee makes the transition from his former place in society to a position of higher status.[22] Dua-Khety admonishes his son Pepy during their journey to the Resident City where the youth is to be placed in the "school of scribes," among the children of the most eminent men of the land. On the surface, the speaker and addressee seem to stem from the lower echelons of society. However, Egyptian tradition attributes the work to the infamous sage Khety, who is also associated with the production of the Instruction of Amenhemet I.[23] This tradition suggests that the work represents the advice of a prominent sage to his son, a young aristocrat who is preparing to enter a school for elite scribes.

In general, the instructional compositions from the Old and Middle Kingdoms possess a distinct, courtly flavor. However, this aristocratic color is modulated in the New Kingdom writings. In contrast to the elite authors and addressees of the Old and Middle Kingdom instructions, the New Kingdom Instruction of Any represents a democratization of the genre.[24] While the work contains the typical form of a father instructing his son, it presents two significant developments in the instructional tradition. First, rather than posing as a noble or famous figure within the bureaucracy, the protagonist is portrayed as a middle class temple scribe—a relatively subordinate member of the official hierarchy.[25] Second, the ostensive recipient of the admonitions is not disclosed until the epilogue, where Any's son, the scribe Khonshotep, protests that his father's instructions are too difficult to understand and implement. These features suggest the work attests to the development of the middle class within the expanding bureaucracy of the Eighteenth Dynasty, since the speaker and addressee appear to be subordinate scribes within the pharaonic administration.[26] Nonetheless, the significance of their social position should not be underestimated, for within the

---

21 For the text, see W. Helck, *Die Lehres des Dwȝ–Ḫtjj, Textzusammenstellung* (Kleine Ägyptische Texte 3; Wiesbaden: Harrassowitz, 1970); "Die Lehre des Cheti" (Brunner, *Die Weisheitsbücher der Ägypter*, 155–68); "The Satire on the Trades: The Instruction of Dua-Khety" (*LAE* 431–37); Quirke, *Egyptian Literature*, 121–26; "The Satire of the Trades" (*AEL* 1:184–92).

22 For a discussion of liminality as a social setting for the Instructions of Kagemni, Ptahhotep, Merikare, Amenhemet I and Dua-Khety, see L. G. Perdue, "Liminality as a Social Setting for Wisdom Instructions," *ZAW* 93 (1981): 114–26.

23 See "Die Lehre des Papyrus Chester Beatty IV" (Brunner, *Die Weisheitsbücher der Ägypter*, 229–30), ll. 215–19.

24 For the text, see "Die Lehre des Ani" (Brunner, *Die Weisheitsbücher der Ägypter*, 196–214); "The Instruction of Any" (*AEL* 2:135–46).

25 H. Brunner, "Lehre des Ani," *LÄ* 3:976; J. F. Quack, *Die Lehren des Ani: Ein neuägyptischer Weisheitstext in seinem kulturellen Umfeld* (OBO 141; Göttingen: Vandenhoeck & Ruprecht, 1994), 79–80; M. Lichtheim, *Moral Values in Ancient Egypt* (OBO 155; Göttingen: Vandenhoeck & Ruprecht, 1997), 29.

26 "The Instruction of Any" (*AEL* 2:135).

New Kingdom everyday administrative power was placed into the hands of the middle authorities.[27]

Among the sapiential works of the New Kingdom, The Instruction of Amenemope may be the best-known instructional composition.[28] While the form of the work differs from earlier exemplars, it incorporates a conventional narrative framework that places it in continuity with the instructional tradition. The prologue delineates the principle features of the document's discursive setting: Amenemope, an official in the administration of royal estates, delivers the "teaching for life" to his youngest son, Horemmaakheru, a priestly scribe operating within the temple of Min. Similar to the Instruction of Any, the implied author and addressee appear to be middle class officials within the pharaonic administration. However, this social designation is vague, since middle class officials functioned in a variety of capacities. If the Duties of the Vizier provide any indication of the organization of the pharaonic administration during the New Kingdom,[29] then Amenemope seems to have been a high-ranking government official, who had been appointed by the vizier and was responsible to the vizier.[30] In this case, the implied author would be a relatively significant member of the royal administration, who delivers the "teaching for life" to future generations in general and his youngest son in particular.

The democratization of the instructional tradition in the New Kingdom continues in the Late Period. In contrast to its sapiential antecedents, the demotic instructions of Ankhsheshonq possess a popular discourse setting and incorporate forms that differ significantly from its instructional predecessors. However, in conjunction with its counterparts, the work's narrative prologue places it in direct continuity with Egyptian instructional tradition.[31] Similar to its

---

27   Brunner, *Die Weisheitsbücher der Ägypter*, 63.

28   For the text, see "Die Lehre des Amenemope" (Brunner, *Die Weisheitsbücher der Ägypter*, 234–56); "The Instruction of Amenemope" (*LAE* 223–43); "The Instruction of Amenemope" (*AEL* 2:146–63); V. P.-M. Laisney, *L'Enseignement d'Aménémopé* (Rome: Pontifical Biblical Institute, 2007).

29   For the text, see G. P. F. van den Boorn, *The Duties of the Vizier: Civil Administration in the Early New Kingdom* (Studies in Egyptology; London: Kegan Paul, 1988). Van den Boorn places the composition of the text in the early New Kingdom, which corresponds with the general range of dates assigned to the Instruction of Amenemope. See I. Shirun-Grumach, "Lehre des Amenemope," *LÄ* 3:971; K. D. F. Römheld, *Wege der Weisheit: Die Lehren Amenemopes und Proverbien 22,17–24,22* (BZAW 184; Berlin: de Gruyter, 1989), 7; Washington, *Wealth and Poverty*, 11–14.

30   For a discussion of the place and function of the "overseer of fields" within the civil administration of the New Kingdom, see van den Boorn, *The Duties of the Vizier*, 320–30; S. G. J. Quirke, "Administration: State Administration," in *The Oxford Encyclopedia of Ancient Egypt* (ed. D. B. Redford; 3 vols; Oxford: Oxford University Press, 2001), 1:14.

31   For the text, see "Die Spruchsammlung des Anch-Scheschonki" (Brunner, *Die Weisheitsbücher der Ägypter*, 257–91); "The Instruction of 'Onchsheshonqy" (*LAE* 497–529); "The Instruction of Ankhsheshonq" (*AEL* 3:159–84).

generic prototypes, the text takes the form of an address from a father to his son. The work is cast in the Twenty-second Dynasty,[32] where Ankhsheshonq is presented as a priest of Re, who was incarcerated for failing to inform Pharaoh of a plot on his life. In order to fulfill his paternal duty, Ankhsheshonq writes instructions for his son on potsherds, which are read before Pharaoh and his court on a daily basis. In view of the prologue, the text purports to be the teaching of a priest, which addresses two distinct audiences. The rhetorical audience of the text is Ankhsheshonq's son, while the real audience appears to be the pharaonic court.

In light of the ostensive authors and addressees presented in these instructional texts, at least two conclusions may be drawn. First, the sapiential works are framed by narratives, titles, or hortatory introductions that present a father transmitting instruction either to his son or, in the case of Kagemni, to his children. Second, the implied authors and addressees of Egyptian instructional texts range from the king and vizier to middle class officials and impending scribal aristocrats within the pharaonic administration. These features suggest that Egyptian instructional texts share a continuous documentary history and a common discursive setting that exhibits a discrete courtly color.

The discursive setting of Egyptian instructional works situates them within a courtly environment. However, this aristocratic setting becomes problematic if the texts are fictional or if the implied addressee does not correspond with the actual intended audience of the constituent compositions. Therefore, rather than simply relying on the discourse setting of these works to assess the degree to which they may be considered courtly documents, the subject matter of these texts may indicate the nature of their addressee and the perspective of their writers.[33] The contents may determine whether the instructions contain subjects and themes that pertain exclusively to the royal administration or whether the material extends beyond the concerns of the bureaucracy.

2.1.2 The Content of Egyptian Instructional Literature

The earliest instructional texts seem to discuss matters that transcend social boundaries and pertain to a large sociological range of individuals. On the one hand, the Instruction of Hardjedef delineates the importance of establishing a house and making proper mortuary preparations—a particular concern of the Old Kingdom that extended throughout Egyptian history. In addition, the Teaching of the Vizier Kagemni commends the value of modesty, self-control, and reticent speech—virtues that cut across social boundaries and encompass the

---

32   See H. J. Thissen, "Lehre des Anch-Scheschonqi," *LÄ* 3:974.
33   Parkinson, "Individual and Society," 142.

socio-moral ethos of the community. On the other hand, the Instruction of Ptahhotep presents material that appears to address a smaller group of individuals. While the piece considers the cardinal virtues of self-control, listening, obedience, generosity, justice, truthfulness and discretion, the document places these virtues within hypothetical situations that describe the relationship between two principle groups: those in a position of hierarchical superiority and those in a position of hierarchical subordination.[34] The former group is called to be a model of discipline, while the latter is to be marked by obedience, especially toward the king.[35] Though the virtues and vices presented in the work are not the specific property of a particular class, these ethical principles are illustrated through theoretical relationships between bureaucratic officials and subordinate administrators. These personages are called to embody the "ways of the ancestors" and "perform Maat" so they might serve as an example to others.[36]

The aristocratic character of the Instruction of Ptahhotep is also reflected in the teachings for Merikare and Amenhemet I. These royal testaments are presented as treatises on kingship, which discuss the political responsibilities and diplomatic prerogatives of the monarchy. While the Teaching for King Merikare does not provide a comprehensive presentation of the king's administrative duties, the document outlines the fundamental elements of his domestic and international policy. The work addresses the different ways in which the king is to deal with factions, government officials, and the Egyptian people, and justifies the need for border control and troop conscription by highlighting the king's responsibility to speak, establish, and observe Maat. In contrast to Merikare's optimistic instructions, the Teaching of King Amenhemet I is distinguished by its pessimistic tone. Whereas Merikare focuses on the advantages of prudent officials, Amenhemet warns his son of the threats posed by royal advisors. Together, these instructions contain many of the same moral precepts and present official duties that pertain to the elite. Though the content of the instructions betrays a strict royal focus, the works address issues that are restricted to the royal post and possess a cosmic dimension that is particularly associated with the king.[37]

---

34   Lichtheim, *Moral Values*, 23–24; P. Vernus, "Le discours politique de l'*Enseignement de Ptahhotep*," in *Literatur und Politik im pharaonischen und ptolemäischen Ägypten: Vorträge der Tagung zum Gedenken an Georges Posener 5.–10. September 1996 in Leipzig* (ed. J. Assmann and E. Blumenthal; Cairo: Institut Français d'Archéologie Orientale, 1999), 139–52.

35   See "The Instruction of Ptahhotep" (*AEL* 1:61–80), maxims 5, 8, 15, 16, 17, 24, 25, 26, 28, 30, 31, 34, 36. Also, for the possibility of change in social positions, see maxims 10, 13, 14, 30.

36   "Die Lehre des Ptahhotep" (Brunner, *Die Weisheitsbücher der Ägypter*, 104–05); Vernus, "Le discours politique," 151–52; Junge, *Lehre Ptahhoteps*, 148–59; E. Otto, "Law and Ethics," in *Religions of the Ancient World: A Guide* (ed. S. I. Johnston; Cambridge: Harvard University Press, 2004), 86–87.

37   Baines, "Kingship," 21.

The royal tone and topos of the teachings for Merikare and Amenhemet I is also evident in two anonymous works from the Middle Kingdom: the Loyalist Instruction[38] and the Teaching of a Man for his Son.[39] Both texts are divided into two distinct parts that seek to serve a similar purpose. The first segment of the Loyalist Instruction catalogues the divine qualities of the king in hymnic style, while the second portion admonishes the addressee to treat the lower classes of society with benevolence. In the same way, the beginning of the Teaching of a Man for his Son extols the virtues of the king and describes the concrete benefits that accompany the loyal administrator, while the second half addresses the qualities of diligence, silence, and reliability, which are to be developed within the character of the young official. In general, it seems that both texts attempt to inculcate a sense of loyalty toward the divine Pharaoh and admonish their listeners to act as faithful representatives of the pharaonic institution. Though the authors of these texts remain anonymous,[40] their subject matter and concern with social mobility suggests the material is particularly relevant to high or middle class officials within the royal bureaucracy.[41]

The Instruction of Dua-Khety emulates the courtly tenor of its instructional counterparts. Whether the text is a satire or a serious piece of literature,[42] the document may be divided into two parts. The first segment presents several vignettes on various trades. In the main, these vignettes serve as a foil to promote the advantages of the scribal office. The latter half of the work then provides general rules of behavior, which center on the protocol of scribal students in relation to officials. These features suggest the work addresses a class of future

---

38 For the text, see G. Posener, *L'enseignement loyaliste: Sagesse égyptienne du Moyen Empire* (Centre de recherches d'historie et de philologie 2; Hautes études orientales 5; Geneva, 1976); "Die Loyalistische Lehre" (Brunner, *Die Weisheitsbücher der Ägypter*, 178–84); "The Loyalist Instruction from the Sehetepibre Stela (*LAE* 172–74); Quirke, *Egyptian Literature*, 108–11.

39 For the text, see K. A. Kitchen, "Studies in Egyptian Wisdom Literature: I. The Instruction by a Man for His Son," *OrAnt* 8 (1969): 189–208; Helck, *Die Lehre des Djedefhor und Die Lehre eines Vaters an seinen Sohn*, 25–72; "Die Lehre eines Mannes fur seinen Sohn" (Brunner, *Die Weisheitsbücher der Ägypter*, 185–92); "The Instruction of a Man for his Son (First Section)" (*LAE* 175–77); Quirke, *Egyptian Literature*, 102–07.

40 For proposals concerning the identity of the author's of the loyalistic literature, see G. Posener, "Lehre, loyalistische," *LÄ* 3:982; Parkinson, "Teachings," 109; Loprieno, "Loyalistic Instructions," 405–06.

41 H. W. Fischer-Elfert, "Instructions of a Man for his Son," in *The Oxford Encyclopedia of Ancient Egypt* (ed. D. B. Redford; 3 vols. Oxford: Oxford University Press, 2001), 2:170.

42 See Helck, *Die Lehres des Dw3-Htjj*, 161–62; J. L. Foster, "Some Comments on Khety's Instruction for Little Pepi on His Way to School (Satire on the Trades)," in *Gold of Praise: Studies on Ancient Egypt in Honor of Edward F. Wente* (SAOC 58; Chicago: The Oriental Institute of the University of Chicago, 1999), 121–29; "The Satire of the Trades" (*AEL* 1:184).

scribes, who are preparing to enter either the royal administration or a private post.[43]

In contrast to the courtly flavor of these instructional works, the Instruction of Any does not appear to present distinctive, aristocratic values. Any moves from a concern with bureaucratic success to traditional advice concerning religious piety, moderation, reticent speech, care for the marginalized, and the threat of strange women. The work addresses the benefits of studying "the writings" and admonishes its addressee to act according to his rank. Nevertheless, the material does not have a strict aristocratic focus.

The Instruction of Amenemope, however, appears to present the virtues and values of the responsible official. In order to exemplify the principal qualities of the virtuous person, Amenemope compares two archetypal personages: the unruly individual and the disciplined individual. The unruly person is pugnacious, contentious, and violent, while the disciplined person is quiet, self-controlled, kind toward others and humble before God. Among his instructions, Amenemope admonishes his addressee to abstain from cheating, avoid quarrels, speak the truth in court, respect those in authority, and exercise kindness toward the marginalized. In typical New Kingdom style, the work fuses personal piety with moral behavior to align the individual with the beneficent sphere of world order. The conventional virtues presented in the work are accessible to many. However, for Amenemope, these ethical principles are not simply practical guidelines that lead to a successful life; they are also virtues that characterize the skilled scribe and the ideal courtier.[44]

Similar to its instructional counterparts, the demotic Instruction of Ankhsheshonq contains a pastiche of conventional concerns. However, in contrast to earlier exemplars, the Instruction of Ankhsheshonq is cast in monostichic prose with sayings that exhibit no apparent concern for topical organization.[45] Among the instructions, statements, and proverbs delineated in the work, Ankhsheshonq highlights those characteristics that mark the wise man, the fool, the virtuous woman, the evil woman, the wealthy man, and the poor. Moreover, the work emphasizes the need for people to act in the interest of others and includes more references to agricultural matters than any of its instructional predecessors. These features have led many to conclude that the

---

43   L. H. Lesko, "Some Comments on Ancient Egyptian Literacy and Literati," in *Studies in Egyptology Presented to Miriam Lichtheim* (2 vols.; ed. S. Israelit-Groll; Jerusalem: Magnes, 1990), 2:661.

44   See "The Instruction of Amenemope" (*AEL* 2:162), chapter 30. Also see Shirun-Grumach, *LÄ* 3:971; Baines, "Society," 194–95; Lichtheim, *Moral Values*, 42.

45   See M. Lichtheim, *Late Egyptian Wisdom Literature in the International Content: A Study of Demotic Instructions* (OBO 52; Göttingen: Vandenhoeck & Ruprecht, 1983), 1–12.

work is addressed to a rustic, lower class audience, based in the village.[46] Whether or not the images presented in the aphorisms serve as a reliable indication of their origin, it seems that the instruction provides common cultural advice, with no particular aristocratic focus.

In view of the content of Egyptian instructional texts, several conclusions may be drawn. In general, Egyptian instructional works contain material that seems to be directed toward and particularly relevant for the official class. Though some of these works impress general social values on their addressees, these virtues and vices are typically framed within relationships between members of the official hierarchy. When the material presented in these works is read within the discursive setting of the constituent pieces, it seems that Egyptian instructional texts are not only attributed to a variety of individuals within the pharaonic administration, but the majority of these works also discuss subjects and themes that are either limited to or ostensively directed toward the official class.

This conclusion is reinforced by the production and function of literature in ancient Egypt. Since the majority of the Egyptian population remained illiterate, it seems that either the central elite or the sub-elite were responsible for the production of written media.[47] While instructional texts may have been courtly or pastoral "travesties" that were composed and delivered orally,[48] by virtue of being written they became the property of an elite class and the restricted property of the written culture.[49] Thus, despite the absence of aristocratic elements in some of the compositions, Egyptian instructional works seem to have been the

---

46   B. Gemser, "The Instructions of 'Onchsheshonqy and Biblical Wisdom Literature," *SJT* 7 (1960): 102–28; repr. in *Studies in Ancient Israelite Religion* (ed. J. L. Crenshaw; New York: Ktav, 1976), 134–60; L. G. Perdue, *Wisdom and the Cult: A Critical Analysis of the Views of Cult in the Wisdom Literatures of Israel and the Ancient Near East* (SBLDS 30; Missoula: Scholars Press, 1977), 59; Lichtheim, *Late Egyptian Wisdom Literature*, 4; H. J. Thissen, *Die Lehre des Anchscheshonqi (p. BM 10508)* (Papyrologische Texte und Anhandlungen 32; Bonn: Habelt, 1984), 1.

47   See J. Baines and C. Eyre, "Four Notes on Literacy," *Göttinger Miszellen* 61 (1983): 65–96; J. Baines, "Literacy and Ancient Egyptian Society," *Man* 18 (1983): 572–99; H. te Velde, "Scribes and Literacy in Ancient Egypt," in *Scripta Signa Vocis: Studies About Scripts, Scriptures, Scribes and Languages in the Near East Presented to J. H. Hospers by His Pupils, Colleagues and Friends* (ed. H. L. J. Vanstiphout et al.; Groningen: Egbert Forsten, 1986), 253–64; L. D. Morenz, *Beiträge zur Schriftlichkeitskultur im Mittleren Reich und in der 2. Zwischenzeit* (Ägypten und Altes Testament; Wiesbaden: Harrassowitz, 1996), 17; L. H. Lesko, "Literature, Literacy, and Literati," in *Pharaoh's Workers: The Villagers of Deir El Medina* (ed. L. H. Lesko; London: Cornell University Press, 1994), 134–36; idem, "Literacy," in *The Oxford Encyclopedia of Ancient Egypt* (ed. D. B. Redford; 3 vols; Oxford: Oxford University Press, 2001), 2:297–99; D. Franke, "Kleiner Mann (*nds*)—was bist Du?," *Göttinger Miszellen* 167 (1998): 33–48; Parkinson, *Poetry and Culture*, 66; Quirke, *Egyptian Literature*, 37–38; D. B. Redford, "Ancient Egyptian Literature: An Overview," *CANE* 2223.

48   For a discussion of "travesties" in Egyptian literature, see M. V. Fox, *The Song of Songs and Ancient Egyptian Love Songs* (Madison: University of Wisconsin Press, 1985), 292–94; Parkinson, "Individual and Society," 140–45; idem, *Poetry and Culture*, 77–78.

49   C. Eyre, "The Semna Stelae," 1:162–65; Parkinson, *Poetry and Culture*, 67.

products and property of the Egyptian elite. These works represent an elite phenomenon that promoted virtues and values encompassing the socio-moral ethos of society. Together, they presented a basic worldview, an ethical vision that outlined key cultural values of Egyptian society.

2.1.3 The Worldview of Egyptian Instructional Literature

The worldview or ethical system promoted in Egyptian literature in general and instructional texts in particular centered on the concept of Maat. As a "moral system," Egyptian society was dependent upon a set of ethical guidelines that would ensure the maintenance of social life.[50] These guidelines were grounded in the concept of Maat ("truth, justice"), which constituted the veritable foundation of Egyptian ethics, religion, and civilization. Maat was perceived as the pristine condition of primordial order by which the gods and humanity were to live.[51] It was the principle that governed all actions, and the standard by which all deeds were judged.[52] Far from being a mechanistic force, Maat required social solidarity and human action for its realization,[53] and instructional texts provided the medium through which individuals were taught to act in conformity with Maat.[54]

While Maat imposed obligations on all social classes, the task of maintaining and realizing Maat was the particular responsibility of the pharaonic institution. As the microcosmic representative of the sun god, the king functioned as the sole mediator between humanity and the gods, establishing order in place of disorder (*isft*), extending the boundaries of the land,[55] enhancing the prestige of the state, providing for the needs of society,[56] and ruling in conformity with Maat, making

---

50   Baines, "Society," 130.

51   H. H. Schmid, *Gerechtigkeit als Weltordnung: Hintergrund und Geschichte des alttestamentlichen Gerechtigkeitsbegriffs* (BHT 40; Tübingen: Mohr, 1968), 46–61; E. Hornung, *Conceptions of God in Ancient Egypt: The One and the Many* (trans. J. Baines; Ithaca: Cornell University Press, 1982), 213–16; M. Lichtheim, *Maat in Egyptian Autobiographies and Related Studies* (OBO 120; Göttingen: Vandenhoech & Ruprecht, 1992), 18–19; J. Assmann, *The Search for God in Ancient Egypt* (trans. D. Lorton; Ithaca: Cornell University Press, 2001), 3. Also see "The Instruction of Ptahhotep" (*AEL* 1:64), maxim 5; "The Instruction Addressed to King Merikare" (*AEL* 1:106–107), ll. 131–38.

52   E. Hornung, *Idea into Image: Essays on Ancient Egyptian Thought* (trans. E. Bredeck; New York: Timken Publishers, 1992), 136.

53   J. Assmann, *Maât, l'Egypte pharaonique et l'idée de justice sociale* (Conférences, essais et leçons du Collége de France; Paris: Julliard, 1989), 127–28; M. V. Fox, "World Order and Maʿat: A Crooked Parallel," *JANES* 23 (1995): 37–48.

54   Assmann, *Maât*, 35; Hornung, *Idea*, 138; F. Dunand and C. Zivie-Coche, *Gods and Men in Egypt: 3000 BCE to 395 CE* (trans. D. Lorton; Ithaca: Cornell University Press, 2004), 147.

55   See "The Instruction of King Amenhemet I for his Son Sesostris I" (*AEL* 1:137), ll. 2.10–2.11.

56   See "The Instruction Addressed to King Merikare" (*AEL* 1:106–107), ll. 47–52; "The Instruction of King Amenhemet I for his Son Sesostris I" (*AEL* 1:137), ll. 2.12–3.3.

certain that the cults were maintained and the gods were appeased.[57] In addition, the royal administration served as an intermediary between the king and the rest of society.[58] As the functional extension of the pharaonic institution, these officials sought to establish Maat by fulfilling the expectations inherent in their social and administrative roles. In so doing, they functioned as a conduit for Maat, extending it from the royal sphere to the general populace. In view of the importance of the state in the realization of Maat, it is not surprising that Egyptian instructional texts show a particular concern for the elite, for they were the media through which Maat was realized and the instrument that made society function.[59]

Egyptian instructional texts served as a repository of traditional social virtues and the primary means of socialization. As the codified norm of socio-moral values, the instructional literature trained members of the official class to observe the fundamental principles of the moral order, to function within their official positions, and to achieve success.[60] Though these works rarely touch on topics whose relevance is limited to the professional elite, they describe the basic principles of social existence. The "father" represents the embodiment of experience, insight, and cultural tradition, which he transmits to his son in order to initiate the recipient into society and its culture.[61] Rather than functioning as manuals that describe the specific tricks of the bureaucratic trade, these works served as a written deposit of key cultural traditions that were used to socialize members of the ruling class.[62] They were not composed as school "textbooks," but were intended to orient readers to the social world.[63] In so doing, these documents attempted to inculcate the concept of Maat within the elite and thus maintain the order of social life.

In light of the discourse setting of Egyptian instructional literature, the subject matter they contain, and the fundamental role of the pharaonic administration in the maintenance of society, Egyptian instructional texts may be

---

57   Assmann, *Maât*, 115–28; D. P. Silverman, "Divinity and Deities in Ancient Egypt," in *Religion in Ancient Egypt: Gods, Myths, and Personal Practice* (ed. B. E. Shafer; Ithaca: Cornell University Press, 1991), 58–73.

58   Doxey, *Egyptian Non-Royal Epithets*, 26.

59   Assmann, *Maât*, 115–16.

60   Perdue, *Wisdom and the Cult*, 26.

61   See J. Assmann, "Das Bild des Vaters im Alten Ägypten," in *Das Vaterbild in Mythos und Geschichte* (ed. H. Tellenbach; Berlin: Kohlhammer, 1976), 20–29; P. Nel, "The Concept 'Father' in the Wisdom Literature of the Ancient Near East," *JNSL* 5 (1977): 53–66.

62   J. Assmann, "Kulturelle und literarische Texte," in *Ancient Egyptian Literature: History and Forms* (Probleme der Ägyptologie 10; Leiden: Brill, 1996), 60–82; idem, *The Mind of Egypt*, 125; D. M. Carr, *Writing on the Tablet of the Heart: Origins of Scripture and Literature* (Oxford: Oxford University Press, 2005), 77.

63   See Baines, "Literacy," 580; Weeks, *Early Israelite Wisdom*, 19; idem, *Instruction and Imagery in Proverbs 1–9* (Oxford: Oxford University Press, 2007), 16–32; Parkinson, *Poetry and Culture*, 236.

considered courtly documents. As the products and property of the official class, these texts ostensibly direct their advice to members of the elite, contain material that is either limited to or particularly relevant for the elite, and function within the wider project of enculturation in order to ensure the realization of Maat within society.

While Egyptian instructions contain several courtly elements, the instructional genre is not limited to Egypt; Mesopotamia and Syria also produced instructional texts that were shaped in accordance with their own ideas and cultural contexts. In order to avoid drawing strict analogies between Egypt and other societies in the ancient world, it is necessary to examine the discursive, thematic, and conceptual features of Mesopotamian and Syrian instructional texts within their social and cultural environment.

2.2 Mesopotamian and Syrian Instructional Literature

Though "wisdom" may not be an appropriate generic designation for certain Mesopotamian or Syrian literary works,[64] several documents contain features that are comparable to Egyptian instructional texts. Similar to their Egyptian counterparts, most Mesopotamian and Syrian instructions possess a conventional discursive setting. These sapiential works are cast in the form of an address from a father to his son and discuss particular themes that are characteristic of the ancient Near Eastern instructional tradition. In addition, these documents typically identify a speaker and addressee and display a consistent documentary history from the third millennium through the first millennium BC. Though Mesopotamian and Syrian instructions differ from their Egyptian analogues in terms of epistemology and cultural tradition, their formal and thematic features situate these works within a relatively stable international literary tradition. The discursive setting and thematic emphases of each work deserves a brief comment.

2.2.1 The Discourse Setting of Mesopotamian and Syrian Instructional Literature

While Mesopotamia and Syria's instructional tradition is not as extensive as Egypt's, at least two texts delineate a specific discursive setting. The first is The Instructions of Shuruppak.[65] As the oldest known exemplar of the instructional

---

64   G. Buccellati, "Wisdom and Not: The Case of Mesopotamia," *JAOS* 101 (1981): 35–47; Lambert, *BWL* 1.

65   For the text, see "Instructions of Suruppak" (*BWL*, 92–95); C. Wilcke, "Philologische Bemerkungen zum *Rat des Suruppag* und Versuch einer neuen Übersetzung," *ZA* 68 (1978): 196–232; M. Civil, "Notes on the 'Instructions of Suruppak'," *JNES* 43 (1984): 281–98; B. Alster, *The Instructions of Suruppak: A Sumerian Proverb Collection* (Mesopotamia: Copenhagen Studies in

genre, the work is presented as an address by the antediluvian ruler Shuruppak to his son Ziusudra, the pious king and sole survivor of the flood who was granted immortality by the gods.[66] Similar to its Egyptian counterparts, the Instructions of Shuruppak are cast in the conventional form of a father instructing his son. However, in contrast to Egyptian instructions, the frame narrative is restated twice in the document and the recipient is addressed repeatedly as "my son" in the main body of the work.[67] The concluding section of the document presents the text as a written deposit of teaching for future generations, but the admonitions in the main body of the work are directed specifically toward Ziusudra. Though the speaker and addressee of the document seem to be fictional personages, placed within the text to enhance its authority and create a sense of continuity with the past,[68] they are presented as kings and heroes nonetheless.

The Words of Ahiqar represent the second instructional text that delineates a concrete discourse setting.[69] As one of the most widely disseminated works in the ancient world, Ahiqar is known through several later recensions that stem from different geographical locations.[70] Though these later versions present a different arrangement of the material and provide a more developed narrative than the

Assyriology 2; Copenhagen: Akademisk Forlag, 1974); "Shuruppak," translated by B. Alster (*COS* 1.176: 569–70).

66 See "The Eridu Genesis," translated by T. Jacobsen (*COS* 1.158: 513–15).

67 See Römheld, *Die Weisheitlehre im alten Orient*, 85–96, 110–11; J. Day, "Foreign Semitic Influence on the Wisdom of Israel and Its Appropriation in the Book of Proverbs," in *Wisdom in Ancient Israel: Essays in Honour of J. A. Emerton* (ed. J. Day et al.; Cambridge: Cambridge University Press, 1995), 65–66; Alster, *The Instructions of Suruppak*, ll. 6–12, 35, 39, 66, 78–87, 138, 148–57, 165, 170, 197, 212, 223, 265. Within the instructions proper, Alster argues that the address "my son" functions as a substitute for the frame narrative. See B. Alster, *Studies in Sumerian Proverbs* (Mesopotamia: Copenhagen Studies in Assyriology 3; Copenhagen: Akademisk Forlag, 1975), 107, 216.

68 See Kramer, *The Sumerians*, 224; B. Alster, "Literary Aspects of Sumerian and Akkadian Proverbs," in *Mesopotamian Poetic Language: Sumerian and Akkadian* (Cuneiform Monographs 6; Groningen: Styx, 1996), 9. For a discussion of Shuruppak and Ziusudra within Mesopotamian literary tradition, see "Instructions of Suruppak" (*BWL*, 93–94); P.-A. Beaulieu, "The Social and Intellectual Setting of Babylonian Wisdom Literature," in *Wisdom Literature in Mesopotamia and Israel* (SBLSymS 36; Atlanta: Society of Biblical Literature, 2007), 4–8.

69 For the Aramaic text, see J. M. Lindenberger, *The Aramaic Proverbs of Ahiqar* (JHNES; Baltimore: Johns Hopkins University Press, 1983); "Ahiqar," translated by J. M. Lindenberger (*OTP* 2: 479–508); I. Kottsieper, *Die Sprache der Ahiqarsprüche* (BZAW 194; Berlin: de Gruyter, 1990); A. Yardeni and B. Porten, *Textbook of Aramaic Documents from Ancient Egypt: Volume 3: Literature, Accounts, Lists* (Hebrew University, Dept. of the History of the Jewish People, Texts and Studies for Students; Jerusalem: Hebrew University, 1993), 24–57.

70 For the versions, see F. C. Conybeare, J. R. Harris and A. S. Lewis, *The Story of Ahiqar from the Aramaic, Syriac, Arabic, Armenian, Ethiopic, Old Turkish, Greek and Slavonic Versions* (2nd ed; Cambridge: Cambridge University Press, 1913). Also see Tob 1:21–22; 2:10; 11:18; and 14:10 for details that are not included in the Aramaic narrative.

older Aramaic text, each of these works is arranged within a dual setting. The framework story provides the exterior setting of the text, which is cast in the seventh century, during the reign of Esarhaddon.[71] Here Ahiqar is presented as the official counselor and seal-bearer of the king, who seeks permission from Esarhaddon to groom his nephew Nadin to succeed him in his official post. When the king approves of the appointment, the narrative recounts Nadin's betrayal and Ahiqar's preservation under Nabusumiskun, an officer of the king. The Aramaic version then shifts to an interior setting, according to which Ahiqar chastises his nephew with a series of maxims. In a departure from the order of the Aramaic text, the Syriac, Arabic, and Armenian versions include a series of detailed instructions delivered by Ahiqar to his nephew at the time of his ascension to the vizierate.[72] Moreover, these versions extend the Aramaic narrative by describing Ahiqar's emergence from hiding, his success in Egypt, his restoration to favor, and his revenge on Nadin, who overdoses on Ahiqar's instruction and bursts. Despite their diversity, each of these documents is cast in a royal setting and purport to be the admonitions Ahiqar delivered to his "son" Nadin. This discourse setting situates the piece within a courtly context, that is, among high officials within the royal bureaucracy.

In view of the ostensive speakers and addressees presented in these discursive texts, at least three conclusions may be drawn. First, the works are framed by narratives or hortatory introductions that identify the discourse setting of the document. Second, these didactic pieces are cast in the form of a father's instructions for his son and employ the standard idiom "my son" throughout the main body of the work. Third, the ostensive speakers and addressees of these texts are either kings or viziers within the royal bureaucracy. These features suggest that Mesopotamian and Syrian instructions share several formal similarities with Egyptian instructional texts. Similar to their Egyptian

---

71   Though the frame narrative places the story within a seventh century Mesopotamian setting, the language and religious perspective of the sayings favor a northern Syrian context. Rather than assuming that the Aramaic text is a translation of an Akkadian work, recent scholarship suggests the composition was composed originally in two different Aramaic dialects. The frame narrative is written in the Imperial Aramaic dialect of the neo-Assyrian period, while the aphorisms are written in a more archaic dialect that is comparable to Old Aramaic. These features have led scholars to conclude that the narrative and gnomic portions of the text stem from different regions and were combined at a later date. In view of the lack of Persian loanwords in the narrative section and the archaic language of the sayings, it appears the two sections were combined before the mid-sixth century. In this case, the Aramaic text may be dated to the late seventh or early sixth century B.C. For a discussion, see J. C. Greenfield, "The Dialects of Early Aramaic," *JNES* 37 (1978): 93–99; idem, "The Wisdom of Ahiqar," in *Wisdom in Ancient Israel: Essays in Honour of J. A. Emerton* (ed. J. Day et al., Cambridge: Cambridge University Press, 1995), 43–52; Lindenberger, *The Aramaic Proverbs of Ahiqar*, 16–27.

72   See Perdue, who argues that the instructional material inserted by the later versions at the time of Nadin's succession is an example of a liminal social setting, which is also common in Egyptian instructions ("Liminality," 121–22).

counterparts, the instructional material is embedded within a formal framework, cast in the form of paternal instructions, and addressed to high-ranking members within the royal bureaucracy.

The discourse setting of Mesopotamian and Syrian instructional works places the documents within a courtly environment. This dialogical context not only identifies the speaker and addressee of the text, but it also serves as a framework within which to understand the meaning and pragmatic significance of the instructions proper. However, as noted above, it is necessary to examine the subject matter of the instructional texts to assess the degree to which the material corresponds with the discourse setting of the document. This form of analysis may provide a more reliable indication of the nature of these didactic works and illuminate the degree to which these instructional pieces may be considered courtly documents.

2.2.2 The Content of Mesopotamian and Syrian Instructional Literature

The instructional literature from Mesopotamia and Syria incorporates a pastiche of general concerns derived from the natural, cosmic, ritual, and ethical dimensions of the world. This is apparent in each sapiential piece, which exhibit a wide range of distinctive cultural emphases. The Instructions of Shuruppak include a variety of popular sayings derived from daily life. The document is replete with aphorisms pertaining to horticultural activities and fauna—characteristic motifs employed in Sumerian proverb collections to describe the natural world and illustrate human behavior.[73] Among the randomly arranged prohibitions, positive commands, and traditional sayings, the writer warns his addressee of the dangers involved in becoming a guarantor, associating with another man's wife, and engaging in quarrels. In addition, the document commends familial solidarity, fine speech, and submission to authority, and provides advice regarding the acquisition of servants and the displacement of worthless people. The contrasts between the foolish and the wise and the wicked and the pious suggest that the text's central concern is to transmit proper patterns of social order, which were grounded in the wisdom of Utu, the god of justice.[74]

---

73 See Alster, "Literary Aspects of Sumerian and Akkadian Proverbs," 2–9; idem, *The Instructions of Suruppak*, ll. 15–18, 49, 53, 217–18, 220–22, 228–29. In spite of Shuruppak's use of popular proverbs, the instruction differs from Sumerian proverb collections. Sumerian proverb collections do not contain direct admonitions or precepts and are not arranged within a formal frame. However, the Instructions of Shuruppak are cast within a formal frame and contain precepts that express rules for moral conduct. These features suggest that the Instructions of Shuruppak constitute a "literary poem" rather than a formal proverb collection. See Alster, *Studies in Sumerian Proverbs*, 15; idem, *Proverbs of Ancient Sumer: The World's Earliest Proverb Collections* (2 vols.; Bethesda: CDL Press, 1997), 1:xxiv.

74 See Alster, *The Instructions of Suruppak*, ll. 76–77.

As a whole, the document does not appear to present any distinctive, aristocratic values. Rather, the social references and inherent imagery of the admonitions seem to reflect the disposition of those involved in the management of large households.[75]

The Counsels of Wisdom is a fragmentary piece that does not provide a concrete discursive setting. This document is directed toward an anonymous "son" and addresses a variety of themes, ranging from domestic and interpersonal affairs to specific counsel pertaining to the vizierate.[76] In general, the piece is divided into ten sections, each of which presents a series of admonitions regarding a particular topic. The topics covered include conduct toward evil companions, proper and improper speech, kindness toward the marginalized, marriage, interpersonal relationships, and religious piety—common cultural values that encompass the ethical norms of society. However, one section includes specific vocational advice. Here the speaker warns his "son" against coveting the prince's wealth. As the servant and seal-bearer of the king with sole access to the royal treasury, the son is advised to act with integrity and guard against the temptations inherent in his administrative position. These admonitions have led many to conclude that the work represents the advice of a high bureaucratic official to his son who will succeed him as vizier to the king.[77] Whether or not this conclusion is accepted, the text contains practical values and specific vocational advice that is particularly relevant to a high-ranking member within the royal bureaucracy.

The Akkadian Advice to a Prince also exhibits a courtly flavor.[78] Similar to the Counsels of Wisdom, the piece does not possess a definitive discursive setting and contains a series of admonitions directed toward members of the royal institution. However, in contrast to the Counsels of Wisdom, Advice to a Prince is composed in the casuistic style of omens.[79] This Akkadian text emphasizes the royal administration's responsibility to maintain justice and adhere to the legal rights guaranteed to the citizens in the cities of Sippar, Nippur, and Babylon. If the king or his administrators fail to recognize these divinely established privileges, the gods will abandon their temples and raise up foreign armies to

---

75 B. Alster, "Proverbs from Ancient Mesopotamia: Their History and Social Implications," *Proverbium* 10 (1993): 9–10.

76 For the text, see "Counsels of Wisdom" (*BWL*, 96–107); "Counsels of Wisdom" (B. R. Foster, *Before the Muses: An Anthology of Akkadian Literature* [2nd ed.; Bethesda: CDL Press, 1996], 1:326–29). In theory, it seems that the prologue included the ostensive author of the document. However, in light of the fragmentary nature of the work, the attribution is unclear.

77 See "Counsels of Wisdom" (*BWL*, 96); McKane, *Proverbs: A New Approach*, 151.

78 For the text, see "Advice to a Prince" (*BWL*, 110–15); "Advice to a Prince" (Foster, *Before the Muses*, 2:745–47).

79 See G. E. Bryce, "Omen-Wisdom in Ancient Israel," *JBL* 94 (1975): 22–23.

decimate the land.[80] Though the document does not identify an author or administration, the writer seems to have been either a priest or a court scribe who directed his counsels toward the king and his administration to protect the interests of his own class.[81]

The Words of Ahiqar also present themes that pertain to court functionaries. The document combines courtly wisdom with folk wisdom through a series of formal proverbs, fables, and numerical sayings arranged in pairs or small groups according to subject matter, formal structure, or genre.[82] The sayings cover a wide variety of topics, ranging from family discipline, prudent speech, diligence, and humility to respect for the king and proper behavior towards inferiors and superiors.[83] Though many sayings are fragmentary and some of the instructions are general in character, the document presents a series of political virtues and practical admonitions regarding the courtier's behavior vis-à-vis the king. These features suggest that the piece was accessible to many, but particularly relevant for officials within the royal administration.[84]

The content of Mesopotamian and Syrian instructional texts suggests these didactic works contain a significant amount of material related to the official class. The Counsels of Wisdom fuse general political virtues with specific vocational advice that pertains to the vizierate. Advice to a Prince delineates the bureaucratic responsibilities of the monarchy and directs its omen-patterned counsels toward the king and his administration. The Words of Ahiqar integrate popular wisdom with aristocratic advice concerning an individual's relationship to the king, while the Instructions of Shuruppak describe the social virtues needed to maintain order within society. In general, Mesopotamian and Syrian instructional texts are not only attributed to or directed toward prominent individuals within the bureaucracy, but these works also contain subjects and themes that are either limited to or particularly relevant for the official class. These didactic pieces seek to inculcate certain virtues in the lives of their recipients and present a fundamental moral vision for their addressee. They serve as an ethical repository that delineates traditional, cultural values intended to

---

80   The gods mentioned in the document are Ea, Shamash, Enlil, Marduk, Anu, Erra, Adad, and Nabu.

81   For proposals regarding the author and addressee of the document, see "Advice to a Prince" (*BWL*, 111); Bryce, "Omen-Wisdom," 23; S. W. Cole, "The Crimes and Sacrileges of Nabu-Suma-Iskun," *ZA* 84 (1994): 220–52. Also see V. A. Hurowitz, who suggests that the author attempted to present the document as a composition of the god Ea ("Advice to a Prince: A Message from Ea," *SAAB* 12 (1998): 39–53).

82   Lindenberger, *The Aramaic Proverbs of Ahiqar*, 21.

83   For a discussion of the relationship between the Instruction of Ankhsheshonq and the Syriac and Armenian versions of Ahiqar, see Lichtheim, *Late Egyptian Wisdom Literature*, 13–22; "Die Spruchsammlung des Anch-Scheschonki" (Brunner, *Die Weisheitsbücher der Ägypter*, 259); Weeks, *Early Israelite Wisdom*, 172–73.

84   Lindenberger, *The Aramaic Proverbs of Ahiqar*, 21.

shape a specific socio-moral vision for their beneficiaries. The fundamental features of this worldview deserve specific comment.

2.2.3 The Worldview of Mesopotamian and Syrian Instructional Literature

Similar to Egypt's ethical vision, Mesopotamian and Syrian instructional texts focus on the concept of cosmic and social order. According to Mesopotamian tradition, the god Enki divided the cosmos into celestial entities and cultural phenomena, each of which was regulated by a *me*.[85] These *me*'s functioned as a set of rules that ensured the proper maintenance of order within the divine and terrestrial realms.[86] They were properties instituted by the gods that enabled civilized human life and principles that determined human success. These fundamental patterns of civilization were transmitted from the gods to humanity through seven semi-divine, antediluvian sages (*apkallu*), who in turn passed their divinely endowed wisdom and social expertise on to a group of human, postdiluvian "scholars" (*ummanu*).[87] This group of *ummanu* preserved these social principles and disseminated them through literature in order to transmit the tenets of order within the cosmos.

Mesopotamian and Syrian instructional texts reflected on these socio-religious principles and translated them into written media to align the individual with the proper pattern of social order. However, as literary works, these documents were not written for public consumption or directed toward the general populace. Since the majority of the population was illiterate, these instructional works were accessible only to the social elite.[88] Writing was used to bolster bureaucratic and social control, and the social function of writing restricted these texts to a select group.[89] While these documents contain popular material that was accessible to a wide variety of people, by virtue of being written

---

85   See "Inanna and Enki," translated by G. Farber (*COS* 1.161: 522–26).

86   See Kramer, *The Sumerians*, 115–16; T. Jacobsen, *The Treasures of Darkness* (New Haven: Yale University Press, 1976), 84–85; D. T. Potts, *Mesopotamian Civilization: The Material Foundations* (Ithaca: Cornell University Press, 1997), 185–86.

87   For a discussion of the *apkallu* tradition, see B. Foster, "Wisdom and the Gods in Ancient Mesopotamia," *Or* 43 (1976): 344–54; S. Denning-Bolle, *Wisdom in Akkadian Literature: Expression, Instruction, Dialogue* (Mededelingen en verhandelingen van het Vooraziatisch-Egyptisch Genootschap "Ex Oriente Lux" 28; Leiden: Ex Oriente Lux, 1992), 48–56.

88   See J. L. Crenshaw, "Education in Ancient Israel," *JBL* 104 (1985): 608; S. Parpola, "The Man without a Scribe and the Question of Literacy in the Assyrian Empire," in *Beiträge zu altorientalischen und mittelmeerischen Kulturen: Festschrift für Wolfgang Röllig* (ed. B. Pongratz-Leisten et al.; Neukirchen-Vluyn: Neukirchener Verlag, 1997), 315–24; Carr, *Writing on the Tablet*, 20; L. E. Pearce, "The Scribes and Scholars of Ancient Mesopotamia," *CANE* 2265.

89   See Potts, *Mesopotamian Civilization*, 236; J. L. Crenshaw, *Education in Ancient Israel: Across the Deadening Silence* (ABRL; New York: Doubleday, 1998), 29–40.

these compositions became the property of an elite class and the restricted property of the written culture.

In view of their limited audience, it appears these didactic works were composed either in the royal court or in the context of scribal education in order to teach literacy and to inculcate cultural values into the lives of their recipients.[90] The educational system in Mesopotamia was designed to train young officials to function within particular administrative and ritual positions.[91] Educational institutions served as the media through which central values were fostered, future members of the bureaucracy were socialized, and the ideological foundation of the bureaucratic class was formed.[92] However, while Mesopotamian and Syrian instructional works served as an indispensable vehicle for cultural education within these institutions, these literary works did not function as simple vocational manuals or lexical and grammatical guides. Rather it seems that Mesopotamian and Syrian instructional texts attempted to inculcate proper ethical and cultural values into their recipients to cultivate virtues that would enable the official class to perform their bureaucratic functions and to achieve harmony within society.

The task of maintaining order within society was the particular responsibility of the royal institution. On the one hand, the king was perceived as the preeminent sage and the wise man *par excellence*. The monarchy was governed by a number of *me*'s and ordained by the gods for the specific purpose of establishing order in society through warfare, social justice, building programs, and cultic rituals.[93] On the other hand, the royal bureaucracy was the instrument through

---

90 Sjöberg, "The Old Babylonian Eduba," 171; S. N. Kramer, "The Sage in Sumerian Literature: A Composite Portrait," in *The Sage in Israel and the Ancient Near East* (ed. J. G. Gammie and L. G. Perdue; Winona Lake: Eisenbrauns, 1990); 32; R. F. G. Sweet, "The Sage in Mesopotamian Palaces and Royal Courts," in *The Sage in Israel and the Ancient Near East* (ed. J. G. Gammie and L. G. Perdue; Winona Lake: Eisenbrauns, 1990), 104; N. Veldhuis, "Sumerian Proverbs in Their Curricular Context," *JAOS* 120 (2000): 383–99; Carr, *Writing on the Tablet*, 31.

91 There is a general consensus that students within the educational system came from the elite households and that instruction took place within the private home of the father/teacher. See C. J. Gadd, *Teachers and Students in the Oldest Schools* (London: University of London, 1956), 24–25; Kramer, "The Sage in Sumerian Literature," 37; Carr, *Writing on the Tablet*, 82; Pearce, "The Scribes and Scholars of Ancient Mesopotamia," 2265.

92 P. Michalowski, "Charisma and Control: On Continuity and Change in Early Mesopotamian Bureaucratic Systems," in *The Organization of Power: Aspects of Bureaucracy in the Ancient Near East* (ed. M. Gibson and R. D. Biggs; Chicago: The Oriental Institute of the University of Chicago, 1987), 63–66; Kramer, "The Sage in Sumerian Literature," 32–33.

93 See L. Kalugila, *The Wise King: Studies in Royal Wisdom as Divine Revelation in the Old Testament and Its Environment* (ConBOT 15; Lund: CWK Gleerup, 1980), 39–56; Kramer, "The Sage in Sumerian Literature," 40–44; Sweet, "The Sage in Mesopotamian Palaces and Royal Courts," 99–102; idem, "The Sage in Akkadian Literature: A Philological Study," in *The Sage in Israel and the Ancient Near East* (ed. J. G. Gammie and L. G. Perdue; Winona Lake: Eisenbrauns, 1990), 51–56; J. N. Postgate, *Early Mesopotamia: Society and Economy at the Dawn of History* (London: Routledge, 1992; repr., London: Routledge, 1994), 262–74; W. G. Lambert, "Kingship in Ancient Mesopotamia,"

which order was realized in society. As the functional extension of the royal institution, the temple and palace scribes regulated the administrative, economic and bureaucratic tasks of the state by administering justice, redistributing wealth, training officials, and fulfilling the expectations inherent in their administrative roles.[94] In so doing, they contributed to the royal task of establishing order and made society functional. In view of the fundamental role of the bureaucracy in the ancient oriental world, it is not surprising that Mesopotamian and Syrian instructional texts show a particular concern for the official class, for they were the divinely ordained vehicle that maintained order within the cosmos and the glue that held society together.[95]

In light of the discourse setting of Mesopotamian and Syrian instructional texts, the subject matter they contain, and the fundamental role of the bureaucracy in the maintenance of order within society, Mesopotamian and Syrian instructional texts may be considered courtly documents. Similar to their Egyptian counterparts, Mesopotamian and Syrian instructional works direct their admonitions toward the official class, contain subjects and themes that are either limited to or particularly relevant for the official class, and function within the wider project of education-enculturation in order to ensure the continuation of order within society.

2.3 Conclusion

These conclusions are not novel. Many scholars have recognized that ancient Near Eastern instructional texts presuppose a courtly context and contain subjects and themes that pertain to officials within the bureaucracy. As the exclusive property of the written culture, these documents combine traditional cultural values with specific vocational advice to orient readers to the social world and build character. Whether these instructional works are considered to be cultural texts, school "textbooks," courtly or pastoral "travesties," pieces of royal propaganda, or the creative musings of professional writers, their aristocratic character is generally accepted.

Ancient oriental instructional texts play a significant role in the investigation of the book of Proverbs, for they provide a generic framework through which to

---

in *King and Messiah in Israel and the Ancient Near East: Proceedings of the Oxford Old Testament Seminar* (JSOTSup 270; Sheffield: Sheffield Academic Press, 1998), 54–70. Also see "The Eridu Genesis" (*COS* 1.158: 514).

94   See A. L. Oppenheim, *Ancient Mesopotamia: Portrait of a Dead Civilization* (Chicago: University of Chicago Press, 1964), 96–104; Potts, *Mesopotamian Civilization*, 208; Sweet, "The Sage in Mesopotamian Palaces and Royal Courts," 101; Pearce, "The Scribes and Scholars of Ancient Mesopotamia," 2273–77.

95   Carr, *Writing on the Tablet*, 33.

read and assess the materials in the compendium. However, a problem arises when the nature and function of these sapiential texts are transposed to the book of Proverbs. While Proverbs shares several formal, generic features with ancient Near Eastern instructional texts, the latter cannot be used to elucidate phenomena within ancient Israel without an understanding of the social context of the sapiential discourse. Since strict social analogies cannot be drawn between these ancient Near Eastern societies and Israel, it is necessary to examine the book of Proverbs within its distinct, literary context in order to assess the degree to which it may be considered a courtly piece. This is the task to which we now turn, beginning with Proverbs 1–9.

Chapter 3

The Value of Wisdom: Proverbs 1–9

The formal and thematic similarities between ancient Near Eastern instructional texts and the book of Proverbs bears witness to Israel's intellectual involvement in the international phenomenon of wisdom literature. Israel's sages not only incorporated a shared stream of literary forms, idioms, and motifs that are characteristic of the instructional tradition, but they also shaped the material to address the socio-religious needs of the Israelite community. This process of acquisition-adaptation is evident in Proverbs, which exhibits both formal, generic similarities to ancient Near Eastern instructional texts as well as some formidable differences.

3.1 Proverbs 1–9 vis-à-vis the Ancient Near Eastern Instructional Tradition

The book of Proverbs includes several features that are characteristic of ancient Near Eastern instructional tradition. In general, the compendium contains conventional sayings and basic formulas that appear in Mesopotamian instructions and Ahiqar.[1] In addition, the document incorporates longer poetic compositions that resemble Egyptian instructions.[2] Moreover, the material is cast within a discourse setting that places the work within the international stream of wisdom literature. The image of a father transmitting advice to a son is a dominant motif of ancient oriental instructional works and a defining feature of the genre.[3]

The formal and thematic features of Proverbs situate the work within the ancient oriental sapiential tradition. Nonetheless, the compilers of these materials

---

1   See Day, "Foreign Semitic Influence on the Wisdom of Israel and its Appropriation in the Book of Proverbs," 55–70.

2   See C. Kayatz, *Studien zu Proverbien 1–9* (WMANT 22; Neukirchen-Vluyn: Neukirchener Verlag, 1966), 26–75; J. M. Thompson, *The Form and Function of Proverbs in Ancient Israel* (Paris: Mouton, 1974), 39–94; R. N. Whybray, *Wisdom in Proverbs: The Concept of Wisdom in Proverbs 1–9* (SBT 45; Naperville: Allenson, 1965), 61–71; idem, *The Composition of the Book of Proverbs*, 11–13.

3   S. Weeks, *Instruction and Imagery*, 12.

were not slaves to mechanical laws of genre.[4] While Proverbs exhibits formal, generic similarities to ancient Near Eastern didactic wisdom, the book contains at least three distinctive features. First, Proverbs invokes the authority of the mother alongside the father in the instructions (1:8; 6:20). Though the mother does not represent an independent voice in the instructions proper, her role in the lectures is a distinguishing feature of Proverbs' pedagogy.[5] Second, in terms of content, Woman Wisdom is presented as an autonomous figure who extends the scope of the material to include the communal and cosmic realms of society.[6] Third, the formal preamble to the book (1:1–7) departs from the traditional title formula employed in ancient Near Eastern instructional texts, as the work does not identify the specific addressee of the discourse.[7]

Together, these elements of continuity and discontinuity between Proverbs 1–9 and ancient Near Eastern instructional texts have given rise to questions concerning Israel's dependence on and imitation of foreign precedents. In light of the generic similarities between these works, scholars have appealed to ancient oriental instructions to illuminate the social setting of Proverbs 1–9. That is, they employ Near Eastern instructions to understand the father-son relationship. In so doing, scholars situate the material in two principle settings: the school and the family.

The evidence for formal schools in Egypt and Mesopotamia is incontrovertible.[8] In the case of Mesopotamia, thousands of student exercises have been discovered, ranging from lexical lists and small literary excerpts to copies of major compositions.[9] The Mesopotamian scribal matrix collected and updated a limited corpus of standard texts that were used to inculcate cultural values and to teach literacy. In the main, education took place in the *edubba*

---

4   K. A. Kitchen, "The Basic Literary Forms and Formulations of Ancient Instructional Writings in Egypt and Western Asia," in *Studien zu altägyptischen Lebenslehren* (OBO 28; Göttingen: Vandenhoeck & Ruprecht, 1979), 243.

5   See C. R. Fontaine, "The Sage in the Family and Tribe," in *The Sage in Israel and the Ancient Near East* (ed. J. G. Gammie and L. G. Perdue; Winona Lake: Eisenbrauns, 1990), 161; Day, "Foreign Semitic Influence," 66; Weeks, *Instruction and Imagery*, 39. Also see B. Alster, *Studies in Sumerian Proverbs*, 137; and "The Satire of the Trades" (*AEL* 1:191), where Dua-Khety identifies the teachings of the mother with his own at the conclusion of his instructions.

6   F.-J. Steiert, *Die Weisheit Israels—ein Fremdkörper im Alten Testament?: Eine Untersuchung zum Buch der Sprüche auf dem Hintergrund der ägyptischen Weisheitslehren* (Freiburger Theologische Studien 143; Freiburg: Herder, 1990), 217–19.

7   See Kitchen, "The Basic Literary Forms and Formulations," 243–45; Steiert, *Die Weisheit Israels*, 215; Weeks, *Instruction and Imagery*, 39.

8   See Gadd, *Teachers and Students*, passim; Kramer, *The Sumerians*, 224–45; Sjöberg, "The Old Babylonian Eduba," 159–79; Michalowski, "Charisma and Control," 55–68; Assmann, *The Mind of Egypt*, 123–27; Carr, *Writing on the Tablet*, 17–109.

9   P. D. Gesche, *Schulunterricht in Babylonien im ersten Jahrtausend v. Chr* (AOAT 275; Münster: Ugarit-Verlag, 2000), 9–24.

("school"), which was often the master scribe's own home.[10] Though the student body was not limited to biological kin,[11] educational roles were shaped by domestic relationships. The teacher adopted the role of a father and the student assumed the role of his son.[12] This familial structure formed the basis of an apprenticeship system, in which students were socialized and groomed for professional posts.

The educational system in Egypt is comparable to Mesopotamia's. In general, literary texts were used in educational settings to inculcate social values and to teach literacy. The earliest forms of education were based in the domestic unit. However, the familial relationship within an educational setting extended beyond the biological family unit to include other students. Education did not take place in a special structure; rather instruction occurred in the home of the master scribe.[13] Within the educational system, instructional texts played a formative role in the socialization of prospective bureaucratic functionaries. However, as noted in chapter two, these works were not created as school textbooks. The curricular use of the instructional genre does not appear until the New Kingdom,[14] and the authors of these works are not presented as schoolteachers. Though many of these didactic works were used in schools during the New Kingdom and the Late Period, they were not composed as school textbooks. Rather, instructional works seem to have been created outside of the educational sphere in order to inculcate cultural values and transmit vocational advice to their recipients.[15]

In short, the evidence for formal schools in Egypt and Mesopotamia is undeniable. The earliest forms of education did not take place in separate schools with professional teachers, but in a family-based, apprenticeship-like atmosphere within the homes of scribal masters.[16] Here both the biological children of the scribal teacher as well as those outside of the immediate family unit received instruction. In later periods, separate, identifiable schools were formed and a stable curriculum of key cultural texts was instituted to socialize students.

However, despite the extensive evidence for educational institutions in the ancient oriental world, the existence of formal schools in Israel is not as clear. On

---

10   Gadd, *Teachers and Students*, 25; J. L. Crenshaw, *Education in Ancient Israel: Across the Deadening Silence* (ABRL; New York: Doubleday, 1998), 19; K. Volk, "Edubba'a und Edubba'a-Literatur; Rätsel und Lösungen," *ZA* 90 (2000): 5–8; Carr, *Writing on the Tablet*, 20.

11   Michalowski, "Charisma and Control," 58–64; Carr, *Writing on the Tablet*, 20–21.

12   Gadd, *Teachers and Students*, 15; Kramer, *The Sumerians*, 232.

13   Assmann, "Kulturelle und literarische Texte," 72. For a discussion of the different types of schools that emerged in the Middle Kingdom, see "The Satire of the Trades" (*AEL* 1:185); Brunner, *Altägyptische Erziehung*, 17; Assmann, "Schrift, Tod und Identität," 82–87; Carr, *Writing on the Tablet*, 68.

14   Parkinson, *Poetry and Culture in Middle Kingdom Egypt*, 236.

15   Assmann, "Das Bild des Vaters im Alten Ägypten," 24; Crenshaw, *Education in Ancient Israel*, 23; Weeks, *Early Israelite Wisdom*, 19.

16   Carr, *Writing on the Tablet*, 113.

the one hand, textual and epigraphic evidence suggests that some sort of education took place in ancient Israel.[17] Biblical texts date from various periods and reflect the presence of literate individuals (Judg 8:13–17; Isa 8:16; Jer 8:8; Hab 2:2; Job 31:35–37; Prov 25:1), while inscriptions, seals, ostraca, and graffiti point to a widespread knowledge of writing.[18] Nonetheless, since Hebrew is not as abstruse as other Near Eastern languages, literacy in ancient Israel does not mean that there was need for a formal, integrated school system.[19] On the other hand, biblical authors never mention schools and texts that seem to allude to formal educational establishments can be understood without postulating such an institution (Isa 28:9–13; 50:4–9; Prov 22:17–21).[20] Though several texts mention the education of the general populace (Qoh 12:9; 1 Chron 17:7–9) or intimate a specialized form of scribal training (2 Sam 8:15–18; 20:23–26; 1 Kgs 4:1–6; Prov 25:1), these passages do not provide a clear indication of the content of the curricula or the scope of the instruction. At best, they illuminate the multifaceted nature of education in ancient Israel. Among the textual remains, Sirach 51:23 represents the earliest extant reference to an educational institution in Syria-Palestine. However, the nature of the institution is ambiguous. On the whole, epigraphic evidence and the existence of literary texts presuppose that some sort of education took place in ancient Israel prior to the second century B.C. While

---

17   See Lemaire, *Les écoles et la formation de la Bible*; 7–33; idem, "The Sage in School and Temple," 165–81; D. W. Jamieson-Drake, *Scribes and Schools in Monarchic Judah: A Socio-Archeological Approach* (JSOTSup 109; Sheffield: Almond Press, 1991).

18   See A. Millard, "The Knowledge of Writing in Iron Age Palestine," *TynBul* 46 (1995): 207–17; R. S. Hess, "Literacy in Iron Age Israel," in *Windows into the Old Testament History: Evidence, Argument, and the Crisis of "Biblical Israel"* (ed. D. W. Baker et al.; Grand Rapids: Eerdmans, 2002), 82–95; G. Davies, "Hebrew Inscriptions," in *The Biblical World* (ed. J. Barton; London: Routledge, 2002); 1:270–86; idem, "Some Uses of Writing in Ancient Israel in the Light of Recently Published Inscriptions," in *Writing and Ancient Near Eastern Society: Papers in Honour of Alan R. Millard* (ed. C. Mee et al.; New York: T&T Clark, 2005), 155–74. Also see M. Haran, "On the Diffusion of Literacy and Schools in Ancient Israel," in *Congress Volume: Jerusalem 1986* (ed. J. A. Emerton; Leiden: Brill, 1988), 81–95.

19   C. H. Kraeling and R. M. Adams, eds., *City Invincible; A Symposium on Urbanization and Cultural Development in the Ancient Near East Held at the Oriental Institute of the University of Chicago, December 4–7, 1958* (Chicago: University of Chicago, 1960), 123; Weeks, *Early Israelite Wisdom*, 151–53.

20   See F. W. Golka, "Die israelitische Weisheitsschule oder 'des Kaisers neue Kleider'," *VT* 33 (1983): 257–70; ET, *The Leopard's Spots*, 4–15; Crenshaw, "Education in Ancient Israel," 602–04; idem, *Education in Ancient Israel*, 90–96; Weeks, *Early Israelite Wisdom*, 132–56. For those who posit a theory of formal schools in ancient Israel, see Klostermann, "Schulwesen im alten Israel," 193–232; Dürr, *Das Erziehungswesen im Alten Testament und im Antiken Orient*; Hermisson, *Studien zur israelitischen Spruchweisheit*, 97–136; Lemaire, *Les écoles et la formation de la Bible*; G. I. Davies, "Were There Schools in Ancient Israel?", in *Wisdom in Ancient Israel: Essays in Honour of J. A. Emerton* (ed. R. P. Gordon et al.; Cambridge: Cambridge University Press, 1995), 199–211; E. W. Heaton, *Solomon's New Men: The Emergence of Ancient Israel as a National State* (New York: Pica Press, 1974); idem, *The School Tradition of the Old Testament: The Bampton Lectures for 1994* (Oxford: Oxford University Press, 1994).

the nature of this variegated, educational system is not clear, the discourse setting of Proverbs 1–9 may help to illuminate the character of some Israelite instruction.

3.2 The Discourse Setting of Proverbs 1–9

As noted above, the discourse setting of Proverbs 1–9 is conveyed through the father-son relationship. This idiom is the chief literary device that is maintained throughout the prologue (1:8, 10, 15; 2:1; 3:1, 11, 21; 4:1, 10, 20; 5:1, 20; 6:1, 3, 20; 7:1, 24). The idiom occurs throughout ancient Near Eastern instructions, where it indicates either blood relationship or the bond between a teacher and his pupil.[21] However, since strict social analogies cannot be drawn between ancient Near Eastern societies and Israel,[22] it is necessary to examine Proverbs 1–9 in order to determine the discourse setting of the material. We will begin by considering the school setting, and then assess the evidence for a domestic context in Proverbs 1–9.

3.2.1 The Social Setting of Proverbs 1–9

If the father-son idiom in Proverbs 1–9 is a cipher for a teacher-pupil relationship, it places the discourse setting of the instructions in the school. Several details in Proverbs have been interpreted to suggest this setting. First, in contrast to its ancient Near Eastern counterparts, Proverbs does not name an explicit addressee. Whether this anonymity is an Israelite innovation in the genre or a deliberate ploy to democratize the work, the lacuna leaves the relationship between father and son undefined. Second, the speeches of Woman Wisdom in the bustling bazaar may refer to public classrooms (1:20–21; 8:2–3).[23] Third, allusions to tuition payments are scattered throughout Proverbs 1–9 (3:14; 4:7; 8:10).[24] This is particularly evident in Proverbs 4:7, where קנה may carry the commercial connotation "buy" rather than a more general reference to "get."[25]

---

21   P. Nel, "The Concept 'Father' in the Wisdom Literature of the Ancient Near East," 53–66.

22   P. Nel, "A Proposed Method for Determining the Context of the Wisdom Admonitions," *JNSL* 6 (1978): 39; Weeks, *Early Israelite Wisdom*, 16-18.

23   Lemaire, *Les écoles et la formation de la Bible*, 53; B. Lang, *Wisdom and the Book of Proverbs: A Hebrew Goddess Redefined* (New York: The Pilgrim Press, 1986), 29–31.

24   Lemaire, *Les écoles et la formation de la Bible*, 57.

25   Davies, "Were There Schools in Ancient Israel?", 199–200; Crenshaw, *Education in Ancient Israel*, 96–97.

Fourth, Proverbs 5:13 clearly refers to teachers. Here the son identifies those who addressed him as מוֹרָי and מְלַמְּדָי, rather than "my father" or "my mother."[26] Together, these features have been interpreted to suggest that the father-son idiom functions as a formal designation for the teacher-pupil relationship.

However, in contrast to the school setting, the father-son idiom may also indicate a familial relationship. This notion is supported by both external and internal evidence. On the one hand, the biological relationship between a father and a son in a didactic setting is evident in several ancient Near Eastern instructional works. Egyptian didactic wisdom texts are cast as instructions from a father to his biological son, who is often named in the title. Since bureaucratic positions were often hereditary in both Egypt and Mesopotamia, this blood relationship is not surprising.[27] The same was true in Israel.[28] Israelite fathers not only passed their vocations on to their sons, but they were also responsible for their social, moral, and religious training (Gen 18:19; Exod 12:24; Deut 4:9–11; 6:20–25).[29] On the other hand, the domestic sense of the father-son designation is apparent in the sapiential lectures. The inclusion of the mother within the instructions is a significant feature of the discourse (1:8; 6:20). Though the maternal voice is not given expression in the lectures (cf. 31:1–9), the appellation seems to indicate a domestic setting, for it assumes a relational dimension that transcends the teacher-pupil relationship.[30] The familial flavor of the instructional

---

26   Lemaire, *Les écoles et la formation de la Bible*, 55; Davies, "Were There Schools in Ancient Israel?", 200; G. D. Pemberton, "The Rhetoric of the Father: A Rhetorical Analysis of the Father/Son Lectures in Proverbs 1–9" (Ph.D. diss.; The University of Denver, 1999), 95–96.

27   See W. Helck, "Amtserblichkeit," *LÄ* 1:228–29; Michalowski, "Charisma and Control," 58; Baines, "Society, Morality, and Religious Practice," 132; D. B. Redford, *Egypt, Canaan, and Israel in Ancient Times* (Princeton: Princeton University Press, 1992), 390; D. Lorton, "Ethics and Law Codes: Egypt," in *Religions of the Ancient World: A Guide* (ed. S. I. Johnston; Cambridge: Harvard University Press, 2004), 514; Carr, *Writing on the Tablet*, 21–22. While Egyptian sons were compelled to follow in the professions of their father and scribal and bureaucratic offices were often hereditary, the Instruction of Merikare presents the possibility of social mobility, with success based on merit. In later periods, the growing bureaucratic needs of the pharaonic institution created opportunities for commoners to become scribes and extended the scribal office to include individuals from any social class. See Washington, *Wealth and Poverty*, 40.

28   See 1 Kgs 4:3; 2 Sam 8:17; 20:25; Jer 26:24; 29:3; 36:10; 39:14; 1 Chron 18:16.

29   B. K. Waltke, "The Book of Proverbs and Ancient Wisdom Literature," *BSac* 136 (1979): 232; E. Lipinski, "Royal and State Scribes in Ancient Jerusalem," in *Congress Volume: Jerusalem 1986* (ed. J. A. Emerton; Leiden: Brill, 1988), 157–64; Golka, *The Leopard's Spots*, 11; Carr, *Writing on the Tablet*, 130.

30   While Lang ("Schule und Unterricht im Alten Israel," in *La Sagesse de l'Ancien Testament.* [ed. M. Gilbert; BETL 51; Gembloux: Duculot, 1979; repr., Leuven: Leuven University Press, 1990], 193–95) argues that the father and mother constitute a conventional word pair and the inclusion of the mother is attributed to the stylistic demands of parallelism, the variation apparent in several aphorisms (Prov 17:21; 23:24) seems to indicate that the writer could have employed other expressions to coincide with the father (Crenshaw, "Education in Ancient Israel," 614 n. 61).

material is particularly evident in Proverbs 4:3–4. Here the father describes the setting in which he received instruction from his own father. Few would deny that the grandfather's speech was delivered in a domestic setting. Although the rhetorical setting of the lecture in 4:1–9 cannot be equated with the rhetorical setting of the grandfather's speech,[31] it is unlikely the references to the father and mother in 4:3–4 envisage a family setting, while their collocations elsewhere in the book point to a school context. Whether or not the father-son discourses were created and circulated independent of one another, they have been incorporated in a larger literary context that attributes the instructions to both the father and the mother (1:8; 6:20; cf. 31:1–9).

The weight of the internal evidence suggests that the father-son idiom designates a domestic setting.[32] This familial context is represented in ancient Near Eastern instructional works and envisioned through the inclusion of the mother within Proverbs 1–9. The mention of the mother's teaching is significant, for women rarely played a formative role in educational institutions throughout the ancient oriental world.[33] However, their role within the domestic unit was indispensable. The family was the primary locus of education and socialization in ancient Israel; it served as a foundational social unit and played a fundamental role in the preservation and transmission of social mores to the next generation. Though the introductory lectures incorporate several features that could evince a school setting, the supposed evidence for this context can be understood without postulating such an institution. In general, the evidence for the existence of public classrooms is derived from late Greek and Jewish sources.[34] Moreover, the allusions to tuition payments within the discourse seem to be symbolic injunctions rather than literal commands, as the speaker incorporates economic rhetoric to highlight the inestimable value of wisdom in comparison to material goods.[35] The ostensive reference to "teachers" and "instructors" in 5:13 serves as

---

31   Pemberton, "The Rhetoric of the Father," 93–94.

32   Whybray, *Wisdom in Proverbs*, 42; idem, "The Sage in the Israelite Royal Court," in *The Sage in Israel and the Ancient Near East* (ed. J. G. Gammie and L. G. Perdue; Winona Lake: Eisenbrauns, 1990), 139; C. R. Fontaine, "Wisdom in Proverbs," in *In Search of Wisdom: Essays in Memory of John G. Gammie* (ed. B. B. Scott et al.; Louisville: Westminster John Knox, 1993), 101–03; Weeks, *Early Israelite Wisdom*, 15; Fox, "The Social Location of the Book of Proverbs," 231–32; R. E. Murphy, *Proverbs* (WBC 22; Nashville: Thomas Nelson, 1998), xxi; R. J. Clifford, *Proverbs* (OTL; Louisville: Westminster John Knox, 1999), 7–8; R. Schäfer, *Die Poesie der Weisen: Dichotomie als Grundstruktur der Lehr- und Weisheitsgedichte in Proverbien 1–9* (WMANT 77; Neukirchen-Vluyn: Neukirchener Verlag, 1999), 22; Carr, *Writing on the Tablet*, 130; Dell, *The Book of Proverbs*, 30.

33   See R. Harris, "The Female 'Sage' in Mesopotamian Literature (with an Appendix on Egypt)," in *The Sage in Israel and the Ancient Near East* (ed. J. G. Gammie and L. G. Perdue; Winona Lake: Eisenbrauns, 1990), 3–17; C. V. Camp, "The Female Sage in Ancient Israel and in the Biblical Wisdom Literature," in *The Sage in Israel and the Ancient Near East* (ed. J. G. Gammie and L. G. Perdue; Winona Lake: Eisenbrauns, 1990), 185–203.

34   See Lang, *Wisdom and the Book of Proverbs*, 29–31.

35   Sandoval, *The Discourse of Wealth and Poverty*, 87–89.

the strongest evidence for a formal, educational setting. However, within the larger literary context of Proverbs 1–9, these designations may also refer to the teaching activity of parents.[36] The internal features of the introductory lectures suggest that the father-son idiom designates a domestic setting. This setting is significant, for it forms a conceptual grid through which to view the book of Proverbs in general and the introductory lectures in particular.

The domestic setting of the introductory lectures and interludes plays an important role in the book of Proverbs. Together, the lectures and interludes serve as an extended introduction to the book, providing a hermeneutical framework within which to read the document.[37] As the introduction to the work, the prologue contains several distinct features that are also incorporated in the concluding compositions. Similar to the introductory lectures, the words of Lemuel (31:1–31) are cast within a domestic context. Here the silent, maternal voice is given particular expression, as the queen mother addresses specific themes reminiscent of the instructions within the prologue (31:1–9; 1:3; 2:9; 5:1–23; 7:1–27). In addition, the heroic panegyric (31:10–31) includes a series of images that bind the אֵשֶׁת־חַיִל with the prologue in general and Woman Wisdom in particular.[38] These features suggest that Proverbs 1–9 and 30–31 form an interpretive envelope around the book.[39] These discrete compositions highlight a fundamental component of the work's discourse setting and provide a lens through which to read and assess the pastiche of sayings presented in the sentence literature. They situate the sapiential material within a domestic context and delineate the dialogical setting in which the material is cast.

---

36 Crenshaw, *Education in Ancient Israel*, 233.

37 S. R. Driver, *An Introduction to the Literature of the Old Testament* (Gloucester: Peter Smith, 1972), 395; B. S. Childs, *Introduction to the Old Testament as Scripture* (Philadelphia: Fortress, 1979), 552–53; O. Plöger, *Sprüche Salomos (Proverbia)* (BKAT 17; Neukirchen-Vluyn: Neukirchener Verlag, 1984), xxxvi; Steiert, *Die Weisheit Israels*, 217; S. L. Harris, *Proverbs 1–9: A Study of Inner-Biblical Interpretation* (SBLDS 150; Atlanta: Scholars Press, 1995), 3; M. V. Fox, *Proverbs 1–9: A New Translation with Introduction and Commentary* (AB 18A; New York: Doubleday, 2000), 346; B. K. Waltke, *The Book of Proverbs: Chapters 1–15* (NICOT; Grand Rapids: Eerdmans, 2004), 10–13; Murphy, *The Tree of Life*, 28; Sandoval, *The Discourse of Wealth and Poverty*, 57.

38 See J. Becker, *Gottesfurcht im Alten Testament* (AnBib 25; Rome: Pontifical Biblical Institute, 1965), 211–13; Camp, *Wisdom and the Feminine in the Book of Proverbs* (Bible and Literature Series 11; Sheffield: Almond, 1985), 179–208; T. P. McCreesh, "Wisdom as Wife: Proverbs 31:10–31," *RB* 92 (1985): 25–46; J. Blenkinsopp, *Sage, Priest, Prophet: Religious and Intellectual Leadership in Ancient Israel* (Library of Ancient Israel; Louisville: Westminster John Knox, 1995), 35; Bergant, *Israel's Wisdom Literature*, 80; H. F. Fuhs, *Das Buch der Sprichwörter: Ein Kommentar* (FB 95; Würzburg: Echter Verlag, 2001), 15; Yoder, *Wisdom as a Woman of Substance*, 2.

39 Camp, *Wisdom and the Feminine*, 179; A. Meinhold, *Die Sprüche, Teil 1: Sprüche Kapitel 1–15* (ZBK 16.1; Zürich: Theologischer Verlag, 1991), 26; Whybray, *The Composition of the Book of Proverbs*, 159; R. C. Van Leeuwen, "The Book of Proverbs: Introduction, Commentary, and Reflections," *NIB* 5:24; Fuhs, *Das Buch der Sprichwörter*, 15; W. P. Brown, "The Pedagogy of Proverbs 10:1–31:9," in *Character and Scripture: Moral Formation, Community, and Biblical Interpretation* (ed. W. P. Brown; Grand Rapids: Eerdmans, 2002), 153.

Within this domestic setting, the instructions in Proverbs 1–9 present a series of lectures and interludes.[40] These discourses do not exhibit a logical progression of thought from instruction to instruction; rather they address the issue of seduction from different perspectives and through distinct rhetorical strategies.[41] The prologue opens with a title (1:1) and a preamble (1:2–7), followed by ten lectures that develop a single theme in a tripartite structure (1:8–19; 2:1–22; 3:1–12, 21–35; 4:1–9, 10–19, 20–27; 5:1–23; 6:20–35; 7:1–27). These lectures are interrupted by five interludes (1:20–33; 3:13–20; 6:1–19;[42] 8:1–36; 9:1–18), which develop particular themes introduced in the parental discourses.[43] Though the addressee is introduced to different voices within the instructions proper, the father assumes the role of the speaker throughout the prologue. He introduces the son to the value of wisdom and interprets the deceptive rhetoric of different characters to transform the naïve predilection of the addressee.[44] Together, the lectures and interludes constitute a continuous, uninterrupted discourse, rather than a series of isolated instructions.[45] Though these addresses may have been produced as independent speeches,[46] they are cast as a progressive program of instruction bound together by a series of archetypal personages and root metaphors.[47] The lectures and interludes in Proverbs 1–9 coalesce into a single, sustained instruction. This instruction is situated within a specific discourse setting that possesses a distinct, courtly flavor.

The introductory lectures and interludes incorporate a series of aristocratic elements. These elements are expressed through metaphors, images, and terms that appear throughout the prologue. In order to assess these features, it is necessary to identify the voice of the tradition, for the voice of the tradition provides the contextual factors needed to determine the "interaction situation"[48] of the material. The interaction situation represents the relationship between the speaker and the addressee through age, gender, and social status, among other

---

40   I have adopted the terms "lecture" and "interlude" from Fox, *Proverbs 1–9*, 44.

41   Pemberton, "The Rhetoric of the Father," *passim*.

42   While 6:1–19 begins with the typical address to "my son" and presents a message that is comparable to the other lectures, the discourse lacks a formal exhortation and motivation, which are fundamental characteristics of the lectures in Proverbs 1–9. See Fox, *Proverbs 1–9*, 225-27.

43   Fox, *Proverbs 1–9*, 328–29.

44   Weeks, *Instruction and Imagery*, 42.

45   Weeks, *Instruction and Imagery*, 44.

46   See B. Lang, *Die weisheitliche Lehrrede: Eine Untersuchung von Sprüche 1–7* (SBS 54; Stuttgart: KBW Verlag, 1972), 100; Meinhold, *Die Sprüche*, 1:42–46; Whybray, *The Composition of the Book of Proverbs*, 11–61; L. G. Perdue, *Proverbs* (IBC; Louisville: John Knox, 2000), 61; Dell, *The Book of Proverbs*, 48.

47   See Harris, *Proverbs 1–9*, 160–62.

48   Seitel, "Proverbs: A Social Use of Metaphor," 130.

things.[49] Within Proverbs 1–9, the discourse is situated in a domestic context and presented as the instructions of a father to his son. Though the identity of the father is not stated explicitly in the prologue, the preamble (1:1–7) provides an indication of the principal speaker.

3.2.2 The Speaker of Proverbs 1–9

The title of the book of Proverbs attributes the work to Solomon (1:1). This "authorial" designation is not limited to Proverb 1–9, but applies to the book in its entirety. While several collections are attributed to "authors" other than Solomon (22:17, 24:23; 30:1; 31:1), the prologue serves as the introduction to the entire book and provides a framework within which to read the component parts of the discourse. The title does not claim that Solomon was the "author" of the work in the modern sense of the term. On the one hand, the expression may indicate that Solomon was the collector or patron of the various anthologies. On the other hand, the sages may have attributed the collections to Solomon in order to legitimize their work and demonstrate that their teachings were an extension of the intellectual tradition that emerged during Solomon's tenure.[50]

The issue of "authorship" in Proverbs is comparable to other ancient Near Eastern didactic wisdom texts. These instructions range from cases of "honorary" and attributed authorship to pseudepigraphy.[51] Opinions on the authenticity of their authorial attributions vary among scholars. In certain cases, the attributions are considered to be genuine, while others are regarded as pseudepigraphic. However, since the ancient oriental world did not produce a comprehensive theory of authorship and there is no objective means to identify any proverbs as Solomonic,[52] the search for the "author" of Proverbs may be misconceived. Rather than functioning as a declaration of the document's "author," the title of Proverbs may introduce the voice of the tradition, the speaker of the document.

---

49 Seitel, "Proverbs: A Social Use of Metaphor," 130. Seitel's discussion of the interaction situation is limited to individual proverbs. Building on this proposal, the present study attempts to extend the fundamental principles of this situation to the level of the discourse as a whole.

50 See W. A. Brueggemann, "The Social Significance of Solomon as a Patron of Wisdom," in *The Sage in Israel and the Ancient Near East* (ed. J. G. Gammie and L. G. Perdue; Winona Lake: Eisenbrauns, 1990), 117–32; L. G. Perdue, "Wisdom Theology and Social History in Proverbs 1–9," in *Wisdom, You Are My Sister: Studies in Honor of Roland E. Murphy, O. Carm., on the Occasion of His Eightieth Birthday* (CBQMS 29; Washington, D.C.: The Catholic Biblical Association of America, 1997), 92–101.

51 For a discussion of the different forms of authorship in the ancient oriental world, see K. van der Toorn, *Scribal Culture and the Making of the Hebrew Bible* (Cambridge: Harvard University Press, 2007), 27–49.

52 See W. M. Schniedewind, *How the Bible Became a Book* (Cambridge: Cambridge University Press, 2004), 7; van der Toorn, *Scribal Culture*, 45–48.

The voice in the preamble of Proverbs may represent the editor or transmitter of Solomon's wisdom.[53] The title of the work is comparable to Egyptian instructional texts, which include the personal name of the author/compiler formulated in the third person with epithets.[54] These titles not only refer to the "author" of the work, but they also identify the voice that is heard throughout the document. The same may be true of Proverbs. The opening verses of Proverbs portray the king as a teacher of wisdom and place Solomon in an implied role as the father.[55] Moreover, the attribution to Solomon represents the only linear-sequential antecedent to the father (1:8), suggesting that the editors included the title to clarify the identity of the speaker in the document.

This notion is reinforced by the early reception history of the book of Proverbs. The Septuagint version of Proverbs rearranges the material in the book to create one seamless Solomonic composition.[56] The Greek translation replaces "the words of the wise" (22:17; 24:23) with a first person direct address and conceals the attributions to Agur (30:1) and Lemuel (31:1) to strengthen the single Solomonic voice. Although the LXX represents a secondary arrangement of the document and the alterations may be the result of the translator's *Vorlage* or his Hellenistic milieu,[57] it seems the translators attempted to clarify the voice of the tradition. In so doing, they identified Solomon as the document's principal speaker.

3.3 The Content of Proverbs 1–9

The identity of the speaker provides the contextual clues needed to determine the interaction situation of the instructions. This situation is cast in the form of parental teaching, delivered by a royal figure to his son in a domestic setting. The interaction situation provides a framework within which to assess the metaphors, images, and terms that punctuate the instructions, for it enables the reader to identify the manner in which the speaker "matches up" or correlates the

---

53 Fox, *Proverbs 1–9*, 73.

54 K. A. Kitchen, "Proverbs and Wisdom Books of the Ancient Near East: The Factual History of a Literary Form," *TynBul* 28 (1977): 76–79.

55 R. J. Clifford, "The Community of the Book of Proverbs," 289; Schniedewind, *How the Bible Became a Book*, 75–76; A. F. Wilke, *Kronerben der Weisheit: Gott, König und Frommer in der didaktischen Literatur Ägyptens und Israels* (FAT 20; Tübingen: Mohr, 2006), 1.

56 For a discussion of the additions and omissions in the LXX and its *Vorlage*, see J. Cook, *The Septuagint of Proverbs: Jewish and/or Hellenistic Colouring of the LXX Proverbs* (VTSup 69; Leiden: Brill, 1997); E. Tov, "Recensional Differences between the Masoretic Text and the Septuagint of the Book of Proverbs," in *The Greek and Hebrew Bible: Collected Essays on the Septuagint* (VTSup 72; Leiden: Brill, 1999), 419–32.

57 Washington, *Wealth and Poverty*, 127; Schniedewind, *How the Bible Became a Book*, 7.

discourse with his addressee.[58] The addressee of the instructions is identified in both the preamble and the instructions proper. However, in preparation for our discussion of the addressee of Proverbs 1–9 it is necessary to evaluate the courtly elements within the discourse. We will begin with the lectures, and then evaluate the courtly features in the interludes of Proverbs 1–9.

3.3.1 The Lectures of Proverbs 1–9

The lectures in Proverbs 1–9 seek to promote communal virtues and values.[59] Their message is clear: do not steal, murder, or commit adultery; rather pursue wisdom, justice, and marital fidelity. Together, the lectures constitute a cycle of instructions that attempts to provide the addressee with an antidote for seductive speech.[60] Each lecture addresses the temptations that confront young men and develops its argument through different rhetorical objectives and strategies.[61] The father employs a variety of metaphors and images to present his argument and persuade his son to choose the right path. The nature of these features deserves specific comment.

The first lecture (1:8–19) develops its principal topic through a rhetorical scheme that is emulated by the subsequent instructions. The discourse opens with an exordium (1:8–9), followed by a lesson (1:10–18) and a conclusion (1:19).[62] The instruction proper begins with a warning against joining a gang of desperados who entice the naïve with their promise of wealth by means of murder (1:10–14). The parents present the invitation of the sinners and then subvert their speech by exposing the self-destructive nature of their claims (1:15–19). Far from being a lesson on the repercussions of robbery and murder, the parent's speech illustrates the communal and individual judgment that accompanies those who operate outside the boundaries of the socio-moral order.[63]

Within the opening lecture, the parents incorporate ornamental imagery to describe their teaching. This imagery reappears in many of the lectures, where it is used in reference either to instruction or its rewards (1:9; 3:3, 22; 4:9; 6:21; 7:3).

---

58   Seitel, "Proverbs: A Social Use of Metaphor," 131.
59   Brown, *Character in Crisis*, 23–25; Sandoval, "Revisiting the Prologue of Proverbs," *JBL* 126 (2007): 471.
60   J. N. Aletti, "Seduction et parole en Proverbes I–IX," *VT* 27 (1977): 129–44; Fox, *Proverbs 1–9*, 324.
61   See Pemberton, "The Rhetoric of the Father," *passim*.
62   For the rhetorical structure of the lectures, see Whybray, *The Composition of the Book of Proverbs*, 13; Fox, *Proverbs 1–9*, 324.
63   Aletti, "Seduction et parole," 137; Brown, *Character in Crisis*, 32; J. E. Miles, *Wise King — Royal Fool: Semiotics, Satire and Proverbs 1–9* (JSOTSup 399; London: T&T Clark International, 2004), 46–53.

In Proverbs 1:9, the teaching of the parents is characterized as a לִוְיַת חֵן ("fair garland") and עֲנָקִים ("pendants")—multivalent metaphors that express the attraction of the parent's instruction. These ornamental images may function in several ways. On the one hand, they may be symbolic apotropaic or mnemonic devices (Deut 6:6–9; 11:18–20).[64] On the other hand, the garland and necklace may denote honor and high social status.[65] This nuance is apparent when these terms are compared with their occurrences elsewhere in the Old Testament. The word לִוְיָה occurs elsewhere only in Proverbs 4:9, where it parallels עֲטֶרֶת תִּפְאֶרֶת ("beautiful crown")—an object associated with royal adornment and the trappings of a high office.[66] The term עֲנָק occurs in Judges 8:26 and Song of Songs 4:9, where it refers to the royal accoutrements draped around the necks of the Midianite camels and the necklace of the woman that sends her lover into frenzied passion, respectively. In each case, these ornaments serve as signs of status, with royal overtones. They are aristocratic accessories that evoke images of honor, distinction, and even royalty.[67]

The second lecture (2:1–22) emulates the structural design of the first, opening with a lengthy exordium (2:1–11), followed by a lesson (2:12–20) and a conclusion (2:21–22).[68] This lecture builds on the first and delineates the *Lehrprogramm* of the parental instructions that follow, highlighting the right relationship with God (2:5–8; 3:1–12), communal relations with other people (2:9–11; 3:21–35), the dangers of wicked men (2:12–15; 4:10–19, 20–27), and the warnings against the Strange Woman (2:16–19; 5:1–23; 6:20–35; 7:1–27).[69] The father leads his son through the educational process, which begins with instruction and the son's incorporation of the directives (2:1–4), and ends with God granting the gift of wisdom (2:5–6).[70] The father exhorts the son to assimilate his teaching and pursue wisdom, for God will reward his quest and protect him from the schemes of sinful men and the Strange Woman. To combat the anti-social ethos of these deceptive characters, wisdom provides the neophyte

---

64   Kayatz, *Studien*, 107–11; Waltke, *Proverbs: Chapters 1–15*, 187–88.

65   See R. B. Y. Scott, *Proverbs, Ecclesiastes: Introduction, Translation, and Notes* (AB 18; Garden City: Doubleday, 1965), 38; Kayatz, *Studien*, 111–17; Meinhold, *Die Sprüche*, 1.53; R. N. Whybray, *Proverbs* (NCB; Grand Rapids: Eerdmans, 1994), 38; Fox, *Proverbs 1–9*, 83.

66   See Exod 28:2, 40; Isa 3:18; 28:1, 4; Jer 13:18, 20; Ezek 16:17, 39; Esth 1:4, E. E. Platt, "Jewelry, Ancient Israelite," *ABD* 3:831.

67   For a discussion of similar ornaments in Egypt and Assyria, see Kayatz, *Studien*, 107–17; K. R. Maxwell-Hyslop, *Western Asiatic Jewellery c. 3000–612 B.C.* (Methuen's Handbooks of Archaeology; London: Methuen, 1971), 251–54; Camp, *Wisdom and the Feminine*, 31; Fox, *Proverbs 1–9*, 85; Waltke, *Proverbs: Chapters 1–15*, 187–88.

68   For an analysis of the parallelism in the lecture, see D. Pardee, *Ugaritic and Hebrew Poetic Parallelism: A Trial Cut ('nt I and Proverbs 2)* (VTSup 39; Leiden: Brill, 1988).

69   Meinhold, *Die Sprüche*, 1:43.

70   Fox, *Proverbs 1–9*, 132.

with a series of communal virtues (2:9). These virtues possess a pronounced courtly flavor.

The principles of righteousness (צֶדֶק), justice (מִשְׁפָּט), and equity (מֵישָׁרִים) form a constellation of virtues that carry moral as well as communal connotations (1:3; 2:9).[71] These terms are often combined in a hendiadys and convey the Israelite concept of social justice.[72] Though each term bears a distinctive meaning, together they express a single concept that encapsulates the moral and ethical qualities necessary to live, judge and govern rightly.[73] Many suggest that the concept of מִשְׁפָּט and צֶדֶק functioned in the same way as Maat in Egypt and the *mes* in Mesopotamia.[74] In this case, the terms refer to a cosmic order that permeates social institutions and was guaranteed by God through the just reign of the royal institution.[75] Whether or not Israel incorporated this Near Eastern notion, it seems that righteousness, justice and equity represented the Israelite concept of social justice. This justice was to be administered by all people, but was particularly relevant for socio-political leaders who were responsible for the maintenance of society and the execution of its laws (Deut 16:20–18:22).[76]

The third and fourth lectures illustrate the contours of these moral and communal virtues through proper behavior toward God (3:1–12) and other people (3:21–35). The third lecture begins with an exordium (3:1–4) followed by a lesson (3:5–10) and a conclusion (3:11–12). Here the father implores his son to accept his teachings and live a life of piety, expressed through trusting, fearing, and honoring YHWH. The father's instruction outlines a program of behavior that extends from the religious to the social sphere, as the virtues of obedience, trust and humility manifest themselves in communal favor and ethical conduct (3:4, 6). The final admonition of the lesson proper develops the addressee's obligations from inner piety to its outward expression in worship (3:9–10).[77] These verses not only position the cult within the program of wisdom literature, but they also illuminate the distinctive nature of the addressee. The references to הוֹנֶךָ ("your wealth"), תְּבוּאָתֶךָ ("your produce"), אֲסָמֶיךָ ("your barns"), and יְקָבֶיךָ ("your wine vats") assume the addressee is an established member of the community who owns landed property. These features suggest the "son" is a

---

71   Brown, *Character in Crisis*, 26.

72   M. Weinfeld, "'Justice and Righteousness'—משפט וצדק—the Expression and Its Meaning," in *Justice and Righteousness: Biblical Themes and Their Influence* (ed. H. G. Reventlow and Y. Hoffman; Sheffield: Sheffield Academic Press, 1992), 228–46.

73   See Deut 16:18; Isa 16:5; 32:1; Ps 72:2; 89:14; Weinfeld, "Justice and Righteousness," 234–36.

74   L. G. Perdue, "Cosmology and the Social Order in the Wisdom Tradition," in *The Sage in Israel and the Ancient Near East* (ed. J. G. Gammie and L. G. Perdue; Winona Lake: Eisenbrauns, 1990), 458; Crenshaw, *Education in Ancient Israel*, 57.

75   See Schmid, *Gerechtigkeit als Weltordnung*, 46–61.

76   Weinfeld, "Justice and Righteousness," 246.

77   Waltke, *Proverbs: Chapters 1–15*, 247.

descendent of a wealthy land-owning family who can be trusted with increased wealth.[78]

The fourth lecture develops the communal orientation of the social values presented in Proverbs 2:9–11 through proper relations with other people (3:21–35).[79] This lecture seeks to promote harmonious social relationships by illustrating how a person's behavior affects the community. Similar to its instructional counterparts, the lecture opens with an exordium (3:21–26), followed by a lesson (3:27–31) and a conclusion (3:32–35). In the exordium, the father calls the son to secure the practical faculties of sound judgment and discretion (3:21). These virtues are described as חֵן לְגַרְגְּרֹתֶיךָ ("adornment for your neck")—an expression reminiscent of the ornamental imagery in Proverbs 1:9 and a courtly metaphor that describes the honorable nature of these values (3:22; 1:9; 4:9). The father emphasizes the importance of these practical faculties, arguing that they will lead to security in both the communal (3:27–31) and religious realms of the cosmos (3:32–35). In the main, the lifestyle advocated in the lesson is portrayed relationally.[80] The father presents a series of vignettes to illustrate the way in which these virtues affect the community (3:27–31) and determine the fate of the individual (3:32–35).

The final three lectures graphically describe the אִשָּׁה זָרָה ("strange woman") and the אִשָּׁה נָכְרִיָּה ("foreign woman"), who threaten to undermine the established structures of the family and the community (2:16–19; 5:1–23; 6:20–35; 7:1–27). These lectures introduce the addressee to a composite literary figure, a *femme fatale*, who shares several common descriptions. These descriptions have given rise to a variety of interpretations concerning the nature and function of the "strange" or "foreign" woman.[81] First, the composite literary figure may be characterized as an ethnically foreign woman. Here זָרָה and נָכְרִיָּה function as social designations that denote foreignness by reason of nationality or ethnicity. Accordingly, the Strange Woman represents the dangers associated with exogamous marriage and embodies the economic problems that threaten the genealogical lineage, land tenure, and cultic rights of members in the Golah community.[82] Second, the Strange Woman may function as a poetic expression of

---

78   N. C. Habel, "Wisdom, Wealth, and Poverty Paradigms in the Book of Proverbs," *BiBh* 14 (1988): 29; R. N. Whybray, *Wealth and Poverty*, 101–02.

79   Brown, *Character in Crisis*, 35.

80   Brown, *Character in Crisis*, 35.

81   For an analysis of the אִשָּׁה זָרָה in the LXX, see J. Cook, "זרה אשה (Proverbs 1–9 Septuagint): A Metaphor for Foreign Wisdom?," *ZAW* 106 (1994): 458–76; M. V. Fox, "The Strange Woman in Septuagint Proverbs," *JNSL* 22 (1996): 31–44.

82   See 4Q184, lines 9–12; Camp, *Wisdom and the Feminine*, 256–71; H. C. Washington, "The Strange Woman (אִשָּׁה זָרָה/נָכְרִיָּה) of Proverbs 1–9 and Post-Exilic Judean Society," in *Second Temple Studies 2. Temple and Community in the Persian Period* (ed. T. C. Eskenazi and K. H. Richards; Sheffield: JSOT, 1994), 217–42; C. Maier, *Die 'Fremde Frau' in Proverbien 1–9: Eine Exegetische und Sozialgeschichtliche Studie* (OBO 144; Göttingen: Vandenhoeck & Ruprecht, 1995), 92–108; Weeks, *Instruction and Imagery*, 155.

"foreignness," that is, as a symbol of apostasy that builds on the deuteronomic and deuteronomistic traditions associated with foreign women.[83] Third, the זָרָה אִשָּׁה or אִשָּׁה נָכְרִיָּה may represent a prostitute, whether foreign or native (7:1–27).[84] Fourth, the Strange Woman may constitute the human embodiment of a foreign goddess. This proposal assumes that the character and behavior of the Strange Woman is based on a type-scene in epic literature, according to which a goddess offers a deceptive marriage proposal to a hero who recognizes the deceitful nature of the offer and rejects it.[85] Fifth, the Strange Woman may symbolize a social outsider who acts outside of the socio-religious boundaries of the community.[86] Here the Strange Woman is a symbol of "the Other," an idealized portrait of evil and social chaos in its multiple dimensions.[87]

These diverse proposals reflect the multivalent descriptions of the אִשָּׁה זָרָה and נָכְרִיָּה within the discourse. However, when these descriptions are taken together, the father seems to present her as a single figure, viz., the wife of another man and an unchaste woman who betrays her husband.[88] On the whole, the parental lectures portray the Strange Woman as married (2:17; 5:10, 16–17; 6:26, 29, 34; 7:19). She represents a promiscuous woman who violates her marriage covenant (2:17) and seeks to lure young men into an adulterous relationship (6:26; 7:10–21).[89] There is nothing in the lectures to suggest that the actions of the woman are a form of cultic prostitution.[90] If this were the case,

---

83   N. Nam Hoon Tan, *The 'Foreignness' of the Foreign Woman in Proverbs 1–9: A Study of the Origin and Development of a Biblical Motif* (BZAW 381; Berlin: Walter de Gruyter, 2008), 81–105.

84   G. Boström, *Proverbiastudien: Die Weisheit und das fremde Weib in Sprüche 1–9* (LUÅ 3; Lund: Gleerup, 1935), 103–55; K. van der Toorn, "Female Prostitution in Payment of Vows in Ancient Israel," *JBL* 108 (1989): 193–205; D. A. Garrett, "Votive Prostitution Again: A Comparison of Proverbs 7:13–14 and 21:28–29," *JBL* 109 (1990): 681–82.

85   R. J. Clifford, "Woman Wisdom in the Book of Proverbs," in *Biblische Theologie und gesellschaftlicher Wandel. Für Norbert Lohfink* (ed. W. Groß et al.; Freiburg: Herder, 1993), 61–72.

86   L. A. Snijders, *The Meaning of* zar *in the Old Testament* (OTS 10; Leiden: Brill, 1954), 89–104; McKane, *Proverbs: A New Approach*, 185.

87   G. A. Yee, "'I Have Perfumed My Bed with Myrrh': The Foreign Woman (*iššâ zārâ*) in Proverbs 1–9," *JSOT* 43 (1989): 53–68; A. Brenner, "Some Observations on the Figuration of Woman in Wisdom Literature," in *A Feminist Companion to Wisdom Literature* (ed. A. Brenner; Sheffield: Sheffield Academic Press, 1995), 53; C. V. Camp, "What's So Strange About the Strange Woman?," in *The Bible and the Politics of Exegesis: Essays in Honor of Norman K. Gottwald on His Sixty-Fifth Birthday* (ed. P. L. Day et al.; Cleveland: Pilgrim Press, 1991), 17–31; idem, "Woman Wisdom and the Strange Woman: Where Is Power to Be Found?," in *Reading Bibles, Writing Bodies: Identity and the Book* (ed. T. K. Beal and D. M. Gunn; London: Routledge, 1997), 94; Fontaine, *Smooth Words*, 42–43.

88   Fox, *Proverbs 1–9*, 139–41; Waltke, *Proverbs: Chapters 1–15*, 124.

89   See G. P. Hugenberger, *Marriage as a Covenant: A Study of Biblical Law and Ethics Governing Marriage Developed from the Perspective of Malachi* (VTSup 52; Leiden: Brill, 1994), 296–302.

90   See J. Day, "Does the Old Testament Refer to Sacred Prostitution and Did It Actually Exist in Ancient Israel?," in *Biblical and Near Eastern Essays: Studies in Honour of Kevin J. Cathcart* (ed. C. McCarthy and J. F. Healey; London: T&T Clark International, 2004), 8–9. Day argues that the

then the father should have characterized her as a קְדֵשָׁה. Moreover, the adjectives
זָרָה and נָכְרִיָּה do not necessarily designate ethnic foreignness. Elsewhere, these
terms refer to Israelites who are members of another family (Gen 31:15; Deut
25:5; Ps 69:9; Prov 6:24) or individuals who are not members of the priesthood
(Lev 22:12). These features suggest that the Strange Woman is not ethnically
foreign; rather she is characterized as strange or off limits because she is the wife
of another.[91] The predominant issue throughout the final lectures is adultery. The
father presents the Strange Woman as an unfaithful wife in search of a one-night
stand, and one who stands outside of the immediate family unit. She is an
archetypal representative of any seductive, adulterous woman who spurns the
conventions of society.[92] This multi-dimensional figure serves as a pedagogical
device shaped by the father to illustrate the socio-religious consequences that
follow from giving in to her speech (2:18; 5:5, 8–14; 6:32–35; 7:27).

The Strange Woman uses speech to seduce the naïve youth. It is not her
beauty, her eyelids, her brazen face, her perfume or the extravagant linens that
line her bed that lure the youth into sexual promiscuity; rather her smooth words
are the mechanism for seduction (2:16; 5:3; 6:24; 7:5, 14–21).[93] While the father
focuses on the smooth words of the Strange Woman, her actual speech is not
presented until the final lecture (7:1–27). The speech of the Strange Woman is
cast in a correctional type-scene, where the father looks down through his
window to observe the youth's encounter with the seductress (7:9–13).[94] Though
this type-scene is typically attributed to women (Josh 2:13–21; Judg 5:26–30; 1

reference to הַיּוֹם שִׁלַּמְתִּי נְדָרָי should not be understood as a payment received by the woman to
settle a vow at the temple, for שִׁלַּמְתִּי is a perfect ("today I have paid my vows") and the wisdom
literature is unconcerned with cultic practices.

91   Camp, *Wisdom and the Feminine*, 118–19; C. A. Newsom, "Woman and the Discourse of
      Patriarchal Wisdom," in *Gender and Difference in Ancient Israel* (ed. P. L. Day; Minneapolis:
      Fortress, 1989), 142–60; repr. in *Reading Bibles, Writing Bodies: Identity and the Book* (ed. T. K. Beal
      and D. M. Gunn; London: Routledge, 1997), 127; Fox, *Proverbs 1–9*, 134.
92   Camp, *Wisdom and the Feminine*, 116; Fox, *Proverbs 1–9*, 139–41.
93   Aletti, "Seduction et parole," 129–44; S. Amsler, "La sagesse de la femme," in *La sagesse de
      l'Ancien Testament* (BETL 51; Leuven: Leuven University Press, 1979; repr., 1990), 112–16.
94   See O'Connell, "Proverbs VII 16–17: A Case of Fatal Deception in a 'Women and the
      Window'," *VT* 41 (1991): 235–41. The LXX changes the masculine pronoun and the verb to
      feminine forms, making the Strange Woman the subject rather than the father. However, it is
      difficult to see such a sudden shift to a female voice, especially in a lecture delivered by the
      father where the woman is in the streets, not in the window. Though the vignette in chapter 7 is
      cast in the form of a "woman in the window" type-scene, this literary motif is not limited to
      women (Gen 26:8). For a discussion of the issues, see Snijders, *The Meaning of zar in the Old
      Testament*, 98; W. F. Albright, "Some Canaanite-Phoenician Sources of Hebrew Wisdom," in
      Wisdom in Ancient Israel and in the Ancient Near East: Presented to Professor Harold Henry Rowley
      (VTSup 3; Leiden: Brill, 1955), 10; Plöger, *Sprüche Salomos*, 77; F. van Dijk-Hemmes, "The I
      Persona in Proverbs 7," in *On Gendering Texts: Female and Male Voices in the Hebrew Bible* (ed. A.
      Brenner and F. van Dijk-Hemmes; Leiden: Brill, 1993), 57–62; Brenner, "Some Observations on
      the Figuration of Woman in Wisdom Literature," 53; Waltke, *Proverbs: Chapters 1–15*, 362.

Sam 19:11–12; 2 Sam 6:16; 2 Kgs 9:30, 33), the motif is not limited to a feminine posture (Gen 26:8–10). In many cases, the type-scene is centered on a royal figure.[95] Abimelech, Michal, and Jezebel are portrayed looking through their windows, while ivory plaques from Samaria, Assyria, Cyprus and Syria depict noble women adorned with elaborate headdresses peering though an ornate aperture.[96] This scene sets the stage for the youth's encounter with the adulteress. The lecture focuses on the discourse of the woman and illuminates her noble status.

The character of the Strange Woman is presented through a series of erotic images and expressions that are interspersed throughout her discourse. In order to lure the youth into her bedchamber, the Strange Woman claims to be a responsible member of the community, a faithful supporter of the cult, and one with fresh meat available for consumption (7:14; Lev 17:11–21). In addition, the woman describes the banquet she has prepared for the youth, complete with exotic, foreign furnishings. She appeals to the youth's senses, claiming her couch has been draped with מַרְבַדִּים ("covers") and חֲטֻבוֹת אֵטוּן מִצְרָיִם ("dyed drapes of Egyptian linen"), that is, with expensive, imported fabrics that symbolize her high social status (7:16; 31:22).[97] She completes the scene by describing the precious spices that cover her bed (7:17). Together, these evocative symbols heighten the scene of sexual love (Cant 4:6, 11, 14–16; 5:5, 13) and illuminate the status of the woman.[98] The furniture and spices within the woman's household,[99] coupled with the status of her husband (7:19–20), suggests the אִשָּׁה זָרָה is a married, upper-class Israelite woman who seizes the opportunities afforded by her absentee husband to gratify her sexual desires.[100] The father offers a lucid portrait of the character and rhetorical tactics of a noble adulteress—a woman who seems to pose a serious threat to the addressee.

The discourse of the Strange Woman marks the conclusion of the parental lectures. However, the noble adulteress is not an isolated literary figure. This

---

95   See Gen 26:8–10; 1 Sam 19:11–12; 2 Sam 6:16; 2 Kgs 9:30, 33; Van Leeuwen, "The Book of Proverbs," *NIB* 5:84.

96   P. J. King and L. E. Stager, *Life in Biblical Israel* (Library of Ancient Israel; Louisville: Westminster John Knox, 2001), 30–31.

97   See D. R. Edwards, "Dress and Ornamentation," *ABD* 2:235.

98   In view of the multivalent nature of the imagery, O'Connell and Clifford interpret the linens and spices as ambivalent symbols that refer to commodities used in funeral rites. This proposal is possible but unconvincing, since the interpretation is dependent upon New Testament and late Greek burial customs. If funerary rites were consistent in Hebrew culture, then one would expect the authors to demonstrate that these commodities were used in Old Testament burial customs. However, since the Old Testament does not specify the adornments or ingredients employed in burial rites, the suggestion is speculative. See O'Connell, "Proverbs VII 16–17: A Case of Fatal Deception in a 'Women and the Window'," 237–38; Clifford, *Proverbs*, 88–89.

99   For a discussion of the aristocratic character of these commodities, see 2 Kgs 20:13; Ps 45:7–8; Cant 3:6–7; Meinhold, *Die Sprüche*, 1:128; Waltke, *Proverbs: Chapters 1–15*, 379–81.

100 Lang, *Wisdom and the Book of Proverbs*, 101; Pemberton, "The Rhetoric of the Father," 260–61.

femme fatale has a positive counterpart in the son's own wife (5:15–19),[101] who is given particular expression in the heroic panegyric (31:10–31). These women are mirror images of one another: one embodies wisdom (31:30); the other symbolizes death (7:27).[102] Whereas the אִשָּׁה זָרָה imports luxurious fabrics from Egypt to entice prospective sexual partners (7:16), the אֵשֶׁת־חַיִל produces her own linens in order to enhance her household (31:13, 19, 22).[103] This female antithesis is also reflected in the interludes of Proverbs 1–9, where Woman Wisdom stands in stark contrast to Woman Folly. These transcendent figures share some of the qualities attributed to their human counterparts. Nonetheless, they are presented as autonomous characters who deliver their own discourses—discourses that contain several courtly features.

3.3.2 The Interludes of Proverbs 1–9

The interludes in Proverbs 1–9 reinforce the message of the lectures by developing certain ideas that are introduced in the instruction. These poems supplement the parental lectures by highlighting the addressee's obligations to seek wisdom and the consequences that follow from despising reproof (1:28–32; 3:13; 8:1, 17, 32–35).[104] The interludes develop the abstract notion of wisdom found in the lectures and elevate the discourse from a literal to a metaphorical level.[105] Woman Wisdom assumes the same cultural voice that speaks through the father.[106] She emerges as a multifaceted literary character who substantiates the parental discourses and elaborates on their significance.

The images associated with the Woman Wisdom have given rise to several questions concerning her origin(s).[107] In general, two theories concerning the

---

101 Fox, *Proverbs 1–9*, 262; Fontaine, *Smooth Words*, 42–45.

102 Brown, "The Pedagogy of Proverbs 10:1–31:9," 154.

103 Brown, "The Pedagogy of Proverbs 10:1–31:9," 154.

104 Fox, *Proverbs 1–9*, 328–29. Fox argues that the interludes are a later stratum inserted into the cycle of lectures at different periods to introduce new themes and ideas. Whether or not the interludes developed as a series of "midrashic commentaries" created by the scribes in order to elaborate on the lectures, they have been placed within a larger literary context that shares common motifs and a comparable rhetorical function. In general, Fox's compositional proposal is provocative, but hypothetical. Since the final literary text of Proverbs is the only resource available to the interpreter, it will serve as the basis for the discussion. See Fox, *Proverbs 1–9*, 326–29.

105 Clifford, *Proverbs*, 2; Fox, *Proverbs 1–9*, 352.

106 Newsom, "Woman and the Discourse of Patriarchal Wisdom," 119; Brown, *Character in Crisis*, 40; Dell, *The Book of Proverbs*, 22.

107 In essence, an understanding of Wisdom's pedigree is contingent on the date of Proverbs 1–9, for arguments concerning Wisdom's origins are inseparable from questions concerning the date of the composition. For a discussion of the provenance of Proverbs 1–9 based on linguistic and generic features, see Albright, "Some Canaanite-Phoenician Sources," 1–15; M. J. Dahood,

origin(s) of Woman Wisdom have dominated recent discussions. On the one hand, those who explore the origins of Woman Wisdom from the perspective of the history of religions suggest that she embodies features associated with several foreign and Semitic goddesses.[108] This proposal assumes that Woman Wisdom developed under the influence of female deities in other Near Eastern cultures.[109] She served as a literary compensation for the eradication of goddess worship in ancient Israel religion, that is, as an orthodox substitute who satisfied the need for the feminine to be represented in the deity.[110] On the other hand, those who employ a sociological approach to the origins of Woman Wisdom suggest she is a literary or theological creation produced to meet the needs of the Israelite community in the Persian Period. This proposal assumes that Wisdom was shaped by the real social roles of women in society and created as an ideological

---

Proverbs and Northwest Semitic Philology (Scripta Pontificii Instituti Biblici 113; Roma: Pontificim Institutum Biblicum, 1963); Kayatz, *Studien*, 15–75; Kitchen, "Proverbs and Wisdom Books of the Ancient Near East," 69–114; Washington, *Wealth and Poverty*, 111–33; Yoder, *Wisdom as a Woman of Substance*, 19–38.

108 Proposals include the Mesopotamian goddess Ishtar (Boström, *Proverbiastudien*, 156–74), the Egyptian goddess Maat (W. Schenke, *Die Chokma [Sophia] in der jüdischen Hypostasen-Spekulation: Ein Beitrag zur Geschichte der religiösen Ideen im Zeitalter des Hellenismus* [Kristiana: Jacob Dybwad, 1913]; Kayatz, *Studien*, 93–119; U. Winter, *Frau und Göttin: Exegetische und ikonographische Studien zum weiblichen Gottesbild im alten Israel und in dessen Umwelt* [OBO 53; Göttingen: Vandenhoeck & Ruprecht, 1987], 511–14; S. Schroer, *Die Weisheit hat ihr Haus gebaut: Studien zur Gestalt der Sophia in den biblischen Schriften* [Mainz: Matthias-Grünewald, 1996], 12–62), a Hellenized form of the Egyptian goddess Isis (B. L. Mack, "Wisdom Myth and Myth-ology: An Essay in Understanding a Theological Tradition," *Int* 24 [1970]: 46–60; J. S. Kloppenborg, "Isis and Sophia in the Book of Wisdom," *HTR* 75 [1982]: 57–84), the Semitic goddess Asherah (J. E. McKinlay, *Gendering Wisdom the Host* [JSOTSup 216; Sheffield: JSOT, 1996]), or an unknown Canaanite goddess (Lang, *Wisdom and the Book of Proverbs*, 57–70).

109 Others argue that Woman Wisdom is a hypostasis of YHWH's wisdom. However, this theory does not adequately describe the persona of Wisdom in Proverbs 1–9, for she is presented as an autonomous figure who is subordinate to YHWH (1:20–33; 8:22–31). For those who argue that Wisdom is a hypostasis, see H. Ringgren, *Word and Wisdom: Studies in the Hypostatization of Divine Qualities and Functions in the Ancient Near East* (Lund: H. Ohlson, 1947); R. Marcus, "On Biblical Hypostases of Wisdom," *HUCA* 25 (1950): 157–71; Whybray, *Wisdom in Proverbs*, 76–104; A. Cooper, "'The Lord Grants Wisdom': The World View of Proverbs 1–9," in *Bringing the Hidden to Light: The Process of Interpretation. Studies in Honor of Stephen A. Geller* (ed. K. F. Kravitz and D. M. Sharon; Winona Lake: Eisenbrauns, 2007), 32.

110 See M. Barker, *The Great Angel: A Study of Israel's Second God* (Louisville: Westminster John Knox, 1992), 48–59; J. M. Hadley, "From Goddess to Literary Construct: The Transformation of Asherah into Hokmah," in *A Feminist Companion to Reading the Bible: Approaches, Methods and Strategies* (ed. A. Brenner and C. Fontaine; London: Dearborn, 1997), 360–99; M. D. Coogan, "The Goddess Wisdom—'Where Can She Be Found?' Literary Reflexes of Popular Religion," in *Ki Baruch Hu: Ancient Near Eastern, Biblical, and Judaic Studies in Honor of Baruch A. Levine* (ed. W. W. Hallo et al., Winona Lake: Eisenbrauns, 1999), 203–09; D. Penchansky, "Is Hokmah an Israelite Goddess, and What Should We Do About It?," in *Postmodern Interpretations of the Bible: A Reader* (ed. A. K. M. Adam; St. Louis: Chalice, 2001), 81–92.

response to the social conditions of the post-exilic period.[111] She provided the community with a family-centered social configuration,[112] and functioned as the authoritative mediator who reconciled the chaotic sense of reality with a harmonious cosmos.

These approaches to Wisdom's origins highlight the mythological and historical images that are woven into her multifaceted portrayal. However, neither approach accounts for the agglomeration of images or attributes attributed to Wisdom. The main impediment to locating Woman Wisdom's background in a particular goddess tradition is that Wisdom bears only partial resemblance to these female deities. While these foreign and Semitic deities may have provided a background for the formation of Woman Wisdom, there is no direct link between any one goddess and חָכְמָה.[113] The sociological approach captures several aspects of Wisdom's literary character, but the proposal overstates the ethos of the interludes. The discourses are not cast in an atmosphere of social disorder or communal decay; rather these poems acknowledge the reality that society includes aberrant individuals who will receive their just deserts (1:31–32; 8:36; 9:18).[114] Within this environment, Wisdom embodies a series of roles associated with real women, but she does not mediate God's word to humankind and her involvement with statecraft militates against her exclusive association with the activities of real women (8:15–16).[115]

While neither approach to Wisdom's origins accounts for the variety of features woven into her impressionistic portrayal, few would deny that Woman Wisdom is a literary personification. The sages employed this rhetorical convention to elevate Wisdom to the symbolic register and provide a general, conceptual framework through which to evaluate her multifaceted literary character.[116] Through personification the diverse images of prophet, teacher, counselor, goddess, lover, and mother are subsumed and concretized in a composite figure.[117] The sages used this literary device as a pedagogical tool to

---

111   See G. Baumann, *Die Weisheitsgestalt in Proverbien 1–9* (FAT 16; Tübingen: Mohr, 1996); A. M. Sinnott, *The Personification of Wisdom* (SOTSMS; Burlington: Ashgate, 2005).

112   See Camp, *Wisdom and the Feminine*, 69–147; M. A. Klopefnstein, "Auferstehung der Göttin in der spätisraelitischen Weisheit von Prov 1–9?," in *Ein Gott allein? JHWH-Verehrung und biblischer Monotheismus im Kontext der israelitischen und altorientalischen Religionsgeschichte* (ed. W. Dietrich and M. A. Klopfenstein; Fribourg: Fribourg University, 1994), 531–42; S. Schroer, "Wise and Counseling Women in Ancient Israel: Literary and Historical Ideals of the Personified *Hokma*," in *A Feminist Companion to Wisdom Literature* (ed. A. Brenner; Sheffield: Sheffield Academic Press, 1995), 67–84; C. R. Fontaine, "The Social Roles of Women in the World of Wisdom," in *A Feminist Companion to Wisdom Literature* (ed. A. Brenner; Sheffield: Sheffield Academic Press, 1995), 24–49; idem, *Smooth Words*, 15–149; Yoder, *Wisdom as a Woman of Substance*, 41–71.

113   N. Shupak, *Where Can Wisdom Be Found?*, 269–70.

114   Fox, *Proverbs 1–9*, 342.

115   Fox, *Proverbs 1–9*, 334, 338–40.

116   Camp, *Wisdom and the Feminine*, 215–16; Sinnott, *The Personification of Wisdom*, 18–19.

117   Camp, *Wisdom and the Feminine*, 215–17; Sinnott, *The Personification of Wisdom*, 19–20.

transform abstract knowledge into an attractive form and to elaborate on the inchoate personifications of חָכְמָה in the lectures.[118] The interludes in Proverbs 1–9 personify Wisdom as an autonomous, fully developed literary character who embodies several courtly characteristics. These characteristics are conveyed through particular metaphors, motifs, and expressions in each of the Wisdom interludes.

The first interlude complements the parent's opening lecture (1:20–33). The juxtaposition of the parent's warning with Wisdom's indictment links the father's teaching with the voice of חָכְמָה and extends the parental discourse into the realm of the community.[119] In prophetic fashion, Wisdom speaks through the voice of the father and addresses three groups of people: פְּתָיִם, לֵצִים, and כְּסִילִים (1:22).[120] She delivers a carefully crafted speech in the center of communal life and outlines the repercussions of rejecting her call.

Wisdom's indictment is set in the public arena (1:20–21; 8:1–3; 9:1–3). She delivers a scourging rebuke in the streets and the city gate, where the masses are gathered to conduct business, the elders are seated to discuss local affairs, and the government is convened to administer justice.[121] This setting indicates Wisdom's integral position with regard to the thresholds of life.[122] Her presence at the בָּעִיר שְׁעָרִים (1:21; 8:3) identifies her association with the proceedings of public life, and symbolizes her specific involvement in commercial, judicial, and government affairs—subjects she develops in chapter 8 (8:14–16).[123]

The second interlude constitutes an encomium of Wisdom that foreshadows her aretalogy in chapter 8 (3:13–20). This interlude is cast as a macarism, praising the benefactions of Wisdom in hymnic fashion.[124] In contrast to the first

---

118 For the inchoate forms of personification in the lectures, see Prov 2:3; 4:6–9; 6:22; 7:4. Also see Fox, *Proverbs 1–9*, 332.

119 Newsom, "Woman and the Discourse of Patriarchal Wisdom," 119; R. C. Van Leeuwen, "Liminality and Worldview in Proverbs 1–9," *Semeia* 50 (1990): 115.

120 For those who argue that Wisdom is portrayed as either a prophet or a teacher in 1:20–33, see B. Gemser, *Sprüche Salomos* (HAT 16; Tübingen: Mohr, 1963), 16–17; McKane, *Proverbs: A New Approach*, 273; M. Gilbert, "Le discours menaçant de Sagesse en Proverbes 1,20–33," in *Storia e tradizioni di Israele: Scritti in onore di J. Alberto Soggin* (ed. D. Garrone and F. Israel; Brescia: Paideia, 1991), 99–119; Camp, "Woman Wisdom and the Strange Woman," 87; Harris, *Proverbs 1–9*, 68–109; Blenkinsopp, *Sage, Priest, Prophet*, 44; Sinnott, *The Personification of Wisdom*, 69–81.

121 See Jer 48:38; Amos 5:16; Zech 8:4, 5; Ezra 10:9; Neh 8:1, 3; 2 Chron 29:4, Lang, *Wisdom and the Book of Proverbs*, 22–29, King and Stager, *Life in Biblical Israel*, 191.

122 See Van Leeuwen, "The Book of Proverbs," *NIB* 5:89; Waltke, *Proverbs: Chapters 1–15*, 394–95; Perdue, *Wisdom Literature: A Theological History*, 52–53.

123 See Deut 16:18; 17:8; 21:19; 22:15; Josh 20:4; 1 Sam 4:18; 2 Sam 15:2; 18:4, 24; 19:8; 1 Kgs 22:10; Amos 5:10, 12; Job 29:7; 31:21; Prov 22:22; 31:23; Ruth 4:1, 11. For discussion of the city gate as the place of legal procedures, see H.-J. Boecker, *Law and the Administration of Justice in the Old Testament and Near East* (trans. J. Moiser; Minneapolis: Augsburg, 1980), 31–33; King and Stager, *Life in Biblical Israel*, 234.

124 For discussion of the macarism, see Fox, *Proverbs 1–9*, 161.

interlude, Wisdom does not deliver a discourse. Rather, the father elaborates on the benefits associated with his own teaching by describing the social and material rewards that accompany Woman Wisdom (3:1–12; 13–20).[125] Wisdom is compared with a series of precious commodities (3:14–15) and extolled for the gifts she possesses (3:16–18). Among these gifts, Wisdom dispenses עֹשֶׁר וְכָבוֹד (3:16; 8:18)—an expression used primarily in reference to royal figures.[126] Whether עֹשֶׁר and כָּבוֹד are collocated or used in close proximity to one another, they form a single concept that carries the connotation of royal honor and prestige.[127] This expression, coupled with a series of verbal and thematic parallels (3:13, 14, 19–20; 8:10, 17, 32, 34, 35), links the discourse with chapter 8, where Wisdom develops the images and motifs introduced in the initial interludes through a lucid aretalogy.

The poem in chapter 8 elaborates on the themes raised in the previous discourses to present the most revealing portrait of Wisdom's literary character (8:1–36). Here the father speaks through Wisdom, who highlights her character, benefits, and authority with a view toward persuading the addressee to embrace her.[128] Within the context of Proverbs 1–9, Wisdom's aretalogy serves as a foil to the noble adulteress in chapter 7.[129] Her discourse functions as a heuristic device through which the father subverts the speech of the אִשָּׁה זָרָה and develops his argument.[130]

In conjunction with the first interlude, Wisdom addresses a series of individuals in the public thoroughfares (1:20–21; 8:2–3). She assumes the mantle of a teacher and addresses three groups of people: פְּתָאיִם, בְּנֵי אָדָם, and כְּסִילִים (8:4–5, 32). Though Wisdom addresses humankind in general, she narrows her audience to the naïve and the obtuse dolt. She issues a powerful panegyric

---

125 Waltke, *Proverbs: Chapters 1–15*, 255; Sandoval, *The Discourse of Wealth and Poverty*, 83.

126 Many scholars propose that Wisdom is portrayed in the guise of Maat in 3:16. The image of Wisdom holding longevity in her right hand and riches and glory in her left is comparable to Maat. However, the iconographic resemblance between the two figures is not precise and several deities in the ancient world are also portrayed in a similar fashion. For a discussion of these issues, see Kayatz, *Studien*, 105; Fox, "World Order and Maꜥat," 37–48; idem, *Proverbs 1–9*, 161; Perdue, *Wisdom Literature: A Theological History*, 50–51.

127 As a phrase, עֹשֶׁר וְכָבוֹד is used only in reference to royal figures (1 Chron 29:28; 2 Chron 17:5; 18:1; 32:27). The single exception is Proverbs 22:21, where honor and prestige are bestowed on the one who is humble and fears YHWH. Moreover, when עֹשֶׁר and כָּבוֹד are used in close proximity to one another, they are typically attributed to either kings or bureaucratic officials (1 Kgs 3:13; Esth 1:4; 5:11; 2 Chron 1:11, 12).

128 See Newsom, "Woman and the Discourse of Patriarchal Wisdom," 128; Yoder, *Wisdom as a Woman of Substance*, 3.

129 Van Leeuwen, "The Book of Proverbs," *NIB* 5:89; Clifford, *Proverbs*, 94; Fox, *Proverbs 1–9*, 265; Waltke, *Proverbs: Chapters 1–15*, 392.

130 G. A. Yee, "The Theology of Creation in Proverbs 8:22–31," in *Creation in Biblical Traditions* (ed. R. J. Clifford and J. J. Collins; Washington, D.C.: The Catholic Biblical Association of America, 1992), 86.

punctuated by courtly motifs to describe her character and demonstrate her authority. These courtly images not only identify Wisdom's indispensable value, but they also reveal her fundamental role in governmental affairs.

The clearest depiction of Wisdom's activity in the terrestrial realm is found in the third strophe (8:12–21). Here Wisdom describes her role in the civil order (8:12–16) and outlines the gifts that she bestows on those who love her (8:17–21). Woman Wisdom opens her encomium with a self-identification formula that resembles numerous royal inscriptions and divine aretalogies throughout the ancient oriental world (8:12).[131] She claims the faculties of עֵצָה, תּוּשִׁיָּה, and גְּבוּרָה— political skills that are wielded by rulers to execute effective governance (8:14). In general, the noun עֵצָה is typically associated with political consultation and denotes the capacity both to conceive a plan and to communicate it to others.[132] Together with תּוּשִׁיָּה and גְּבוּרָה, these terms seem to refer to political or military advice.[133] Wisdom is portrayed as the possessor of these political faculties and the proprietress of the skills needed for statecraft. She is the medium through which מְלָכִים, רוֹזְנִים, שָׂרִים, נְדִיבִים and כָּל־שֹׁפְטֵי reign, formulate righteous decrees, and execute justice (8:15–16).[134] This catalog of expressions from the semantic field of governance demonstrates that all just, governmental functions are done in accordance with Wisdom's gifts. From kings and princes to foreign officials and members of the ruling class, Wisdom claims that she is the fundamental principle of effective governance.

The courtly motifs presented in verses 12–17 are also reflected in verses 18–21. Here Wisdom moves from her possession of political faculties and their value for statecraft to the material and social benefits she bestows on those who love her. Wisdom elaborates on the rhetoric of wealth delineated in chapter 3 and relates a series of precious commodities in order to highlight her inestimable value. She reiterates the assertion from 3:16, claiming the attributes of royal honor and prestige (עֹשֶׁר־וְכָבוֹד, 8:18). By means of the comparative construction (טוֹב־מִן), Wisdom asserts that her value is greater than the commercial gains of silver and gold (8:19). Moreover, she promises to fill the treasuries of those who love her (8:21). Elsewhere the noun אוֹצָר refers to storehouses or vaults containing valuable metals, precious commodities, furnishings, or spices. The term designates the treasuries or storehouses that belong to YHWH (Josh 6:19,

---

131 See Kayatz, *Studien*, 76–93; Fox, "World Order and Maʿat," 44–47; idem, *Proverbs 1–9*, 271.

132 See 2 Sam 15:31, 34; 16:20, 23; 17:7, 14, 23; 1 Kgs 1:12; 12:8, 13, 14; 18:20; Isa 11:2; 19:3, 11; 30:1; 36:5; Jer 19:7; 49:30; Ezek 7:26; 11:2; Prov 20:18; Ezra 10:8; 1 Chron 12:9; 2 Chron 22:5.

133 Lang, *Wisdom and the Book of Proverbs*, 73–74; Van Leeuwen, "The Book of Proverbs," *NIB* 5:91; Murphy, *Proverbs*, 50; Waltke, *Proverbs: Chapters 1–15*, 402; Perdue, *Wisdom Literature: A Theological History*, 55.

134 For a description of the social status and political position of these rulers and judges, see R. de Vaux, *Ancient Israel: Its Life and Institutions* (trans. J. McHugh; New York: McGraw-Hill, 1961), 1:69–70; F. S. Frick, *The City in Ancient Israel* (SBLDS 36; Missoula: Scholars Press, 1977), 111–12; Fox, *Proverbs 1–9*, 274.

24), the temple (1 Kgs 7:51; 14:26; 15:18; 2 Kgs 24:13; Mal 3:10), a nation (Joel 1:17), or the royal palace (1 Kgs 14:26; 2 Kgs 12:18; 24:13). If Wisdom's promise to fill the treasuries of her devotees has any relevance for the addressee of Proverbs, it seems her role is that of a benefactress of the palace treasuries. Within the present context, there is no allusion to the temple or a corporate body and YHWH is not in view. Rather Wisdom is portrayed as the matron of rulers and a supporter of the royal repository. To complete her character résumé, Wisdom describes the social virtues that regulate her behavior (8:19). She embodies צְדָקָה and מִשְׁפָּט, communal values that promote a just order and political qualities that equip rulers to govern wisely.[135] She not only empowers rulers to execute righteous judgment (8:15–16), but she also represents a way of life that is guided by communal virtues and values (8:18, 20).

Wisdom's résumé in Proverbs 8:12–21 provides an explicit account of her activity in the terrestrial realm. Within Proverbs 1–9, Woman Wisdom performs several earthbound functions. She indicts those who reject her (1:20–33), loves those who respond to her, and hates those who forsake her (8:17, 21, 36). She delivers her discourses in the streets and the city gate, but does not identify her explicit involvement in commerce or communal gatherings (1:20–21; 8:2–3). Moreover, she bestows material goods and social virtues on her devotees when they assimilate her teachings and implement the principles of wisdom in their lives (8:21). However, Wisdom's particular involvement in human affairs is ambiguous. She is depicted as a composite literary character who performs her role by being rather than by doing.[136] In view of Wisdom's inchoate activities within the prologue, Proverbs 8:12–21 presents the most explicit depiction of her involvement in human affairs and her value in the terrestrial realm. Wisdom does not direct the discourse toward rulers; rather she enumerates a litany of royal motifs to extol her socio-political qualities and identifies a specific group of people through whom these qualities are manifested. She is portrayed as the one who possesses the faculties of statecraft: shrewdness, counsel, competence, power, justice, and righteousness. She does not control the events of human history;[137] rather she endows leaders with the virtues needed to govern effectively. In the main, the discourse plays a significant role in literary development of Woman Wisdom. The speaker specifies Wisdom's activity in historic time and depicts her as a royal patroness, the principal of just government, and the instrument of ordered society.[138]

---

135   L. Kalugila, *The Wise King*, 105; Weinfeld, "Justice and Righteousness," 234–35.

136   Fox, *Proverbs 1–9*, 355.

137   Fox, *Proverbs 1–9*, 355.

138   This is not to say that Woman Wisdom is an *Ordnungsmacht*, following von Rad (*Weisheit in Israel*, 189–228). Rather Wisdom is portrayed as the possessor of statecraft and the means by which leaders establish an ordered society.

This portrait of Wisdom's involvement in historic time is balanced by an account of her involvement in primordial time (8:22–31). The fourth strophe of the poem develops 3:19–20 and identifies Wisdom's position in relation to creation, YHWH, and humanity.[139] Here Wisdom recounts her birth in the primordial past and her presence at the construction of the cosmos to emphasize her chronological priority in creation, her special relationship with YHWH, and her unique knowledge of the basic structures, patterns and components of reality (8:22–29).[140] The presence of Wisdom at the ordering of the cosmos confirms her authoritative status and legitimizes her ability to bestow the faculties of statecraft upon rulers.[141] By observing YHWH's construction of the cosmic order, Wisdom is able to provide rulers with the skills necessary to establish social order. Her role in the terrestrial realm is not divorced from her role in the cosmological; rather Wisdom's knowledge of the fundamental patterns of reality provides her with the resources to endow the human race in general and socio-political leaders in particular with the skills necessary to live in concert with the cosmic order.

The final strophe of the poem marks the conclusion of Wisdom's speech and serves as a bridge to her invitation in chapter 9 (8:32–36). Here Wisdom imitates the rhetoric of the father and assumes the persona of a homeowner (5:7; 7:24; 8:34). She resumes the role of a teacher and elaborates on the exhortation presented in the exordium, urging her audience to listen to her so they might live and receive divine favor (3:2; 22, 4:22; 8:35). Wisdom's invitation, coupled with the architectural images, foreshadows the discourse in chapter 9 (8:34; 9:14), where Woman Wisdom and Woman Folly admonish the פֶּתִי to accept their invitation, cross their threshold, and dine at their banquet.

---

139   For an analysis of the structure of 8:22–31, see J. N. Aletti, "Proverbes 8:22–31: Étude et structure," *Bib* 57 (1976): 25–37; G. A. Yee, "An Analysis of Prov 8:22–31 According to Style and Structure," *ZAW* (1982): 58–66.

140   These verses have given rise to several questions concerning the nature of Wisdom's genesis. The verb קנה may mean "acquire" or "obtain." This connotation is attested elsewhere in Proverbs in connection with wisdom, knowledge and good sense (Prov 1:5; 4:5, 7; 15:32; 16:16; 17:16; 18:15; 19:8). However, in several texts, קנה carries the connotation "create" (Gen 4:1; 14:19, 22, Ps 139:13). This nuance seems to fit the present context better than "acquire," since קנה is used in conjunction with נסך and חיל (8:23, 24, 25). The verb נסך conveys the notion of being "poured out" or "formed" (Ps 139:13; Job 10:11), while חיל denotes the activity of writhing in birth pains (Deut 32:18; Job 39:1; Ps 29:9; 90:2). Both verbs are passive in the present context, reflecting YHWH's procreation of Wisdom. In light of these verbs, it seems that קנה carries the connotation "create" rather than "acquire" in 8:22 (cf. LXX, Targ., Syr.). For a discussion of the issues, see B. Vawter, "Prov 8:22: Wisdom and Creation," *JBL* 9 (1980): 205–16; Fox, *Proverbs 1–9*, 279–83; Waltke, *Proverbs: Chapters 1–15*, 408–13; Sinnott, *The Personification of Wisdom*, 25–27. Also see W. H. Schmidt, "קנה," *TLOT* 3:1147–1153; A. Baumann, "חיל," *TDOT* 4:345–47.

141   The repetition of the verb חקק (8:15, 29) grounds Wisdom's ability to counsel rulers in YHWH's ordering of creation. See Van Leeuwen, "The Book of Proverbs," *NIB* 5:93–94; Waltke, *Proverbs: Chapters 1–15*, 407–08.

The final interlude (9:1–18) summarizes the major themes and images
presented in the discourses of Proverbs 1–9. Here the speaker integrates the root
metaphors of women, ways, houses and invitations that punctuate the lectures
and interludes through the rival discourses of Woman Wisdom and Woman
Folly.[142] Similar to the relationship between the addressee's wife and the Strange
Woman, these antithetical figures are mirror images of one another: one
embodies wisdom and life (9:1, 6), the other, folly and death (9:13, 18). In fact,
Wisdom's antithesis bears the attributes of the אִשָּׁה זָרָה: she is turbulent (7:11;
9:13), she is ignorant (5:6; 9:13), and her path leads to the Rephaim in Sheol (2:18;
5:5; 7:27; 9:18). Woman Folly's seductive machinations complement the tactics of
the אִשָּׁה זָרָה, as both figures attempt to persuade the naïve through their seductive
speech. The epilogue of Proverbs 1–9 presents two contrasting domiciles that
embody several courtly characteristics. These characteristics are conveyed
through particular images and expressions associated with both Woman Wisdom
and Woman Folly.

In view of her royal patronage and her unique relationship with YHWH
(8:12–31), Wisdom emerges as a noble hostess in chapter 9 (9:1–6). The speaker
elaborates on Wisdom's authority and dignity through a vivid portrait of the
banquet she prepares for her devotees (9:1–3). Wisdom builds a large house,
prepares a lavish banquet, and issues an open invitation to the פֶּתִי and the חֲסַר־לֵב.
This building-feasting topos is a conventional ancient Near Eastern literary motif
that grounds human wisdom in the divine ordering of the cosmos (1 Kgs 8:62–
66).[143] In essence, Wisdom's home serves as a multivalent symbol that illuminates
her indispensable value as well as her noble status; it identifies Wisdom's
fundamental role in the establishment of a household (Prov 14:1; 24:3; 31:10–31)
and depicts her as a wealthy matrician.[144] The seven pillars of Wisdom's home
symbolize its perfection (6:16; 24:16; 26:25), and indicate its spacious and
sophisticated construction.[145] Moreover, Wisdom's retinue of attendants signifies

---

142 Van Leeuwen, "The Book of Proverbs," *NIB* 5:100.

143 For a discussion of this literary motif and its connection to Proverbs 9, see M. Lichtenstein,
"The Banquet Motifs in Keret and in Proverbs 9," *JANES* 1 (1968/69): 19–31; R. J. Clifford,
"Proverbs IX: A Suggested Ugaritic Parallel," *VT* 25 (1975): 298–306; J. Klein, "Building and
Dedication Hymns in Sumerian Literature," *Acta Sumerologica* 11 (1989): 28–67; Meinhold, *Die
Sprüche*, 1:152; V. A. Hurowitz, *I Have Built You an Exalted House: Temple Building in the Bible in
Light of Mesopotamian and Northwest Semitic Writings* (JSOTSup 115; Sheffield: JSOT, 1992); R. C.
Van Leeuwen, "Cosmos, Temple, House: Building and Wisdom in Mesopotamia and Israel," in
Wisdom Literature in Mesopotamia and Israel (SBLSymS 36; Atlanta: Society of Biblical Literature,
2007), 67–90.

144 Lang, *Wisdom and the Book of Proverbs*, 92; Waltke, *Proverbs: Chapters 1–15*, 432; Yoder, *Wisdom as a
Woman of Substance*, 100.

145 The nature of Wisdom's home has given rise to a variety of interpretations. Many suggest that
Wisdom's house is portrayed as a temple and that her attendants are inviting devotees to a cultic
meal. However, archeological evidence suggests that Wisdom's home reflects the structure of
houses constructed for the wealthy. In general, there is nothing in the text to suggest that

her high social stature, for any literary character that has a נַעֲרָה is a person of substance.[146] These features complement the portrayal of Wisdom's literary character in Proverbs 1–9 and accentuate an additional dimension of her persona. On the whole, the interludes present Woman Wisdom as a wealthy matrician who functions as a patroness of rulers, a faithful devotee of YHWH, and a noble hostess.

The discourse of Woman Folly shares several elements with the invitation of Woman Wisdom. Woman Folly employs a rhetorical scheme that resembles the invitation of Woman Wisdom: she directs her discourse toward the פֶּתִי and the חֲסַר־לֵב (9:4, 16), she offers her invitation at the heights of the city (9:3, 14), and she issues the same call as Woman Wisdom (9:4, 16). In addition, the characterization of Woman Folly is comparable to Woman Wisdom. In conjunction with the אִשָּׁה זָרָה, Woman Folly is depicted as a noble hostess who attempts to lure the naïve into her home through provocative rhetoric peppered by erotic images (7:14–20; 9:13–18). She is portrayed as an honorable matron who sits upon a כִּסֵּא at the doorway of her house near the heights of the city (9:14).[147] Within the book of Proverbs, a כִּסֵּא symbolizes a seat of honor and prestige (16:12; 20:8, 28; 25:5; 29:14).[148] This descriptive feature not only enhances the seductive nature of Woman Folly, but it also demonstrates her elevated status.[149] The writer portrays her as a prominent hostess who entices the naïve with her smooth words and her self-indulgent meal.

Wisdom's home is a cultic shrine. If the temple were in view, then the author would have characterized her meal in terms of a cultic slaughter (זבח), rather than a profane slaughter (טבח). In light of the association between Wisdom's home and the domiciles of the wealthy, some suggest that the residence is a palace. This conclusion is based on the size of the house and the building activity associated with its construction, which has royal connotations (2 Sam 5:11–12; 1 Kgs 6:1–2; 7:1, 9–12; 9:10). However, the text does not provide enough evidence to substantiate the conclusion. When Wisdom's home is read within the larger literary context of the book (31:10–31), it seems that the residence is depicted as a patrician's house. For a discussion of these issues, see Albright, "Some Canaanite–Phoenician Sources," 1–15; McKane, *Proverbs: A New Approach*, 362–65; G. W. Ahlström, "The House of Wisdom," in *Svensk Exegetisk Årsbok* (ed. H. Ringgren; Uppsala: Gleerup-Lund, 1979), 74–76; Plöger, *Sprüche Salomos*, 101–04; Lang, *Wisdom and the Book of Proverbs*, 90–96; Clifford, "Woman Wisdom in the Book of Proverbs," 61–72; Waltke, *Proverbs: Chapters 1–15*, 432–33 n. 44; F. Mies, "'Dame Sagesse' en Proverbes 9 une personnification féminine?," *RB* 108 (2001): 167–69.

146 L. G. Perdue, *Wisdom and Creation: The Theology of Wisdom Literature* (Nashville: Abingdon, 1994), 96; C. S. Leeb, *Away from the Father's House: The Social Location of* Na'ar *and* Na'arah *in Ancient Israel* (JSOTSup 301; Sheffield: Sheffield Academic Press, 2000), 43; Fontaine, *Smooth Words*, 38.

147 Several scholars suggest that Woman Folly is a prototype of a harlot (Lang, *Wisdom and the Book of Proverbs*, 97–98; Perdue, *Proverbs*, 147–52). However, in light of her literary counterpart, the זָרָה אִשָּׁה, it seems that Woman Folly is portrayed as a noble adulteress rather than a cult prostitute.

148 See J. Oswalt, "כִּסֵּא," *TWOT* 1:448. Oswalt concludes that all but seven references to כִּסֵּא in the Old Testament designate a royal or a divine throne.

149 See Perdue, *Wisdom and Creation*, 100; Miles, *Wise King — Royal Fool*, 97; Waltke, *Proverbs: Chapters 1–15*, 444.

3.3.3 Section Conclusion

To summarize, the lectures and interludes in Proverbs 1–9 contain a variety of courtly elements. Within the lectures, the parents describe the attractive quality of their instructions through ornamental imagery, evoking images of royal status and honor (1:9; 3:22; 4:9). They present a constellation of socio-moral values needed to live and govern rightly and illustrate the contours of these virtues through proper behavior toward God and other people (2:9; 3:1–12; 3:21–35). Moreover, the parents introduce the addressee to the seductive tactics of a noble adulteress (2:16–19; 5:1–23; 6:20–35; 7:1–27), who seems to present a real threat to their listeners.[150] Together with the parental lectures, the interludes elaborate on the inchoate personifications of Wisdom and extend the virtues and values of the home into the socio-religious sphere. Woman Wisdom is presented as a multifaceted literary figure who delivers her discourses in the center of communal life (1:20–21; 8:2–3; 9:3). She endows her devotees with royal honor and prestige (3:16; 8:18) and functions as a royal patroness, providing rulers with the skills necessary to establish social order (8:12–21). She is portrayed as a daughter of YHWH, a noble hostess, and one who understands the fundamental patterns of reality (8:22–31; 9:1–6). Wisdom's negative counterpart is also depicted as an aristocratic figure. Woman Folly delivers her erotic invitation from her throne atop the city (9:14), enticing those who pass by with her seductive rhetoric. Together, these courtly features play a significant role in the instructions of Proverbs 1–9; they punctuate the sapiential material and provide a framework through which to evaluate both the addressee and the interaction situation of the material.

3.4 The Addressee of Proverbs 1–9

The ostensive addressee of Proverbs 1–9 is identified in both the preamble and the main body of the work. The preamble articulates the fundamental purpose of the document and presents the intended addressee of the material (1:1–7).[151]

---

150 Whybray argues that the noble adulteress described in chapter 7 is "unlikely to have set out to seduce a penniless and uncouth young man from outside her own social circle" (Whybray, *The Composition of the Book of Proverbs*, 56).

151 See McKane, *Proverbs: A New Approach*, 262; Plöger, *Sprüche Salomos*, 8; Van Leeuwen, "The Book of Proverbs," *NIB* 5:32; Murphy, *Proverbs*, 3; Clifford, *Proverbs*, 32; Fox, *Proverbs 1–9*, 58. Many scholars have suggested that verse 5 is an interpolation, since it interrupts the series of infinitives construct with a set of finite verbs (F. Renfroe, "The Effect of Redaction on the Structure of Prov 1,1–6," *ZAW* 101 [1989]: 290–93; Whybray, *Proverbs*, 31; idem, *The Composition of the Book of Proverbs*, 51–56). Whether or not this shift is taken as evidence for the literary-historical development of the preamble, verse 5 serves as a logical continuation of the preamble's purposes (Fox, *Proverbs 1–9*, 62).

Based on the syntax of the preamble, the opening verses may be divided into two principal parts: a statement of purpose and an invitation to the book. The first section outlines the educational goal of the document and identifies the principal addressee of the instructions (1:2–4). In the main, the work seeks to promote a variety of ethical principles, ranging from cognitive and instrumental virtues to moral dispositions and communal values.[152] The litany of intellectual values (1:2) and practical virtues (1:4) frame a series of communal principles (1:3), which comprise the centerpiece of the prolegomena.[153] The absence of an introductory *lamed* prefix in verse 3b highlights the importance of the document's social virtues: צֶדֶק, מִשְׁפָּט, and מֵישָׁרִים. From a structural standpoint, these virtues mark the climax of the preamble and form a significant topos in the instructions of Proverbs 1–9.[154]

The second section of the prologue offers an invitation to the addressee and describes the nature of the instructions that follow (1:5–6). The string of finite verbs in verse 5 interrupts the chain of infinitives construct in verses 2–4. These verbs seem to function as jussives, expressing a wish or desire. Though the initial verb, יִשְׁמַע, is isolated and ambiguous in form, the second verb, יוֹסֶף, is typically understood as a jussive.[155] This suggests that the series of finite verbs in verse 5 should be taken as jussives, presenting the addressee with an invitation to engage the book's purposes.[156] The invitation urges the addressee to assume the role of a wise individual who is able to process and interpret the figures and tropes presented in the instructions.[157] This subject position is a fundamental prerequisite for an interpretation of the material. The cluster of literary expressions listed in verse 6 does not refer to the discrete genres incorporated in the book; rather it highlights the multivalent nature of the discourse and alerts the addressee to the interpretive process he must undertake.[158] Together, verses 2–6 present the purpose of the book through a program of character formation and issue an invitation that identifies the intellectual faculties needed to interpret the instructions.

---

152 Brown, *Character in Crisis*, 23–30.

153 Brown, *Character in Crisis*, 29.

154 Brown, *Character in Crisis*, 22–49; Sandoval, "Revisiting the Prologue of Proverbs," 461.

155 See GKC §69v; §107m, n; §151a; Fox, *Proverbs 1–9*, 53, 62; Waltke, *Proverbs: Chapters 1–15*, 173; Longman, *Proverbs*, 91; Sandoval, "Revisiting the Prologue of Proverbs," 462.

156 Sandoval, "Revisiting the Prologue of Proverbs," 462.

157 Sandoval, "Revisiting the Prologue of Proverbs," 462–63.

158 The terms מָשָׁל, מְלִיצָה, דִּבְרֵי חֲכָמִים, and חִידָה may refer to distinct literary genres within the book. This is apparent in the case of the מָשָׁל and the דִּבְרֵי חֲכָמִים, which are associated with the sayings in chapters 10:1–22:16 and 22:17–24:34, respectively. However, the "riddle" and the "figure" are absent from the collections (Van Leeuwen, "The Book of Proverbs," *NIB* 5:33; Murphy, *Proverbs*, 5; Fox, *Proverbs 1–9*, 65–67). This seems to suggest that the cluster of forms in verse 6 does not refer to particular literary genres in the book, but to the multivalent nature of the instructions (Sandoval, "Revisiting the Prologue of Proverbs," 469).

The audience addressed in the preamble is identified as the "naïve youth" or the "callow youth" (1:4).[159] Many recognize that the preamble addresses the simple youth, but they also identify a secondary addressee: the חָכָם and the נָבוֹן (1:5).[160] This duality is found in several ancient Near Eastern instructional texts. The instructions of Ptahhotep and Amenemope, for example, direct their teachings toward a dual audience. The former transmits the "ways of the ancestors" to both his son and those who are willing to hear, while the latter delivers the "teaching for life" to future generations in general and his youngest son in particular.[161] However, if verse 5 functions as an invitation to the addressee, rather than a declaration of a secondary audience, then the principal addressee of the preamble seems to be the naïve youth. This notion finds further support in the interludes of Proverbs 1–9. As noted above, the interludes address a variety of individuals, ranging from humanity in general to the scoffer, the fool and the naïve in particular (1:22; 8:4–5, 9:4, 16). Wisdom directs her discourses to the human race in order to emphasize her universal relevance, but she narrows her addressees to the obstinate and the untutored. Wisdom's invitation to the לֵץ and the כְּסִיל, however, appears to be rhetorical, for within the book of Proverbs these personages are unable to learn.[162] Since the פְּתָיִם are malleable and capable of being shaped by the educational process, it seems that they are the principal addressees of the interludes. The פְּתָיִם form a group of inexperienced, gullible youths who function as the primary addressee of both the preamble and the interludes (1:4; 1:22, 32; 8:5; 9:4, 16).[163]

In conjunction with the preamble and the interludes, the parental lectures present a second primary addressee: the son. The parents appeal to the son in each of the lectures (1:8, 10, 15; 2:1; 3:1, 11, 21; 4:10, 20; 5:1, 7, 20; 6:20; 7:1, 24). However, on several occasions the audience is addressed in the plural בָּנִים (4:1; 5:7; 7:24). This plural injunction is intrusive, for these addresses are couched within a larger cycle of lectures directed toward בְּנִי.[164] Whether the plural address is a generic convention or a rhetorical device that highlights the general relevance of the father's teaching, it does not seem to introduce an additional addressee of the instructions. The indefinite construction suggests the father employs the

---

159 The terms פְּתָאִים and נַעַר form a distributed hendiadys, which Fox glosses as "the callow young." See Fox, *Proverbs 1–9*, 61.

160 Plöger, *Sprüche Salomos*, 10; Whybray, *Proverbs*, 30–31; Van Leeuwen, "The Book of Proverbs," *NIB* 5:32; Clifford, *Proverbs*, 35; Schäfer, *Die Poesie der Weisen*, 10; Perdue, *Proverbs*, 69; Fuhs, *Das Buch der Sprichwörter*, 38; Fox, *Proverbs 1–9*, 53, 58; Yoder, *Wisdom as a Woman of Substance*, 3; Waltke, *Proverbs: Chapters 1–15*, 177–79; Longman, *Proverbs*, 98.

161 See "The Instruction of Ptahhotep" (*AEL* 1:63); "The Instruction of Amenemope" (*AEL* 2:148–49, 162).

162 Fox, "Who Can Learn?", 68; idem, *Proverbs 1–9*, 41–42.

163 Fox, "Who Can Learn?", 68.

164 It should be noted that in chapters 5 and 7 the injunction is an anomalous plural, since the verbs that precede and follow the address are in the singular (cf. LXX).

plural בָּנִים to emphasize the trans-generational nature of his teaching and ground his discourses in the chain of tradition (4:1–9).[165] In light of these observations, it appears that the son is the ostensive addressee of the lectures, while the references to the בָּנִים represent the successive generations of sons who can benefit from the father's teaching.

While the preamble and the lectures identify two distinct audiences, these addressees are not mutually exclusive. The preamble presents the primary addressee of the book, the פֶּתִי or נַעַר (1:4), who is represented by the addressee in the text, בְּנִי (cf. 7:7).[166] The פֶּתִי addressed in the preamble is called to take up the subject position of the son in the lectures in order to receive social and moral training that will enable him to develop into a responsible member of the community.[167] This notion is reinforced by Wisdom's aretalogy, which imitates the rhetoric of the parental lectures and associates the naïve with the son (8:5, 32). These features suggest the simple youth is the primary addressee of the discourse. This designation is rather ambiguous, but the subject matter of the instructions and term נַעַר provide some indication of the book's principal addressee.

The subject matter of the lectures and interludes present a variety of details that help to identify the nature of the simple youth. The parental discourses assume the addressee is able to steal, murder, join a gang of rogues, associate with perverse people, and engage a wealthy, captivating adulteress (1:10–19; 2:12–19; 4:10–19; 7:1–27). The addressee appears to possess strong sexual appetites (6:24–35), own landed property (3:9–10), and recognize the value of material wealth (3:14–16). Moreover, the lectures indicate that the addressee is either married or at a marriageable age (5:1–23). Together, these details suggest the simple youth is either a young adult or a young male preparing to enter the community as an independent adult.[168]

The term נַעַר also provides an indication of the nature of the book's principal addressee. Within the Old Testament, the term is used with individuals of various ages, ranging from an unborn child to a young man and a seasoned warrior (Gen 22:5; 1 Sam 2:11; Judg 13:5, 7; 1 Chron 12:28). In addition, the נְעָרִים were also associated with a variety of social roles; they functioned as personal attendants to patriarchs (Gen 18:7), prophets (2 Kgs 5:1–27), and kings in the domestic realm

---

165 Newsom, "Woman and the Discourse of Patriarchal Wisdom, 124; Waltke, *Proverbs: Chapters 1–15*, 276, 311, 384. The plural address is also employed by Woman Wisdom. To conclude her aretalogy in chapter 8, Wisdom moves from addressing the masses to direct her exhortations toward the בָּנִים. Here it seems that Wisdom's initial address to humanity and the obstinate serves as a foil for her principal addressee, who is identified as the educable פְּתָיִם and the בָּנִים (8:5, 32). In so doing, Wisdom emulates the rhetoric of the parents, as she incorporates language reminiscent of the lectures (וְעַתָּה בָנִים שִׁמְעוּ־לִי, 5:7; 7:24; 8:32).

166 Fox, *Proverbs 1–9*, 326.

167 Newsom, "Woman and the Discourse of Patriarchal Wisdom," 116–17.

168 Sandoval, "Revisiting the Prologue of Proverbs," 464–65.

(1 Kgs 11:28), and spies (Josh 6:22), informants or retainers in military contexts (1 Sam 9:5–7; 14:1). Whether the נַעַר was an infant, an adolescent, or a soldier, age was not the primary focus of the designation. Rather than serving to identify the age of an individual, it seems the designation may indicate the person's status.

Several studies have attempted to identify the social status of the נַעַר, offering varying results. On the one hand, MacDonald and Stager identify a נַעַר as a person of high status or position. MacDonald focuses on the etymology of the term to demonstrate that the נְעָרִים were a distinctive class of young, literate males of noble birth who occupied prominent service posts in society.[169] Stager elaborates on MacDonald's work, claiming the term נַעַר was a social designation for a potential elder.[170] For Stager, a נַעַר was either a firstborn male awaiting the death of the *pater familias* or a younger son who entered military, priestly, or governmental service because he stood little chance of inheriting much patrimony.[171] On the other hand, Carolyn Leeb argues that the unifying characteristic of the נְעָרִים is neither their social status nor their function within society, but their common social location "away from their father's house."[172] Leeb identifies two primary social situations associated with the נְעָרִים. In the first, the נְעָרִים are dependents who function in domestic, agricultural, or military capacities. Here the נְעָרִים are dependent on their masters or commanders and estranged from both the protection and provision of their *pater familias*.[173] In the second social situation the נְעָרִים are "at risk individuals," placed in dangerous circumstances.[174] The נְעָרִים in these vulnerable situations are not servants, but princes, kings, or nobles in a liminal state.[175] This situation corresponds with the circumstances of the נַעַר in Proverbs 1–9. As noted above, the addressee in Proverbs 1–9 is set within a liminal situation. This state is illustrated through the competing voices that vie for the addressee's allegiance, as well as the root metaphors of women, ways, houses and invitations that punctuate the discourse. If the נַעַר in Proverbs 1–9 is one of the "at risk," liminal נְעָרִים in the Old Testament, then the primary addressee is young men of noble descent. In this

---

169 J. MacDonald, "The Status and Role of the Na'ar in Israelite Society," *JNES* 35 (1976): 147–70.

170 L. E. Stager, "The Archaeology of the Family in Ancient Israel," *BASOR* 260 (1985): 25.

171 Stager, "The Archaeology of the Family in Ancient Israel," 26–27. Also see H. P. Stähli, *Knabe– Jüngling–Knecht: Untersuchungen zum Begriff* Na'ar *im Alten Testament* (BBET 7; Frankfurt: Peter Lang, 1978), 96–217. Stähli distinguishes two semantic domains for נַעַר: (1) a servant, and (2) an unmarried, dependent individual.

172 Leeb, *Away from the Father's House*, 41.

173 Leeb, *Away from the Father's House*, 44–90.

174 Leeb, *Away from the Father's House*, 91–124.

175 Leeb acknowledges that the "at risk" נְעָרִים are not servants. She lists several liminal נְעָרִים in dangerous situations: Jeroboam (1 Kgs 11:28), Solomon (1 Chron 22:5; 28:20), Rehoboam (2 Chron 13:7), Josiah (2 Chron 34:3), Hadad of Edom (1 Kgs 11:17), Isaac (Gen 22:12), David's sons (2 Sam 13:32), Absolom (2 Sam 14:21), Abijah (1 Kgs 14:3), and Bathsheba's child (2 Sam 12:16), among others. See Leeb, *Away from the Father's House*, 91–124.

case, the prologue presents the discourse as a series of instructions delivered by a royal voice to a noble addressee within a domestic context.[176]

This conclusion is reinforced by the subject matter of the lectures and interludes. By referring to the primary addressee as a naïve נַעַר, the document envisions a person in need of instruction and one who has the intellectual capacity both to process and interpret the material.[177] Moreover, the aristocratic nature of the addressee accounts for the courtly elements scattered throughout the discourse. The lectures and interludes underscore wisdom's value through luxurious commodities (3:16; 8:18), emphasize the importance of communal virtues necessary for social order (1:3; 2:9; 3:27–31), and incorporate royal, ornamental imagery to delineate the nature of the parent's teaching (1:9; 3:22; 4:9). In addition, the women who appear in the discourses are noble figures: the strange woman is a rich, affluent adulteress (7:16–20); Woman Folly is characterized as an erotic temptress who sits upon her throne near the heights of the city; and Woman Wisdom appears as a wealthy proprietress, who dispenses the skills necessary for just governance. As noted above, the prologue assumes a noble, distinguished addressee; a person who owns landed property (3:9–10), recognizes the value of material wealth (3:14–16), and is susceptible to the tactics of a wealthy, captivating adulteress (1:10–19; 2:12–19; 4:10–19; 7:1–27). In light of the discourse setting of the prologue, it seems the royal speaker incorporates a series of courtly metaphors, images, and expressions that correspond with the social position of his addressee.

3.5 Conclusion

The lectures and interludes of Proverbs 1–9 incorporate sapiential virtues and courtly elements to present the value of wisdom and transform the addressee's naïve predilection. Together, the extended lectures and interludes form a dialogical context that gives particular expression to the fundamental features of

---

176 Several scholars have made similar proposals regarding the audience of Proverbs 1–9. Based on the urban locales mentioned throughout the prologue and its reticence concerning the poor, Whybray argues that it represents the interests of a wealthy, upper-class audience ("City Life in Proverbs 1–9," 243–450). Crenshaw suggests that the material in Proverbs 1–9 may be directed toward prospective courtiers, but acknowledges that nothing in the collection lies outside the realm of ordinary citizens ("The Sage in Proverbs," 211). In addition, Yoder argues that the language and worldview of Proverbs 1–9 indicate the instructions were intended for an affluent, commercial class audience (*Wisdom as a Woman of Substance*, 103).

177 Sandoval, "Revisiting the Prologue of Proverbs," 465. Also see the instances in which נַעַר is employed in Proverbs: 7:7; 20:11; 22:6, 15; 23:13; 29:15. These occurrences suggest that the נַעַר is not a child, but a late adolescent or young adult whose conduct and response to instruction reveal his character.

the setting in which the material is conveyed. They identify the performance context or discourse setting of the material and provide the rhetorical context through which the constituent compendia of the document are to be read. This discourse setting has a distinct, courtly flavor. The material is set within a domestic context, where a royal voice instructs the noble youth in communal virtues and practical values. The royal speaker incorporates a variety of aristocratic images and expressions to correlate his discourse with the interests, aspirations, and temptations of the addressee.[178] He highlights the value of wisdom and provides the noble youth with a lens through which to assess the ethical vision delineated in the sentence literature.

---

178 Seitel, "Proverbs: A Social Use of Metaphor," 131.

Chapter 4

Rudimentary Wisdom: Proverbs 10–24

The formal differences between the instructions in Proverbs 1–9 and the "sentence literature" in chapters 10–29 are striking. The extended lectures and interludes presented in the prologue give way to a collection of short, pithy, "sayings" that appear to arise from a variety of social settings and periods, with no apparent concern for topical or logical organization. The atomistic character of the sentence literature has given rise to a number of questions concerning the origin, evolution, and arrangement of the individual aphorisms in the book of Proverbs. The general impression is that the sentence literature represents a collection of Israel's traditional lore that was produced by distinct social groups in various locations. Nonetheless, there is no consensus regarding the origin of the aphorisms in the sentence literature, the sociological milieu of the collectors, the organization of the sentences, or the literary context within which they should be read.

4.1 The Literary Context of the Sentence Literature

The search for the origin of a proverb is an arduous task. While scholars situate the formation of Israel's sapiential lore in either an aristocratic or a plebian context, the variegated materials in the book of Proverbs betray both a strict court/school or family/folk setting.[1] When exploring the origin or social location

---

1 See the discussion in 1.1. In addition to family/folk and court/school origins, others have suggested that wisdom and law derived from a common origin: a *Sippenweisheit* or a *Gruppenethos*. This premise is based on comparable forms and themes apparent in both the legal and sapiential traditions. While the content and ethos of the legal and wisdom traditions are similar, the admonition form cannot establish the setting of a statement. In order to determine the relationship between law and wisdom, it is necessary to distinguish between the law and the codification of the law (Nel, *The Structure and Ethos of the Wisdom Admonitions in Proverbs*, 60–61). For a discussion of the relationship between law and wisdom, see J.-P. Audet, "Origines comparées de la double tradition de la loi et de la Sagesse dans le Proche-Orient ancien," in *International Congress of Orientalists* (Moscow: Actes du Congrès, 1964), 1:352–57; E. Gerstenberger, *Wesen und Herkunft des 'apodiktischen Rechts'* (WMANT 20; Neukirchen-Vluyn: Neukirchener, 1965); Richter, *Recht und Ethos*; Nel, *The Structure and Ethos of the Wisdom*

of the aphorisms in the sentence literature, it is necessary to distinguish between the oral stage and the written stage of composition. Based on the general character of the sentence literature, a popular background for some of the material seems to be a reasonable assumption. This assumption does not necessarily conflict with the view that the court or some guild of literati associated with the court was responsible for the compilation and redaction of the sentence literature, for these settings are not mutually exclusive: one refers to the oral origin of a saying, the other to its literary origin. The distinction between the oral stage and the written stage of production serves as an essential criterion for establishing the origin of the material in the sentence literature. However, this distinction does not account for the setting or social location of a given proverb.

Any attempt to isolate the origin of a proverb, whether oral or written, is hypothetical. Since proverbs are situationally oriented, open-ended sayings that cut across social barriers and remain relevant to a wide variety of people,[2] it is difficult to determine the origin of a saying in a collection. The original context of a saying in a collection is usually irrecoverable, and the content of a saying cannot provide an absolute indication of its origin.[3] The meaning of a proverb is made clear only when it is cast in a performance context, where the accompanying social situation can help to identify the function and significance of the saying.[4] Performance analysis is most problematic in the book of Proverbs, however, for the sayings have been removed from their original context(s) and assembled into a collection.[5] Yet this loss of a live, cultural context does not mean that a proverb in a collection is "dead."[6] Once a proverb is grafted into a collection it receives a new performance context, viz., the literary context, the *Sitz im Buch*.[7] Whether individual sayings in the sentence literature originated in an aristocratic or a plebeian context, their arrangement and re-contextualization into a collection

---

Admonitions in Proverbs; J. Blenkinsopp, *Wisdom and Law in the Old Testament: The Ordering of Life in Israel and Early Judaism* (Oxford Bible Series; Oxford: Oxford University Press, 1983); J. L. Crenshaw, "Prohibitions in Proverbs and Qoheleth," in *Priests, Prophets and Scribes: Essays on the Formation and Heritage of Second Temple Judaism in Honour of Joseph Blenkinsopp* (ed. J. W. Wright et al.; Sheffield: Sheffield Academic Press, 1992), 115–24.

2   R. E. Murphy, "Form Criticism and Wisdom Literature," *CBQ* 31 (1969): 483; Brown, *Character in Crisis*, 14.

3   Fontaine, *Traditional Sayings*, 12–13; idem, "Proverb Performance in the Hebrew Bible," *JSOT* 32 (1985): 94; Römheld, *Die Weisheitlehre im Alten Orient*, 3; Murphy, *The Tree of Life*, 4.

4   Firth, "Proverbs in Native Life," 134; Seitel, "Proverbs: A Social Use of Metaphor," 125–43; Kirshenblatt-Gimblett, "Toward a Theory of Proverb Meaning," 111–21; Fontaine, *Traditional Sayings*, 55.

5   Fox, *Proverbs 10–31*, 484.

6   W. Mieder, "The Essence of Literary Proverb Study," *Proverbium* 23 (1974): 892.

7   See Van Leeuwen, *Context and Meaning in Proverbs 25–27*, 2; K. M. Heim, *Like Grapes of Gold Set in Silver: An Interpretation of Proverbial Clusters in Proverbs 10:1–22:16* (BZAW 273; Berlin: Walter de Gruyter, 2001), 24; Fox, "Wisdom and the Self-Presentation of Wisdom Literature," 153–54; Sandoval, *The Discourse of Wealth and Poverty*, 37.

creates a literary context for the reader. In order to understand the individual sayings in the sentence literature it is necessary to explore the two types of literary context in the book of Proverbs: the immediate context and the distant context. Each deserves a brief comment.

The immediate literary context is concerned with the arrangement and juxtaposition of the individual sayings in the sentence literature. While this form of analysis is based on the heuristic assumption that the editors of the sentence literature attempted to produce literary contexts for individual sayings that would compensate for their de-contextualization in a collection,[8] it accounts for a variety of elements that link individual sayings or groups of sayings together. The principles of sound and sense are the fundamental criteria employed to identify the existence of proverbial units. The former detects literary organization by means of paronomasia, word play, catchwords, and verbal repetition, while the latter highlights common images, themes or topics within a constituent section.[9] These principles of arrangement help identify coherent groupings in the sentence literature and the contexts within which individual proverbs are to be read. They demonstrate that the sentence literature is not a random, haphazard collection of independent sayings, but a sophisticated compendium of proverbial lore. The deliberate arrangement of certain sayings within the sentence literature is not surprising, for ancient Near Eastern proverb collections and instructional texts exhibit comparable compositional principles.[10] Nonetheless, it is difficult to

---

8   Van Leeuwen, *Context and Meaning*, 30–31; Heim, *Like Grapes of Gold*, 24.

9   Several authors employ these principles in varying degrees in order to identify coherent units within the sentence literature. See G. Boström, *Paronomasi i den äldre hebraiska maschalliteraturen* (LUÅ 23; Lund: Gleerup, 1928); Schmidt, *Studien zur Stilistik der alttestamentlichen Spruchliteratur*, 58–60; Hermisson, *Studien zur israelitischen Spruchweisheit*, 171–83; O. Plöger, "Zur Auslegung der Sentenzensammlungen des Proverbienbuches," in *Probleme biblischer Theologie: Gerhard von Rad zum 70. Geburtstag* (ed. H. W. Wolff; Münich: Kaiser Verlag, 1971), 402–16; T. Hildebrandt, "Proverbial Pairs: Compositional Units in Proverbs 10–29," *JBL* 107 (1988): 207–24; Van Leeuwen, *Context and Meaning*, 18–19; J. Krispenz, *Spruchkompositionen im Buch Proverbia* (Europäische Hochschulschriften 349; Frankfurt: Peter Lang, 1989); Meinhold, *Die Sprüche*, 1:23–26; T. P. McCreesh, *Biblical Sound and Sense: Poetic Sound Patterns in Proverbs 10–29* (JSOTSup 128; Sheffield: Sheffield Academic Press, 1991); Garrett, *Proverbs*, 46–48; Whybray, *The Composition of the Book of Proverbs*; R. Scoralick, *Einzelspruch und Sammlung* (BZAW 232; Berlin: Walter de Gruyter, 1995); A. Scherer, *Das weise Wort und sein Wirkung: Eine Untersuchung zur Komposition und Redaktion von Proverbia 10,1–22,16* (WMANT 83; Neukirchen-Vluyn: Neukirchener Verlag, 1999), 35–46; Heim, *Like Grapes of Gold, passim*; Wilke, *Kronerben der Weisheit*, 18–23. Other scholars acknowledge the use of these editorial principles, but conclude the material is neither dependent on nor enhanced by a consideration of these proverbial units. See McKane, *Proverbs: A New Approach*, 10, 413; Weeks, *Early Israelite Wisdom*, 20–40.

10   See E. I. Gordon, *Sumerian Proverbs* (New York: Greenwood, 1968), 19, 26, 154–55; Alster, *Studies in Sumerian Proverbs*, 13–14; Lambert, *BWL*, 213, 223; Lindenberger, *The Aramaic Proverbs of Ahiqar*, 21; M. Lichtheim, "Observations on Papyrus Insinger," in *Studien zu altägyptischen Lebenslehren* (OBO 28; Göttingen: Vandenhoeck & Ruprecht, 1979), 284–305; idem, *Late Egyptian Wisdom*, 63–65, 109–16.

discern a comprehensive structure, a consistent *Ordnungsprinzip*, and a logical unity among the individual sayings within the sentence literature as a whole. Each individual saying is an independent, self-contained entity. However, juxtaposition with other sayings may create wider themes and applications that modify or qualify the sense of the individual proverb. Thus, when exploring the meaning of a proverb in the sentence literature, it is necessary to interpret individual sayings both independently and within their larger editorial context.[11]

In conjunction with the immediate context, the distant context of the sentence literature accounts for two features. First, it considers both similarities and differences between the topics and themes presented in individual sayings that are not contiguous.[12] This form of analysis recognizes the variegated perspectives and nuanced development of significant topics throughout the sentence literature such as wealth and poverty, the king, and matters of justice. Second, the distant context acknowledges the fundamental role of Proverbs 1–9 within the document as a whole. In order to understand the meaning of a proverb in a collection it is necessary to determine the structure of the literary work, for the structure supplies the reader with a lens through which to view the various components of the discourse as well as the discourse as a whole.[13] As noted in chapter three, within the book of Proverbs chapters 1–9 serve as the introduction to the work, providing a hermeneutical framework within which to read the document.[14] This framework delineates the discourse setting in which the teaching is delivered and provides a lens through which to read and assess the litany of sayings in the sentence literature. The importance of the prologue should not be underestimated, for this setting not only identifies the social and dialogical situation in which the material is cast, but it also serves as a logical introduction to the collections that follow.

The introductory lectures and interludes of the book of Proverbs offer the addressee simple, rudimentary instruction. The father rarely enumerates the substance of his teaching, and Woman Wisdom does not explain the insights she

---

11   Several commentators employ this methodological principle. See Plöger, *Sprüche Salomos*, 118–19, *et passim*; L. Alonso Schöckel and J. Vilchez, *Proverbios*, 255; Meinhold, *Die Sprüche*, 1:23–26; idem, *Die Sprüche, Teil 2: Sprüche Kapitel 16–31* (ZBK 16.2; Zürich: Theologischer Verlag, 1991), *passim*; Garrett, *Proverbs*, 46–48; Murphy, *Proverbs*, 64–67; Waltke, *Proverbs: Chapters 1–15*, 21, 447–639; idem, *Proverbs: Chapters 15–31*, *passim*; Fox, *Proverbs 10–31*, 478.

12   Van Leeuwen, *Context and Meaning*, 3.

13   P. Ricoeur, *Interpretation Theory: Discourse and the Surplus of Meaning* (Fort Worth: The Texas Christian University Press, 1976), 77; idem, *The Rule of Metaphor* (Toronto: The University of Toronto Press, 1977), 212–13; Sandoval, *The Discourse of Wealth and Poverty*, 15.

14   Camp, *Wisdom and the Feminine*, 179; Steiert, *Die Weisheit Israels—ein Fremdkörper im Alten Testament?*, 217; Meinhold, *Die Sprüche*, 1:26; Whybray, *The Composition of the Book of Proverbs*, 159; Van Leeuwen, "The Book of Proverbs: Introduction, Commentary, and Reflections," *NIB* 5:24; Fuhs, *Das Buch der Sprichwörter*, 15; Brown, "The Pedagogy of Proverbs 10:1–31:9," 153; Sandoval, *The Discourse of Wealth and Poverty*, 116.

offers in her speeches.[15] The lectures and interludes are not primarily concerned with transmitting information; rather they serve to introduce the addressee to different characters and present the value of wisdom's way.[16] The introduction is punctuated by a series of invitations to acquire wisdom and embrace parental teaching, but the essence of the wise life is not described in great detail. Indeed, it would be difficult to paint a realistic portrait of the wise life from chapters 1–9 alone. The sentence literature, however, provides the reader with a kaleidoscopic and paradigmatic portrait of the wise life.[17] These sayings catalog the characteristics of the wise, the fool, the righteous, and the wicked—archetypes who are introduced in the prologue but remain flat or one-dimensional without increasing in rotundity and profundity.[18] The sentence literature profiles the distinctive, defining features of these personages to provide "characterizations of character;"[19] that is, it identifies particular virtues, values, qualities, and traits embodied in certain character types. In so doing, the terse, pithy aphorisms present a complex, multidimensional portrait of various literary characters to shape the disposition of the addressee. While the value of wisdom is given categorical preeminence in the prologue, the essence of the wise life is given particular expression in the sentence literature. The introduction inculcates receptivity and provides the addressee with a socio-religious map to navigate through the myriad of sayings in the sentence literature.[20] It establishes the performance context or discourse setting through which to explore the meaning and pragmatic significance of the individual proverbs within their wider textual environment.

In light of the prologue's formative role within Proverbs, it is necessary to explore the degree to which the material in the sentence literature corresponds with the courtly discourse setting delineated in chapters 1–9. To accomplish this goal, this chapter will examine the moral and literary character of the materials in Proverbs 10:1–24:34, highlighting the courtly features of the collections and the thematic development of the material.[21] We will begin with the sayings in Proverbs 10:1–22:16, and then explore the instructions in chapters 22:17–24:34.

---

15   Frydrych, *Living under the Sun*, 61.

16   Clifford, *The Wisdom Literature*, 51; Pemberton, "The Rhetoric of the Father," 91, *et passim*.

17   Frydrych, *Living under the Sun*, 40–41.

18   Murphy, *Wisdom Literature*, 65; A. Berlin, *Poetics and Interpretation of Biblical Narrative* (Bible and Literature Series 9; Sheffield: Almond, 1983), 23–32; M. Sternberg, *The Poetics of Biblical Narrative* (Bloomington: Indiana University Press, 1987), 321–64.

19   Brown, *Character in Crisis*, 19.

20   Van Leeuwen, "The Book of Proverbs," *NIB* 5:31.

21   With regard to the thematic development of the material, see the discussion of William Brown's work below.

4.2 Elementary Wisdom: Solomon 1A (10:1–15:33)

The traditional subtitle (10:1a) and pronounced shift in form, tone, and style distinguishes the sentence literature from the extended instructions in Proverbs 1–9. These features do not mark the introduction of an independent unit; rather they initiate a transition that links the introductory discourses with the collections that follow. Several elements bind the first collection of the sentence literature to the discourses in Proverbs 1–9. The editorial subheading and initial aphorism in Proverbs 10:1 facilitates the transition from the prologue to the first collection (10:1–22:16).[22] This saying forms a janus between the collections, as it refers to the father, the mother, and the son, pointing back to the setting of the parental lectures and foreshadowing the fundamental role of the domestic unit in the sayings that follow.[23] The sentence literature also contains several implicit and explicit injunctions to "my son" (10:1, 17; 12:1, 15; 13:1; 15:5; 19:27; 23:15, 19, 26; 24:13, 21; 27:11), which extend the discourse setting of the introduction into the collections.[24] Moreover, as noted above, the sentence literature elaborates on topics and themes presented in the prologue. The sentence literature highlights the characteristic qualities of the wise, the fool, the righteous and the wicked, and employs the root metaphor of the way. The "wise" and the "righteous" continue to serve as positive archetypes who represent the way of life, while the "fool" and the "wicked" continue to function as negative archetypes who symbolize the way of death.[25] These personages not only bind the collections together through shared vocabulary and imagery, but they also provide a hermeneutical guide for the reader.[26] The prologue describes socio-moral values through a series of characters and root metaphors in order to provide an ethical framework through which to evaluate the sayings in the sentence literature.

The general, ethical framework delineated in the prologue is given particular expression in Solomon 1A (10:1–15:33). The antithetical sayings in Proverbs 10–15 present a morally bifurcated worldview in which the righteous/wise are set against the wicked/fool. While these moral and intellectual polarities, their

---

22   The editorial subheading in Proverbs 10:1a and the educational saying in 22:17 mark the boundaries of the first collection.

23   Clifford, *The Wisdom Literature*, 65; Frydrych, *Living under the Sun*, 140–42; Waltke, *Proverbs: Chapters 1–15*, 14.

24   Fox, "Wisdom and the Self-Presentation of Wisdom Literature," 160.

25   Sandoval, *The Discourse of Wealth and Poverty*, 56. The three terms used for the "way" (דֶּרֶךְ, נְתִיבָה, אֹרַח) in the book of Proverbs are distributed throughout the instructions and the sentence literature.

26   See N. C. Habel, "The Symbolism of Wisdom in Proverbs 1–9," *Int* 26 (1972): 131–57; C. V. Camp, "Woman Wisdom as Root Metaphor: A Theological Consideration," in *The Listening Heart: Essays in Wisdom and the Psalms in Honor of Roland E. Murphy* (ed. K. G. Hoglund et al.; Sheffield: JSOT, 1987), 45–76; Van Leeuwen, "Liminality and Worldview in Proverbs 1–9," 111–44; Sandoval, *The Discourse of Wealth and Poverty*, 56–57.

synonyms and equivalent phrases, overlap in certain instances (10:16–17, 31; 11:9, 30), the antithetical sets are not interchangeable.[27] The wise/fool and the righteous/wicked designate different spheres and have distinct semantic fields: the former presents an intellectual evaluation, while the latter provides a moral evaluation.[28] These two sets of appellations are not synonymous, but their relationship may be described as co-referential—the antitheses do not have the same meaning or sense, but they refer to the same reality, the same referent in a given context.[29] The righteous/wise, the wicked/fool, and related vocabulary in either semantic field describe the positive and negative, the moral and intellectual character traits of the same type of person. These moral and intellectual polarities present alternative ways of life that divide individuals into two different classes: the righteous/wise and the wicked/fool.

The co-referential relationship between the righteous and the wise, on the one hand, and the wicked and the fool, on the other, provide an ethical context through which to evaluate the sayings in the first collection.[30] These antitheses present a static, bipolar world in which all people belong to one of two distinguishable groups based on their behavior. The antithetical appellations outline the basic contours of the character-consequence nexus (*Haltung-Schicksal Zusammenhang*)[31] through a description of the general, unqualified rewards and punishments that are meted out to the appropriate characters. The abstract nature of the character-consequence nexus in Proverbs 10–15 is a significant feature of Solomon 1A.[32] The simplistic character of this scheme does not mean the complex is an artificial construct. Rather the indefinite character-consequence connection serves as a foundational building block for the thematic development that takes place throughout the successive sections of the document. The general, bifurcated worldview and the facile description of the character-consequence connection present the fundamental structure of the socio-moral order and provide the addressee with an elementary paradigm of the wise life. Together,

---

27   Scott, "Wise and Foolish, Righteous and Wicked," 153; Westermann, *Roots of Wisdom*, 84; Scoralick, *Einzelspruch und Sammlung*, 67–73; Murphy, *Proverbs*, 267–68.

28   See N. Shupak, *Where Can Wisdom Be Found?*, 265–67; Heim, *Like Grapes of Gold*, 85–101.

29   P. Cotterell and M. Turner, *Linguistics and Biblical Interpretation* (London: SPCK, 1979), 160–61; Heim, *Like Grapes of Gold*, 81–101; Frydrych, *Living under the Sun*, 25; Waltke, *Proverbs: Chapters 1–15*, 93.

30   R. N. Whybray, "Yahweh-Sayings and Their Contexts in Proverbs 10,1–22,16," in *La sagesse de l'Ancien Testament* (ed. M. Gilbert; Leuven: Leuven University Press, 1990), 153–65; J. Goldingay, "The Arrangement of Sayings in Proverbs 10–15," *JSOT* 61 (1994): 75–83.

31   Character-consequence nexus is a more accurate designation than act-consequence nexus (*Tat-Ergehen Zusammenhang*) in the book of Proverbs, for the sayings generally link consequences to character traits, attitudes, and lifestyles, rather than individual actions. See Skladny, *Die ältesten Spruchsammlungen in Israel*, 8, 72; Boström, *The God of the Sages*, 90, 117–33; T. Hildebrandt, "Motivation and Antithetical Parallelism in Proverbs 10–15," *JETS* 35 (1992): 259; Waltke, *Proverbs: Chapters 1–15*, 73.

32   Van Leeuwen, "The Book of Proverbs," *NIB* 5:105.

these features form an ethical matrix that describes the basic rules the addressee needs to navigate successfully through the world, and prepares him for the exceptions to these rules that will appear in the collections that follow.[33]

The theoretical nature of the character-consequence connection, coupled with the preponderance of antithetical sayings concerning the righteous/wicked and the wise/fool, has prompted many scholars to divide the first Solomonic collection into two sections: chapters 10:1–15:33 and 16:1–22:16.[34] The form, content, and style of each sub-collection reinforce this division. Solomon 1A is characterized by antithetical parallelism, while Solomon 1B (16:1–22:16) contains a rich variety of poetic forms.[35] In addition, Solomon 1A gives particular

33   R. C. Van Leeuwen, "Wealth and Poverty: System and Contradiction in Proverbs," *HS* 33 (1992): 32–34; idem, "The Book of Proverbs," *NIB* 5:105.

34   Skladny, *Die ältesten Spruchsammlungen in Israel*, 7–46; A. Barucq, *Le livre des Proverbes* (SB; Paris: Librairie Lecoffre, 1964), 17; Meinhold, *Die Sprüche*, 1:26; Whybray, *The Composition of the Book of Proverbs*, 89, 131; Van Leeuwen, "The Book of Proverbs," *NIB* 5:105; Crenshaw, *Old Testament Wisdom*, 61–62; Clifford, *Proverbs*, 108; Perdue, *Wisdom Literature: A Theological History*, 58; Fox, *Proverbs 10–31*, xviii–xix. Other scholars follow a similar structural paradigm, but mark the boundary of Solomon 1A at different places. For example, Scherer and Wilke contend that 15:33 represents the beginning of Solomon 1B. Waltke argues that 15:30–33 functions as an introduction to the second sub-collection, while Kovacs identifies 15:28 as the opening statement of Solomon 1B. See Scherer, *Das weise Wort und sein Wirkung*, 190–202; Wilke, *Kronerben der Weisheit*, 158, Waltke, *Proverbs: Chapters 1–15*, 16; idem, *Proverbs: Chapters 15–31*, 5–8; B. W. Kovacs, "Sociological-Structural Constraints upon Wisdom: The Spatial and Temporal Matrix of Proverbs 15:28–22:16" (PhD diss., Vanderbilt University, 1978), 307–516.

35   Based on the content and inherent setting of the individual sayings in the collections, scholars have postulated a particular class-ethic (*Standesethik*) for Solomon 1A and 1B: the former section appears to represent the ethos of small farmers or an urban proletariat (Skladny, *Die ältesten Spruchsammlungen in Israel*, 23; Whybray, *Wealth and Poverty in the Book of Proverbs*, 31, 114), while the latter contains values particularly relevant for royal officials (Skladny, *Die ältesten Spruchsammlungen in Israel*, 46). These inferences are based on valid observations, but the observations do not necessarily mean the collections represent a distinct class-ethic, for different classes often share common concerns, attitudes, and values (Whybray, "The Social World of the Wisdom Writers," 227–50; M. Sneed, "Wisdom and Class: A Review and Critique," *JAAR* 62 [1994]: 651–72; idem, "A Middle Class in Ancient Israel," in *Concepts of Class in Ancient Israel* [ed. M. Sneed; Atlanta: Scholars Press, 1999], 53–69). In general, scholars argue that the sages responsible for the collection and redaction of the sentence literature stem from the "upper class." However, the specific character of this upper class milieu varies among scholars, as proposals range from the ruling elite, the wealthy, and the "goldsmith-banker class," to the "well-placed middle class." See A. Kuschke, "Arm und reich im Alten Testament mit besonderer Berücksichtigung der nachexilischen Zeit," *ZAW* 57 (1939): 47; R. Gordis, "The Social Background of Wisdom Literature," *HUCA* 18 (1943/44): 77–118; Hermisson, *Studien zur israelitischen Spruchweisheit*, 94–96; von Rad, *Weisheit in Israel*, 112–13; Kovacs, "Is There a Class-Ethic in Proverbs?", 173–89; J. Brown, "Proverb-Book, Gold-Economy, Alphabet," *JBL* 100 (1981): 169–91; B. V. Malchow, "Social Justice in the Wisdom Literature," *BTB* 12 (1982): 121; J. D. Pleins, "Poverty in the Social World of the Wise," *JSOT* 37 (1987): 61–78; R. J. Coggins, "The Old Testament and the Poor," *ExpTim* 99 (1987–88): 11–14; Boström, *The God of the Sages*, 11; W. J. Houston, "The Role of the Poor in Proverbs," in *Reading from Right to Left: Essays on the Hebrew Bible in Honour of David*

attention to the contrast between the righteous/wise and wicked/fool, whereas Solomon 1B exhibits a lack of concern with these antithetical groups. While each collection has its own unique characteristics, these sub-units address comparable themes and contain sayings found in other collections,[36] which suggests some unity of perspective among the materials.[37] The sentence literature covers a wide range of everyday occurrences and assesses various forms of conduct to provide a kaleidoscopic portrait of the world. Each proverb presents a particular perspective on the world from a specific, narrow angle. None of the individual sayings offers a comprehensive picture of reality; rather the sapiential world is constructed through a combination of the perspectives that the individual sayings provide.[38] The aphorisms do not necessarily provide an objective depiction of world; instead they supply the addressee with a paradigmatic lens through which to view the world. The sentence literature describes the world from two main behavioral perspectives: behavior within the context of human relationships, and behavior within the context of relationship with God.[39] In order to assess the courtly nature of the collections and the thematic development of the material, it is necessary to explore the anthropocentric and theocentric dimensions of the sapiential worldview. We will begin with Solomon 1A and then examine the material in Solomon 1B.

4.2.1 The Anthropocentric Dimension of Solomon 1A

The anthropocentric and theocentric dimensions of the world presented in Solomon 1A include a wide range of topics that apply to commoners, courtiers, and kings. The anthropological perspective of the sentence literature is expressed through the character and comportment of the individual as well as the relationship between the individual and the traditional social structures of the family, the community, and the monarchy. While the sentence literature addresses the individual and describes the effects of behavior in individual terms, the book of Proverbs does not regard the individual as an isolated self. Rather, the character and actions of the individual are often set within a communal context (e.g. 10:21; 11:10–15). The social structures of the human world situate the individual within a collective order and serve as a grid through which to assess the

---

J. A. *Clines* (ed. J. C. Exum and H. G. M. Williamson; Sheffield: Sheffield Academic, 2003), 229–40; Perdue, *Wisdom Literature: A Theological History*, 59.

36　For an analysis of proverbial repetitions in the sentence literature, see D. C. Snell, *Twice-Told Proverbs and the Composition of the Book of Proverbs* (Winona Lake: Eisenbrauns, 1993).

37　Dell, "How Much Wisdom Literature Has Its Roots in the Pre-Exilic Period?", 259.

38　Frydrych, *Living under the Sun*, 43.

39　Frydrych, *Living under the Sun*, 11; M. V. Fox, "The Epistemology of the Book of Proverbs," *JBL* 126 (2007): 678–80.

components of the sapiential worldview. Indeed, these social structures form the pillars of the social perspective expressed in the sentence literature. The sentence literature presents wisdom as a means for both individual success and social order.[40] In so doing, it provides a paradigm that promotes harmonious relationships between the individual and society as a whole. The monarchy, the community, and the family constitute the fundamental social units of the sapiential world. We shall examine the ethos of each social structure in turn.

4.2.1.1 The Monarchy

The royal institution functions as the guarantor of harmonious society in Solomon 1A. While the sayings concerning the king and the court are more fully developed in Solomon 1B, the royal institution commands at least three proverbs in Proverbs 10–15. These sayings address two principal topics: the necessity of competent advisors and the demand of a just reign for communal success. The first is expressed in Proverbs 11:14:

בְּאֵין תַּחְבֻּלוֹת יִפָּל־עָם	Where there is no guidance a people falls,
וּתְשׁוּעָה בְּרֹב יוֹעֵץ	but there is safety in a multitude of counselors.

This saying conveys the need for counsel in matters of national interest.[41] The noun עָם situates verse 14 in a national context, as it refers to a collective, ethnic community (cf. 14:28).[42] The well-being and protection of this group is dependent, however, on counsel and direction. The community required many counselors to develop national policies and guard against partisan political agendas. The technical term יוֹעֵץ, coupled with its synonymous counterpart תַּחְבֻּלוֹת,[43] highlight the expertise needed to manage the community in a responsible manner (cf. 15:22; 20:18; 24:6). While this saying may apply to leaders of a kinship group in general or to battle tactics in a military context in particular,[44] the aphorism emphasizes the necessity of experienced advisors for

---

40 Frydrych, *Living under the Sun*, 134.

41 McKane, *Proverbs: A New Approach*, 429; Garrett, *Proverbs*, 125–26; Van Leeuwen, "The Book of Proverbs," *NIB* 5:118; Murphy, *Proverbs*, 82; Waltke, *Proverbs: Chapters 1–15*, 495–96.

42 See D. I. Block, *The Foundations of National Identity: A Study in Ancient Northwest Semitic Perceptions* (Ann Arbor: UMI, 1982), 12–83. Block concludes that עָם is a warm, relational expression that denotes a people belonging to a particular deity or ruler.

43 Etymologically, תַּחְבּוּלָה seems to be a nautical term derived from חֶבֶל, which conveys the image of rope pulling for the purpose of steering a ship. Elsewhere the noun is used in conjunction with "plans" (מַחֲשָׁבוֹת) and "counsel" (עֵצָה) (Prov 12:5; 20:18; 24:6). In the main, it seems the term refers to the virtue of guidance or steering that is used to direct others. See Fox, *Proverbs 1–9*, 63; תַּחְבֻּלוֹת, *HALOT* 4:1716; Waltke, *Proverbs: Chapters 1–15*, 96.

44 See Clifford, *Proverbs*, 123; Fox, *Proverbs 10–31*, 536.

the survival of the community. This task was the particular duty of the royal institution, which employed counselors and advisors to execute civic policies that would produce communal success.

The communal significance of the royal institution is also reflected in the two explicit *Königssprüche* in Solomon 1A. These sayings outline the social orientation of the king and his court:

בְּרָב־עָם הַדְרַת־מֶלֶךְ	In a multitude of people is the glory of a king,
וּבְאֶפֶס לְאֹם מְחִתַּת רָזוֹן	but being without people is a ruler's ruin. (Prov 14:28)

רְצוֹן־מֶלֶךְ לְעֶבֶד מַשְׂכִּיל	The king's favor is toward a prudent servant,
וְעֶבְרָתוֹ תִּהְיֶה מֵבִישׁ	but his wrath is toward a shameful one. (Prov 14:35)

As independent, self-contained aphorisms, these sayings reflect on the relationship between the king and his people: the former locates royal glory in the king's service for the community; the latter admonishes the king to eliminate corruption in the court and urges officials to embody competence in their duties. However, within their larger editorial context these *Königssprüche* frame a series of sayings that describe the social conditions of a just reign (14:28–35). In conjunction with verse 34, the *Königssprüche* form an inclusio through the terms מֶלֶךְ and לְאֹם (14:28, 34, 35), on the one hand, and the word play between רָזוֹן and רְצוֹן, on the other (14:28, 35).[45] These features serve as a framework within which to read the intervening aphorisms in verses 29–33. They mark the boundaries of a subunit that describes the reciprocal relationship between the ruler and the ruled: the ruler must be devoted to the people and the people must embody basic virtues to ensure national security.

The subunit describes this relationship between the king and the populace through five characterizations. The first addresses the issue of justice. The initial *Königsspruch* reminds the ruler that his glory does not consist in wealth or weapons; rather his splendor resides in his just, competent rule, which strengthens popular allegiance and guards against communal skepticism (14:28). The second characterization describes the value of self-control (14:29–30). Here self-control is described from the perspective of an individual's outward countenance (14:29), and then from the standpoint of his inward disposition (14:30).[46] Together, these sayings outline the intellectual and emotional value of

---

45   Plöger, *Sprüche Salomos*, 174–76; Meinhold, *Die Sprüche*, 1:242–46; idem, "Das Wortspiel רצון–רזון in Prov 14,28–35," *ZAW* 110 (1998): 615–16; Garrett, *Proverbs*, 145–47; A. Lelièvre and A. Maillot, *Commentaire des Proverbes. Les Proverbes de Salomon chapitres 10–18* (LD 1; Paris: Éditions du Cerf, 1993), 146; Heim, *Like Grapes of Gold*, 187–89; Wilke, *Kronerben der Weisheit*, 138–58.

46   For the correspondence between אֶרֶךְ אַפַּיִם ("long of nose, patient") and לֵב מַרְפֵּא ("a calm heart") on the one hand, and קְצַר־רוּחַ ("short of spirit, a quick temper") and קִנְאָה ("passion") on the other, see H. A. Brongers, "Die Partikel ‬lma'an in der biblisch-hebräischen Sprache," *OtSt* 18

patience and quietude—virtues that enrich the moral order and the individual's life, and principles that reinforce the king's ability to execute justice and increase the welfare of the community.

The third characterization discusses social behavior and its enduring consequence (14:31–32). This proverbial pair associates oppression of the poor (14:31) with wickedness (14:32), and kindness toward the needy (14:31) with righteousness (14:32) to form the theological basis for social ethics in the book of Proverbs. Verse 31 asserts that all human beings, irrespective of their social standing, have a dignity that derives from their common Creator (17:5; 22:2; 29:13). This saying does not function as a critique of the current social order; rather it expresses the fundamental conviction that all people are created in the *imago Dei* (Gen 1:26). The principle of kindness toward the marginalized is a basic tenet of both royal and communal ethics in the ancient oriental world.[47] In theory, the king was required to protect and provide for the weak in order to establish order in society (cf. 31:4–9), while individuals had to recognize that their common constitution took precedence over the existing social arrangement in order to grant the disenfranchised their dignity and maintain harmony in society.[48] By actualizing these principles the king and the individual could seek refuge in YHWH in the advancement of life, while the wicked were consumed by their evil (14:32).[49]

(1973): 277; Murphy, *Proverbs*, 107; Heim, *Like Grapes of Gold*, 188; Waltke, *Proverbs: Chapters 1–15*, 605–08.

47   See "Statue B," §7:38–43 (D. O. Edzard, *Gudea and His Dynasty* [RIME 3/1; Toronto: University of Toronto Press, 1997], 36); "Laws of Ur-Namma," (A IV 162–68, C II 30–39) (M. T. Roth, *Law Collections from Mesopotamia and Asia Minor* [2nd ed.; ed. P. Michalowski; SBLWAW 6; Atlanta: Scholars Press, 1997], 16); "Laws of Hammurabi," (XLVII 59–78) (Roth, *Law Collections from Mesopotamia and Asia Minor*, 133–34); "Aqhat," (col. 5 lines 6–8) (S. B. Parker, *Ugaritic Narrative Poetry* [ed. S. B. Parker; SBLWAW 9; Atlanta: Scholars Press, 1997], 58); "The Instruction Addressed to King Merikare" (*AEL* 1:100); "The Instruction of King Amenemhet I for His Son Sesostris I" (*AEL* 1:136); Deut 15:1–11; Ps 72.

48   Houston, "The Role of the Poor in Proverbs," 238–39.

49   The MT of Proverbs 14:32 appears to describe the hope of the afterlife, as the righteous seeks refuge in his death. The LXX and Syriac versions read בְּתֻמּוֹ ("in his integrity") rather than בְּמוֹתוֹ ("in his death"), suggesting a metathesis of מ and ת with the insertion of ו in the MT. This emendation is reasonable, but the reading of the MT is preferred for three reasons. First, the verb חסה never takes an abstraction like תֹם as its object (Van Leeuwen, "The Book of Proverbs," *NIB* 5:144; Waltke, *Proverbs: Chapters 1–15*, 582–83 n. 53). Second, the verb occurs thirty-seven times with the sense "to seek refuge" in something rather than "to find/have a refuge" (McKane, *Proverbs: A New Approach*, 475). With the exception of Proverbs 14:32b and two other instances in which the verb occurs, חסה takes YHWH as its object (e.g. Isa 14:32; Ps 2:12; 5:12; 7:2; 11:1; 71:1; Prov 30:5). Moreover, when the verb occurs in the *Qal* participle or in a relative clause it denotes "one who seeks refuge in YHWH." This seems to suggest that יְהוָה is the unstated object of חסה in Proverbs 14:32b (Plöger, *Sprüche Salomos*, 176; Meinhold, *Die Sprüche*, 1:245; Heim, *Like Grapes of Gold*, 190; Waltke, *Proverbs: Chapters 1–15*, 582 n. 52). Third, since the subject is active, it appears that the process of dying, rather than the state of death, is in view

The fourth characterization highlights the formative role of Wisdom with both the discerning person and the fool (14:33). The association of Wisdom with the fool has prompted many scholars to emend the MT, for the book of Proverbs depicts the intractable as an archetype who is unable to embrace wisdom (2:22; 17:16).[50] However, this emendation undermines the plain meaning of the text. The educational saying asserts that Wisdom "settles down" (תָּנוּחַ)[51] in the heart of the discerning, and reveals herself "in the midst of" (בְּקֶרֶב)[52] fools. Wisdom's residence in the heart of the discerning is quite different from her manifestation among fools. To be sure, the prologue is punctuated by Wisdom's appeals in the presence of the insolent. The fool may not have a heart for wisdom, but his ability to learn is not inconceivable (8:5b).[53] Wisdom presents herself to the intractable through the character of the discerning, who serves as a medium whereby she may influence her detractors.[54] In so doing, she provides the king and the individual with an indispensable resource for dealing with fools.

The fifth characterization enhances the communal character of the subunit by emphasizing the mutual relationship between the king and the people (14:34–35). The juxtaposition of verses 34 and 35 is significant, for it identifies the king as the socio-moral barometer of the nation—as the king goes, so goes the people. As noted above, verse 34 corresponds to the initial *Königsspruch*, setting the aphorism in a national context through the noun לְאֻמִּים ("peoples").[55] In general, the saying asserts that the status of a nation is not evaluated by the scope of its territory, the size of its treasury, or the extent of its military; rather the piety of the people is the decisive factor for assessing a nation's prestige. Within its wider context, verse 34 issues an implicit admonition to the king to embody the values of the community, exemplify righteousness, and guide the people through his conduct. This tacit exhortation is given particular expression in verse 35. Here the moral posture of the king and his servants is brought to the fore. On the one hand, verse 35 calls the royal official (עֶבֶד)[56] to demonstrate prudence and

---

(Waltke, *Proverbs: Chapters 1–15*, 582–83 n. 53). Together, these features suggest that Proverbs 14:32 does not necessarily describe the hope of the afterlife, but the security that YHWH provides in the advancement of life.

50   See Gemser, *Sprüche Salomos*, 67; Plöger, *Sprüche Salomos*, 167; Van Leeuwen, "The Book of Proverbs," *NIB* 5:145See Meinhold, *Die Sprüche*, 1:242; Murphy, *Proverbs*, 102 n. 33a.

51   In the Qal, נוח denotes "to settle down" or "to have rest." See F. Stolz, "נוח," *TLOT* 2:723.

52   Here בְּקֶרֶב carries the sense of "in the midst of," for it appears with a plural object. When the phrase occurs with a singular object it means "in the heart of" (26:24). See Waltke, *Proverbs: Chapters 1–15*, 610.

53   Fox, *Proverbs 1–9*, 42.

54   Heim, *Like Grapes of Gold*, 190–91.

55   See Block, *The Foundations of National Identity*, 136–37.

56   While עֶבֶד is a fluid term that refers to a variety of people in distinct social locations, it appears to denote a royal official within the context of the subunit. For a catalogue of seal inscriptions where עֶבֶד is ubiquitous as a general designation for courtiers, ministers, or scribes in the service of the king, see G. I. Davies, *Ancient Hebrew Inscriptions: Corpus and Concordance* (Cambridge:

competence in their actions in order to secure the favor of the king and avert his
fury. On the other hand, the saying admonishes the king to cultivate loyal,
capable administrators by rewarding the competent and reproving the corrupt.
Together, verses 34–35 describe the joint relationship between the king and his
people: the king depends on faithful, judicious servants to carry out the
responsibilities of the royal institution, while the people depend on the king to
promote prudent advisors and remove incompetent administrators from their
bureaucratic posts.

On the whole, the portrait of the royal establishment that emerges in
Proverbs 10–15 is rather simple: the royal institution requires prudent advisors to
secure communal welfare (11:14; 14:35), while the king is responsible to maintain
justice by acting on behalf of the people (14:28), protecting the rights of the
disenfranchised (14:31–32), and inspiring righteousness through his character and
leadership (14:29–30, 33, 34–35). Though many of the aphorisms in Proverbs
14:29–34 may apply to individuals in nonpolitical situations, these sayings are cast
in a subunit concerned with national welfare and describe moral and intellectual
qualities that are relevant to the royal institution. The broad applicability of these
principles is not surprising, for the royal establishment was not above the socio-
moral values of the community (Deut 17:14–20). The monarchy was intended to
serve as the fount of justice, the model of responsible leadership, and the
embodiment of the community's ethos. In view of the discourse setting
delineated in the prologue, the sayings concerned with the royal institution
provide the noble youth with a fundamental paradigm of leadership: a just,
competent leader must promote prudent advisors, serve the people by promoting
justice and righteousness, and embody irreproachable character among his
subjects. The aphorisms highlight the social significance of the royal
establishment in the maintenance of a harmonious society, a concern that is also
expressed through the actions and behavior of the individual in the community.

4.2.1.2 The Community

The community plays a significant role in the sapiential perspective of Solomon
1A. While a preponderance of sayings in the sub-collection address the character
and comportment of the individual, this individual emphasis is balanced by
concern with the communal implications of a person's character and conduct. As
noted above, Solomon 1A presents a static, bipolar world in which the
righteous/wise are set against the wicked/fool. These co-referential appellations

---

Cambridge University Press, 1991), 453; N. Avigad, *Corpus of West Semitic Stamp Seals* (rev. and
comp. by B. Sass; Jerusalem: The Institute of Archaeology, The Hebrew University of Jerusalem,
1997), 49–53, 173–75, 466.

and their corresponding terms form a socio-moral paradigm that divides individuals into two groups based on their character. The virtues and vices associated with these personages outline the contours of the individual's identity and serve as a lens through which to understand the communal implications of a person's conduct. The sayings in Solomon 1A address the social effects of an individual's behavior through three principal topics: character, communication, and wealth. Each deserves specific comment.

Several aphorisms in Proverbs 10–15 highlight the social significance of the individual through the positive and negative effects of their character on the community. In essence, a person possesses the power to enrich the community or to destroy its socio-moral fabric:

זֵכֶר צַדִּיק לִבְרָכָה וְשֵׁם רְשָׁעִים יִרְקָב	The memory of the righteous becomes a blessing, but the name of the wicked rots.[57] (Prov 10:7)
פְּרִי־צַדִּיק עֵץ חַיִּים וְלֹקֵחַ נְפָשׁוֹת חָכָם	The fruit of a righteous person is a tree of life, and the one who takes lives is wise.[58] (Prov 11:30)
יָתֵר מֵרֵעֵהוּ צַדִּיק וְדֶרֶךְ רְשָׁעִים תַּתְעֵם	A righteous person shows the way to his neighbor, but the way of the wicked leads them astray.[59] (Prov 12:26)

---

57   The *BHS* emends יִרְקָב ("will rot, decay") to יוּקַב ("will be cursed") to strengthen the antitheses. However, יִרְקָב preserves the antitheses, for the contrast is between the righteous individual's enduring influence and the eradication of the wicked person's name in the community.

58   The combination of the verb לָקַח with the direct object נֶפֶשׁ has prompted many scholars to emend חָכָם to חָמָס (e.g., McKane, *Proverbs: A New Approach*, 432; Murphy, *Proverbs*, 84), since the word pair typically means "to take life away" (1 Sam 24:12; Ps 31:14; Prov 1:19). This reading assumes the stichoi are set in antithetical parallelism and that חָמָס corresponds to the LXX's reading παρανόμων ("transgressor, lawless one"). However, this emendation is unconvincing, for Proverbs 11:30 seems to develop the antithetical set in 11:28b through synonymous parallelism. Moreover, the LXX of Proverbs 11:30 differs from the MT in several ways, making it difficult to rely on its reading. Other scholars have attempted to retain חָכָם by either re-pointing לקח or interpreting נְפָשׁוֹת לֹקֵחַ in various ways (Dahood, *Proverbs and Northwest Semitic Philology*, 24; D. C. Snell, "'Taking Souls' in Proverbs 11:30," *VT* 33 [1983]: 363–64; Plöger, *Sprüche Salomos*, 143; W. H. Irwin, "The Metaphor in Prov. 11,30," *Bib* 65 [1984]: 97–100). While וְלֹקֵחַ נְפָשׁוֹת may have an unexpected meaning, the rendering of the MT should be retained. When לקח is read in light of the agricultural imagery in verset A, וְלֹקֵחַ נְפָשׁוֹת חָכָם produces an intentional irony with the sense "and the wise gathers/harvests (i.e., saves) lives" (Irwin, "The Metaphor in Prov. 11,30," 97–100). See Fox, *Proverbs 10–31*, 545.

59   The relationship between the lines in verse 26 is difficult to determine. The sense of verset A is contingent on the interpretation of יָתֵר. The verb may be a *Hiphil* derived from תור, meaning "to guide, search out, show the way" (McKane, *Proverbs: A New Approach*, 447; Meinhold, *Die Sprüche*, 1:213; Murphy, *Proverbs*, 88 n. 26.a.; Waltke, *Proverbs: Chapters 1–15*, 518). However, the verb may also derive from the root יתר ("to remain over"), which carries the sense "to be better than" in conjunction with the particle מִן (Targ.; Heim, *Like Grapes of Gold*, 157). The former proposal provides an appropriate contrast with verset B. The pronominal suffix in verset B may refer to the wicked or to others; both alternatives are possible and the line appears to have each option

Together, these sayings describe the social orientation of the individual. The reputation of the righteous serves as a blessing that reverberates throughout the community after their death, while the name of the wicked deteriorates with their bodies in the grave (10:7). The character and conduct of the righteous produce life-giving fruit that nourishes the people (11:30a), while the wise provide life that rescues others from death (11:30b; 13:14). Moreover, the righteous person is able to steer others in the right direction, whereas the wicked lead themselves and others astray (12:26). The aphorisms illustrate the social significance of an individual's character by describing its effect on the community: the righteous strengthen the social environment through their character and comportment, while the wicked wreak havoc on the populace (cf. 10:26; 11:11).

The sentence literature also describes the communal implications of communication in interpersonal social relationships. In Solomon 1A, sayings concerned with the effects of proper and improper speech predominate. These sayings describe the power of speech to heal or destroy, to rejuvenate or mutilate others in the community:

מְקוֹר חַיִּים פִּי צַדִּיק	The mouth of the righteous is a fountain of life,
וּפִי רְשָׁעִים יְכַסֶּה חָמָס	but the mouth of the wicked conceals violence. (Prov 10:11)
שִׂפְתֵי צַדִּיק יִרְעוּ רַבִּים	The lips of a righteous person nourish many,
וֶאֱוִילִים בַּחֲסַר־לֵב יָמוּתוּ	but fools die for lack of sense. (Prov 10:21)
בְּפֶה חָנֵף יַשְׁחִת רֵעֵהוּ	With the mouth the godless destroys his neighbor,
וּבְדַעַת צַדִּיקִים יֵחָלֵצוּ	but the righteous are delivered through their knowledge. (Prov 11:9)
מַעֲנֶה־רַּךְ יָשִׁיב חֵמָה	A gentle answer turns back wrath,
וּדְבַר־עֶצֶב יַעֲלֶה־אָף	but a harsh word stirs up anger. (Prov 15:1)

Communication is fundamental to communal life in the sapiential perspective.[60] The sentence literature commends sincere, reticent speech that is delivered at the appropriate time, and condemns effusive, rash jabber (10:19; 12:19; 13:3; 15:23, 28). A person's speech has the capacity to benefit the community and promote harmonious relationships or to damage society and interpersonal relations.

---

    in view. These features suggest that verse 26 intends a contrast between those who know the right path and lead others in the right direction and those who lead themselves and others astray. For an additional proposal, see J. A. Emerton, "A Note on Proverbs xii.26," *ZAW* 76 (1964): 191–93, who reads verset A, "The righteous is delivered (*Hophal* of נתר) from harm." This emendation is possible, but unconvincing.

60   In addition to the aphorisms listed above, see Prov 10:10, 18; 11:12, 13; 12:6, 17, 18, 20; 14:5, 25; 15:2, 4, 7, 23.

Indeed, speech can mean the difference between life and death (10:10, 11; 14:25; 15:4), success and suffering (11:9–11), peace and conflict (12:18; 15:1), trust and uncertainty (11:13). The spoken word can be directed toward both good and bad ends. It uncovers the inward disposition of the individual and has a profound effect on the community in general and interpersonal relations in particular.

The sentence literature's concern with economic ethics constitutes an additional dimension of the individual's communal orientation in the sapiential perspective. The economic discourse in Solomon 1A elaborates on the social values delineated in the prologue to provide the addressee with a more comprehensive picture of the significance of economic matters in the context of the community (cf. 3:27–28; 6:1–11). This discourse provides a multidimensional portrait of economic relationships through three principal topics: business ethics, generosity, and social justice. The first is presented in Proverbs 11:15 (cf. 6:1–5; 17:18; 20:16; 22:26–27; 27:13; 28:8):

רַע־יֵרוֹעַ	One will be treated badly
כִּי־עָרַב זָר	when one becomes surety for a stranger,
וְשֹׂנֵא תֹקְעִים בּוֹטֵחַ	but one who hates clapping [hands] is secure.
	(Prov 11:15)

This saying offers a pointed warning against serving as a financial guarantor for other people. Whether the motivation for this practice stems from the guarantor's compassion or desire for profit,[61] the saying emphasizes the precarious situation of the economic representative. On the one hand, the guarantor is subject to the machinations of the lender. On the other hand, the financial representative is at the mercy of the זָר ("stranger"),[62] who may default on his loan and leave the guarantor liable. In the main, the aphorism does not offer a critique of surety practices or attempt to censure the motives of the guarantor; rather it highlights the risks involved in the economic policy. While standing surety for a stranger has the potential to strengthen social relationships, it seems the risks outweigh the rewards. The saying expresses a traditional ancient Near Eastern socio-economic principle that stresses the dangers involved in financial dealings.[63]

---

61 See A. Scherer, "Is the Selfish Man Wise?: Considerations of Context in Proverbs 10.1–22.16 with Special Regard to Surety, Bribery and Friendship," *JSOT* 76 (1997): 61–64.

62 While זָר may denote an ethnic foreigner, its use in an economic relationship is undefined. In the present context, the traditional rendering "foreigner" or "unfamiliar person" seems to be in view. Whether or not זָר contains an ethnic sense in Proverbs 11:15, the conventional meaning of the term retains the perilous connotation emphasized in the aphorism.

63 See "The Instruction of Any" §6 (*AEL* 2:139); "The Instruction of Ankhsheshonq" §16 (*AEL* 3:171–72); Sir 29:14–20. In Sirach 29:14–20, the author's concern is with standing surety for a neighbor, not a stranger.

The second social principle presented in the economic discourse of Solomon 1A is the virtue of generosity. The most elaborate expression of this value is captured in the following proverbial group (Prov 11:24–26):

יֵשׁ מְפַזֵּר	24	There is one who scatters
וְנוֹסָף עוֹד		and who is increased still more,
וְחוֹשֵׂךְ מִיֹּשֶׁר		and one who withholds what is right [and comes]
אַךְ־לְמַחְסוֹר		only to lack.
נֶפֶשׁ־בְּרָכָה תְדֻשָּׁן	25	Those who bless will be fattened,
וּמַרְוֶה גַּם־הוּא יוֹרֶא		and those who give water will also receive water.
מֹנֵעַ בָּר	26	As for the one who withholds grain,
יִקְּבֻהוּ לְאוֹם		people will curse him,
וּבְרָכָה לְרֹאשׁ מַשְׁבִּיר		but blessing [is] on the head of the one who dispenses it.

Together, these paradoxical aphorisms promote social justice and civic responsibility through the virtues of generosity and distribution. The sayings employ images from the realms of agriculture, animal husbandry, and horticulture to underscore the practical necessities that the generous disseminate to the community. The benevolent promote communal well-being through their liberal distribution of what is essential for the preservation of everyday life, while misers suffer for their niggardliness. This general principle is given particular expression in verse 26, which is cast in a form appropriate to the economic and political elite. Here the image of the one who withholds grain is comparable to the economic injustice sanctioned by the upper class in Amos' preaching (Amos 5:11; 8:4–8), while the one who sells grain is reminiscent of the vizier Joseph in Egypt (Gen 41:56; 42:4).[64] Though the virtues of generosity and distribution are accessible to a wide variety of people, the use of these images in conjunction with the implicit power of the supplier suggests the aphorisms highlight the economic responsibilities of the ruling class.[65] Those responsible for the sustenance of the community and the regulation of the marketplace were expected to exercise generosity in order to promote social harmony and communal welfare.

This implicit appeal to social justice is specified in several sayings throughout the economic discourse of the sentence literature. Within Proverbs 10–15, the issue of social justice is articulated most clearly in 14:20–21 (cf. 13:23):

גַּם־לְרֵעֵהוּ יִשָּׂנֵא רָשׁ	20	A poor person is hated even by his neighbor,
וְאֹהֲבֵי עָשִׁיר רַבִּים		but those who love the rich are many.

---

64   Plöger, *Sprüche Salomos*, 142; R. N. Whybray, *Proverbs* (NCB; Grand Rapids: Eerdmans, 1994),
     180; Van Leeuwen, "The Book of Proverbs," *NIB* 5:120; Fuhs, *Das Buch der Sprichwörter*, 201;
     Waltke, *Proverbs: Chapters 1–15*, 508; Sandoval, *The Discourse of Wealth and Poverty*, 174, Fox,
     Proverbs 10–31, 544.
65   See Sandoval, *The Discourse of Wealth and Poverty*, 174.

בָּז־לְרֵעֵהוּ חוֹטֵא   21   The one who despises his neighbor is a sinner,

וּמְחוֹנֵן עֲנָיִים אַשְׁרָיו   but blessed is the one who shows favor to the poor.[66]

This proverbial pair offers both an observation and a critique of social relationships based on wealth.[67] As an independent, self-contained aphorism, verse 20 seems to present a simple, social observation of the interpersonal relations wealth promotes and obstructs: the rich have a multitude of friends, while the poor are companionless. However, this saying is far from a neutral observation of the "the way the world wags." The aphorism locates the locus of commitment in the wealth of the rich rather than their character or values.[68] This implicit critique of the superficial basis of social relationships is clarified in verse 21.[69] Here the one who hates the poor is described as a sinner, and the proper response to the needy is portrayed in terms of kindness. The proverbial pair addresses the issue of social justice through an evaluation of the nature and stability of ideal interpersonal relationships. Since the rich and the poor have a common dignity derived from their Creator (14:31), the individual is called to esteem the poor as worthy of favor and mutual respect.

The virtues presented in the economic discourse of Solomon 1A provide a lens through which to understand the social observations regarding the rich and the poor, the lazy and the diligent. The aphorisms in Solomon 1A concerned with the former antithetical pair assess the value of wealth and the disparagement of poverty from a variety of angles. On the one hand, riches adorn the righteous (14:24), protect their possessor from disaster (10:15), and accompany a life of virtue (10:16; 11:28; 15:6), while poverty results in the absence of social security and communal degradation (10:15; 14:20). On the other hand, wealth is characterized as ephemeral and of limited value when it is acquired by wicked means or compared with the profit of virtue (10:16; 11:4, 18, 28). Proverbs 10–15 exhibits a tension between the value of wealth and the importance of virtue: wealth is an invaluable asset in the economical realm, but it has little value when it is procured by injustice or employed at the expense of the community's benefit. In light of the ethical principles presented in the economic discourse of Solomon 1A, it seems that the observations concerning the plight of the poor and the wealth of the reputable do not simply function as general assessments of the

---

66   The Ketib and several ancient versions read עֲנָיִים ("poor"), while the Qere reads עֲנָוִים ("humble"). The Ketib should be retained, for it preserves the conventional word pair עָנִי-עָשִׁיר (14:20–21). So also Murphy, *Proverbs*, 102 n. 21.a.; Heim, *Like Grapes of Gold*, 181; Waltke, *Proverbs: Chapters 1–15*, 580 n. 37.

67   Sandoval, *The Discourse of Wealth and Poverty*, 195.

68   Sandoval, *The Discourse of Wealth and Poverty*, 196.

69   See S. Storøy, "Why Does the Theme of Poverty Come into the Context of Prov 14:20?" in *Text and Theology: Studies in Honour of Professor Dr. Theol. Magne Saebø* (ed. A. Tångberg; Oslo: Verbum, 1994), 298–318.

social world; they also serve as an implicit critique of the social realities they observe.[70]

The social observations concerning the rich and the poor are often associated with the lazy/diligent sayings, for wealth and poverty are seen as a direct result of hard work or sloth.[71] However, the relationship between these antithetical pairs is not clear-cut, for the lazy/diligent sayings are not primarily concerned with the social origins of the rich or the poor.[72] These sayings do not attempt to demonstrate that the reward for diligence is wealth and the punishment for laziness is poverty; rather they serve to underscore the advantages of hard work and honest labor and the dangers associated with procrastination, negligence, idle talk, and vain pursuits (10:4; 12:11, 24, 27, 13:4, 11; 14:23; 15:19). The setting, imagery, and tone of the lazy/diligent sayings have prompted many scholars to postulate a particular performance context for the aphorisms.[73] Whether they function ideologically to legitimate the aristocratic bias of the upper class, polemically to reign in potential abuse by the economic elite, or practically to commend hard work as the means for commoners to avoid poverty, the lazy/diligent sayings seek to persuade the addressee of the value of certain virtues and the perils of particular vices.[74] These sayings address both moral (12:27; 15:19) and economic principles in order to present a multifaceted portrait of the socio-economic world that seeks to balance the benefits of industriousness with the dangers of indolence.

The variety of sayings concerning character, communication, and wealth underline the fundamental role of the community in Proverbs 10–15 and provide a framework within which to view the significance of the individual's character and conduct. Several aphorisms highlight the positive and negative effects of a

---

70   Sandoval, *The Discourse of Wealth and Poverty*, 186–93.

71   So Pleins, "Poverty in the Social World of the Wise," *JSOT* 37 (1987): 68; idem, *The Social Visions of the Hebrew Bible* (Louisville: Westminster John Knox, 2001), 465–70; T. P Townsend, "The Poor in Wisdom Literature," *BiBh* 14 (1988): 8–9; Van Leeuwen, "Wealth and Poverty: System and Contradiction in Proverbs," 28.

72   Houston, "The Role of the Poor in Proverbs," 229–40; idem, *Contending for Justice: Ideologies and Theologies of Social Justice in the Old Testament* (Library of Hebrew Bible/Old Testament Studies 428; London: T&T Clark, 2006), 121–22; Sandoval, *The Discourse of Wealth and Poverty*, 137–38.

73   See Pleins, "Poverty in the Social World of the Wise," *JSOT* 37 (1987): 61–78; Habel, "Wisdom, Wealth, and Poverty Paradigms in the Book of Proverbs," 37–40; J. L. Crenshaw, "Poverty and Punishment in the Book of Proverbs," *QR* 9 (1989): 30–43; repr. in *Urgent Advice and Probing Questions: Collected Writings on Old Testament Wisdom* (ed. J. L. Crenshaw. Macon: Mercer University Press, 1995), 396–405; R. N. Whybray, "Poverty, Wealth and Point of View in Proverbs," *ExpTim* 100 (1988–89): 332–36; idem, *Wealth and Poverty in the Book of Proverbs*, 4; B. C. Birch, *Let Justice Roll Down: The Old Testament, Ethics, and Christian Life* (Louisville: Westminster John Knox, 1991), 337; Washington, *Wealth and Poverty*, 185; Westermann, *Roots of Wisdom*, 18–20; Houston, "The Role of the Poor in Proverbs," 229–40.

74   Sandoval, *The Discourse of Wealth and Poverty*, 136–42.

person's character to identify the communal significance of their lifestyle. Other sayings address the social orientation of the individual through the faculties of speech. The sentence literature's concern with proper and improper speech is not surprising, for the motif is a conventional theme in ancient Near Eastern didactic wisdom texts.[75] The same is true with regard to the socio-economic principles delineated in the sub-collection. Communal generosity and kindness toward the disenfranchised are characteristic virtues of ancient oriental wisdom.[76] Wealth means power, and economic authority should be used for the betterment of the community rather than for self-aggrandizement. The sayings concerned with the community situate individuals within their larger social environment and provide the addressee with various principles that promote harmonious relationships. In light of the discourse setting of the document, the sapiential perspective of life in the community offers the noble youth a basic paradigm for social success: the addressee must embody a courtly character through judicious speech, diligence, communal generosity, and social justice in order to strengthen the community and exemplify its ethos. The community plays a significant role in the sapiential perspective of Solomon 1A; its role within the socio-moral vision of the book of Proverbs corresponds with the institution that serves as the foundational building block of society: the family.

4.2.1.3 The Family

Within the sapiential worldview, the family is the most important social unit. The family was a cohesive group with a collective identity, in which individual members performed their respective roles within a tightly-knit hierarchical structure.[77] As noted in chapter three, the instructions in Proverbs 1–9 are cast within a family setting. This social setting provides a concrete context within which to read and assess the meaning and pragmatic significance of the sayings in the sentence literature. However, the domestic setting of the prologue is not simply a heuristic guide for the reader, for the sentence literature contains a

---

75   See "The Instruction Addressed to Kagemni" (*AEL* 1:60); "The Instruction of Ptahhotep" (*AEL* 1:63–64, 67, 70–71); "The Instruction of Any" (*AEL* 2:137–38, 140, 143); "The Instruction of Amenemope" (*AEL* 2:148, 150, 153–55, 158–59, 161); "Counsels of Wisdom" (*BWL*, 101, 105).

76   See F. C. Fensham, "Widow, Orphan, and the Poor in Ancient Near Eastern Legal and Wisdom Literature," *JNES* 21 (1962): 129–39; repr. in *Studies in Ancient Israelite Wisdom*, 161–71. Also see n. 63.

77   For a discussion of the family in ancient Israel, see C. Meyers, "The Family in Early Israel," in *Families in Ancient Israel* (Louisville: Westminster John Knox, 1997), 1–47; J. Blenkinsopp, "The Family in First Temple Israel," in *Families in Ancient Israel* (Louisville: Westminster John Knox, 1997), 48–103; D. I. Block, "Marriage and Family in Ancient Israel," in *Marriage and Family in the Biblical World* (ed. K. M. Campbell; Downers Grove: InterVarsity, 2003), 33–102.

number of sayings concerned with the domestic unit. The mention of the family unit at the document's seams (1:8; 10:1; 31:1–2), coupled with the implicit exhortations to the son in Solomon 1A (10:1, 17; 12:1, 15; 13:1; 15:5), suggest the family is the fundamental locus of sapiential instruction. Within this familial context, several sayings in the sentence literature address explicit issues related to the domestic unit. Among these issues, Solomon 1A discusses three principal topics associated with the family: the importance of parental instruction, the significance of a responsible, cohesive domestic group, and the nature of a noble wife. Each topic deserves specific comment.

The prologue's concern with the value of parental teaching and discipline is reflected in Proverbs 10–15. Several aphorisms underscore the necessity of familial instruction and the benefit of its acceptance (cf. 10:1b; 15:20):

בֵּן חָכָם מוּסַר אָב	A wise son [listens to] a father's instruction,
וְלֵץ לֹא־שָׁמַע גְּעָרָה	but a scoffer does not listen to rebuke. (Prov 13:1)
אֱוִיל יִנְאַץ מוּסַר אָבִיו	A fool despises his father's instruction,
וְשֹׁמֵר תּוֹכַחַת יַעְרִם	but the one who listens to correction is shrewd. (Prov 15:5)
חוֹשֵׂךְ שִׁבְטוֹ	The one who withholds his rod
שׂוֹנֵא בְנוֹ	is one who hates his son,
וְאֹהֲבוֹ שִׁחֲרוֹ מוּסָר	but the one who loves him seeks him diligently with discipline (Prov 13:24)

In general, these sayings highlight the pedagogical responsibilities of both the parents and the son. On the one hand, parents are required to transmit basic social values to their children (13:1; 15:5) and discipline them in accordance with the motives and methods of the Lord (13:24; cf. 3:12). On the other hand, the son is required to accept the instruction of his parents and ensure the psychological well-being of his progenitors (10:1b; 15:20). If parents fail to instruct or discipline their children, they demonstrate their hate by surrendering them to the way of evil (13:24a). If the son fails to receive instruction, he spurns the hierarchical structure of the household (15:5) and produces parental grief (10:1b; 15:20). Together with the prologue, these aphorisms heighten the significance of domestic instruction. Whereas the lectures emphasize the importance of receptivity to parental teaching through the instructional form (1:8; 2:1; 3:1; 4:1, 10, 20; 5:1; 6:20; 7:1–3, 24), Solomon 1A delineates the pedagogical responsibilities of both the parents and the son through terse observations (13:1, 24; 15:5). While the parental lectures focus on the fallacious moral vision of rival discourses through the inevitable outcome of their adherents (1:8-19; 4:10–19; 5:1–23; 6:20–35; 7:1–27), Solomon 1A focuses on the disposition and emotional destruction produced by the one who repudiates familial instruction (10:1b;

15:20). The aphorisms elaborate on the inchoate ethical vision of the prologue and widen the ethical purview of the sapiential discourse. They present the family as the locus for instruction, the medium for socialization, and the primary means by which wisdom is appropriated in the sapiential perspective.

In addition to the importance of familial instruction, the sentence literature also describes the codependent nature of the domestic unit. For Solomon 1A, the family constituted a cohesive group that was responsible for the behavior of its members:

עוֹכֵר בֵּיתוֹ יִנְחַל־רוּחַ	The one who troubles his household inherits wind,
וְעֶבֶד אֱוִיל לַחֲכַם־לֵב	and a fool is a slave to the wise in heart. (Prov 11:29)
טוֹב יַנְחִיל בְּנֵי־בָנִים	A good person leaves an inheritance for his grandchildren,
וְצָפוּן לַצַּדִּיק חֵיל חוֹטֵא	but the wealth of a sinner is stored up for a righteous person. (Prov 13:22)
עוֹכֵר בֵּיתוֹ בּוֹצֵעַ בָּצַע	The one who is greedy for dishonest gain troubles his household,
וְשׂוֹנֵא מַתָּנֹת יִחְיֶה	but the one who hates bribes will live. (Prov 15:27)

These aphorisms demonstrate that the conduct of an individual family member possesses the power to bring honor or disrepute on the household (cf. 5:1–14). The ramifications of this conduct extend far beyond the members of the nuclear family to include the resident's chattel, real estate, and reputation, for בַּיִת functions as a metonymy for the family's heritage and social prestige (11:29; 15:27). Since the family was a cohesive group with a collective identity, the behavior of an individual member either enhanced the status of the household or engendered conflict and communal alienation (12:7; 13:22). Within Solomon 1A, it appears the family either floundered or flourished on the behavior of its constituents.

Together with familial instruction and the codependent nature of the domestic unit, Solomon 1A gives particular attention to the fundamental features of a noble wife. The attention given to the subject is not surprising, since the prologue is punctuated by female figures who seek to entice the noble youth. In view of the pervasive role of woman in both the introductory lectures and interludes, it seems Solomon 1A builds upon the inchoate ethical vision of the prologue to provide a more detailed portrait of marital relations. The collection moves from the metaphorical register to the historical register, from the abstract to the concrete, to present the value of a virtuous wife:

אֵשֶׁת־חֵן תִּתְמֹךְ כָּבוֹד
וְעָרִיצִים יִתְמְכוּ־עֹשֶׁר

A gracious woman takes hold of honor,
but ruthless men take hold of riches.[78] (Prov 11:16)

נֶזֶם זָהָב בְּאַף חֲזִיר
אִשָּׁה יָפָה וְסָרַת טָעַם

As a ring of gold in a swine's snout
[so is] a beautiful woman who has turned from discretion.
(Prov 11:22)

אֵשֶׁת־חַיִל עֲטֶרֶת בַּעְלָהּ
וּכְרָקָב בְּעַצְמוֹתָיו מְבִישָׁה

A valiant wife is the crown of her husband,
but like rottenness in his bones is a shameful wife.
(Prov 12:4)

חַכְמוֹת נָשִׁים בָּנְתָה בֵיתָהּ
וְאִוֶּלֶת בְּיָדֶיהָ תֶהֶרְסֶנּוּ

The wise among women builds her house,[79]
but a foolish woman tears it down with her own hands.
(Prov 14:1)

These aphorisms focus on the moral and intellectual virtues of an ideal wife. They are not concerned with the physical charms of a suitable maiden; rather they provide an ethical vision of a noble woman. This vision is constructed through a series of ethical values that are comparable to the moral and intellectual virtues of Woman Wisdom. Similar to Woman Wisdom, a noble wife possesses a gracious disposition that produces social honor (כָּבוֹד) and communal admiration (11:16; cf. 3:16; 8:18). She enhances the status of her husband (12:4; cf. 4:9; 31:23) and employs wisdom in the management of her household (14:1; cf. 9:1; 24:3–4; 31:10–31).[80] In contrast to the deceptive physical charms of the Strange Woman (6:24–25; 7:10–23) and the perverted disposition of the unprincipled wife (11:22; 12:4b; 14:1b), these aphorisms identify the locus of true feminine beauty, viz., virtue. This notion is reinforced by the shocking imagery of Proverbs 11:22. Here beauty without virtue is comparable to a golden ring in the snout of a pig. Though physical beauty is valuable (i.e., a golden ring and a beautiful woman), when it is located in an inappropriate place or tainted by vice, it is grotesque.[81]

---

78 The LXX adds two versets between vv. 16a and 16b. Though several translations incorporate these additional lines (NRSV, NEB, NAB), the MT is preferred. It seems that the LXX translator did not understand the nature of the parallelism and elaborated on the aphorism through two versets (Tov, "Recensional Differences between the Masoretic Text and the Septuagint of the Book of Proverbs," 422).

79 Many revocalize חַכְמוֹת to read חָכְמָה and omit נָשִׁים to conform the verset to Proverbs 9:1 (see BHS; Gemser, Sprüche Salomos, 168; Murphy, Proverbs, 101). However, since חכמות is never personified in the sentence literature and נָשִׁים may have been included to highlight the difference between Woman Wisdom and real women, the MT is preferred. See Camp, Wisdom and the Feminine, 137–40; Plöger, Sprüche Salomos, 168; Heim, Like Grapes of Gold, 171; Waltke, Proverbs: Chapters 1–15, 576 n. 1, 2.

80 See J. Hausmann, Studien zum Menschenbild der älteren Weisheit (Spr 10ff.) (FAT 7; Tübingen: Mohr, 1995), 150–51; Fox, Proverbs 10–31, 548.

81 K. N. Heim, "A Closer Look at the Pig in Proverbs xi 22," VT 58 (2008): 13–27, esp. 24–25; Fox, Proverbs 10–31, 541.

Together, these aphorisms build upon the moral vision of prologue to provide the noble youth with an ethical framework for marriage preparation.[82] Several sayings incorporate language and imagery reminiscent of the lectures and interludes to transform the metaphorical into the historical, the cosmological into the anthropological. Whereas the prologue describes an illusive form of beauty (6:24–25; 7:10–23), Solomon 1A presents the essence of true beauty: virtue. In addition, while the prologue promotes marriage as the socio-moral elixir to the seductive machinations of the Strange Woman (5:15–20), Solomon 1A describes the fundamental qualities of a marriageable maiden. The aphorisms elaborate on the ethical vision of the prologue to provide the noble youth with a concrete portrait of a virtuous woman who may serve as the foundation of a stable home.

To summarize, the anthropocentric dimension of the world presented in Solomon 1A places the individual in relation to the perceived social environment to highlight the value of particular virtues, perspectives, and principles. Solomon 1A offers an impressionistic portrait of the individual in community that (re)constructs the addressee's perception of the world and shapes his character. The same is true with regard to the theocentric dimension of Solomon 1A. Several sayings within Proverbs 10–15 reflect on the virtues and vices presented in the anthropocentric frame of reference through a theocentric view of the world. To gain a more holistic perspective of the sapiential worldview, it is necessary to examine the theocentric dimension of Proverbs 10–15.

4.2.2 The Theocentric Dimension of Solomon 1A

The theocentric dimension of the world presented in Solomon 1A is constructed through a series of sayings that describe the attitude and actions of YHWH in relation to the individual.[83] While many claim that early Israelite wisdom was a secular tradition concerned with practical matters that eventually underwent a religious, Yahwistic reinterpretation,[84] it appears the "YHWH sayings" are not the product of a later, theological stage of development. Rather the YHWH sayings are integral to the sapiential worldview; they complement the more "mundane" aphorisms by affirming their significance and elaborating on their theological

---

82 Heim, "A Closer Look at the Pig in Proverbs xi 22," 26.

83 Boström, *The God of the Sages*, 105.

84 J. Fichtner, *Die altorientalische Weisheit in ihrer israelitisch-jüdischen Ausprägung* (BZAW 62; Giessen: Töpelmann, 1933), 24–25; W. McKane, *Prophets and Wise Men* (SBT 44; Naperville: Allenson, 1965); idem, *Proverbs: A New Approach*, 11–21; Scott, "Wise and Foolish, Righteous and Wicked," 145–65.

dimensions.[85] Within Proverbs 10–15, the YHWH sayings provide a theological assessment of three principal topics introduced in the anthropological perspective of the world, viz., character, communication, and social justice. Each deserves a brief comment.

Since character formation is the fundamental goal of the wisdom literature, it is not surprising that the sentence literature balances the communal orientation of an individual's character with its theological significance. Several sayings in Proverbs 10–15 focus on the attitude and actions of YHWH toward certain characters. The attitude of YHWH is given particular expression in the תּוֹעֲבָה-sentences:

תּוֹעֲבַת יְהוָה עִקְּשֵׁי־לֵב		People with perverse hearts are an abomination to YHWH,
וּרְצוֹנוֹ תְּמִימֵי דָרֶךְ		but his favor is with those who are blameless in their way. (Prov 11:20)
זֶבַח רְשָׁעִים תּוֹעֲבַת יְהוָה	8	The sacrifice of the wicked is an abomination to YHWH,
וּתְפִלַּת יְשָׁרִים רְצוֹנוֹ		but the prayer of the upright finds his favor.
תּוֹעֲבַת יְהוָה דֶּרֶךְ רָשָׁע	9	An abomination to YHWH is the way of the wicked,
וּמְרַדֵּף צְדָקָה יֶאֱהָב		but the one who pursues righteousness he loves. (Prov 15:8–9)

These תּוֹעֲבָה-sentences present YHWH's emotive value judgment on an individual's character. In the first, divine favor is contingent on the lifestyle of the individual: YHWH detests those with a twisted disposition, but he delights in those who are committed to him (11:20; 12:2). This general character assessment is then cast in a concrete description in the second proverbial pair (15:8–9).[86] Here the criterion for YHWH's favor is not the meticulous performance of cultic rituals, but the ardent pursuit of righteousness. This pair illuminates the dynamic relationship between YHWH and the individual. Sacrifices and supplications do not have automatic, built-in consequences; rather it is the character of the intercessor that precipitates divine favor. The pair not only acknowledges the role of the cult in the wisdom literature (cf. 3:9; 15:29; 21:3, 27), but it also highlights

---

85   F. M. Wilson, "Sacred and Profane? The Yahwistic Redaction of Proverbs Reconsidered," in *The Listening Heart: Essays in Wisdom and the Psalms in Honor of Roland E. Murphy* (ed. K. G. Hoglund et al.; Sheffield: JSOT, 1989), 328. Also see R. E. Murphy, "Wisdom—Theses and Hypotheses," 40; M. L. Barré, "'Fear of God' and the World View of Wisdom," *BTB* 11 (1981): 41–42; Boström, *The God of the Sages*, 36–38; R. N. Whybray, "Thoughts on the Composition of Proverbs 10–29," in *Priests, Prophets and Scribes: Essays on the Formation and Heritage of Second Temple Judaism in Honour of Joseph Blenkinsopp* (ed. J. W. Wright et al.; Sheffield: Sheffield Academic Press, 1992), 108–09; Fox, *Proverbs 10–31*, 482-83.

86   See Hildebrandt, "Proverbial Pairs," 212–13, who identifies the semantic, syntactic, and thematic coherence between Proverbs 15:8–9.

the fundamental principle that governs human and divine interaction. Proverbial Yahwism recognizes the significance of the cult in human-divine relations, but it places conformity with the divine character above compliance with cultic practice.[87]

In addition to YHWH's emotional assessment of an individual's disposition, the sentence literature gives particular expression to his active involvement in the lives of certain characters:

לֹא־יַרְעִיב יְהוָה נֶפֶשׁ צַדִּיק	YHWH will not allow the soul of the righteous to hunger,
וְהַוַּת רְשָׁעִים יֶהְדֹּף	but the desires of the wicked he thrusts aside. (Prov 10:3)
טוֹב יָפִיק רָצוֹן מֵיְהוָה	A good person obtains favor from YHWH,
וְאִישׁ מְזִמּוֹת יַרְשִׁיעַ	But a crafty person he condemns. (Prov 12:2)

These aphorisms demonstrate that YHWH is not a passive, impersonal agent who supervises a retributive paradigm in which actions have inherent, built-in consequences; rather they present YHWH as active agent in the world. The aphorisms exhibit little concern for specific actions; instead they focus on YHWH's response to the character and lifestyle of certain people. The first saying portrays YHWH as the supplier and the sustainer of the righteous (10:3), while the second depicts YHWH as a judge who dispenses just deserts to the appropriate characters (12:2). These aphorisms highlight YHWH's active role in the sapiential world. He is depicted as an administrator of rewards and punishment for an individual's actions, lifestyle, and even their hidden intentions (15:3, 11).

The theocentric dimension of Solomon 1A also includes several sayings that underscore YHWH's ardent assessment of proper and improper speech:

תּוֹעֲבַת יְהוָה שִׂפְתֵי־שָׁקֶר	Lying lips are an abomination to YHWH,
וְעֹשֵׂי אֱמוּנָה רְצוֹנוֹ	but those who act faithfully find his favor. (Prov 12:22)
תּוֹעֲבַת יְהוָה מַחְשְׁבוֹת רָע	Evil plans are an abomination to YHWH,
וּטְהֹרִים אִמְרֵי־נֹעַם	But pleasant words are pure. (Prov 15:26)

Together, these aphorisms demonstrate that communication may incite YHWH's revulsion or engender his favor. In the sapiential perspective, the spoken word extends beyond interpersonal social relations to include divine-human relations; it not only serves as an indication of a person's disposition, but it also has implications for the individual's relationship with YHWH.

---

87   Frydrych, *Living under the Sun*, 94–95.

In conjunction with its theocentric evaluation of character and communication, Solomon 1A highlights YHWH's active involvement in matters of social justice. Proverbs 10–15 provides a theological rationale for the social principles presented in the anthropocentric dimension of the collection through a description of Yahweh's relationship with economic affairs and the plight of the marginalized:

מֹאזְנֵי מִרְמָה תּוֹעֲבַת יְהוָה
וְאֶבֶן שְׁלֵמָה רְצוֹנוֹ

Deceitful balances are an abomination to YHWH,
but a full weight finds his favor. (Prov 11:1)

בֵּית גֵּאִים יִסַּח יְהוָה
וְיַצֵּב גְּבוּל אַלְמָנָה

YHWH tears down the house of the proud,
but he makes firm the boundary of the widow.
(Prov 15:25)

The initial תּוֹעֵבָה-sentence expresses YHWH's judgment on commercial practices and describes his implicit involvement in the enterprise, for if the consequences regarding economic injustice were automatic, YHWH's assessment would be irrelevant.[88] The concern for economic justice in commercial activities is a significant motif in the ancient oriental world.[89] This is not surprising, since it serves as an ethical principle that promotes socio-moral justice.[90] The same is true in Proverbs 11:1. Within the sapiential worldview, economic fraud provokes YHWH's moral outrage, for it is irreconcilable with his character. Similar to communication, the implications of deceitful business practices extend beyond the community to include the individual's relationship with YHWH. While the aphorism is not directed toward a specific social group, it assumes that YHWH is intimately involved in commercial affairs and that he responds to the retailer according to his economic exploits.[91] In so doing, the saying provides a theological assessment of business practices and constructs a concrete economic ethic for the addressee.[92]

YHWH's involvement in the economic affairs of the marketplace is consistent with his actions on behalf of the disenfranchised. Proverbs 15:25

---

88   Frydrych, *Living under the Sun*, 103.

89   See Lev 19:35–37; Deut 25:13–16; Ezek 45:10; Hos 12:7–8; Amos 8:5; Mic 6:11. For a discussion of weights, measures, and commercial activities in the ancient oriental world, see R. B. Y. Scott, "Weights and Measures of the Bible," *BA* 22 (1959): 22–40; K. R. Veenhof, *Aspects of Old Assyrian Trade and Its Terminology* (Studia et Documenta ad Iura Orientis Antiqui Pertinentia 10; Leiden: E. J. Brill, 1972), esp. 59–61; D. C. Snell, *Life in the Ancient Near East: 3100–332 B.C.E.* (New Haven: Yale University Press, 1997), 42–43; King and Stager, *Life in Biblical Israel*, 195–98; C. M. Monroe, "Money and Trade," in *A Companion to the Ancient Near East* (ed. D. C. Snell; Malden: Blackwell, 2005), 155–68.

90   Also see "The Instruction of Amenemope" (*AEL* 2:156–57).

91   Boström, *The God of the Sages*, 201.

92   Sandoval, *The Discourse of Wealth and Poverty*, 143–45.

supplements the communal concern for the poor in the anthropocentric dimension of Proverbs 10–15 through a description of YHWH's concern for the אַלְמָנָה ("widow"). The widow serves as a synecdoche for all those who are vulnerable to socio-economic exploitation. While the Israelite community in general and the king in particular were responsible to provide for and protect the disenfranchised on the horizontal level, YHWH functioned as their champion on the vertical level.[93] He assumed responsibility for their welfare and ensured the conservation of their ancestral allotments (15:25). In the main, the saying describes YHWH's involvement on behalf of the weak and provides a theological rationale that links social ethics with religious values.

On the whole, the theocentric dimension of Solomon 1A complements the anthropocentric frame of reference by affirming its values and developing its theological significance. The YHWH sayings reflect on topics presented in the anthropological discourse, providing a holistic perspective that unites the two essential sides of the sapiential worldview. They demonstrate that human knowledge of self cannot be divorced from knowledge of YHWH, for an individual's character and conduct has implications in both the human world and the divine realm. The religious sayings underscore the intimate relationship between lifestyle and the fate of the individual, and highlight YHWH's active role in the retribution-reward schema.

4.2.3 Section Conclusion

Together, the anthropocentric and theocentric dimensions of Proverbs 10–15 supply the addressee with a basic introduction to the socio-religious sphere. Solomon 1A elaborates on virtues, vices, and personas introduced in the prologue to provide an elementary paradigm of the wise life. The general, bifurcated world and austere virtues, values, and principles presented in Solomon 1A produce a fundamental image of the cosmos. This basic socio-religious paradigm shapes the character of the noble youth, introduces him to the basic contours of the socio-religious world, and outlines the ethical agenda that he must pursue. The compendium depicts a world through which the addressee must navigate, a world whose ideals he must embody. In so doing, Solomon 1A forms a basic, ethical foundation for the thematic development that takes place in Proverbs 16:1–22:16. This development is significant, for the material moves from the general to the specific, from the conceptual to the concrete. Solomon 1B reinforces particular

---

93   See Exod 22:21–24; Deut 10:18; 14:28–29; 16:11, 14; 24:17, 19–21; 26:12–13; 27:19; Lev 19:9; Job 24:3; 29:12–16; 31:16–21; Prov 14:21; Isa 1:17, 23; 10:2; Jer 7:6; 22:3; Zech 7:10; Mal 3:5; Fensham, "Widow, Orphan, and the Poor in Ancient Near Eastern Legal and Wisdom Literature," 161–71.

topics, modulates certain themes, and provides a more detailed portrait of the socio-religious world.

4.3 Intermediate Wisdom: Solomon 1B (16:1–22:16)

The notion of a thematic or "pedagogical" development in the successive collections of the book of Proverbs is given particular attention by William P. Brown.[94] In view of the "overarching movement" from the prologue to the heroic panegyric (31:10–31) and the maturation of moral character delineated in these compositions, Brown explores whether a comparable development is apparent within the intervening collections of the book of Proverbs (10:1–31:9).[95] He focuses on the formal and thematic features of the constituent collections within Proverbs 10:1–31:9 in order identify the development of the material, the role of the individual compendia, the rationale behind their present arrangement in the MT, and their contribution to the process of moral formation.[96] Since Brown's developmental model plays a foundational role in the present study, it is necessary to provide a brief summary of his work.

In general, Brown divides his work into five parts, each of which examines the poetic texture and thematic emphases of the individual compositions within Proverbs 10:1–31:9. The initial section focuses on the first Solomonic collection (10:1–22:16). In light of the formal features of the collection, Brown divides the compendium into two segments: Proverbs 10:1–15:32 and 15:33–22:16. He identifies several common motifs in the sub-collections and gives particular attention to the "thematic movement" of the material. For Brown, Solomon 1B evinces "a curricular advancement in such areas as human relations, communication, ethics, money, governance, and theology."[97] The sub-collection moves from family to friendship, from character to concept, and from silence to elocution; it provides a more fully developed portrait of wealth and poverty, the

---

94   Brown, "The Pedagogy of Proverbs 10:1–31:9," 150–82. Brown notes Van Leeuwen's observation concerning the development within the first Solomonic collection from a simple to "a more complex view of acts and consequences" (Van Leeuwen, "The Book of Proverbs," *NIB* 5:23; Brown, "The Pedagogy of Proverbs 10:1–31:9," 152 n. 12). Within the commentary proper, Van Leeuwen elaborates on this statement, arguing that Proverbs 10–15 present "the ABC of wisdom, the basic rules the young need to live well. Starting with chap. 16, the exceptions to the basic rules of life will appear much more frequently" ("The Book of Proverbs," *NIB* 5:105). This conclusion precipitated my own thinking regarding a thematic movement within the book of Proverbs prior to my introduction to Brown's work. Since many of my own conclusions correspond with those presented in Brown's essay, his work will play a foundational role in the present study.

95   Brown, "The Pedagogy of Proverbs 10:1–31:9," 153.

96   Brown, "The Pedagogy of Proverbs 10:1–31:9," 153–54.

97   Brown, "The Pedagogy of Proverbs 10:1–31:9," 158.

royal institution, and the role of YHWH in the socio-religious world. In view of the rhetorical characteristics and thematic progression of Solomon 1B, Brown concludes that the compositional unit reinforces certain themes and addresses topics that do not find precedent in Solomon 1A. In so doing, it exhibits a "didactic movement" that widens the moral purview of the sapiential material.[98]

The second section of the study examines the formal characteristics and thematic emphases of the "Words of the Wise" (22:17–24:22; 24:23–34). Here Brown focuses on the ethos of the instructional material, the pedagogical development within the collections, and the implied addressee of the compendia. Among the various themes presented in the discussion, Brown gives particular attention to divine activity, honest speech, individual character, social justice, and royal service. He identifies the way in which the instructions reinforce specific themes from the first Solomonic collection and advance particular topics in the sapiential material. In view of the thematic development within the compendia, the domestic setting of the instructions, and the attention given to royal service, Brown suggests the "Words of the Wise" are directed toward an addressee who "stands liminally between the righteous and the wicked, even between the common and the royal."[99]

The third section of the work focuses on the Hezekian collection (25:1–29:27). Similar to the previous segments, Brown examines the formal features and thematic emphases within the compositional unit in order to explore the didactic movement of the material. For Brown, the stylistic features and poetic sophistication of the collection suggest the material serves "not only to proscribe but also to *model* the art of elocution."[100] The formal progression of the material corresponds with thematic development of particular topics. Brown examines the collection's treatment of the king, the Torah, the righteous and the wicked, the fool, the marginalized, and YHWH, among others. He demonstrates that the Hezekian collection reiterates familiar themes from the earlier compendia through diverse literary forms; it affirms the value of traditional topics, but reorients these issues through a dynamic frame of reference. This is particularly apparent in the collection's critical assessment of the monarchy, its emphasis on the Torah and interpersonal conflicts, as well as the "overtly politicized" nature of individual character. Together, these formal and thematic features lead Brown to conclude that the Hezekian collection evinces a significant progression in the material. The compositional unit achieves "a higher level of discursive elocution;"[101] it moves from the domestic sphere to a conflictive social world "populated with wicked and just rulers, good and deceitful neighbors, the greedy

---

98   Brown, "The Pedagogy of Proverbs 10:1–31:9," 164.
99   Brown, "The Pedagogy of Proverbs 10:1–31:9," 169.
100   Brown, "The Pedagogy of Proverbs 10:1–31:9," 171.
101   Brown, "The Pedagogy of Proverbs 10:1–31:9," 175.

rich and the righteous poor, friends and enemies."[102] The collection transforms character into a political construct and "thrusts the reader into the fray of political wrangling."[103]

The fourth section of the work explores the poetic texture and thematic emphases of the Words of Agur (30:1–33). Here Brown identifies the general tenor of the piece, catalogs the distinct literary forms incorporated in the composition, and surveys the principal topics delineated in the collection. For Brown, the Words of Agur widen the scope of the sapiential discourse. The composition moves from a familial ethos to the ethos of creation and "elicits a sense of *mystrium tremendum*" in order to accentuate the value of humility and the wonders of wisdom manifested in the created order.[104] Brown gives particular attention to the virtue of humility, the nature of deceptive discourse, and the issue of wealth and poverty. He describes the different ways in which the compositional unit reinforces these traditional motifs and elaborates on their significance. In so doing, Brown concludes that the Words of Agur contribute to the pedagogical movement of the sapiential discourse. This bizarre collection highlights the virtues of humility, honest speech, and moderation from a theological perspective; it situates these moral values in the context of creation and incorporates various phenomena from the natural world to "advance the measure of wisdom," inspire wonder of the divine, and "expand the moral scope" of the material.[105]

The final section of the study examines the "Words of King Lemuel" (31:1–9). For Brown, this royal instruction not only represents the most extended direct address among the collections, but it also contains two distinct features. First, in contrast to the previous material, the instruction gives particular expression to the maternal voice. Second, the superscription moves beyond an authorial ascription to provide the specific identity of the "*implied* reader."[106] In so doing, the composition brings the pedagogical movement of the collections full circle and reveals "its specific subject *and* object, a mother and her royal son."[107] Brown delineates the fundamental themes presented in the instruction and identifies how these motifs contribute to the issue of competent leadership. He traces the development of the discourse setting of the sapiential material as well as the progressive portrait of the king—a ruler who moves from the embodiment of exalted power to the object of critique to one accountable for his public and private actions.

---

102 Brown, "The Pedagogy of Proverbs 10:1–31:9," 175.
103 Brown, "The Pedagogy of Proverbs 10:1–31:9," 175.
104 Brown, "The Pedagogy of Proverbs 10:1–31:9," 177.
105 Brown, "The Pedagogy of Proverbs 10:1–31:9," 178.
106 Brown, "The Pedagogy of Proverbs 10:1–31:9," 178.
107 Brown, "The Pedagogy of Proverbs 10:1–31:9," 178–79.

On the whole, Brown's study is an important contribution to the nature and function of the individual collections in the book of Proverbs. Though the work is general in character, Brown identifies several features that suggest a formal and thematic movement among the constituent collections in Proverbs 10:1–31:9. He demonstrates that the compendia evince a formal progression that heightens the level of discursive elocution and enhances the moral purview of the sapiential material. In addition, Brown describes the various ways in which the individual collections reinforce traditional themes and advance particular topics. He demonstrates that the material moves from a simple bipolar world to a complex conflicted world, from the domestic sphere to the royal court, and from an ambiguous addressee to an explicit addressee. This "didactic movement" not only contributes to the project of moral formation, but it also suggests the collections have been deliberately collated. Brown's study recognizes a profound, hermeneutical dynamic within the collections of Proverbs and reflects on its significance for the moral formation of the reader.

Brown's developmental model will play an important role in the present study. The subsequent discussion will build on the foundation laid by Brown in paying close attention to the formal and thematic movement within the individual collections of the book of Proverbs. Where I agree with Brown on aspects of development, the discussion will be brief. In the main, I will simply provide an exegetical basis for his conclusions. However, where I nuance Brown's proposals or move beyond his conclusions, I will identify the distinctive contributions of the present study. With this basic framework, the subsequent investigation will explore the formal and thematic development within the individual compositional units of the book of Proverbs in order to determine the degree to which the compendia correspond with the courtly discourse setting of the prologue.

4.3.1 The Anthropocentric Dimension of Solomon 1B

In general, Proverbs 16:1–22:16 elaborates on the materials presented in Solomon 1A to provide a more comprehensive portrait of the socio-religious world. While these sub-collections share many features, the rhetorical characteristics and thematic emphases of Solomon 1B evince a didactic movement in the material.[108] The static, bipolar world and terse antithetical sayings in Proverbs 10–15 give way to a dynamic, variegated frame of reference expressed through diverse poetic forms.[109] The formal development of the sapiential discourse coincides with the thematic movement of the material. Solomon 1B widens the socio-religious

---

108 Brown, "The Pedagogy of Proverbs 10:1–31:9," 157–58.
109 For a discussion of the formal differences between Solomon 1A and Solomon 1B, see Brown, "The Pedagogy of Proverbs 10:1–31:9," 156–58.

purview of the sapiential world through its nuanced development of particular themes and its interest in subjects that receive only a brief treatment in Solomon 1A.[110] Within the anthropocentric dimension of Proverbs 16:1–22:16, this development is apparent in the sayings concerned with the fundamental social units of the sapiential world: the monarchy, the community, and the family.

4.3.1.1 The Monarchy

Solomon 1B contains a series of sayings related to the royal institution. These sayings build on the *Königssprüche* in Solomon 1A to form an impressionistic portrait of the ideal king's power and personality.[111] They enhance the king's communal orientation by highlighting his judicial authority, his moral character, and his sovereign power. These motifs are conveyed in each of the *Königssprüche* in Proverbs 16:1–22:16. However, they are given particular expression in 16:10–15:

קֶסֶם עַל־שִׂפְתֵי־מֶלֶךְ בְּמִשְׁפָּט לֹא יִמְעַל־פִּיו	10	An inspired verdict is on the lips of the king; in judgment his mouth is not unfaithful.
פֶּלֶס וּמֹאזְנֵי מִשְׁפָּט לַיהוָה מַעֲשֵׂהוּ כָּל־אַבְנֵי־כִיס	11	A just balance and scales are YHWH's; all the weights in the bag are his work.
תּוֹעֲבַת מְלָכִים עֲשׂוֹת רֶשַׁע כִּי בִּצְדָקָה יִכּוֹן כִּסֵּא	12	An abomination to kings is doing wickedness, for a throne is established through righteousness.
רְצוֹן מְלָכִים שִׂפְתֵי־צֶדֶק וְדֹבֵר יְשָׁרִים יֶאֱהָב	13	Kings take pleasure in righteous lips, and the one who speaks upright things he loves.
חֲמַת־מֶלֶךְ מַלְאֲכֵי־מָוֶת וְאִישׁ חָכָם יְכַפְּרֶנָּה	14	The wrath of the king is a messenger of death, but a wise person appeases it.
בְּאוֹר־פְּנֵי־מֶלֶךְ חַיִּים וּרְצוֹנוֹ כְּעָב מַלְקוֹשׁ	15	In the light of a king's face is life, and his favor is like a cloud of spring rain.

---

110 Brown, "The Pedagogy of Proverbs 10:1–31:9," 158.

111 Brown acknowledges that the royal institution is more fully developed in the latter half of the first Solomonic collection. In general, he focuses on royal character and office through the individual *Königssprüche* in Proverbs 16:1–22:16. However, Brown fails to discuss the content of the royal sayings in Solomon 1A. In addition, he limits the royal context of Solomon 1A to the two explicit *Königssprüche* within the collection (14:28, 35). In contrast, the present study includes these royal sayings within a larger compositional unit devoted to the social orientation of the royal institution (14:28–35, cf. 11:14). In so doing, the present study provides a more comprehensive framework through which to trace the development of the royal institution between the compositional units. Though Brown demonstrates that Solomon 1B evinces a thematic progression with regard to the degree to which the compendium considers the king, he does not examine the individual aphorisms within their immediate literary context or describe how Solomon 1B expands upon the portrait of the royal institution delineated in Solomon 1A. See Brown, "The Pedagogy of Proverbs 10:1–31:9," 163.

The juxtaposition of the subunits concerned with YHWH (16:1–9) and the king (16:10–15) creates an editorial context within which to understand the meaning and pragmatic significance of the material. Together, these subsections present the fundamental basis of cosmic order: YHWH superintends the socio-religious order and mediates his justice through his official representative, the king.[112] The royal sayings in the subunit address the nature of the king through three characterizations: the socio-economic authority of the king, the moral character of the ideal king, and the sovereign power of the wise king. Each deserves specific comment.

The first quatrain presents the socio-economic authority of the wise king (16:10–11). Here the king is portrayed as infallible in the administration of justice, but subject to YHWH's rule. The initial aphorism describes the king's inerrant judgment through the pejorative term קֶסֶם. Elsewhere in the Old Testament קֶסֶם refers to illegitimate forms of pagan divination and false prophecy (e.g., Deut 18:10; 1 Sam 15:23; Jer 14:14; Ezek 13:6). However, the noun has a positive connotation in the present context, for it is parallel to מִשְׁפָּט and alludes to a legitimate method of reaching a decision in the judicial sphere. While קֶסֶם may refer to an authorized means of divination (e.g., the Urim and Thummin),[113] when the aphorism is read within its larger editorial context (16:1) it appears the noun denotes YHWH's capacity to endow the king with a just verdict through wisdom (8:14–16; 2 Sam 14:17, 20; 16:23; 1 Kgs 3:16–28; Isa 11:1–5).[114] As YHWH's official representative, the king exercised his judicial responsibilities by adjudicating difficult cases through inspired decisions in order to establish justice. In addition to the legal arbitration of the king, the ideal monarch also mediated YHWH's justice through economic equity (16:11). Though the king is not mentioned in verse 11, the repetition of מִשְׁפָּט links the king's judicial activity with his maintenance of economic affairs (16:10–11). Since just economic practices are the creation and the concern of YHWH, the wise king executes economic equity by enforcing standard weights and measures.[115] In contrast to the other sayings regarding scales and weights (11:1; 20:10, 23), the present aphorism describes the

112 See Schmid, *Gerechtigkeit als Weltordnung*, 83–89; idem, *Altorientalische Welt in der alttestamentliche Theologie* (Zürich: Theologischer Verlag, 1974), 100–101.

113 See E. W. Davies, "The Meaning of *qesem* in Prv 16,10," *Bib* 61 (1980): 554–56. Davies reads Proverbs 16:10 in light of Ezekiel 21:23–28 and argues קֶסֶם refers to a process of lot casting based on its use with "to shake/cast arrows" (קִלְקַל בַּחִצִּים). This proposal is possible, but less than convincing, for casting arrows is quite different from casting lots. Moreover, Ezekiel classifies casting arrows, consulting idols, and examining the liver under the designation of קֶסֶם. Since consulting idols and examining the liver are prohibited in the Old Testament, it follows that casting arrows are also proscribed. See D. I. Block, *The Book of Ezekiel: Chapters 1–24* (NICOT; Grand Rapids: Eerdmans, 1997), 686–87; Waltke, *Proverbs: Chapters 15–31*, 17 n. 61.

114 See Alonso Schöckel and J. Vilchez, *Proverbios*, 347; Meinhold, *Die Sprüche*, 2:269; Clifford, *Proverbs*, 159; Waltke, *Proverbs: Chapters 15–31*, 17; Wilke, *Kronerben der Weisheit*, 176.

115 Fox, *Proverbs 10–31*, 615.

subject in a positive manner. The saying does not offer YHWH's value judgment on commercial practices (תּוֹעֲבַת יְהוָה); rather it emphasizes his role in the institution of economic justice and places the maintenance of commercial ethics under the authority of the king. In the main, the initial quatrain highlights the judicial and economic prerogatives of the ideal king. The aphorisms depict the king as the instrument through which Yahweh mediates his justice in the socio-economic realm (cf. 21:1).

The second quatrain describes the moral character of the wise king (16:12–13).[116] The initial aphorism delineates the ideal king's moral posture towards the wickedness of others through an emphatic value judgment followed by a motivation.[117] While תּוֹעֵבָה typically occurs with YHWH, here it refers to the king's moral sensibilities. Similar to YHWH's (6:16; 15:8, 9; 17:5) and Woman Wisdom (8:7), the ideal king detests the wicked actions of his people in general and his officials in particular (20:8, 26; 29:12). His moral orientation has significant implications, for the order and stability of the kingdom rests on the righteous character of YHWH's agent of justice (16:12; 20:28).[118] The second aphorism identifies the king's attitude toward righteous speech (16:13): the king takes pleasure in honest words and dispenses his covenant commitment (יֶאֱהָב) to those who emulate Wisdom's vernacular (8:8; 16:13; 22:11). Together, these sayings depict the revulsion of kings against wicked acts and their delight in proper speech. They outline the contours of the wise king's moral character, and describe the fundamental virtues that underlie his judicial and economic responsibilities.

The third quatrain specifies the sovereign power of the wise king (16:14–15). The initial aphorism depicts the king's wrath as a herald that portends death (16:14), while the second portrays his favor through meteorological images (16:15). The favor and wrath of the king are significant themes in Solomon 1B. On the one hand, the temperament of the king is compared with a roaring,

---

116 For the relationship between the aphorisms, see Plöger, *Sprüche Salomos*, 192; Hildebrandt, "Proverbial Pairs," 209 n. 7; Meinhold, *Die Sprüche*, 2:270–71; Heim, *Like Grapes of Gold*, 212.

117 The construct phrase תּוֹעֲבַת מְלָכִים introduces a subjective genitive rather than an objective genitive, making others the agents of עֲשׂוֹת רֶשַׁע rather than the king (cf. LXX, Targ., Vulg.). For an extended discussion of the issue, see Heim, *Like Grapes of Gold*, 213–14.

118 Following Hellmut Brunner, several scholars argue that the concept of righteousness as the foundation of the royal throne (16:12; 20:28; 25:5) is comparable with Egyptian royal ideology. This proposal is based on the fact that the hieroglyph for both the royal pedestal and *ma'at* are identical. The imagery in Proverbs 16:12 and the significance of the throne in Israelite royal ideology reflect the concepts associated with *ma'at* and the pharaonic throne, but these similarities do not necessarily lead to the conclusion that Egyptian thought influenced the description in 16:12, for this imagery is found elsewhere in the Old Testament (cf. Ps 89:15; 97:2). For a discussion of these issues, see H. Brunner, "Gerechtigkeit als Fundament des Thrones," *VT* 8 (1958): 426–28; Boström, *The God of the Sages*, 123; Perdue, *Wisdom Literature: A Theological History*, 64; Wilke, *Kronerben der Weisheit*, 170–72.

growling lion that rages against insubordinate subjects to maintain order in his kingdom (19:12; 20:2).[119] On the other hand, the favor of the king is compared with images of natural renewal (16:15; 19:12).[120] As Yahweh's immediate agent, the king possesses the power to enforce order in society and bestow a full, abundant life on his subjects. His power to administer life and death is not only a royal prerogative, but also a prerogative of the divine king.

To summarize, Solomon 1B builds on the *Königssprüche* in Proverbs 10–15 to provide a more elaborate portrait of the royal institution. In the main, the *Königssprüche* within the sub-collection give particular expression to the king's socio-economic authority, moral character, and sovereign power. They depict the king as YHWH's official representative, who mediates his judicial authority, regulates his economic standards, and dispenses his just rewards and punishments. The subunit presents an ideal portrait of the principal responsibilities and supreme power of the wise king. In so doing, the *Königssprüche* provide a series of instructions that are particularly relevant for those who interact with the king and depend on his favor for their well-being.

4.3.1.2 The Community

The thematic progression of the royal institution accords with the nuanced development of various themes concerning the individual in the community. Solomon 1B reinforces specific themes and develops particular topics that receive a superficial treatment in Proverbs 10–15.[121] The thematic development of the material is apparent in several topics throughout Proverbs 16:1–22:16. Among these topics, the sub-collection's treatment of character, communication, and wealth evince a thematic movement in the material.

Solomon 1B elaborates on the importance of character in a variety of ways. On the one hand, the sub-collection promotes basic virtues introduced in Proverbs 10–15. Several sayings illustrate the social significance of a person's character by describing its effect on the community: the wicked, violent person causes communal destruction (16:29; cf. 1:10–19; 4:10–19; 10:6) and brutalizes his neighbor (21:10), while the righteous acts on behalf of the community (21:26). On the other hand, the sub-collection exhibits a movement away from the conduct and consequences of particular character types to a description of the

---

119   See T. L. Forti, *Animal Imagery in the Book of Proverbs* (VTSup 118; Leiden: Brill, 2008), 58–62.

120   The images of spring rain, dew, and a growling lion are used in reference to YHWH elsewhere in the Old Testament (e.g., Deut 11:14; 33:28; 1 Kgs 17:1; Hos 5:14; 6:3; 13:7–8; Hag 1:10; Zech 8:12; 10:1), thus strengthening the interrelationship between Yahweh and the king in the sapiential perspective. For a discussion of these images in Proverbs 10–15, see Brown, "The Pedagogy of Proverbs 10:1–31:9," 163.

121   Brown, "The Pedagogy of Proverbs 10:1–31:9," 158.

concrete qualities these characters embody.[122] This movement is evident in the
sayings concerning the righteous and the wicked. These appellations occur less
frequently in Solomon 1B.[123] However, when they appear, the righteous and the
wicked are typically associated with the virtue of justice (cf. 17:15, 26; 19:28;
21:15):[124]

שֹׁחַד מֵחֵיק רָשָׁע יִקָּח	A wicked person accepts a bribe from the bosom
לְהַטּוֹת אָרְחוֹת מִשְׁפָּט	to divert the paths of justice. (Prov 17:23)
שְׂאֵת פְּנֵי־רָשָׁע לֹא־טוֹב	To show favoritism to the wicked is not good,
לְהַטּוֹת צַדִּיק בַּמִּשְׁפָּט	so that the righteous is thrust aside from justice.
	(Prov 18:5)
שֹׁד־רְשָׁעִים יְגוֹרֵם	The violence of wicked people drags them away,
כִּי מֵאֲנוּ לַעֲשׂוֹת מִשְׁפָּט	because they refuse to do justice. (Prov 21:7)

While the theme of justice is attested in Proverbs 10–15 (12:5; 13:23), the motif is
given particular attention in Solomon 1B.[125] The righteous and the wicked are
portrayed as individuals in positions of power. They punish the innocent, flog
officials (17:26), and influence the judicial process. In the main, the righteous and
the wicked are depicted as magistrates whose disposition toward justice is the
primary determinant of their character. The righteous sustain the social order
through their impartial execution of justice, while the wicked subvert the social
order through their partiality (17:23; 18:5), preference for evil (21:7), and
perversion of the judicial system (17:26). Whereas Solomon 1A evaluates the
conduct and consequences of the individual's lifestyle through general virtues,
Solomon 1B assesses the individual's character through the judicial sphere.[126] In
so doing, Solomon 1B exhibits a move from the abstract qualities of individual
character types to the concrete, legal virtues they exemplify.[127]

The thematic movement between the sub-collections is also evident with
respect to their treatment of communication. Solomon 1B reinforces various
dialogical principles presented in the Proverbs 10–15. Several aphorisms describe

---

122 Brown, "The Pedagogy of Proverbs 10:1–31:9," 160.
123 While the righteous/wicked (צַדִּיק/ רָשָׁע) appear in antithetical parallelism thirty times in Proverbs
      10–15 (10:3, 6, 7, 11, 24, 25, 28; 11:8, 10, 23; 12:3, 5, 7; 13:5, 9, 25; 14:19; 15:28, 29), the pair
      occurs only four times in Proverbs 16:1–22:16 (17:15; 18:5; 21:12, 18). When the adjectives צַדִּיק
      and רָשָׁע are employed independently of one another, צַדִּיק appears six times (17:26; 18:10, 17;
      20:7; 21:15, 26) and רָשָׁע occurs eleven times in the latter half of the collection (16:4, 12; 17:23;
      18:3; 19:28; 20:26; 21:4, 7, 10, 27, 29).
124 Brown, "The Pedagogy of Proverbs 10:1–31:9," 160.
125 Brown, "The Pedagogy of Proverbs 10:1–31:9," 160.
126 Brown, "The Pedagogy of Proverbs 10:1–31:9," 160.
127 Brown, "The Pedagogy of Proverbs 10:1–31:9," 160.

the individual and communal implications of proper and improper speech (e.g., 16:28, 30; 17:20; 18:7; cf. 10:11, 21; 11:9; 13:2; 14:3). Other sayings highlight the inherent power of the tongue (18:21; cf. 12:18, 25), the forensic significance of dishonest speech (19:5, 9, 28; 21:28; cf. 12:17; 14:5, 25), the effects of deceptive discourse (17:4, 7; 19:22; 21:6; cf. 10:18; 12:19; 14:25), and the value of silence (17:27, 28; 21:23; cf. 10:19; 11:12; 13:3).[128] These principles receive comparable attention in each sub-collection. However, Proverbs 16:1–22:16 emphasizes a particular aspect of communication that is mentioned only briefly in the initial compilation: the significance of elocution.[129] While the importance of articulate speech is presented in Proverbs 10–15 (15:2), the subject commands greater consideration in Solomon 1B:

לַחֲכַם־לֵב יִקָּרֵא נָבוֹן		The wise of heart will be called "Discerning,"
וּמֶתֶק שְׂפָתַיִם יֹסִיף לֶקַח		and sweetness of lips increases persuasiveness.
		(Prov 16:21)

לֵב חָכָם יַשְׂכִּיל פִּיהוּ	23	The heart of the wise causes his mouth to be prudent,
וְעַל־שְׂפָתָיו יֹסִיף לֶקַח		and on his lips he adds persuasiveness.[130]
צוּף־דְּבַשׁ אִמְרֵי־נֹעַם	24	Pleasant words are a honeycomb,
מָתוֹק לַנֶּפֶשׁ וּמַרְפֵּא לָעָצֶם		sweet to the soul and healing to the bones.
		(Prov 16:23–24)

Together, these aphorisms are incorporated in a subunit that describe the social benefits of prudent speech (16:20–24).[131] The competent speaker procures communal admiration (16:21) and nourishes the people through his prudence (16:22), while the judicious communicator provides a sweet, soothing balm for his interlocutors (16:24) and increases persuasiveness through his sagacious speech. The discourse unit demonstrates that judicious speech is not only marked by

---

128 For Brown, the virtues of silence and listening are dominant in Solomon 1A, but "scarcely mentioned" in Solomon 1B. He argues that the only reference to these virtues within Solomon 1B is found in Proverbs 17:28 ("The Pedagogy of Proverbs 10:1–31:9," 161). However, he fails to account for other aphorisms within Solomon 1B that address the virtues of listening and silent/reticent speech either explicitly (17:27; 19:27; 21:23) or implicitly (e.g., 18:6, 7, 13).

129 Brown, "The Pedagogy of Proverbs 10:1–31:9," 161–62.

130 Several scholars emend וְעַל to וּבַעַל, with the sense "a master of speech" (Scott, *Proverbs, Ecclesiastes: Introduction, Translation, and Notes*, 105; McKane, *Proverbs: A New Approach*, 490). This emendation is reasonable, but unnecessary, for the phrase יֹסִיף לֶקַח in 16:21b seems to carry the same sense in 16:23b.

131 The unit is bound together through words related to speech (אִמְרֵי, פֶּה, מוּסָר, שְׂפָתַיִם, יִקָּרֵא, דָּבָר) as well as intellectual vocabulary (מַשְׂכִּיל, לַחֲכַם־לֵב, נָבוֹן, שֵׂכֶל, מוּסָר, יֹסִיף לֶקַח). See Alonso Schökel and J. Vilchez, *Proverbios*, 341; Garrett, *Proverbs*, 157; Heim, *Like Grapes of Gold*, 217–20; Waltke, *Proverbs: Chapters 15–31*, 28–30.

restraint, kindness, and silence, but also by eloquence.[132] Solomon 1B builds on the dialogic virtues delineated in Solomon 1A and accentuates the significance of elocution—a virtue accessible to many, but particularly relevant to those responsible for teaching others.

The discourse of wealth and poverty constitutes an additional topic that exhibits a thematic development between the sub-collections. Solomon 1B affirms the economic values presented in Proverbs 10–15 and elaborates on their significance. Several sayings address the virtue of generosity (22:9; cf. 11:15) and matters of social justice (17:5; 21:23; 22:2, 16; cf. 14:31),[133] while others highlight the dangers involved in financial dealings (17:18; 20:16; cf. 11:15).[134] However, in contrast to Proverbs 10–15, Solomon 1B identifies the inherent risks involved in economic relationships through palpable, concrete descriptions. The sub-collection clarifies the economic risks associated with surety practices through a depiction of the payment required from the financial guarantor (20:16), and exposes the social effects of economic exploitation through the repressed condition of the destitute debtor (22:7). In addition, the composition enhances the economic discourse of Proverbs through a series of social observations related to the rich and the poor. Within Solomon 1B, wealth is a source of security (18:11a; cf. 10:15) and accompanies a life of virtue (21:20; 22:4; cf. 15:6), while poverty gives rise to disdain (18:23) and social abandonment (19:4b; 7). However, wealth is also an ephemeral substance with limited value when it is acquired by deceit or compared with the profit of virtue (18:11b; 20:17; 21:6; cf. 11:4, 18, 28). In contrast to Solomon 1A, the tension between the value of wealth and the importance of virtue is minimized in Solomon 1B. While the former collection describes poverty as a distressing condition, the latter promotes poverty over certain character traits:[135]

טוֹב שְׁפַל־רוּחַ אֶת־עֲנָיִּים	Better to be humble with the poor[136]
מֵחַלֵּק שָׁלָל אֶת־גֵּאִים	than to divide the spoil with the proud. (Prov 16:19)

---

132 Brown, "The Pedagogy of Proverbs 10:1–31:9," 161. In addition to the theme of eloquence, Brown also gives particular attention to the subject of honest speech in Solomon 1B ("The Pedagogy of Proverbs 10:1–31:9," 161).

133 Brown, "The Pedagogy of Proverbs 10:1–31:9," 162.

134 Though Brown discusses the issue of wealth and poverty within the first Solomonic collection, he does not address the theme of business ethics and its subsequent development in Solomon 1B.

135 Brown, "The Pedagogy of Proverbs 10:1–31:9," 162.

136 The Ketib reads עֲנִיִּים ("poor"), while the Qere reads עֲנָוִים ("lowly, afflicted"). While the ancient versions and several scholars follow the Qere (e.g., LXX, Vulg., Targ, Plöger, Sprüche Salomos, 194; Murphy, Proverbs, 118 n. 19a.; Waltke, Proverbs: Chapters 1–15, 23), the Ketib is preferred, for the virtue of humility is articulated by the phrase שְׁפַל־רוּחַ ("lowly of spirit"), making the Qere reading tautological. See Heim, Like Grapes of Gold, 216 n. d.; Sandoval, The Discourse of Wealth and Poverty, 132 n. 40.

טוֹב־רָשׁ הוֹלֵךְ בְּתֻמּוֹ	Better is a poor person who walks in his integrity
מֵעִקֵּשׁ שְׂפָתָיו וְהוּא כְסִיל	than one with twisted lips, for he is a fool.[137] (Prov 19:1)
תַּאֲוַת אָדָם חַסְדּוֹ	A person's desire is his kindness;[138]
וְטוֹב־רָשׁ מֵאִישׁ כָּזָב	and it is better to be poor than a liar. (Prov 19:22)
נִבְחָר שֵׁם מֵעֹשֶׁר רָב	Repute is more desirable than great riches;
מִכֶּסֶף וּמִזָּהָב חֵן טוֹב	grace is better than silver and gold. (Prov 22:1)

These aphorisms indicate a significant development in the discourse on wealth and poverty. The comparative sayings integrate ethical principles with economic rhetoric in order to demonstrate that virtue, even if accompanied by poverty, is more valuable than material wealth accompanied by vice.[139] The economic principles delineated in Solomon 1B modify the fiscal aphorisms in the first compilation to provide a more elaborate description of economic ethics. In so doing, they temper both the advantages of wealth and the culpability of poverty by promoting virtue over material resources.[140]

In view of the didactic development and thematic emphases of the material, Solomon 1B exhibits a series of courtly concerns. The composition situates character within the judicial sphere, describes the significance of elocution, and illuminates the value of virtue over wealth to provide the noble youth with a more sophisticated vision of the world. In general, the sayings assume an addressee familiar with the court, liable to judicial exploitation, dependent on the art of elocution, and in need of a framework through which to assess particular values. They delineate a series of principles that are accessible to many, but particularly relevant to those in positions of power.

---

137 This aphorism is not found in the LXX. Several Hebrew manuscripts as well as the Targum and Syriac versions read דְּרָכָיו ("his ways") rather than שְׂפָתָיו ("his lips"). However, this emendation is unnecessary, for it appears the reading is an attempt to harmonize the aphorism with Proverbs 28:6 and facilitate a suitable parallel to הוֹלֵךְ in verset A. See Whybray, *Proverbs*, 275–76; J. Hausmann, *Studien zum Menschenbild*, 89; Waltke, *Proverbs: Chapters 15–31*, 87–88 n. 7.

138 The first stich is ambiguous and difficult to translate, for the term חֶסֶד is a homonym meaning "loyalty, love, benevolence" as well as "shame, disgrace" (*HALOT* 1:336). The LXX reads "income" (תְּבוּאָה) rather than "desire" (תַּאֲוָה), but this emendation does not provide a suitable parallel to verset B. While חֶסֶד may denote "shame, disgrace" (14:34; 25:10), the traditional sense of the word is preferable (McKane, *Proverbs: A New Approach*, 532–33; Plöger, *Sprüche Salomos*, 226; Garrett, *Proverbs*, 172 n. 366; Meinhold, *Die Sprüche*, 2:323; Waltke, *Proverbs: Chapters 15–31*, 92). Nonetheless, both interpretations of חֶסֶד are possible.

139 Sandoval, *The Discourse of Wealth and Poverty*, 133. For an analysis of the functional and rhetorical significance of the "better-than" saying (*Tôb-Spruch*), see G. E. Bryce, "'Better'-Proverbs: An Historical and Structural Study," *The Society of Biblical Literature One Hundred Eighth Annual Meeting: Book of Seminar Papers* (2 vols.; ed. L. C. McGaughy; Missoula: Society of Biblical Literature, 1972), 2:343–54; G. S. Ogden, "The 'Better'-Proverb (Tôb-Spruch), Rhetorical Criticism, and Qoheleth," *JBL* 96 (1977): 489–505.

140 Brown, "The Pedagogy of Proverbs 10:1–31:9," 162.

4.3.1.3 The Family

Together with the monarchy and the community, the composition's treatment of the domestic unit also evinces a thematic development. On the one hand, the sub-collection reinforces particular domestic values presented in Solomon 1A. Several sayings outline the importance of parental instruction (16:20; 17:21, 25; 19:8, 16, 18, 20, 26–27; 22:6, 15), and the significance of a responsible, cohesive domestic group (17:1, 2, 6, 13; 18:22; 19:13, 14; 20:7; 21:9, 12, 19). On the other hand, the sub-collection introduces the addressee to a relational dimension that receives exiguous treatment in the initial compilation: friendship.[141] While several sayings in Proverbs 10–15 address the issue of friendship from a socio-economic angle (14:20–21; cf. 19:4, 6, 7), Solomon 1B assesses the theme through an interpersonal perspective (cf. 16:28):[142]

מְכַסֶּה־פֶּשַׁע מְבַקֵּשׁ אַהֲבָה	The person who covers a transgression
מְבַקֵּשׁ אַהֲבָה	is one who searches for love,
וְשֹׁנֶה בְדָבָר מַפְרִיד אַלּוּף	but whoever repeats a matter separates intimate friends.[143] (Prov 17:9)

בְּכָל־עֵת אֹהֵב הָרֵעַ	A friend is one who loves at all times,
וְאָח לְצָרָה יִוָּלֵד	and a brother is born for adversity. (Prov 17:17)

אִישׁ רֵעִים לְהִתְרֹעֵעַ	A person with many friends may be ruined,[144]
וְיֵשׁ אֹהֵב דָּבֵק מֵאָח	but there is a friend who sticks closer than a brother.[145] (Prov 18:24)

---

141 Brown, "The Pedagogy of Proverbs 10:1–31:9," 158–59.

142 In contrast to Solomon 1A, Brown demonstrates that Solomon 1B gives considerable attention to the topic of friendship. However, he fails to notice that the theme of friendship is addressed implicitly in Solomon 1A (14:20–21). Since the topic of friendship is introduced in Solomon 1A, it seems that the latter half of the collection elaborates on the motif in two principal ways: (1) it expands the social purview of Solomon 1A by giving explicit attention to the topic of friendship, and (2) it addresses the theme through an interpersonal perspective rather than a socio-economic perspective. See Brown, "The Pedagogy of Proverbs 10:1–31:9," 159.

143 The LXX reads שָׂנֵא ("hate") rather than שֹׁנֶה ("repeat") to provide a more precise parallel to אַהֲבָה. Emendation is unnecessary, however, for שֹׁנֶה forms a suitable contrast with מְכַסֶּה־פֶּשַׁע ("covers a transgression").

144 Several LXX manuscripts, the Syriac version, and the Targum read יֵשׁ ("there are") rather than אִישׁ ("a person"). The Sebirin cites 2 Samuel 14:19 and Micah 6:10 to substantiate the change, but אֵשׁ is defective in these verses, making it difficult to justify the emendation in Proverbs 18:24. In addition, scholars have offered various proposals for the verbal root of לְהִתְרֹעֵעַ. While the verb may derive from the root רוע ("to shout, chatter") or represent a Hithpael from the root רעה ("to befriend"), it appears to be a Hithpolel infinitive construct from the root רעע, meaning "makes himself to be broken" or "made to be broken" with an unidentified agent (Gemser, Sprüche Salomos, 216; Heim, Like Grapes of Gold, 249; Waltke, Proverbs: Chapters 15–31, 87). Though each

Solomon 1B gives particular attention to matters of friendship and outlines the contours of interpersonal relations that extend beyond the immediate family unit.[146] Within the composition, true friendship is portrayed as a valuable asset. In contrast to a relative who is born into familial solidarity, a friend chooses covenant fraternity and manifests his devotion through constant commitment in times of adversity (17:17; 18:24). Outside of the domestic unit, friendship is presented as a key relationship. Blood may be thicker than water, but faithful companions are an essential interpersonal resource in the sapiential perspective. Solomon 1B builds on the domestic principles delineated in Solomon 1A and expands the socio-religious purview of the sapiential world through its nuanced development of amicable relationships.[147]

In addition to the topic of friendship, Solomon 1B elaborates on the issue of marital relations.[148] In contrast to Solomon 1A, the compendium does not focus on the attractive virtues or social value of an ideal, marriageable maiden (11:16a; 12:4; 14:1); instead, Solomon 1B describes marital relations from two distinctive perspectives. On the one hand, the composition examines the value of a noble wife from a theological perspective (18:22; 19:14). Within the sapiential worldview, a prudent wife is not acquired through wealth or physical charms; she is a gift from God (19:14b). Similar to the one who finds Woman Wisdom (8:35), the one who finds a wife obtains favor from YHWH (18:22).[149] On the other hand, Solomon 1B describes the disposition of an ignoble wife from a domestic perspective. The contentious wife is the subject of several aphorisms (19:13; 21:9, 19), each of which incorporates the *Leitwort* מִדְיָן ("quarrels, controversies") with vivid images that illuminate the domestic environment produced by this unscrupulous woman.[150] The domicile of the disputatious wife is portrayed as a chaotic domain of perpetual dissention (19:13). In view of this tumultuous environment, the corner of a roof and the arid desert offer more peace and security than the maelstrom of the home (21:9, 19). These striking images provide an impressionistic portrait of a tempestuous domestic environment that stands in contradistinction to the irenic home of a noble wife. Whereas a virtuous wife

---

option is possible, the final proposal is preferred, for it retains the sense of the *Hithpolel* and forms a suitable contrast with verset B by highlighting the nature of enduring friendship.

145   Since the participle אֹהֵב ("one who loves") is paired with רֵעַ in verset A, verset B is rendered "there is a friend who sticks closer to a brother."

146   Brown, "The Pedagogy of Proverbs 10:1–31:9," 159.

147   Brown, "The Pedagogy of Proverbs 10:1–31:9," 159.

148   Though Brown mentions the aphorisms concerned with "identifying the ideal wife" in Solomon 1B (18:22; 21:9, 19), he does not describe the development of the topic. See Brown, "The Pedagogy of Proverbs 10:1–31:9," 159.

149   For an analysis of the comparable elements in Proverbs 18:22 and 8:35, see Snell, *Twice-Told Proverbs*, 39.

150   For an analysis of the comparable elements in Proverbs 21:9, 19, 25:24, see Snell, *Twice-Told Proverbs*, 41, 58.

procures social honor, enhances the status of her husband, and forms the foundation of a stable home (11:16; 12:4a; 14:1a), a contentious wife produces personal torment and domestic conflict. While the virtuous wife embodies a gracious disposition (11:16a), the contentious wife possesses a malevolent disposition. Far from being a divine gift, a cantankerous wife is a domestic curse. Together, these aphorisms widen the moral purview of the sapiential material; they move from an anthropological assessment of a virtuous wife to a theological assessment of her value, and from the socio-moral consequences associated with an unscrupulous wife to the domestic environment produced by a contentious wife. In so doing, they enhance the moral vision of marriage preparation delineated in Solomon 1A and provide the noble youth with a more elaborate framework through which to seek a suitable companion.

In light of the thematic movement apparent in the sayings concerning the monarchy, the community and the family, it seems that the anthropocentric dimension of the world presented in Proverbs 16:1–22:16 supplements the bipolar perspective of Solomon 1A to provide a more nuanced portrait of the world. The sub-collection strengthens the ethical principles presented in Proverbs 10–15 and develops particular themes that receive a superficial treatment in Solomon 1A. The same is true with regard to the theocentric dimension of Proverbs 16:1–22:16. The theocentric dimension exhibits a thematic movement that promotes specific principles presented in the anthropological perspective and advances certain motifs that do not find precedent in Solomon 1A.

4.3.2 The Theocentric Dimension of Solomon 1B

In comparison to Solomon 1A, Proverbs 16:1–22:16 contains a variety of YHWH sayings.[151] In general, these sayings address comparable themes and express the same theological sentiments as those in Proverbs 10–15. Several aphorisms describe YHWH's attitude and actions toward certain characters (16:5, 7; 18:10; cf. 10:3; 11:20; 12:2; 15:8, 9), while others highlight YHWH's value judgment on commercial practices (20:10, 23; cf. 11:1), his involvement in economic activities (16:11), and his role in administering retribution and reward in matters of social justice (17:5; 19:17; 22:2; cf. 14:31; 15:25). These theological assessments are not novel, for they are also articulated in Solomon 1A. However, Solomon 1B assesses three particular topics from a theological perspective that either receive a brief treatment in Proverbs 10–15 or do not find expression in the initial compositional unit.

The first is the issue of justice. As noted above, the theme of justice commands greater attention in Solomon 1B. The material not only evaluates an

---

151   Brown, "The Pedagogy of Proverbs 10:1–31:9," 164.

individual's character through the judicial sphere, but it also presents the divine perspective on justice:[152]

מַצְדִּיק רָשָׁע	The one who justifies a wicked person
וּמַרְשִׁיעַ צַדִּיק	and the one who condemns a righteous person—
תּוֹעֲבַת יְהוָה גַּם־שְׁנֵיהֶם	both of them are an abomination to YHWH. (Prov 17:15)

עֲשֹׂה צְדָקָה וּמִשְׁפָּט	To do righteousness and justice
נִבְחָר לַיהוָה מִזָּבַח	is more desirable to YHWH than sacrifice. (Prov 21:3)

These aphorisms complement the sayings concerning justice in the anthropocentric frame of reference. The first is cast in the judicial sphere (17:15), while the second is set in a cultic context (21:3). The former aphorism describes YHWH's abhorrence of magistrates who pervert the divine ideal by acquitting the wicked and convicting the innocent; the latter echoes a traditional Old Testament ideal (cf. 1 Sam 15:22; Hos 6:6; Mic 6:6–8): conformity with the divine character takes precedence over compliance with cultic ritual, for YHWH prefers ethical conduct to cultic actions (20:25; 21:3; cf. 15:8, 29). Together, the aphorisms offer a theological assessment of justice and provide a divine rationale for the principles delineated in the anthropological dimension of the discourse.

YHWH's transcendence constitutes the second theme that is accentuated in Solomon 1B.[153] While YHWH's sovereignty is introduced in Solomon 1A (15:3, 11), the topic commands greater attention in Proverbs 16:1–22:16 (cf. 16:4; 21:2):

כָּל־דַּרְכֵי־אִישׁ זַךְ בְּעֵינָיו	All the ways of a person [seem] pure in his own eyes,
וְתֹכֵן רוּחוֹת יְהוָה	but YHWH is the one who weighs motives. (Prov 16:2)

מַצְרֵף לַכֶּסֶף וְכוּר לַזָּהָב	The crucible is for silver, and the furnace for gold,
וּבֹחֵן לִבּוֹת יְהוָה	but YHWH is the one who tests hearts. (Prov 17:3)

נֵר יְהוָה נִשְׁמַת אָדָם	The spirit of a person is the lamp of YHWH,[154]
חֹפֵשׂ כָּל־חַדְרֵי־בָטֶן	searching all of his innermost parts. (Prov 20:27)

---

152 Though Brown discusses the role of God in Solomon 1B, he does not address the issue of divine justice. Instead, he examines Proverbs 17:15 and 21:3 in his investigation of character. See Brown, "The Pedagogy of Proverbs 10:1–31:9," 160.

153 In addition to divine justice, Brown does not address the theme of divine transcendence in his investigation. Rather he focuses on the issue of divine inscrutability within Solomon 1B (see below).

154 Fichtner (BHS) emends נֵר ("lamp") to נֹצֵר ("protects, keeps"), citing Proverbs 24:12 and Job 7:20 as grounds for the proposal. Loewenstamm argues that נֵר is a participle derived from the root ניר, and renders the aphorism "God ploughs and examines the soul of man, searches all the innermost chambers" (S. E. Loewenstamm, "Remarks on Proverbs xvii 12 and xx 27," VT 37 [1987]: 121–24). These proposals are possible but unnecessary, for they disrupt the parallelism

The belief that YHWH is sovereign and transcendent is fundamental to the sapiential perspective, for YHWH's ability to exact just rewards and punishments is contingent on his divine character and supreme power. Several aphorisms highlight the omnivision (5:21; 15:3, 11; 22:12), the omnipotence (16:4), and omniscience of YHWH (16:2; 17:3; 20:27; 21:2) to emphasize his absolute insight into every aspect of an individual's life.[155] In so doing, the sayings underline YHWH's ability to evaluate each person in a just manner, and warn the addressee of his accountability to the divine sovereign.

The third theme that is given particular expression in Solomon 1B is related to the second: the supremacy of divine wisdom over human wisdom.[156] In contrast to Solomon 1A (14:12), Proverbs 16:1–22:16 contains a series of sayings concerning the limitations of wisdom and the inscrutability of YHWH's active involvement in the human world (cf. 19:21; 20:24; 21:1):

לְאָדָם מַעַרְכֵי־לֵב וּמֵיְהוָה מַעֲנֵה לָשׁוֹן	To human beings belong the plans of the heart; but the answer of the tongue is from YHWH. (Prov 16:1)
לֵב אָדָם יְחַשֵּׁב דַּרְכּוֹ וַיהוָה יָכִין צַעֲדוֹ	The heart of a person plans his way, but YHWH establishes his step. (Prov 16:9)
בַּחֵיק יוּטַל אֶת־הַגּוֹרָל וּמֵיְהוָה כָּל־מִשְׁפָּטוֹ	The lot is hurled into the bosom, but its every verdict is from YHWH. (Prov 16:33)

אֵין חָכְמָה	30	There is no wisdom,
וְאֵין תְּבוּנָה		and no understanding,
וְאֵין עֵצָה לְנֶגֶד יְהוָה		and no counsel before YHWH.
סוּס מוּכָן לְיוֹם מִלְחָמָה	31	A horse is prepared for the day of war,
וְלַיהוָה הַתְּשׁוּעָה		but the victory belongs to YHWH. (Prov 21:30–31)

Together, these aphorisms reveal a tension between the anthropocentric and theocentric perspectives of the sentence literature, that is, a tension between human wisdom and divine action. The anthropocentric dimension emphasizes the necessity of wisdom, counsel, and prudent planning for national, military, and personal success (11:14; 15:22; 20:18).[157] However, the theocentric frame of reference highlights YHWH's freedom and ability to enforce his sovereign will independent of human cooperation or action. Here YHWH directs all things, from the intellect of the king (16:1, 10; 21:1), to the decisions of the court (16:10,

---

between נֵר ("lamp") and חפשׂ ("to search out") by incorporating images from other spheres of reality (Waltke, *Proverbs: Chapters 15–31*, 149 n. 127).

155   Boström, *The God of the Sages*, 146.
156   Brown, "The Pedagogy of Proverbs 10:1–31:9," 164.
157   Brown, "The Pedagogy of Proverbs 10:1–31:9," 164.

33), to intentions of the commoner (19:21; 20:24). The theocentric dimension assesses human wisdom from a distinct angle and tempers the anthropocentric approach by giving wisdom a divine orientation.[158] It does not negate the value of human wisdom; rather it places human wisdom into perspective by evaluating it on the vertical, religious level instead of the horizontal, social level. In so doing, the theocentric frame of reference supplements the anthropocentric. It demonstrates that human success is not only dependent on counsel (11:14; 15:22; 20:18), but also subject to YHWH's sovereign purposes, and exhorts the addressee to commit his plans to YHWH to ensure their efficacy (16:3).

To summarize, the theocentric dimension of Proverbs 16:1–22:16 reinforces several principles presented in both Solomon 1A and the anthropocentric frame of reference. However, the compositional unit also gives particular expression to theological themes that receive only a brief mention in Proverbs 10–15. Solomon 1B moves from YHWH's attitude and actions toward certain character types, his value judgment on economic activities, and his active role in the retribution-reward schema to a theological assessment of justice, YHWH's transcendence, and the limitations of human wisdom. The composition's treatment of these theological motifs exhibits a thematic development in the material. The compilation supplements the socio-religious ethos of Solomon 1A through its nuanced development of particular themes and its perceptive treatment of specific theological issues. The religious sayings present a complex portrait of the world that seeks to balance YHWH's active participation in the affairs of the individual with the individual's personal responsibility.

4.3.3 Section Conclusion

In light of the rhetorical characteristics and thematic emphases of Proverbs 16:1–22:16 it is not surprising that many scholars have recognized the courtly character of the sub-collection.[159] The compendium contains a series of explicitly royal sayings that describe the ideal, wise king and provide those who interact with and depend on the monarch with invaluable instruction for appropriate behavior in his presence. In addition, the collection assesses the individual's character

---

158   Brown, "The Pedagogy of Proverbs 10:1–31:9," 164.

159   Skladny, *Die ältesten Spruchsammlungen in Israel*, 41–46; Hermisson, *Studien zur israelitischen Spruchweisheit*, 76; Humphreys, "The Motif of the Wise Courtier in the Book of Proverbs," 183; Pleins, "Poverty in the Social World of the Wise," *JSOT* 37 (1987): 61–78; idem, *The Social Visions of the Hebrew Bible*, 456; Perdue, *Wisdom Literature: A Theological History*, 44–45. In addition to those who recognize the courtly flavor of the sub-collection, others suggest that Proverbs 10:1–29:27 is the product of the court. For example, Clifford argues that the book of Proverbs reflects the group identity of royal scribes in service of the king ("The Community of the Book of Proverbs," 281–93), while Fox concludes that the sentence literature was composed by an elite circle of men who served both royal and state interests (*Proverbs 10–31*, 500).

through the judicial sphere, highlights the significance of elocution, and gives particular expression to social justice and kindness toward the marginalized.[160] Together, these features give the collection a distinct, courtly flavor and suggest the primary addressee consists of those preparing for positions of power.

The rhetorical characteristics and thematic emphases of Solomon 1B also indicate a formal development in the material. The move from a static, bipolar world conveyed through terse antithetical sayings to a dynamic, variegated frame of reference expressed through diverse poetic forms heightens the complexity of the discourse.[161] The thematic movement of the discourse corresponds to the formal development of the material. The anthropocentric and theocentric dimensions of Proverbs 16:1–22:16 affirm the socio-religious values delineated in Solomon 1A and emphasize particular themes that receive a brief treatment in Proverbs 10–15.[162] In so doing, Solomon 1B sharpens the socio-religious purview of the proverbial world and provides the addressee with a more comprehensive portrait of reality. The composition moves from the general to the specific, from elementary wisdom to intermediate wisdom.

The formal and thematic progression of the material is significant, for this movement provides a grid through which to assess the identity of the addressee. In conjunction with the prologue and Solomon 1A, Solomon 1B elaborates on previous material and emphasizes particular themes to provide the addressee with specific advice that corresponds with his interests, aspirations, and temptations (16:1–22:16). Indeed, the thematic movement of the sentence literature coincides with the development of the addressee; it modulates specific themes that bring the character of the noble youth into sharper focus. This focus is clarified through the subsequent collections. In order to ascertain the courtly nature of the material and the distinct identity of the noble youth, it is necessary to explore the ethos of the instructions in Proverbs 22:17–24:34. This is the text to which we now turn.

---

160 Malchow, "Social Justice in the Wisdom Literature," 120–23; M. R. Sneed, "The Class Culture of Proverbs: Eliminating Stereotypes," *SJOT* 10 (1996): 296–308; W. J. Houston, "The Role of the Poor in Proverbs," 237.

161 Brown, "The Pedagogy of Proverbs 10:1–31:9," 164.

162 Brown, "The Pedagogy of Proverbs 10:1–31:9," 158.

4.4 Vocational Wisdom: Sayings of the Wise 1 and Sayings of the Wise 2 (22:17–24:34)

Similar to the first Solomonic collection, Proverbs 22:17–24:34 advances particular themes presented in the previous material through two distinct, instructional units. The first is marked off by a titular interjection (22:17) and a formal exordium (22:17–21), while the second is delineated by a conventional sub-title that serves as an introductory statement (24:23).[163] These headings do not function as formal titles to independent works;[164] rather they initiate a transition that bridges the terse aphorisms of the first Solomonic collection with the instructions that follow. This transitional function is apparent in each of the headings. The first heading is cast in the form of direct address and contains both a first-person and a second-person pronominal suffix with no immediate antecedents (22:17). The absence of antecedents suggests that the royal speaker in the prologue reasserts himself in the subsequent instructions.[165] That is, the admonitions in Proverbs 22:17–24:22 resume the direct, instructional discourse of Proverbs 1–9, with the speaker's pointed exhortations to the son (23:15, 19, 22, 26; 24:13, 21). The second heading places the particle גַּם in conjunction with the phrase לַחֲכָמִים (24:23; cf. 22:17). In so doing, the titular interjection links the introductory statement with Proverbs 22:17 and identifies the collection as an appendix to the Sayings of the Wise 1, rather than an independent, isolated compilation.[166] Together, the instructions in Proverbs 22:17–24:34 are integral to

---

163   See Kitchen, "Proverbs and Wisdom Books of the Ancient Near East," 80.

164   Many recognize that Proverbs 22:17 marks the introduction of a new unit, for the material moves from a series of general aphorisms to direct, instructional discourse. However, the shift in the material does not serve as valid grounds for emending the MT to conform to the LXX. Several scholars emend דִּבְרֵי חֲכָמִים הַט אָזְנְךָ וּשְׁמַע דְּבָרָי to הַט אָזְנְךָ וּשְׁמַע דְּבָרֵי חֲכָמִים in order to produce a formal title for the discourse unit (H. Gressmann, "Die neugefundene Lehre des Amen-em-ope und die vorexilische Spruchdichtung Israels," *ZAW* 42 (1924): 274; Scott, *Proverbs, Ecclesiastes: Introduction, Translation, and Notes*, 135; McKane, *Proverbs: A New Approach*, 369; Plöger, *Sprüche Salomos*, 262; Lelièvre and Maillot, *Commentaire des Proverbes II*, 117, 118; Murphy, *Proverbs*, 169 n. 17.a.; Fox, *Proverbs 10–31*, 707–08). This emendation is possible, but unnecessary for two reasons. First, the MT makes sense as it stands, for the expression דִּבְרֵי חֲכָמִים can serve as the object of the verb הַט. Second, the LXX is an unreliable source for structural emendations. The editorial transitions of the LXX differ drastically from the MT, as they omit the title in 10:1 and conceal the attributions to Agur (30:1) and Lemuel (31:1). While the titular interjection in 22:17a introduces a discrete discourse unit, it does not function as a formal title to an independent work. Together with its parallel couplet, Proverbs 22:17 asserts that the speaker has adopted the דִּבְרֵי חֲכָמִים and assimilated them into his instructional repertoire (דְּעְתִּי) for the benefit of his addressee. See A. Luc, "The Titles and Structure of Proverbs," *ZAW* 112 (2000): 252–53; Waltke, *Proverbs: Chapters 15–31*, 217–18 n. 106.

165   Brown, "The Pedagogy of Proverbs 10:1–31:9," 165; Waltke, *Proverbs: Chapters 1–15*, 23–24.

166   See Römheld, *Die Weisheitlehre im alten Orient*, 6; Whybray, *Wealth and Poverty in the Book of Proverbs*, 75.

the book of Proverbs. They affirm particular themes presented in the sentence literature and elaborate on their significance through the instructional form.

The form, tone, and topoi of the instructions in Proverbs 22:17–24:34 are comparable to ancient Near Eastern didactic texts in general and the prologue in particular.[167] In effect, the instructions resume the direct pedagogical discourse of the prologue and preserve the discourse setting presented in the introductory lectures. The speaker assimilates the "words of the wise" and directs his admonitions toward the son (23:15, 19, 26; 24:13, 21), using terms and phrases reminiscent of the instructional material in the prologue.[168] The correspondence between the materials in Proverbs 22:17–24:34 and the lectures in Proverbs 1–9 is given particular expression in the preamble of the first instructional unit (22:17–21). Here the speaker employs pedagogical language from the lectures and imitates the rhetorical scheme of the introductory discourses,[169] opening with a formal exhortation followed by a motivation (22:17–18). Moreover, the speaker declares the purpose of his instructions and specifies the intended addressee of the material (22:19–21). The goal of the admonitions is to inculcate trust in YHWH (22:19) and provide the addressee with "knowledgeable advice" (22:20) in order to transform him into a reliable speaker for those who commission him (22:21). While the text does not clarify the identity of שֹׁלְחֶיךָ, these seem to be a group of important, powerful people who expect reliable reports from their counselors or emissaries.[170] When this purpose statement is read in light of the discourse setting of the book, it appears the royal speaker admonishes the "son"

---

167 For the history of interpretation concerning the relationship between Proverbs 22:17–24:22 and Amenemope, see R. N. Whybray, *The Book of Proverbs: A Survey of Modern Study* (History of Biblical Interpretation Series 1; Leiden: E. J. Brill, 1995), 6–14, 78–84. In addition, for recent discussion on the relationship between Amenemope and Proverbs 22:17–24:22, see P. Overland, "Structure in the Wisdom of Amenemope and Proverbs," in *"Go to the Land I Will Show You": Studies in Honor of Dwight W. Young* (ed. J. Coleson and V. Matthews; Winona Lake: Eisenbrauns, 1996), 275–91; N. Shupak, "The Instruction of Amenemope and Proverbs 22:17–24:22 from the Perspective of Contemporary Research," in *Seeking out the Wisdom of the Ancients: Essays Offered to Honor Michael V. Fox on the Occasion of His Sixty-Fifth Birthday* (ed. R. L. Troxel et al.; Winona Lake: Eisenbrauns, 2005), 203–20; M. V. Fox, "The Formation of Proverbs 22:17-23:11," *WO* 38 (2008): 22–37; idem, *Proverbs 10–31*, 753–69.

168 For example, the phrase שְׁמַע בְּנִי/בָנִים (1:8; 4:1, 10; 5:7; 7:24; 8:32; 23:19), the command to "be wise" (6:6; 8:33; 23:19), the theme of the "way" (e.g., 1:15, 31; 2:8, 20; 3:6, 17; 4:11; 5:21; 6:23; 9:6, 15; 23:19, 26), the father and mother's instruction (1:8; 6:20; 23:22), as well as the injunction to "get wisdom" (4:5, 7; 23:23) are presented in both Proverbs 1–9 and 22:17–24:22.

169 The phrase הַט אָזְנֶךָ ("incline your ear," 22:17) occurs in 4:20; 5:1, 13; שְׁמַע ("hear," 22:17) is scattered throughout the introductory lectures (e.g., 1:8; 4:1; 5:7; 7:24); Proverbs 22:17b is comparable to Proverbs 2:2b, and the sense of "keep them [the words of the wise] in your belly" in 22:18 is captured by Proverbs 4:21; 6:21; 7:3.

170 A. Cody, "Notes on Proverbs 22,21 and 22,23b," *Bib* 61 (1980): 423. Also see W. Bühlmann, *Vom Rechten Reden und Schweigen: Studien zu Proverbien 10–31* (OBO 12; Göttingen: Vandenhoeck & Ruprecht, 1976), 171–211, 327–28, who concludes that carefully crafted speech plays an important role in official circles.

to accept his instructions so that he may be a trustworthy courtier, diplomat, or ambassador to those who send him. The preamble to the instructional material enhances the discourse setting of the prologue and brings the character of the noble youth into sharper focus; it identifies the speaker, addressee, and purpose of the admonitions, and provides a dialogical context through which to assess the material.

Together with the previous collections, Proverbs 22:17–24:34 reinforces particular themes and elaborates on their significance through a series of personalized commands.[171] In general, the instructions present traditional themes pertaining to character, interpersonal relations, communication, and the domestic unit. Several admonitions move from the abstract qualities of the wicked, the fool, and the hothead to concrete council on how to deal with the intractable (22:24–25; 23:9, 17–18; 24:1–2, 7, 19–20, 24–25).[172] Other instructions build on the virtues associated with proper and improper speech and emphasize the value of honest, reliable discourse (23:16; 24:26, 28–29).[173] Moreover, the initial instructional unit outlines the fundamental role of the domestic unit in the appropriation of wisdom (23:13–14, 15–16, 22–25; cf. 24:3–4). The admonitions and didactic sayings reflect on virtues described in the previous collections and reinforce their significance though the instructional form.[174] They inculcate trust in YHWH and form courtly character through a series of specific topics (22:17–21). Among these topics, the monarchy and matters of social justice receive considerable attention. These themes not only develop particular virtues introduced in the previous material, but they also illuminate the identity of the addressee.

The portrait of the king in Proverbs 22:17–24:34 is comparable to Solomon 1B. The king is intimately associated with YHWH and depicted as the agent who preserves socio-moral order through just retribution (24:21–22). This transcendent portrayal of the king constitutes the final admonition in the first instructional unit, warning the addressee of the dangers involved in political collusion.[175] In the main, the admonition promotes a proper attitude toward both

---

171 For a more detailed discussion of the formal features of Proverbs 22:17–24:34, see Brown, "The Pedagogy of Proverbs 10:1–31:9," 165.

172 For a discussion of the role of the fool and the wicked within the instructional units, see Brown, "The Pedagogy of Proverbs 10:1–31:9," 168.

173 See Brown, "The Pedagogy of Proverbs 10:1–31:9," 167.

174 Brown, "The Pedagogy of Proverbs 10:1–31:9," 167.

175 The ancient versions render Proverbs 24:21b in a variety of ways. The crux of the verset is the participle שׁוֹנִים ("those who change"). The LXX reads μηθετέρῳ αὐτῶν ἀπειθήσῃς ("do not disobey either of them [Yahweh and the king]"), which is followed by Fichtner (*BHS*). This reading is questionable, however, for the LXX exhibits significant freedom in its rendering of the following motivation (24:22). Some attempt to solve the problem by reading שׁנה (intransitive) with a transitive sense ("to be different") in order to argue that the verb includes the notion of "rebels" or "detractors" (Vulg., Meinhold, *Die Sprüche*, 2:408). However, this

YHWH and the king and provides the "son" with a paradigm for socio-political success.

The focus on proper attitudes and actions toward the king is given particular expression throughout Proverbs 22:17–24:22. The instructional unit builds on the general principles concerning the royal institution presented in the previous material and emphasizes specific matters related to royal service.[176] The speaker implores the addressee to embody proficiency and skill in his duties so he may serve kings who covet his talents (22:29). He describes wisdom's capacity to equip the individual with pertinent counsel for engineering successful military strategies (24:5–6) and highlights the importance of self-control and discretion through proper banquet etiquette (23:1–3).[177] The speaker employs the banquet scene to outline the significance of restraint and propriety, for the ruler's dinner invitation and table fare present the addressee with an opportunity for success or failure, as temperance or voracity can affect both the ruler's disposition and the addressee's career for good or ill.[178] Together, these admonitions and didactic sayings develop themes concerning the value of wisdom and appropriate conduct before kings by emphasizing specific issues related to royal service. They assume an addressee with significant social standing and accentuate the advantages of competence, wisdom, and self-control to provide the noble youth with a fundamental paradigm for socio-political success.[179]

In addition to the material's emphasis on royal affairs, the theme of social justice receives considerable attention in the composition. On the one hand, the instructional unit affirms particular themes introduced in the sentence literature: the admonitions underscore the inherent dangers associated with surety practices

---

rendering seems to stretch the sense of the verb too far. Others associate שׁנה with the Arabic terms *saniya* ("to be high, exalted") and *sn'* ("great honor") to render the participle "those of high rank" (D. W. Thomas, "The Root *snh* = *sny* in Hebrew, II," *ZAW* 55 [1937]: 174–76; Driver, "Problems in 'Proverbs,'" 189; McKane, *Proverbs: A New Approach*, 249). This seems to be the sense of שׁנים in Proverbs 24:21b. When the verset is read in light of 24:21–22, the admonition does not imply that officials are inherently opposed to Yahweh and the king; rather it assumes that their hunger for power jeopardizes their vocational and personal well-being (Waltke, *Proverbs: Chapters 15–31*, 279–80 n. 45). In the main, the exhortation and admonition encourage the son to respect legitimate authority and avoid those involved in political collusion.

176 Brown, "The Pedagogy of Proverbs 10:1–31:9," 168.

177 For the theme of table manners with superiors in the ancient oriental instructional tradition, see "The Instruction Addressed to Kagemni" (*AEL* 1:59–60); "The Instruction of Ptahhotep" (*AEL* 1:65); "The Instruction of Amenemope" (*AEL* 2:160); Sir 31:12–32:13.

178 Waltke, *Proverbs: Chapters 15–31*, 238.

179 In view of the composition's concern with royal service, Brown suggests "the implied reader is more than simply a lowly subject; instruction is given on the proper way of waging war, highlighting the need for an 'abundance of counselors,' as if the reader were a military official in training (24:5-6; cf. 15:22)" (Brown, "The Pedagogy of Proverbs 10:1–31:9," 168). In addition, Fox concludes that "the pupil being addressed is, ideally, headed for the royal service (Prov 22:29) and will *be* a man of rank (*Proverbs 10–31*, 752).

(22:26–27), the ephemeral nature of wealth (23:4–5), and the socio-religious significance of judicial impartiality (24:23b–25). On the other hand, the instructions emphasize YHWH's concern for the marginalized and advance the discourse of wealth and poverty through specific character defects.[180] Several instructions focus on YHWH's role in the judicial sphere. The speaker attempts to protect the legal rights of the disenfranchised through a description of YHWH's personal involvement on behalf of the marginalized (22:22–23, 28; 23:10–11; 24:10–12). The instructions are given a distinct theological rationale, as YHWH's involvement on behalf of the weak provides a theological basis for social justice.[181] These admonitions assume an addressee in a position of judicial authority, for they seek to curb oppressive activities within the forensic sphere. The critical nature of these injunctions is not surprising, for the protection of the weak and the vulnerable was the fundamental responsibility of the royal institution throughout the ancient oriental world.[182]

Together with the composition's theological concern with the legal rights of the disenfranchised, several instructions describe the threat of poverty through deficient moral character.[183] These admonitions outline the socio-economic consequences associated with an excessive lifestyle in order to promote the virtues of moderation and industry over indulgence (21:17; 23:20–21, 29–35). The speaker warns the "son" of the dangers that accompany unrestrained eating and drinking through the images of יַיִן and בָּשָׂר. In the ancient oriental world, these commodities were luxury goods—products restricted typically to the economic elite.[184] In the main, the speaker seems to incorporate these images to advocate restraint and to censure particular vices that entice his addressee. In conjunction with the admonitions concerning social justice, the discourse on wealth and poverty particularizes the character of the "son." These instructions assume a powerful, affluent addressee and present a series of socio-moral principles to curb specific vices and promote particular virtues that correspond with the circumstances and temptations of the "son."[185]

In short, the instructions in Proverbs 22:17–24:34 contain a variety of courtly elements. The instructional materials resume the direct, pedagogical discourse of the prologue and enhance the discourse setting of the document. Here the royal voice delivers a series of admonitions and didactic sayings, which inculcate trust

---

180 Brown, "The Pedagogy of Proverbs 10:1–31:9," 167.
181 Boström, *The God of the Sages*, 108; Brown, "The Pedagogy of Proverbs 10:1–31:9," 167.
182 See "The Instruction of Ptahhotep" (*AEL* 1:64); "The Instruction Addressed to King Merikare" (*AEL* 1:100); "The Instruction of King Amenhemet I for His Son Sesostris I" (*AEL* 1:136); "The Eloquent Peasant" (*AEL* 1:172); "The Instruction of Amenemope" (*AEL* 2:150–55); "Counsels of Wisdom" (*BWL*, 101–103); Fensham, "Widow, Orphan, and the Poor in Ancient Near Eastern Legal and Wisdom Literature," 161–71. Also see n. 63.
183 Brown, "The Pedagogy of Proverbs 10:1–31:9," 167.
184 Sandoval, *The Discourse of Wealth and Poverty*, 170.
185 Habel, "Wisdom, Wealth, and Poverty Paradigms in the Book of Proverbs," 42–45.

in YHWH and dependable discourse in those who may function as courtiers, diplomats, or ambassadors to powerful patricians (22:17–21). The discourse setting of the instructions coincides with the subject matter of the compendia. The collections emphasize specific, practical matters related to royal affairs, ranging from table etiquette with superiors (23:1–3) and appropriate conduct toward the king to the value of wisdom for engineering military strategies (24:5–6; cf. 22:29). In addition, the instructions highlight the socio-religious significance of justice toward the disenfranchised (22:22–23, 28; 23:10–11; 24:10–12) and promote moderation through products principally consumed by the economic elite (21:17; 23:20–21, 29–35). The attention given to these themes suggests the material is directed toward those in positions of power and influence within society, for the admonitions assume an addressee that has access to the court, judicial authority, sufficient social standing to dine at a ruler's table, and the means to consume luxurious commodities.[186] Similar to the prologue, it seems the speaker incorporates certain features and emphasizes particular themes that coincide with the interests, aspirations, and temptations of his addressee. In so doing, he provides the noble youth with a fundamental paradigm for socio-political success.

4.5 Conclusion

On the whole, Proverbs 10–24 constitutes a complex compendium of wisdom. The constituent compositions build on the inchoate ethical vision of the prologue to produce an impressionistic portrait of the wise life. Solomon 1A (10:1–15:33) highlights the principal features of certain character types introduced in the prologue and serves as a foundational building block for the thematic development that takes place throughout the successive sections of the book. The general, bifurcated worldview and the facile description of the character-consequence connection outline the fundamental structure of the socio-moral order and supply the addressee with an elementary paradigm of the wise life. Solomon 1B enhances the socio-religious purview of the sapiential world through its interest in subjects that receive a superficial treatment in Proverbs 10–15, while the instructional material (22:17–24:34) elaborates on themes delineated in the sentence literature through the instructional form.[187] Together, the material exhibits both a formal and a thematic development that brings the character of the addressee into sharper focus.

---

186   Bryce, *A Legacy of Wisdom*, 153; Habel, "Wisdom, Wealth, and Poverty Paradigms in the Book of Proverbs," 42–45.

187   See Brown, "The Pedagogy of Proverbs 10:1–31:9," 155–69.

The first Solomonic collection elaborates on the introductory lectures and interludes through two distinct compositional units. Solomon 1A places the individual in relation to the perceived social environment in order to outline the value of particular virtues, perspectives, and principles. This unit delineates the communal orientation of the royal institution, the social significance of character, communication, and socio-economic justice, and the importance of the domestic unit. In view of this general worldview, Solomon 1B moves from a static, bipolar world conveyed through terse antithetical sayings to a dynamic, variegated frame of reference expressed through diverse poetic forms.[188] The composition gives particular attention to the royal institution to provide those who interact with the king with invaluable instruction for appropriate behavior in his presence. In addition, the collection assesses the individual's character through the judicial sphere, highlights the significance of elocution, and offers a framework through which to assess the value of virtue over social status. In general, these features assume an affluent, powerful addressee, accustomed to the court, susceptible to judicial exploitation, and responsible for instructing others.

The instructional material (22:17–24:34) resumes the direct discourse of the prologue and enhances the discourse setting of the document. Here the speaker seeks to inculcate trust in YHWH and dependable discourse in those who may function as courtiers, diplomats, or ambassadors to powerful patricians. He gives particular expression to royal affairs and matters of social justice to provide the addressee with a fundamental paradigm for socio-political success. The formal and thematic progression of the material is a significant feature of the work, for this movement brings the identity of the addressee into sharper focus. While the individual aphorisms in the collections describe a variety of traditional virtues accessible to many, the discourse setting of the document and the thematic development of the material clarify the identity of the addressee and affirm his courtly nature.

In short, Proverbs 10–24 incorporates aphorisms that reflect on the anthropocentric and theocentric dimensions of the world to offer a fundamental moral vision that (re)constructs the addressee's perception of reality and shapes his character. The discourse begins with a basic, facile description of the cosmos and then exhibits a thematic movement that develops particular themes that correspond with the interests of the addressee. This thematic development continues in Proverbs 25–29. These collections not only elaborate on topics introduced in the previous material, but they also enhance the identity of the noble youth. In order to assess the courtly nature of the collections and the thematic development of the material, it is necessary to explore the materials in Proverbs 25–29. This is the task to which we now turn.

---

188   Brown, "The Pedagogy of Proverbs 10:1–31:9," 164.

Chapter 5

Advanced Wisdom: Proverbs 25–29

The second Solomonic collection plays a significant role in the book of Proverbs. Similar to the first Solomonic collection (10:1–15:33; 16:1–22:16), the compendium evinces a formal and thematic development. The compilation heightens the artistic sophistication of the material and enhances the anthropocentric and theocentric dimensions of the sapiential worldview;[1] it refines particular topics and reflects on inchoate motifs in the previous collections to shape the character of its distinct addressee. In so doing, the compendium moves from the general to the specific, from intermediate wisdom to advanced wisdom.

In order to identify the nature and function of the second Solomonic collection, it is necessary to examine the moral and literary character of Proverbs 25–29. To accomplish this goal, this chapter will explore the thematic emphases and formal progression of the material, highlighting the courtly features of the collection. We will begin by examining the context of the second Solomonic collection, and then assess the ethos of the individual compositions within Proverbs 25:1–29:27.

5.1 The Courtly Context of Proverbs 25:1–29:27

The editorial superscription (25:1) and pronounced shift in form, tone, and style distinguishes the second Solomonic collection from the Words of the Wise 2 (24:23–34). Though the composition incorporates forms attested in previous material, the compilation has a distinctive character. In contrast to the previous titles (1:1), sub-titles (10:1; 24:23), and titular interjections (22:17), the heading in Proverbs 25:1 alludes to the compositional history of the collection. The superscription may be divided into two parts: the authorial attribution (25:1a) and the compositional ascription (25:1b). In the first, the editorial superscription attributes the material to Solomon (25:1a). The particle גַּם assumes the existence of the previous Solomonic titles (1:1; 10:1), suggesting the editor considered the

---

1   Brown, "The Pedagogy of Proverbs 10:1–31:9," 169–75.

compilation as an addendum to the preceding collections, particularly Proverbs 10:1–22:16.[2] As noted in chapter three, the attribution does not imply that Solomon was the "author" of the collection in the modern sense of the term. Whether the authorial ascription constitutes a case of honorary or attributed authorship, the editor(s) of the material placed the work in the Solomonic tradition and preserved the voice of the royal speaker of the document.

The compositional ascription (25:1b) identifies the editors of the compendium and describes the manner in which the material was collated. This subordinate clause has given rise to several questions concerning the character of the collectors and the extent of their literary activities.[3] On the one hand, Hezekiah's men may be courtiers, clerics, or clerks to whom the king assigned the task of filtering and assembling Israel's traditional sapiential lore.[4] On the other hand, they may constitute a general, social conglomerate of literate individuals, who were either members of the multifaceted scribal establishment or supporters under the king's patronage.[5] These proposals are equally plausible, but they provide no definitive diagnosis of Hezekiah's men, for the size of the group and the social status of each member are unknown.[6] The same is true with regard to

---

2   For a discussion of whether the compilation was produced as an independent document before its incorporation into the book of Proverbs, see Scott, "Wise and Foolish, Righteous and Wicked," 164; Weeks, *Early Israelite Wisdom*, 42–43; idem, *Instruction and Imagery*, 39–40. See also Snell, *Twice-Told Proverbs*, 81. Snell suggests that Proverbs 25–29 is the oldest compilation in the book.

3   Both the LXX and the Syriac versions render אַנְשֵׁי ("men") as "friends." This construal may provide insight into Hezekiah's relationship with those responsible for the compilation of the material, but the differences are too minor to suggest that they represent two independent traditions. See M. Carasik, "Who Were the 'Men of Hezekiah' (Proverbs XXV 1)?" *VT* 44 (1994): 299 n. 33.

4   McKane, *Proverbs: A New Approach*, 577; Whybray, "The Sage in the Israelite Royal Court," 137–38; Carasik, "Who Were the 'Men of Hezekiah'," 298; Blenkinsopp, *Sage, Priest, Prophet*, 32–33; Fox, "The Social Location of the Book of Proverbs," 239; idem, *Proverbs 10–31*, 778; Clifford, *Proverbs*, 8; idem, "The Community of the Book of Proverbs," 281.

5   Scott, *Proverbs, Ecclesiastes*, 21; Fishbane, *Biblical Interpretation in Ancient Israel*, 24–33; Weeks, *Early Israelite Wisdom*, 45; Loader, "Wisdom by (the) People for (the) People," 232–33.

6   Two recent proposals concerning the men of Hezekiah deserve specific comment. Carasik postulates that through inner-biblical exegesis a later glossator formulated Proverbs 25:1 based on Hezekiah's association with wisdom and the "germinal linguistic links" between Proverbs 25 and 2 Kings 18–19. For Carasik, Eliakim the steward, Shebna the scribe, and the senior priests constitute the "men of Hezekiah," rather than an academy of sages (Carasik, "Who Were the 'Men of Hezekiah'," 298). On the whole, Carasik's proposal that Proverbs 25:1 represents a literary phenomenon that is intimately related to the historical superscriptions in the Psalms is stimulating, but many of his inner-biblical parallels are unconvincing. Perdue argues that the plural construct אַנְשֵׁי ("men of") refers to a particular social position held by those who were members of the king's administration. More specifically, he identifies the men of Hezekiah as "court scribes who had the responsibility of assembling, archiving, and transmitting proverbs and other literary materials that were part of the ideology supporting the reign of the monarch" (L. G. Perdue, *The Sword and the Stylus: An Introduction to Wisdom in the Age of Empires* [Grand

the literary activities of Hezekiah's men. The ascription describes their compositional duties through the term הֶעְתִּיקוּ. The verb occurs several times in the *Hiphil* (e.g. Gen 12:8; 26:22; Job 9:5; 32:15) with the general sense "to cause to move." In the present case, it appears הֶעְתִּיקוּ conveys the notion of moving something from one place to another, hence collecting.[7] These men must have been literate, but the extent of their "collecting" activity is unclear. In light of the vivid similes and artistic poems presented in the collection, the verb may suggest that these individuals played a formative role in the selection, arrangement, and modification of the material they had at their disposal. Nonetheless, this conjecture remains hypothetical, for it extends the semantic range of הֶעְתִּיקוּ to include a technical sense that is not extent in its normal usage.[8] In general, the superscription claims that the compilation represents a series of "Solomonic" aphorisms that were collected by a group of literate individuals in close association with Hezekiah. While the specific identity of the collectors and the nature of their compositional activities are uncertain, the royal provenance of the compendium is clear.

The authorial attribution and compositional ascription situate the collection firmly within a courtly context. The royal provenance of the composition is reinforced by the preponderance of sayings concerning the king and his court (25:2–10; 28:15–16; 29:4, 12, 14). The collection assesses the character of the king from a variety of angles and emphasizes various matters associated with royal service, ranging from court etiquette and judicial proceedings to the significance of righteous rule. However, the royal cast and political flavor of the material do not mean the aphorisms were produced in the court. Many of the sayings reflect the ethos of the people and address topics or themes that belong to everyday life.[9] Based on the general character of the second Solomonic collection, it seems reasonable to assume a popular background for some of the material. This assumption does not necessarily conflict with the view that the court or some guild of literati associated with the court was responsible for the compilation and redaction of the material, for these settings are not mutually exclusive: one refers to the oral origin of a saying, the other to its literary origin.[10] Although the sayings and admonitions of the second Solomonic collection appear to arise from a variety of social settings and periods, the authorial attribution and compositional

---

Rapids: Eerdmans, 2008], 95). This proposal is reasonable, but Perdue fails to demonstrate that the construct אַנְשֵׁי designates a scribal position.

7   H. Schmoldt renders the verb "moved from one place to another" ("עתק," *TDOT* 11:456). The LXX, Syriac, and Targum render the verb "to copy, write down," while the Vulgate reads "to transfer." In each case, the compositional activities of Hezekiah's men are vague.

8   Weeks, *Early Israelite Wisdom*, 44.

9   See Naré, *Proverbes salomoniens et proverbes mossi, passim*; Golka, *The Leopard's Spots*, 16–34.

10   See Murphy, "Wisdom—Theses and Hypotheses," 37.

ascription situate the literary compilation of the material in the royal court.[11] The court may not have functioned as the architect of the individual proverbs; rather it may have served as the loom through which both popular and courtly aphorisms were incorporated into the sapiential tradition.[12]

The title of the second Solomonic collection is significant, for it provides the only direct indication of a connection between the wisdom tradition and the royal court. The superscription situates the composition of the work in the court or among individuals in close association with the court and presents a concrete context through which to assess the variety of sayings in the second Solomonic collection. This courtly compendium reiterates and modulates several topics introduced in the first Solomonic collection (10:1–22:16) through two distinct, homologous compositional units: Solomon 2A (25:1–27:27) and Solomon 2B (28:1–29:27).[13] The form, content, and style of each sub-collection reinforce this division. On the one hand, the former compositional unit is characterized by emblematic proverbs, admonitions, the virtual absence of Yahweh sayings, and a predominance of vivid images, expressed through similes and metaphors. On the other hand, the latter subunit contains a preponderance of antithetical sayings (cf. Prov 10–15), a pronounced ethical and religious tone, and a dearth of similes and metaphors. The formal texture of the second Solomonic collection suggests that the compilation is comparable to the first Solomonic collection and may be divided into two distinct subunits, with Proverbs 27:23–27 serving as a janus between the sub-collections.[14] However, in contrast to the first Solomonic collection, the structure of Proverbs 25–29 is rather conspicuous, as the compilation consists of larger proverbial units.[15] In order to assess the degree to which these constituent units correspond with the courtly discourse setting of the prologue in general and the compositional context of Proverbs 25:1 in particular, it is necessary to examine the ethos and didactic movement of the materials in Proverbs 25–29.[16] We will begin with Proverbs 25:2–27:27, and then explore the aphorisms in chapters 28:1–29:27.

---

11   Golka, *The Leopard's Spots*, 16, 112.

12   Fox, *Proverbs 10–31*, 500.

13   There is a virtual consensus that Proverbs 25–29 consists of two discrete compositional units. See Skladny, *Die ältesten Spruchsammlungen in Israel*, 55–66; Barucq, *Le livre des Proverbes*, 193–97; Plöger, *Sprüche Salomos*, 293; Meinhold, *Die Sprüche*, 2:415; Whybray, *The Composition of the Book of Proverbs*, 120–21; Leliévre and Maillot, *Commentaire des Proverbes II*, 185; Murphy, *Proverbs*, 189; Waltke, *Proverbs: Chapters 1–15*, 25.

14   See Malchow, "A Manual for Future Monarchs," 358; Waltke, *Proverbs: Chapters 1–15*, 25.

15   See Skladny, *Die ältesten Spruchsammlungen in Israel*, 56; G. E. Bryce, "Another Wisdom-'Book' in Proverbs," *JBL* 91 (1972): 145–57; idem, *A Legacy of Wisdom*, 135–55; Malchow, "A Manual for Future Monarchs," 353–60; Van Leeuwen, *Context and Meaning in Proverbs 25–27, passim*.

16   In contrast to Brown, the present study examines the thematic development of the material by giving particular attention to the individual compositional units within the second Solomonic collection.

5.2 The Sapiential Vision of Solomon 2A (25:2–27:27)

Solomon 2A (25:2–27:27) exhibits a variety of literary features that suggest a tightly woven, artistically crafted collection. The compendium incorporates several poetic devices—paronomasia, catchwords, verbal repetition, chiasmus, and inclusio—that link individual sayings together, form coherent groupings, and mark the literary parameters of a given unit. These principles of arrangement are employed throughout Solomon 2A to form several discrete, compositional segments (25:2–28; 26:1–12, 13–16, 17–28; 27:1–22, 23–27). The character, content, and tenor of each unit deserve specific comment.

5.2.1 Proverbs 25:2–27

The first compositional sub-unit (25:2–27) considers a variety of themes within a coherent literary structure. The diverse sayings and admonitions scattered throughout the discourse unit are bound together by catchwords, thematic parallels, and paronomasia. In addition, the material is cast within a double chiastic inclusio:

A כָּבֹד ... חֵקֶר (25:2)
   B בְּצֶדֶק ... רָשָׁע (25:5)
   B¹ צַדִּיק ... רָשָׁע (25:26)
A¹ כָּבוֹד ... חֵקֶר (25:27b)

These chiastic inclusios outline the macro-structure of the piece. The first serves as a formal envelope around the discourse unit; the second reinforces the poetic parameters of the piece.[17] Together, these chiastic inclusios delineate the contours of the compositional unit and provide a hermeneutical grid through which to read and assess the intermediate aphorisms.

The hermeneutical significance of the composition's formal frame should not be underestimated. The double inclusios not only define the parameters of the discourse unit, but they also present the fundamental themes of the composition.[18] The initial couplets and concluding verses share specific terms and convey particular themes that enhance the meaning and pragmatic significance of

---

17   While the opposition of רָשָׁע and צֶדֶק is common in the sentence literature in general and Proverbs 10–15 in particular, within Proverbs 25–27 the comparison occurs only in 25:5 and 25:26 (Van Leeuwen, *Context and Meaning*, 71). See also Bryce, "Another Wisdom-'Book' in Proverbs," 154. Bryce argues that the inversion of the terms in their subsequent application in the discourse unit highlights their structural significance within the composition.

18   Bryce, "Another Wisdom-'Book' in Proverbs," 151; Van Leeuwen, *Context and Meaning*, 63; Waltke, *Proverbs: Chapters 15–31*, 309; Wilke, *Kronerben der Weisheit*, 235–36.

the intermediate aphorisms. Within the composition's formal frame (25:2–5, 26, 27b), the discourse may be divided into two sections: vv. 6–15 and vv. 16–27.[19] Two poetic features reinforce this division. On the one hand, each subsection closes with an independent, isolated aphorism (25:15, 27).[20] In contrast to the string of proverbial pairs in each compositional unit, these single aphorisms address particular themes introduced in the initial segment (25:2–5) and mark the parameters of each subsection. On the other hand, the second constituent section (25:16–27) is framed by a chiastic inclusio. The repetition of דְּבַשׁ ("honey") and אכל ("to eat") binds the introductory admonition (25:16) with the concluding saying (25:27a), thus strengthening the structural scheme of the piece and the coherence of the composition as a whole.[21] In general, the discourse consists of three principal sections. The initial segment presents the two primary themes of the discourse unit (25:2–5), the second (25:6–15) and third (25:16–27) elaborate on these motifs through a series of sayings and admonitions.[22]

The initial unit (vv. 2–5) consists of two couplets: vv. 2–3 and vv. 4–5. The former is bound together by the catchwords מְלָכִים and חקר; the latter is linked by the anaphoric verb הגה. Together, these couplets describe the fundamental structure of the socio-religious world and the conflict that threatens to undermine the divine order—themes that constitute the interpretive grid through which the aphorisms in the discourse unit are to be read.[23] The first couplet underscores the hierarchical arrangement of the socio-religious realm (25:2–3). The proverbial pair addresses the multifaceted relationship among God, kings, and subjects through their respective prerogatives and glory.[24] On the one hand, God obtains glory by concealing his complex, mysterious activity within the cosmos (25:2a). On the other hand, kings obtain glory by executing their royal prerogatives, searching out

---

19   Bryce, "Another Wisdom-'Book' in Proverbs," 151; Van Leeuwen, *Context and Meaning*, 61–64; Waltke, *Proverbs: Chapters 15–31*, 309–37. For alternative proposals concerning the structure of Proverbs 25:2–28, see Plöger, *Sprüche Salomos*, 298–305; J. Krispenz, *Spruchkompositionen im Buch Proverbia*, 103–06; Meinhold, *Die Sprüche*, 2:416–34; idem, "Der Umgang mit dem Feind nach Spr 25,21f. als Maßstab für das Menschein," in *Alttestamentlicher Glaube und Biblische Theologie: Festschrift für Horst Dietrich Preuß zum 65. Geburtstag* (ed. J. Hausmann and H.-J. Zobel; Stuttgart: Kohlhammer, 1992), 248–50. Each of these structural proposals is viable. However, in light of the double chiastic inclusio as well as the syntagmatic and paradigmatic patterns in the composition, Proverbs 25:2–27 seems to be a coherent discourse consisting of three primary sections: vv. 2–5, vv. 6–15, and vv. 16–27.

20   Van Leeuwen, *Context and Meaning*, 65; Waltke, *Proverbs: Chapters 15–31*, 309.

21   Bryce, "Another Wisdom-'Book' in Proverbs," 153–55; Van Leeuwen, *Context and Meaning*, 71–72.

22   Bryce, "Another Wisdom-'Book' in Proverbs," 151; Van Leeuwen, *Context and Meaning*, 63; Waltke, *Proverbs: Chapters 15–31*, 309.

23   Bryce, "Another Wisdom-'Book' in Proverbs," 151; idem, *A Legacy of Wisdom: The Egyptian Contribution to the Wisdom of Israel*, 142; Van Leeuwen, *Context and Meaning*, 72.

24   Van Leeuwen, *Context and Meaning*, 73.

and investigating human motives and actions in judicial matters (25:2b).[25] Both God and kings receive glory among their subjects for their inscrutable actions, covering and uncovering enigmatic matters respectively. The king investigates matters pertaining to the state, but he cannot plumb the depths of God's equivocal acts in the cosmos. In the same way, the king's subjects cannot penetrate the profundity of his unfathomable לֵב (25:3; 2 Sam 14:17, 20; 19:27).[26] The couplet describes the intimate relationship between the glory and actions of God and kings and underscores the fundamental difference between them. God conceals and reveals his transcendent activities in the cosmos: no one, not even the king, is able to apprehend his inscrutable actions. Kings investigate various matters in the terrestrial realm; while their wisdom, motives, and intentions are transparent to God (21:1), they remain obscure to their subjects. The initial couplet presupposes a socio-religious hierarchy based on wisdom, authority, and power.[27] In so doing, it describes the fundamental, socio-religious structure of the cosmos and establishes the limits appropriate to each constituent party.

The second couplet (25:4–5) is related to the first. The proverbial pair moves from the king's investigation of matters pertaining to the state to his elimination of wicked officials. In so doing, the proverbial pair enhances the royal prerogatives of the king and describes the second major theme of the compositional unit, viz., the fundamental conflict threatening the socio-religious order.[28] This conflict is expressed through vivid, metallurgical imagery. The metallurgical image forms the basis for the analogy between the individual sayings, as the process of refining and casting silver to fashion a resilient vessel

---

25   While the terms חָקַר ("to search out") and דָּבָר ("word, thing, matter") carry different nuances depending on context, it seems they have a judicial sense in Proverbs 25:2b. This judicial sense is not surprising, for the terms have a technical, legal connotation elsewhere in the Old Testament (e.g., 18:17; 28:11; Job 29:16). Together, חָקַר and דָּבָר highlight the inscrutable nature of the king's wisdom—wisdom that is manifested in his judicial abilities (cf. 1 Sam 18:13; 2 Sam 14:17; 1 Kgs 3:28; 10:3). See Van Leeuwen, *Context and Meaning*, 76–77; idem, "The Book of Proverbs," *NIB* 5:217; Clifford, *Proverbs*, 222; Waltke, *Proverbs: Chapters 15–31*, 311.

26   The juxtaposition of the cosmic merism (25:3a) with the impenetrable nature of the king's heart/mind (25:3b) highlights the king's glory and places him in close relationship with God. The images and expressions used to describe the king in verse 3 are employed elsewhere in the Old Testament with reference to God. The conventional merism, "heavens and earth," is used typically to describe God's sovereign control over the cosmos (30:1–4; Job 26:14; 38:1–39:30; Ps 115:15–16), while the expression אֵין חֵקֶר ("there is no searching") is used only of God's acts in creation and judgment (Job 5:9; 9:10; Ps 145:3; Isa 40:28). By applying these images and expressions to kings, verse 3 associates the king's glory and wisdom with that of God's and connects Israelite royal ideology with creation theology. See Van Leeuwen, *Context and Meaning*, 74–76.

27   Van Leeuwen, *Context and Meaning*, 73.

28   Van Leeuwen, *Context and Meaning*, 77.

corresponds with the judicial responsibilities of the royal institution.[29] As the metallurgist must extract the dross from silver ore to produce a durable vessel (25:4),[30] so the king must depose wicked officials from their bureaucratic posts to establish an enduring dynasty (25:5; cf. 16:12). Together, the aphorisms form a general, socio-religious paradigm that pervades every facet of human life.[31] They describe the inevitable conflict the righteous and the wicked to provide invaluable advice for both kings and courtiers: the king must eliminate wicked officials to promote righteousness and secure his throne, while royal officials must embody the principles of justice and righteousness in their administrative duties or face expulsion from the court (cf. 14:35).[32]

The sayings and admonitions in each section of the discourse elaborate on these motifs to inculcate particular virtues and values in the addressee.[33] This thematic development is evident throughout the second section of the composition (25:6–15), which moves from the basic contours of the socio-religious world to a more detailed portrayal of its multifaceted dimensions.

The second section of the composition (25:6–15) develops the primary themes of the piece through five proverbial pairs. The first consists of an admonition followed by a motivation (25:6–7b). The proverbial pair is linked to the initial segment in general and verses 4–5 in particular by its concern with social hierarchy and life before the king (לִפְנֵי־מֶלֶךְ, 25:5a, 6a). Together, the admonition and motivation promote humility and prudence in relationships among members of the royal court. The aphorism encourages the royal official to recognize his social status and bureaucratic rank, rather than engaging in self-aggrandizement to advance his career prospects (cf. 22:29). The pair moves from a description of the general, hierarchical arrangement of the socio-religious world (25:2–3) to the fluid, authoritative structure of the royal court (25:6–7b).[34] In so doing, the proverbial pair elaborates on a primary theme of the piece and highlights a fundamental principle of the discourse: appropriate behavior in the royal court.

---

29   See Isa 1:21–26; 6:27–30; Ezek 22:18–22; K. H. Singer, *Die Metalle Gold, Silber, Bronze, Kupfer und Eisen im Alten Testament und ihre Symbolik* (FB 43; Würzburg: Echter, 1980), 83–89; Van Leeuwen, *Context and Meaning*, 77–78.

30   Fichtner (*BHS*) retroverts the LXX καθαρισθήσεται καθαρὸν ἅπαν as וְנִצְרַף כֻּלּוֹ and recommends this reading to the Masoretic text's כְּלִי לַצֹּרֵף ("a vessel for the refiner"). However, this reading is unconvincing, for it destroys the parallelism between "refiner" and "king" and restricts the metallurgical process to purification. See R. C. Van Leeuwen, "A Technical Metallurgical Usage of יצא," *ZAW* 98 (1986): 112–13.

31   Van Leeuwen, *Context and Meaning*, 63.

32   See Meinhold, *Die Sprüche*, 2:420.

33   Van Leeuwen, *Context and Meaning*, 80.

34   Van Leeuwen, *Context and Meaning*, 80.

The second proverbial pair (25:7c–8)[35] is intimately related to the third (25:9–10). These aphorisms are bound together by the catchwords רִיב (vv. 8a, 9a), רַע (vv. 8b, 9b), and פֶּן (vv. 8b, 10) as well as by their concern with social humiliation. Together, they promote particular socio-moral values associated with the legal sphere from two distinct angles.[36] On the one hand, the former pair employs optical imagery to urge the addressee to avoid impetuous litigation and safeguard his reputation (25:7c–8).[37] On the other hand, the latter proverbial pair incorporates aural imagery to encourage confidentiality (25:9–10).[38] The admonitions urge the addressee to embody discretion and reliability in judicial matters in order to avoid social ignominy and vocational ruin.[39] In effect, the addressee must value virtue over judicial success and recognize proper social boundaries, rather than engaging in another's personal affairs or divulging another's confidence to promote his political power and position. The quatrain expands the socio-religious structure of the world, as it moves from the fluid, hierarchical arrangement of the royal court to proper social boundaries between peers.[40]

The fourth proverbial pair (25:11–12) elaborates on the judicial concerns of the preceding quatrain (25:7c–10). The aphorisms are bound together by the catchword זָהָב as well as by common imagery and syntax. Together, they describe the significance of perceptive speech and amenable reproof in interpersonal matters in general and legal affairs in particular.[41] The aphorisms describe these

---

35   The Masoretes connected the relative clause אֲשֶׁר רָאוּ עֵינֶיךָ in 25:7c to וְרִיב in verse 7ab. This reading is possible, but it seems the relative clause is linked with the initial stich in verse 8, for the independent relative clause introduces the object, while verse 8a supplies its subject and predicate (P. Jouön, *Grammaire de l'hébreu biblique* [Rome: Pontifical Biblical Institute, 1947], 485, §158l; B. K. Waltke and M. O'Connor, *An Introduction to Biblical Hebrew Syntax* [Winona Lake: Eisenbrauns, 1990], 334, §19.3c). This reading eliminates the ambiguity in both verses 7 and 8 by identifying what the addressee is not to bring hastily to court. See LXX, Syr., Sym., Meinhold, *Die Sprüche*, 2:417, 421; Murphy, *Proverbs*, 188 n. 7a.; Clifford, *Proverbs*, 223.

36   While the aphorisms may pertain to private disputes, the terms רִיב and שָׁמַע, coupled with the technical, forensic terms כְּלִם and דָּבָה, suggest the admonitions refer to a formal, judicial setting (cf. Gen 37:2; Num 13:32; Deut 1:16, 17; 2 Sam 14:16–17; 1 Kgs 3:9, 11; Job 31:35; Prov 10:8; 18:13; 21:28). For a discussion of the terms, see K. W. Whitelam, *The Just King: Monarchical and Judicial Authority in Ancient Israel* (JSOTSup 12; Sheffield: JSOT, 1979), 140–42; Van Leeuwen, *Context and Meaning*, 57–58.

37   Van Leeuwen, *Context and Meaning*, 81.

38   Van Leeuwen, *Context and Meaning*, 81.

39   In conjunction with 25:6–7b, it appears the addressee of the admonitions in verses 7c–10 is a member of the royal court, since the former pertains to court protocol and the latter continues to address the audience in the second person singular.

40   Van Leeuwen, *Context and Meaning*, 81.

41   See H. J. Boecker, *Redeformen des Rechtslebens im Alten Testament* (WMANT 14; Neukirchen: Neukirchener, 1964), 45–47; I. L. Seeligmann, "Zur Terminologie für das Gerichtsverfahren im Wortschatz des biblischen Hebräisch," VTSup 16 (1967): 266; M. Weinfeld, "The Counsel of

virtues through vivid, ornamental imagery to highlight the inherent value of these principles.[42] As a sagacious decision that is delivered in the appropriate circumstance heightens its moral authority (25:11),[43] so a reproving decision that finds acceptance enhances its value (25:12). The couplet moves from an artistically crafted judgment to the reception of its implicit reproof.[44] In so doing, it underscores the importance of justice through appropriate legal decisions and rebuke—virtues that establish righteousness and cultivate proper behavior in the socio-moral sphere.

The fifth proverbial pair (25:13–14) shifts from the judicial sphere to relations with superiors.[45] This couplet is bound together by meteorological imagery and its concern with reliable discourse. The pair assesses the value of faithful communication in interpersonal relations from two angles. The initial aphorism incorporates the image of snow during the harvest season to describe reliable communication from a positive perspective (25:13).[46] Just as cold water revives the weary harvester, so a faithful messenger refreshes the נֶפֶשׁ of his master.[47] The saying develops the hierarchical concern of the composition through the intimate relationship between an emissary and those who dispatch him. In the ancient oriental world, messengers were not only privy to the personal

---

'Elders' to Rehoboam and Its Implications," *Maarav* 3 (1982): 43; Van Leeuwen, *Context and Meaning*, 82–83; idem, "The Book of Proverbs," *NIB* 5:218; Waltke, *Proverbs: Chapters 15–31*, 321.

42   While the sense of the imagery in Proverbs 25:11a is clear, the precise meaning of תַּפּוּחֵי and מַשְׂכִּיֹּות is uncertain. The former occurs five times in the Old Testament (Joel 1:12; Prov 25:11; Song 2:3, 5; 7:9; 8:5), where it denotes some sort of fruit. The latter carries several different nuances, ranging from carved, idolatrous images (Lev 26:1; Num 33:52; Ezek 8:12) to an image produced by the mind (Ps 73:7; Prov 18:11). For a discussion of the terms, see McKane, *Proverbs*, 584; M. Falk, *Love Lyrics from the Bible: A Translation and Literary Study of the Song of Songs* (Sheffield: Almond, 1982), 174; Meinhold, *Die Sprüche*, 2:424; Whybray, *Proverbs*, 364; Murphy, *Proverbs*, 189 n. 11a.; Clifford, *Proverbs*, 224. Also see Sandoval, *The Discourse of Wealth and Poverty*, 121–24.

43   The meaning of the phrase עַל־אָפְנָיו is obscure. In general, scholars render the *hapax legomenon* אָפְנָי as a dual form from אֹפֶן ("wheel") or a plural form that may be countable ("circumstances, moment") or abstract ("time"). The latter proposal is preferred, since the pointing of אָפְנָי in the MT suggests the term cannot be a form of אֹפֶן. This proposal is supported by the cognate Arabic term *iffan* ("time") and the use of בְּעִתֹּו in Proverbs 15:23. See Gemser, *Sprüche Salomos*, 91; Van Leeuwen, *Context and Meaning*, 58–59; A. Tomasino, "אֹפֶן," *NIDOTTE* 1:481; Clifford, *Proverbs*, 224; Waltke, *Proverbs: Chapters 15–31*, 304 n. 25, 320.

44   Waltke, *Proverbs: Chapters 15–31*, 320.

45   Van Leeuwen, *Context and Meaning*, 83.

46   Van Leeuwen, *Context and Meaning*, 83.

47   Several scholars speculate that the image of snow during the harvest refers to a custom in which runners would retrieve snow or ice from the mountains, transport it in jute packing, and then store it in snow houses to cool beverages or delicacies for either the harvesters or the wealthy. Whether or not this is the meaning of the aphorism, the metaphor is clear. For a discussion of the custom, see B. Lang, "Vorläufer von Speiseeis in Bibel und Orient. Eine Untersuchung von Spr 25,13," in *Mélanges bibliques et orientaux en l'honneur de M. Henri Cazelles* (ed. A. Caquot and M. Delcor; Neukirchen-Vluyn: Neukirchener Verlag, 1981), 218–32; Meinhold, *Die Sprüche*, 2:425–26; Garrett, *Proverbs*, 207; Clifford, *Proverbs*, 224; Waltke, *Proverbs: Chapters 15–31*, 322–23.

intentions and confidences of their master, but they also possessed a social status comparable to those who sent them.[48] In effect, a faithful messenger was an envoy of status, who was trusted to conduct business transactions, gather intelligence, and convey written or oral messages in accordance with his master's bidding.[49] The aphorism highlights the value of reliability in master-messenger relations,[50] and elaborates on an additional, hierarchical dimension of the socio-religious world. The second saying employs meteorological imagery to describe faithful communication from a negative perspective (25:14).[51] The picture of clouds and wind that pass without delivering promised rain is comparable to the egotistical windbag, who boasts about a gift only to defraud the expected beneficiary. When the aphorism is read in conjunction with the preceding couplet, it warns against promoting others on the basis of deceptive gifts (cf. 18:16). Together, the sayings heighten the hierarchical concerns of the piece and present both proper and improper means of socio-political success.[52]

The final saying in the initial subsection (25:15) examines the major concerns of the composition and serves as a janus between the discourse units.[53] The first colon discusses social hierarchy through relations with superiors (25:15a); the second emphasizes interpersonal conflict and its resolution (25:15b).[54] Each colon presents the paradoxical power of a particular virtue in order to enhance the principal themes of the compendium. The former colon describes the power of patience to influence social superiors. The second colon presents the capacity of a soft, tender word to alleviate hostility and resolve conflict. Together, the cola articulate the power of a patient disposition and diplomatic speech—virtues that provide the addressee with essential stratagems for dealing with social superiors and settling conflicts. They develop the primary concerns of the composition and serves as a transition to the second major segment of the discourse unit.

The second section of the composition moves from the value of restraint in matters pertaining to the royal court (25:6–15) to the significance of moderation and self-control in interpersonal relations (25:16–27). The segment elaborates on these virtues through two distinct subunits: vv. 16–22 and vv. 23–27. The former

---

48　A. D. Crown, "Messengers and Scribes: The ספר and מלאך in the Old Testament," *VT* 24 (1974): 366–70; S. A. Meier, *The Messenger in the Ancient Semitic World* (HSM 45; Atlanta: Scholars Press, 1988), 21–22, 158–59; Van Leeuwen, "The Book of Proverbs," *NIB* 5:219.

49　Crown, "Messengers and Scribes: The ספר and מלאך in the Old Testament," 366–68.

50　In addition to faithfulness, the qualities of speed, eloquence, diplomacy, and social status were fundamental features of the ideal messenger and elements that informed the selection of the messenger. See Meier, *The Messenger in the Ancient Semitic World*, 22–30.

51　Van Leeuwen, *Context and Meaning*, 83.

52　Van Leeuwen, *Context and Meaning*, 83; Waltke, *Proverbs: Chapters 15–31*, 322.

53　For the verbal and themeatic links between 25:15 and 25:2–5, see Van Leeuwen, *Context and Meaning*, 83; Garrett, *Proverbs*, 207; Waltke, *Proverbs: Chapters 15–31*, 324.

54　Van Leeuwen, *Context and Meaning*, 83.

is delineated by the chiastic inclusio אֱכֹל־שְׂנַא (vv. 16–17, 21–22);[55] the latter is linked by both weather and water imagery (25:23–26).[56] Together, these constituent sections reinforce the principal themes of the piece and provide a more nuanced description of the socio-religious world.

The initial subsection (25:16–22) addresses the significance of social propriety and various matters associated with human conflict through three proverbial units. The first assesses the value of moderation and temperance (25:16–17). The quatrain is linked by common syntax, vocabulary (פֶּן־שָׂבַע), and a concern for restraint.[57] The individual couplets describe the dangers of excess through personal consumption (25:16) and interpersonal relationships (25:17) to highlight the importance of proper limitations. As excess honey induces vomiting, so inordinate time in a neighbor's house produces conflict. In the main, the aphorisms do not proscribe the consumption of appetizing goods or promote social seclusion; rather they warn the addressee of the dangers associated with violating formal boundaries. In so doing, they develop a primary theme of the piece and widen the moral vision of the discourse.

The second unit (25:18–20) elaborates on an implicit concern of the preceding proverbial pair (25:17), viz., potential conflicts between members of the community.[58] This concern is expressed through a description of three character types, all of whom should be avoided. The first is the mendacious witness (25:18). The initial saying incorporates a series of assault weapons to describe the lethal effects of the perjurer. This aphorism enhances the judicial ethos of the composition and develops the sapiential concern with false testimony, as the saying moves from a general portrayal of the character and fate of the perjurer (12:17; 14:5, 25; 19:5; 21:28) to a vivid depiction of the devastation he inflicts on his neighbor. The second saying focuses on an unreliable friend (25:19), who is characterized as impotent and ineffective as a decaying tooth or a dilapidated foot[59]—bodily defects that disappoint and inflict pain during a time of need. The third characterization shifts from the deceptive traitor to the inept speaker (25:20). The aphorism incorporates a set of incongruous images to describe the insensitivity of the incompetent and the significance of social

---

55   Van Leeuwen, *Context and Meaning*, 70; Murphy, *Proverbs*, 189–90; Waltke, *Proverbs: Chapters 15–31*, 325.

56   See Krispenz, *Spruchkompositionen*, 103–06.

57   Van Leeuwen, *Context and Meaning*, 84.

58   In addition to the thematic parallels within the unit, verses 18–20 are also bound together by common syntax and paronomasia. See Van Leeuwen, *Context and Meaning*, 84; Garrett, *Proverbs*, 208; Clifford, *Proverbs*, 225; Waltke, *Proverbs: Chapters 15–31*, 327.

59   The participle מוֹעֶדֶת ("unsteady") may be repointed as a *Qal* participle (מֹעֶדֶת). The emendation is unnecessary, however, for מוֹעֶדֶת may be read as a *Pual* participle of מעד without a preformative מ. See GKC §52s; Murphy, *Proverbs*, 189 n. 19a; Waltke, *Proverbs: Chapters 15–31*, 305 n. 37.

propriety in interpersonal relationships (25:11, 27).[60] On the whole, the second unit provides a vivid description of various sources of conflict within the community. In so doing, it invites the addressee to assess the character of his associates, and provides an implicit warning against integrating the nefarious qualities of these personages into his character.

The third unit (25:21–22) plays a significant role within Proverbs 25:16–22, for it presents an ethical paradigm for resolving social conflicts. Whereas the preceding segments (25:16–17, 18–20) describe human conflict from a negative perspective, verses 21–22 provide a paradoxical solution to social contention.[61] The quatrain presents a traditional, humanistic topos that is expressed in both constitutional and sapiential texts of the ancient oriental world.[62] Rather than exacting vengeance on a vulnerable enemy, the admonition encourages the addressee to exercise charity. The rationale behind this admonition is presented in verse 22: "for you will heap burning coals on his head and YHWH will repay you." While the precise meaning of the expression גֶּחָלִים אַתָּה חֹתֶה עַל־רֹאשׁוֹ is uncertain,[63] in the present context, it seems the metaphor describes the contrition of the hostile enemy and the reconciliation of the disputants, as YHWH's reward extends beyond the compassionate party to restore the relationship between the antagonists.[64] The admonition advances a fundamental theme of the composition by providing the noble youth with a paradigm for resolving social conflicts.

The final unit of the discourse (25:23–26) shifts from particular human conflicts to general disputes in the community.[65] While the individual aphorisms may be read as independent sayings, they are bound together by weather (25:23–24) and water imagery (25:25–26), respectively.[66] The initial quatrain pertains to general social conflicts attributed to inimical speech (25:23–24). The malevolent nature of slanderous discourse is expressed through vivid, meteorological imagery

---

60 Van Leeuwen, *Context and Meaning*, 85. The images in Proverbs 25:20ab have given rise to several textual questions. For a discussion of the issues, see G. R. Driver, "Problems and Solutions," *VT* 4 (1954): 240–41; McKane, *Proverbs*, 588–89; Plöger, *Sprüche Salomos*, 296; Clifford, *Proverbs*, 222; Meinhold, *Die Sprüche*, 2.429; Waltke, *Proverbs: Chapters 15–31*, 306 n. 42; *BHQ*.

61 Van Leeuwen, *Context and Meaning*, 85.

62 See "Counsels of Wisdom" (*BWL* 101); "The Instruction of Ptahhotep" (*AEL* 1:72); "The Instruction of Amenemope" (*AEL* 2:150); "The Instruction of Papyrus Insinger" (*AEL* 3:203); Lev 19:17–18.

63 For proposals concerning the interpretation of the expression, see S. Morenz, "Feurige Kohlen auf dem Haupt," *TLZ* 78 (1953): 187–92; R. C. Van Leeuwen, "Wealth and Poverty: System and Contradiction in Proverbs," *HS* 33 (1992): 60; idem, "The Book of Proverbs," *NIB* 5:220; Boström, *The God of the Sages*, 110; Garrett, *Proverbs*, 208–09; Meinhold, *Die Sprüche*, 2:430; idem, "Der Umgang mit dem Feind," 244–48.T. Longman III, *Proverbs*, 458.

64 Whybray, *Proverbs*, 368; Murphy, *Proverbs*, 193, 195; Waltke, *Proverbs: Chapters 15–31*, 331–32.

65 Van Leeuwen, *Context and Meaning*, 85.

66 See Van Leeuwen, *Context and Meaning*, 85; Krispenz, *Spruchkompositionen*, 103–06; Garrett, *Proverbs*, 210; Clifford, *Proverbs*, 227; Waltke, *Proverbs: Chapters 15–31*, 332.

(25:23).[67] Just as a north wind brings unexpected rain, so a secret, malicious tongue produces unexpected strife when slander is disseminated. The second couplet heightens the conflict presented in 25:23, as it shifts from general social relations to the domestic realm (25:24). Similar to several aphorisms in Solomon 1B (19:13; 21:9, 19), the saying incorporates humor to describe the contentious environment produced by a quarrelsome wife.[68] In so doing, it provides an implicit allusion to the meteorological imagery in the preceding couplet. The saying moves from the unexpected effects of bad weather to the image of a man exposed to the elements, which is considered better than exposure to a turbulent wife.[69] Together, the aphorisms widen the ethical purview of the discourse through their portrayal of social conflicts in general and the vices that precipitate conflicts in particular. They develop the theme of social contention, promote virtues that pertain to various social situations, and underscore the consequences associated with improper speech.

The second quatrain (25:25–26) elaborates on the theme of social conflict from two angles—the first positive, the second negative.[70] The initial aphorism incorporates the image of cold water on a parched throat (נֶפֶשׁ) to highlight its life-giving value (25:25). The saying develops the water imagery presented in the preceding aphorisms (25:13, 21) and moves from the devastating effects of inimical speech (25:23–24) to the value of a good word. The second couplet describes the moral oscillation of the righteous through the image of muddied, polluted waters (25:26). As noted above, the repetition of רָשָׁע and צֶדֶק / צַדִּיק links 25:26 with the initial quatrain (25:4–5). However, in contrast to 25:4–5, the present aphorism describes the inversion of justice.[71] When the righteous compromise their commitment and yield to the wicked, they contaminate the waters of justice and pollute the resources necessary for communal well-being. The aphorism introduces a profound development in the book of Proverbs, for it identifies the manner in which the righteous may be vanquished. While no external agent can depose the righteous (10:3, 30; 12:3, 21; 24:15–16), the

---

67   For a discussion of the imagery, see J. Van der Ploeg, "Proverbs 25:23," *VT* 3 (1953): 189–91; Van Leeuwen, *Context and Meaning*, 60; idem, "The Book of Proverbs," *NIB* 5:220; Murphy, *Proverbs*, 193–94; Waltke, *Proverbs: Chapters 15–31*, 333; *HALOT*, "צָפוֹן," 3:1,046.

68   With a few minor spelling variations, Proverbs 25:24 is a replica of 21:9. For an analysis of the comparable features among Proverbs 21:9, 19 and 25:24, see Snell, *Twice-Told Proverbs*, 41. In addition, for an investigation of the significance of repetition and its role in the pedagogical movement of Proverbs, see C. R. Yoder, "Forming 'Fearers of Yahweh': Repetition and Contradiction as Pedagogy in Proverbs," in *Seeking out the Wisdom of the Ancients: Essays Offered to Honor Michael V. Fox on the Occasion of His Sixty-Fifth Birthday* (ed. K. G. Friebel et al.; Winona Lake: Eisenbrauns, 2005), 172–79.

69   Van Leeuwen, *Context and Meaning*, 85; idem, "The Book of Proverbs," *NIB* 5:220.

70   Waltke, *Proverbs: Chapters 15–31*, 334.

71   Van Leeuwen, *Context and Meaning*, 85.

righteous can depose themselves.[72] The saying qualifies the litany of aphorisms concerning the stability of the righteous and warns the addressee of the dangers associated with the lack of perseverance. Together with 25:25, the couplets employ water imagery to highlight both social restoration and ruin. In so doing, they present the value of a good word and the disastrous effects of moral concession in both interpersonal and communal affairs.

The closing aphorism (25:27) forms an appropriate conclusion to both the second subsection (25:16–27) and the composition as a whole (25:2–27). The verbal links between 25:27 and other aphorisms in the compositional unit have been presented above. These links suggest that the saying functions as an inclusio and provides a hermeneutical lens through which to view the meaning and practical significance of the intermediate aphorisms within their larger editorial context. The initial colon incorporates the image of eating honey to warn the addressee of the dangers associated with excessive indulgence (25:16, 27a).[73] In conjunction with 25:16, the sense of the colon is clear. However, the second colon is notoriously difficult. The MT appears to be corrupt,[74] for the pronominal suffix of כְּבֹדָם has no immediate antecedent and the relation between the cola is obscure.[75] While various emendations have been proposed to resolve the textual ambiguity,[76] it seems best to read "and the searching out of difficult things is without glory."[77] This proposal provides a cogent reading of the entire saying. In

---

72   See Meinhold, *Die Sprüche*, 2:433; Waltke, *Proverbs: Chapters 15–31*, 335–36.

73   R. C. Van Leeuwen, "Proverbs XXV 27 Once Again," *VT* 36 (1986): 107–08.

74   The MT reads וְחֵקֶר כְּבֹדָם כָּבוֹד ("and the search of their glory is glory"). The LXX does not resolve the ambiguity of the MT. Rather it reads חֵקֶר as a *Hiphil* imperative from יקר, adds λόγους to prevent the reader from attributing honor to people, and fails to form a logical parallel with 25:27a. See Van Leeuwen, "Proverbs XXV 27," 106–07.

75   In light of the verbal links between verse 27 and 25:2, the pronominal suffix of כְּבֹדָם may refer to both God and kings. This proposal is grammatically possible, but the antecedents are too far removed. Bühlmann argues that the suffix functions as an impersonal pronoun and renders כָּבוֹד as "burden" (*Vom Rechten Reden und Schweigen*, 179–83). This proposal is unconvincing, however, for the book of Proverbs employs a singular suffix when there is no immediate antecedent (14:26; 20:16) and the semantic range of כָּבוֹד does not include the sense "burden." See Van Leeuwen, "Proverbs XXV 27," 110; Waltke, *Proverbs: Chapters 15–31*, 308 n. 53.

76   See G. R. Driver, "Problems in the Hebrew Text of Proverbs," *Bib* 32 (1951): 190; A. A. MacIntosch, "A Note on Proverbs XXV 27," *VT* 20 (1970): 112–14; McKane, *Proverbs*, 587–88; Bryce, "Another Wisdom-'Book' in Proverbs," 148–150; Bühlmann, *Vom Rechten Reden und Schweigen*, 179–83; Van Leeuwen, "Proverbs XXV 27," 105–114; Garrett, *Proverbs*, 210; Meinhold, *Die Sprüche*, 2:433–34; Leliévre and Maillot, *Commentaire des Proverbes II*, 204–05; Murphy, *Proverbs*, 194; Clifford, *Proverbs*, 227.

77   This rendering repoints כְּבֹדָם as a plural adjective used substantively ("heavy, difficult things") and reads כָּבוֹד as מִכָּבוֹד ("apart from/without glory"), understanding the מ as a case of haplography. See F. Delitzsch, *Biblical Commentary on the Proverbs of Solomon* (trans. M. G. Easton; Grand Rapids: Eerdmans, 1983), 171–72; Bryce, "Another Wisdom-'Book' in Proverbs," 150; Van Leeuwen, "Proverbs XXV 27," 110–11; Leliévre and Maillot, *Commentaire des Proverbes II*, 204; Waltke, *Proverbs: Chapters 15–31*, 308 n. 53.

essence, the aphorism compares the consumption of excessive honey with the intellectual investigation of difficult things. As the ingestion of excess sweets is not good, so the analytical exploration of matters that lie beyond one's epistemological capacity is not honorable. Both cola describe the importance of appropriate boundaries. In so doing, they coalesce with the introductory quatrain (25:2–3) to enhance a primary concern of the composition.[78] The initial quatrain (25:2–3) describes the intellectual limitations appropriate to divine, royal, and human inquiry, while the concluding aphorism proscribes the intellectual investigation of matters that transcend one's limited cognition. The saying moves from a description of proper social and analytical boundaries to a proscription of exploring transcendent profundities, such as the intricacies of the cosmos and the unfathomable לֵב of the king (25:2–3). It presupposes a hierarchical view of the socio-religious sphere, where God, kings, courtiers, and commoners have their proper place, prerogatives, limitations, and glory.[79]

On the whole, the first compositional unit (25:2–27) plays a significant role in the formal and thematic development of the sapiential discourse. The evocative poetic analogies, coupled with the rich variety of literary forms, heighten the rhetorical sophistication of the discourse.[80] In addition, the compositional unit reinforces and develops particular topics introduced in the preceding collections. Several aphorisms address the function of the royal institution (25:2–5; cf. 16:12; 20:8, 26), the importance of the spoken word (25:11–14, 15; cf. 11:9; 15:1; 16:28; 17:27), appropriate behavior in the legal sphere (25:7c–10, 18; cf. 18:5; 22:22–23), and the inevitable conflict between the righteous and the wicked (25:4–5, 26; cf. 10:1–15:33)—prominent themes that are woven throughout the fabric of the sentence literature. However, these familiar themes are not simply reiterated; in certain cases they are also advanced. This is apparent in the aphorisms concerning the royal court, judicial etiquette, and interpersonal conflict.[81]

In terms of the royal court, the compendium elaborates on the aristocratic concerns of the former collections. The compositional unit moves from prudent tactics for placating the wrath of the king (16:14) to virtues that influence his resolve (25:15). Moreover, the material develops the subject of propriety within the socio-political sphere. The composition moves from appropriate table

---

78   Van Leeuwen, *Context and Meaning*, 86.
79   Van Leeuwen, "Proverbs XXV 27," 113–14; idem, *Context and Meaning*, 85–86. Also see Ps 131; Prov 30:1–6; Sir 3:21–22; Bar 3:29–4:1; 2 Esd 4.
80   Brown, "The Pedagogy of Proverbs 10:1–31:9," 171.
81   Though Brown provides a general discussion of these issues in his study, he focuses on particular dimensions of these topics within the context of the second Solomonic collection (Brown, "The Pedagogy of Proverbs 10:1–31:9," 171–75). In particular, he examines these themes through the lens of Solomon 2B (28:1–29:27). In contrast, the present study will examine the thematic development of the material within the compositional unit in view of the previous collections.

manners when dining with superiors (23:1–3) to proper social protocol among members of the royal court (25:6–7b). With regard to judicial values, the material shifts from a general portrayal of the character and fate of the perjurer (12:17; 14:5, 25; 19:5, 9) to a graphic description of the damage he inflicts (25:18). In addition, the compositional unit provides specific legal virtues for dealing with various members of the community (25:7c–10). The discourse situates the issue of social conflict in the political and judicial spheres to describe the value of certain virtues on the concrete level, rather than the abstract.[82] What is more, the compositional unit gives particular expression to appropriate ethical strategies for engaging an enemy.[83] Whereas the preceding collections merely promote a particular disposition toward an adversary (24:17), Proverbs 25:21–22 provides specific advice for dealing with opponents. The composition plays an important role in the thematic movement of the book of Proverbs; it reinforces specific themes and enhances particular topics that widen the ethical purview of the document and illuminate the character of the addressee.

In conjunction with the preceding collections, the thematic movement of the first compositional unit (25:2–27) brings the identity of the addressee into sharper focus. In light of the poetic sophistication and thematic emphases of the composition, it is not surprising that many scholars have considered the compendium as an instruction for prospective courtiers.[84] The sayings and admonitions in the discourse unit are cast within a formal frame that outlines the hierarchical structure of the socio-religious world and the conflict that threatens the divine order (25:2–5, 26, 27). The materials within the composition's formal frame elaborate on this general worldview to present a more detailed description of the socio-religious realm. The composition's concern with matters pertaining to the royal court, the judicial sphere, master-messenger relations, and interpersonal conflicts enhances the multifaceted dimensions of the world and infuses the material with a distinct, courtly flavor. While the virtues promoted in the discourse are accessible to many, the themes presented in the formal frame suggest the material is particularly relevant for members of the royal institution. The material moves from the hierarchical structure of the cosmos, to the authoritative structure of the royal court, to social conflicts and appropriate boundaries among members of the community. In so doing, the discourse unit provides the addressee with a fundamental worldview, an ethical vision of the world in which he must live and through which he must navigate.

---

82   Brown, "The Pedagogy of Proverbs 10:1–31:9," 172.

83   Brown, "The Pedagogy of Proverbs 10:1–31:9," 172–73.

84   Bryce, "Another Wisdom-'Book' in Proverbs," 154–57; idem, *A Legacy of Wisdom*, 147–53; Humphreys, "The Motif of the Wise Courtier in the Book of Proverbs,", 185–87; Van Leeuwen, *Context and Meaning*, 73; Blenkinsopp, *Sage, Priest, Prophet*, 33; Leliévre and Maillot, *Commentaire des Proverbes II*, 186; Murphy, *Proverbs*, 190; Perdue, *The Sword and the Stylus*, 95.

5.2.2 Proverbs 25:28–26:28

The second compositional unit (25:28–26:28) is related to the first (25:2–27). This multifaceted compendium builds on the concerns of the preceding piece (25:2–27) through three principal subsections, with 25:28 serving as a janus between the individual compilations.[85] These poems present a series of archetypal vignettes within a coherent literary structure: the first examines the fool (26:1–12), the second considers the sluggard (26:13–16), while the third explores various characters that instigate social conflict (26:17–28). Together, these subsections enhance the moral disposition of certain personages, heighten the ethical purview of the sapiential material, and elaborate on themes introduced in the previous composition (25:2–27). The individual units describe the importance of social propriety (25:6–7b, 7c–10, 11–12, 20; 26:1–12), the dangers of indolence (26:13–16), and various characters that precipitate social disputes (25:16–17, 21–22, 23–24; 26:17–28). The thematic development of each motif deserves specific comment.

The first poem provides an impressionistic portrait of the fool (26:1–12). In general, the subsection examines the character of the intractable from a variety of angles to highlight the importance of social propriety and provide a framework through which to interpret people, proverbs, and situations in the diverse dimensions of human life.[86] The depiction of the fool is not a mere literary flourish, but a rhetorical montage that accentuates the qualities of the intractable and inculcates the virtue of perception—a faculty of discrimination that is concerned with the recognition of concrete particulars in specific circumstances.[87] Among the circumstances considered, the discourse unit focuses on social and interpersonal dealings with the fool that are deemed either appropriate or inappropriate to develop the theme of propriety.

On the social level, the poem describes the catastrophic repercussions associated with conferring כָּבוֹד on a fool. These repercussions are presented through both general and concrete situations. The opening aphorism delineates the incongruous relationship between honor and the fool through the inversion

---

85 Several features suggest that Proverbs 25:28 serves as a transition between the discourse units. First, the syntactical structure of the aphorism is comparable to the sayings in 25:23–27, as it presents the vehicle in initial colon followed by the tenor in second colon. Second, the saying promotes moderation and self-control through the impotence of the insatiable. These values not only supplement the initial collections concern with restraint, but they also foreshadow the discourse on the fool, who is characterized by a lack of self-control (12:16). Together, these features seem to indicate that 25:28 functions as a janus between the compositional units. See Garrett, *Proverbs*, 211; Waltke, *Proverbs: Chapters 15–31*, 344.

86 Van Leeuwen, *Context and Meaning*, 99, *et passim*; Whybray, *The Composition of the Book of Proverbs*, 123; Murphy, *Proverbs*, 198; Waltke, *Proverbs: Chapters 15–31*, 345.

87 M. C. Nussbaum, *The Fragility of Goodness* (Cambridge: Cambridge University Press, 1986), 300–301.

of the natural order (26:1). The aberrant meteorological patterns accentuate the disastrous consequences of promoting the intractable. Snow in the summer and rain during the harvest season produce devastation, as the natural elements destroy the crops and disintegrate the resources of the community. In the same way, when the fool receives social honor or promotion, the communal effects are disastrous. This general, abstract principle is given concrete expression in several aphorisms within the poem. The discourse moves from the absurdity of honoring a fool to the vivid consequences associated with his social advancement. The incongruity in bestowing status on the fool is reiterated in 26:8. Here the person who promotes the fool is comparable to one who binds a stone in a sling[88]—a futile action that is not fitting, for it renders the weapon ineffectual and endangers the warrior. The same is true of the person who hires the fool or retains him as a messenger. As noted above, messengers were envoys of status in the ancient world. While faithful messengers bring refreshment to their patron (25:13), the foolish emissary inflicts trouble, crippling his master and instigating violence (26:6).[89] These devastating consequences are heightened in 26:10, where the hired fool is depicted as an armed madman, who launches maniacal attacks on his employer and the community as a whole.[90] Together, these aphorisms incorporate arresting images to shape the virtue of perception in the addressee. The sayings assume an affluent, distinguished addressee that is able to confer social honor on others and employ members of the community for both general and specific tasks. They describe the illicit application of social power and position on the intractable to provide the addressee with a paradigmatic framework through which to interpret people and establish appropriate boundaries.

On the interpersonal level, the poem moves from the significance of interpreting people to the importance of construing situations.[91] This aspect of

---

88 While בְּמַרְגֵּמָה may follow a maqtil noun pattern and denote "a heap of stones," it seems the term derives from the verb רגם ("to stone") and incorporates an instrumental *mem* prefix to indicate that it is a device used for hurling stones. Although קֶלַע is the conventional term for "sling" (Judg 20:16; 1 Sam, 17:40, 49, 50; Jer 10:18; Zech 9:15), it appears בְּמַרְגֵּמָה carries the same sense (LXX, Syr., Targ.). See McKane, *Proverbs*, 598; Murphy, *Proverbs*, 200; Waltke, *Proverbs: Chapters 15–31*, 352.

89 This imagery is reflected in the MT. The anonymity of the images has given rise to several improbable emendations that mask the rhetorical force of the colon. For an analysis of these emendations, see McKane, *Proverbs*, 597; Plöger, *Sprüche Salomos*, 310–11.

90 This saying has raised several questions, since the relationship between the cola is obscure and the individual terms may be understood in several different ways. Though רַב could mean "a great one," the predicate מְחוֹלֵל suggests the noun should be read as a substantive from רבב, meaning "archer" (cf. Gen 49:23; Job 16:13; Jer 50:29). For an evaluation of the ancient witnesses and some constructive proposals concerning the translation of the aphorism, see D. C. Snell, "The Most Obscure Verse in Proverbs: Proverbs 26:10," *VT* 41 (1991): 350–56; Waltke, *Proverbs: Chapters 15–31*, 339 n. 17.

91 Van Leeuwen, *Context and Meaning*, 105–06.

social propriety is presented through the practical use of proverbs and the ambiguities inherent in interpersonal conflicts. In the first, the poem describes the ineffectual nature of a proverb in the mouth of a fool (26:7, 9). The fool may understand an aphorism, but he cannot employ its wisdom, for he lacks the capacity to understand the circumstances that correspond with the saying. Knowledge of a proverb does not ensure its proper use; the aphorism must be employed at the appropriate time, in an appropriate way, with an appropriate understanding of the situation to which it applies. The significance of construing situations is reinforced in the juxtaposition of two prominent contradictory pairs (Prov 26:4–5):

אַל־תַּעַן כְּסִיל כְּאִוַּלְתּוֹ	4	Do not answer a fool according to his folly,
פֶּן־תִּשְׁוֶה־לּוֹ גַם־אָתָּה		lest you become like him—even you!
עֲנֵה כְסִיל כְּאִוַּלְתּוֹ	5	Answer a fool according to his folly,
פֶּן־יִהְיֶה חָכָם בְּעֵינָיו		lest he become wise in his own eyes.

These opposing admonitions have given rise to several different interpretations. On the one hand, the contradiction may be more apparent than real. That is, the former couplet may address the manner in which one is to respond to the fool (26:4), while the latter describes the obligation to expose the folly of the intractable (26:5).[92] Rather than responding to the fool with malice, the wise must reprimand the intractable without recourse to their tactics. On the other hand, the individual aphorisms may assume situational variability[93] or express the tension between the didactic responsibilities and potential risks inherent in an encounter with the fool.[94] In the main, the juxtaposition illustrates the general, paradigmatic nature of aphoristic speech and the limitations of moral rules.[95] The admonitions reflect on the ambiguities of life and the significance of speech to cultivate proper perception in the addressee. Whether the juxtaposition refers to different aspects of the same situation or represents the dialectical tension between the responsibilities and risks intrinsic to dialogue with the fool, the admonitions force the addressee to distinguish between what is appropriate and inappropriate. Wisdom is a matter of timing and technique; the wise must read the situation and respond accordingly, whether in reticence, restraint, or reproof.

---

92 This proposal assumes that the ambiguous preposition כְּ may be rendered differently in the individual admonitions (cf. LXX). See Meinhold, *Die Sprüche*, 2:437–38; Waltke, *Proverbs: Chapters 15–31*, 349.

93 McKane, *Proverbs*, 596; Van Leeuwen, "The Book of Proverbs," *NIB* 5:224.

94 See K. G. Hoglund, "The Fool and the Wise in Dialogue," in *The Listening Heart: Essays in Wisdom and the Psalms in Honor of Roland E. Murphy, O. Carm.* (ed. E. F. Huwiler et al., Sheffield: Sheffield Academic Press, 1987), 175–76.

95 For an analysis of the pedagogical significance of contradiction in Proverbs, see Yoder, "Forming 'Fearers of Yahweh': Repetition and Contradiction as Pedagogy in Proverbs," 179–83.

The final aphorism (26:12) serves as a formal conclusion to the poem. The saying enhances the tenor of the piece, as it moves from the interpretation of people, proverbs, and situations to the problem of self-perception.[96] In so doing, the aphorism elaborates on the risks inherent in answering a fool by describing a greater danger for the addressee: the subjective valuation that he is wise. This delusional condition is considered to be worse than the fools, for it fails to recognize proper intellectual parameters (25:2–3) and the limitations of human wisdom (26:4–5).[97] The aphorism represents a significant development in the sapiential material, for it explores the "danger" of wisdom.[98] The insoluble nature of inflated, self-valuation heightens the sense of the poem; it inculcates humility and promotes proper boundaries.

The second poem (26:13–16) is related to the first (26:1–12), for it is bound together by a principal persona and ends with a comparative saying concerning self-valuation (26:5, 12, 16). The discourse unit draws on earlier aphorisms to paint an ironic, exaggerated portrait of the עָצֵל. These earlier sayings play an important role within the poem, for they focus on a particular aspect of the lazy/diligent discourse in the book. In contrast to the preceding poems concerning the indolent (6:9–11; 24:30–34), the present piece does not incorporate wealth and poverty language to provide a rhetorical rationale for diligence.[99] Rather the individual aphorisms form a graphic, satirical vignette that presents the despicable disposition and fatal moral vision of the sluggard. The farcical speech and ludicrous actions of the indolent highlight the moral and intellectual dimensions of his character. In effect, the poem moves from the speech and actions of the sluggard to the subjective rationale for his behavior: he is wiser in his own eyes than seven people who give a judicious answer (26:16).[100] Similar to the deluded (26:12), the indolent promotes a terminal brand of wisdom for which there is no remedy. The vivid portrait of the עָצֵל supplements the discourse on fittingness and the fool (26:1–12). When the poem is read within the discourse setting of the book in general and 25:1–26:12 in particular, it warns the addressee of "obstacles to legitimate success,"[101] impediments that may be inherent in his prominent social position. The ludicrous images do not serve to coerce the עָצֵל into action; rather they illustrate that indolence inhibits social success.

---

96   Van Leeuwen, *Context and Meaning*, 105.
97   Van Leeuwen, *Context and Meaning*, 105–06.
98   Murphy, *Proverbs*, 201.
99   See Brown, "The Pedagogy of Proverbs 10:1–31:9," 174; Sandoval, *The Discourse of Wealth and Poverty*, 134–41.
100 Clifford renders שִׁבְעָה ("seven") "the Seven [sages]," referring to the seven antediluvian *apkallu* of Mesopotamian tradition who transmitted cultural norms to the human race (*Proverbs*, 233). Whether שִׁבְעָה alludes to the wisdom of these legendary figures or simply refers to a large number (26:25), the sense of the comparison is clear.
101 Van Leeuwen, *Context and Meaning*, 108.

The third poem (26:17–28) elaborates on particular themes introduced in 25:2–27, as it describes specific characters who instigate social conflict, especially through their speech.[102] The discourse moves from the meddler (26:17), to the rabble-rouser (26:18–19), to the slanderer (26:20–22), to the disposition and destruction of the mendacious adversary (26:23–28). While many of the aphorisms within the piece may be read as independent, self-contained entities, the poetic texture of the discourse suggests the composition consists of four triplets (26:17–19, 20–22, 23–25, 26–28), each of which is bound together by catchwords, thematic parallels, and paronomasia.[103] Together, the individual subsections form a literary montage of the character and comportment of four antisocial archetypes. The disposition and behavior of each person deserves a brief comment.

The initial triplet (26:17–19) profiles the character of both the meddler and the rabble-rouser through a series of stunning images. On the one hand, the busybody is comparable to one who seizes the ears of a passing cur (26:17), for he cannot resist getting embroiled in the disputes of others. On the other hand, the troublemaker is depicted as a cunning, homicidal maniac,[104] who launches deceitful attacks on his neighbor and passes them off as a practical joke (26:18–19). In the main, the aphorisms elaborate on specific topics introduced in 25:2–27 to illuminate the personal and social devastation precipitated by these individuals. The former aphorism develops the theme of social conflict (25:7c–10; 26:17), while the latter sayings enhance the disposition of the contentious (25:18; 26:18–19).[105] Together, the aphorisms provide the addressee with a more detailed vision of interpersonal relations. They reinforce the dangers inherent in social conflict and proscribe certain qualities.

The second triplet (26:20–22) advances the theme of social conflict through both the external and internal influence of the slanderer. This subsection is bound together by a series of catchwords (מָדוֹן, נִרְגָּן, אֵשׁ, עֵצִים), and linked to the preceding triplet by the term רִיב (26:17, 21). The initial couplet incorporates incendiary images to profile the communal devastation of the malicious gossip (26:20–21). This description of the external dimensions of the slanderer's speech gives way to a graphic depiction of their hidden, internal effects (26:22). The final aphorism within the triplet employs the image of choice delicacies to highlight the

---

102 Van Leeuwen, *Context and Meaning*, 113, 118.

103 See Van Leeuwen, *Context and Meaning*, 116–19; Murphy, *Proverbs*, 198; Waltke, *Proverbs: Chapters 15–31*, 358. For similar structural schemes, see McKane, *Proverbs*, 595; Plöger, *Sprüche Salomos*, 313–16; Meinhold, *Die Sprüche*, 2:443–48; Garrett, *Proverbs*, 214–15; Clifford, *Proverbs*, 233–34.

104 Though מִתְלַהְלֵהַּ is a *hapax legomenon* and the precise nuance of the term is uncertain, it seems the participle carries the sense "to play the fool" (see Sir 35:15; McKane, *Proverbs*, 602). When this connotation is read in light of the modifier הַיֹּרֶה זִקִּים חִצִּים וָמָוֶת, the person is characterized as a dangerous madman.

105 Van Leeuwen, *Context and Meaning*, 119.

tempting, penetrating character of the slanderer's speech; his words have a profound influence on others as they descend into their innermost being, affecting their disposition (26:22). The triplet reinforces the theme of social conflict through the external and internal influence of the slanderer and provides the addressee with an implicit warning. If the addressee tolerates the activities of the slanderer, then he provokes communal disintegration; but if he removes the malicious gossip, he strengthens communal welfare.

The third and fourth triplets develop the internal-external dialectic presented in the preceding subsection through the disposition (26:23–25) and destruction (26:26–28) of the mendacious adversary.[106] The initial triplet moves from the deceptive disposition of the adversary to a pointed admonition. Here the enemy is depicted as a hypocritical pretender, who masks his malignant inner disposition through his delicate outer expression (26:23–24).[107] This deceptive façade forms the basis for the admonition (26:25), which marks the fulcrum of the subsection.[108] The speaker exposes the inner character of the enemy and warns the addressee of the dangers inherent in his seductive speech (26:25):

כִּי־יְחַנֵּן קוֹלוֹ אַל־תַּאֲמֶן־בּוֹ	If his voice is charming, do not trust him,
כִּי שֶׁבַע תּוֹעֵבוֹת בְּלִבּוֹ	for seven abominations are in his heart.

This injunction facilitates the transition to the fourth subsection (26:26–28), which reflects on the perverted disposition of the enemy (26:23–25) and envisions his destruction. This destruction involves both public humiliation and personal affliction. While the adversary may camouflage his internal animosity, his deceitful machinations will be exposed before the community (26:26); the evil he intended to inflict on others will return to claim his own life (26:27); and the

---

106   Van Leeuwen, *Context and Meaning*, 121.

107   The metallurgical image in 26:23a has given rise to two different interpretations. Many scholars follow H. L. Ginsburg ("The North-Canaanite Myth of Anath and Aqhat," *BASOR* 98 [1945]: 21 n. 55) and repoint the consonants כֶּסֶף סִיגִים ("silver dross") to כְּסַפְסִגִים ("like glaze") on the basis of the Ugaritic term *spsg* (Driver, "Problems in the Hebrew Text of Proverbs," 191; Garrett, *Proverbs*, 215; Clifford, *Proverbs*, 230). Others have refuted the Ugaritic evidence by arguing that *spsg* means "a bowl of fluid clay" rather than "glaze" (M. Dietrich, O. Loretz, and J. Sanmartin, "Die angebliche Ug.-He. Parallele *SPSG//SPS(J)G(JM)*," *UF* 8 [1976]: 39; O. Loretz, "Ugaritische und hebräische Lexikographie (IV)," *UF* 15 [1983]: 59–64; H. H. P. Dressler, "The Lesson of Proverbs 26:23," in *Ascribe to the Lord: Biblical and Other Studies in Memory of Peter C. Craigie* [ed. L. Esinger and G. Taylor; Sheffield: JSOT, 1988], 117–25). This proposal not only corresponds with similar texts containing כֶּסֶף and סִיגִים (Isa 1:22; Prov 25:4), but it also reinforces the traditional interpretation of סִיג ("dross, refuse"). While both proposals convey the fundamental point of the image (i.e., what appears as precious is corrupt and disguises something impure), the initial phrase in 26:23 should be rendered "silver dross." See Van Leeuwen, *Context and Meaning*, 111 n. 3; Murphy, *Proverbs*, 197; Waltke, *Proverbs: Chapters 15–31*, 341–42 n. 42.

108   Waltke, *Proverbs: Chapters 15–31*, 362.

abusive organs that disseminate distress will produce their own calamity (26:28). The inevitable destruction of the enemy forms an appropriate conclusion to both the subsection and the poem as a whole. In conjunction with the meddler, the rabble-rouser, and the slanderer, the enemy embodies the fundamental characteristics of social dissent. The final subsection heightens the composition's concern with social conflict, as it moves from the personal pain of the busybody (26:17) to the inner disposition and external destruction of the adversary (26:28). The vignette warns the addressee of the consequences associated with deceptive behavior, and provides him with a lens through which to identify those who instigate social dissension.

The three poems within Proverbs 26 enhance the moral purview of the sapiential material. Together, the constituent pieces outline the fundamental contours of a divisive community, populated by fools (26:1–12), sluggards (26:13–16), and antisocial antagonists (26:17–28)—nefarious characters who advocate a fatal brand of wisdom and abrade the moral foundations of the community.[109] In so doing, they shape a particular moral vision that provides techniques to apply in various situations. The discrete vignettes inculcate perception, identify the limitations of wisdom, and highlight the significance of various virtues, ranging from social propriety and diligence to reticence and discernment. They create a picture of the world in which the addressee must live and illuminate the virtues he must embody.

5.2.3 Proverbs 27:1–22

In contrast to the preceding poems, Proverbs 27:1–22 represents a general, heterogeneous collection of aphorisms that address a variety of topics.[110] This collection is marked off by the former composition's concern with social conflict (26:17–28) and the bucolic poem in 27:23–27.[111] Though the compilation lacks the literary and thematic coherence of the previous pieces, it incorporates several features that suggest it is not an mélange of random aphorisms. On the one hand, the compendium employs a series of poetic devices that link individual aphorisms into larger proverbial pairs.[112] On the other hand, the collection gives particular

---

109 See Brown, "The Pedagogy of Proverbs 10:1–31:9," 175. Though Brown's conclusion regarding the conflictive world of the material pertains to the second Solomonic collection as a whole, it is given particular expression in the compositional units within Proverbs 26.

110 Van Leeuwen, *Context and Meaning*, 125.

111 In addition to these literary units, the composition may be framed by the root הלל ("to praise"), which appears in verses 1–2 and 21.

112 For an investigation of the couplets within the discourse unit, see McKane, *Proverbs*, 608–17; Van Leeuwen, *Context and Meaning*, 123–29; Meinhold, *Die Sprüche*, 2:449–61; Garrett, *Proverbs*, 215–21; Leliévre and Maillot, *Commentaire des Proverbes II*, 241–42, 251–61; Murphy, *Proverbs*, 206–09; Clifford, *Proverbs*, 235; Waltke, *Proverbs: Chapters 15–31*, 371–72.

expression to the topic of friendship (27:5–6, 9–10, 14, 17).[113] In so doing, the composition reinforces particular topics introduced in the preceding collections (16:1–22:16) and advances specific themes to extend the context of ethical conduct to include nonsanguineal relations.[114]

In general, the composition may be divided into two equal halves, each of which concludes with a tripartite saying (27:10, 22; cf. 27:27).[115] The first subsection (27:1–10) develops the limitations of human wisdom, the danger of self-perception, and the insufferable nature of jealousy—themes that punctuate the individual collections in the sentence literature. The initial aphorism reflects on a traditional, sapiential topos: the impotence of human life and wisdom manifested in uncertainty of the future (27:1).[116] This realistic understanding of the human condition qualifies the medley of sayings regarding the necessity of future planning (11:14; 15:22; 20:18; 21:5; 24:6, 27) and highlights the inherent limitations of human knowledge (16:1, 9; 20:24). These cognitive limitations are heightened in 27:2, as the discourse moves from knowledge of the future to knowledge of the self. As evinced in the depiction of the fool and the sluggard, self-valuation is dangerous, since it is shaped by an inevitable bias and susceptible to self-deception (26:12, 16). The admonition reinforces the fallible nature of human judgment (14:12), and moves from a divine evaluation of individuals (16:2; 21:2) to the impartial assessment of an outsider. In the same way, the second couplet (27:3–4) incorporates overpowering images to enhance the indignant disposition of the fool (27:3; cf. 12:16) and the intolerable nature of jealousy (27:4; cf. 6:34; 14:30). The pair presents a series of emotions that progress *a minore ad majus* to describe particular passions that frustrate harmonious relationships.

Similar to the initial subsection, the latter half of the composition reiterates several aphorisms presented in the preceding collections. The pedagogical admonition that opens the second subsection incorporates hortatory language from the prologue (27:11; cf. 6:6; 8:33). This educational aphorism not only resembles the didactic rhetoric of the prologue, but it also alludes to the admonition in 23:15. In the present case, however, the admonition extends beyond a basic appeal to progress in wisdom to a motivation that highlights the co-dependent nature of the domentic unit. Wisdom becomes more than a

---

113 Van Leeuwen, *Context and Meaning*, 129; Meinhold, *Die Sprüche*, 2:449; Whybray, *The Composition of the Book of Proverbs*, 124; Dell, *The Book of Proverbs*, 80.

114 With the exception of Proverbs 27:6, 10, and 22, Brown fails to discuss the thematic development of the material in Proverbs 27. The present study incorporates his hermeneutical model in order to identify the different ways in which the compendium develops particular topics from the earlier collections.

115 See Meinhold, *Die Sprüche*, 2:449; Clifford, *Proverbs*, 230; Waltke, *Proverbs: Chapters 15–31*, 371.

116 See "The Instruction of Amenemope" (*AEL* 2:157–59); Qoh 8:16–17; Sir 11:18–19.

solution to ignorance or a means to virtue; it transforms the son into a domestic weapon, a barricade that shields the family unit from the attacks of outsiders.

In addition to the opening admonition, the latter half of the composition contains a series of aphorisms that represent variations or combinations of sayings introduced in the previous collections. Allusions to earlier aphorisms are evident, for example, in the maxims concerning the foresight of the prudent and the stupidity of the naïve (27:12; cf. 22:3) as well as the dangers associated with economic dealings with foreigners (27:13; cf. 6:1–5; 11:15; 17:18; 20:16; 22:26–27). However, the aphorisms regarding the contentious wife (27:15–16) and a person's reputation (27:21) develop previous sayings to heighten the significance of their topics. The turbulent torture precipitated by the shrewish wife echoes a general sentiment expressed in several sayings in the sentence literature (27:15; cf. 19:13b; 21:9, 19; 25:24).[117] Nevertheless, this sentiment is not simply reaffirmed; it is also developed. In conjunction with verse 16,[118] the quatrain moves from a description of the contentious wife to a graphic portrayal of her irrepressible nature (27:16). Just as one cannot restrain the wind or prevent oil from slipping through their fingers, so a man cannot conceal a turbulent wife. The pair enhances the moral vision of marriage preparation, as it moves from the domestic environment produced by the contentious wife (27:15; cf. 21:9, 19; 25:24) to a vivid description of her uncontrollable disposition (27:16). A similar development is presented in 27:21. The aphorism incorporates metallurgical imagery from 17:3a, but reorients the previous saying through an anthropocentric frame of reference. Whereas YHWH tests the hearts of individuals in 17:3, here a person's mettle is assessed according to the praise he receives (cf. 12:8). While self-valuation is suspect (27:2; cf. 26:12, 16), one's reputation serves as a reliable touchstone of his temperament. The saying elaborates on the initial quatrain (27:1–2) and supplements the theocentric dimension of the proverbial perspective; it provides an anthropocentric medium through which to evaluate the authenticity of one's character and serves as an indispensable framework within which to interpret the disposition of others.

The subsections within 27:1–22 advance specific themes and reiterate particular aphorisms presented in the previous collections. However, among these themes, the composition devotes considerable attention to the nature of

---

117 For an analysis of the comparable elements in Proverbs 27:15 and 19:13, see Snell, *Twice-Told Proverbs*, 52. In addition to 19:13, the *Leitwort* מִדְיָן links 27:15 with the other aphorisms concerning the contentious wife (21:9, 19; 25:24).

118 Together, 27:15–16 constitute a proverbial pair. The latter saying is grammatically linked to the former by the pronominal suffix הָ ("her") and both aphorisms incorporate meteorological imagery. See Murphy, *Proverbs*, 208.

genuine friendship.[119] Rather than exploring the theme from a socio-economic angle (19:4, 6, 7), the compilation examines the dimensions of friendship from an interpersonal perspective (17:9, 17; 18:24). Within the collection, genuine friendship is a means of correction, counsel, and security. It is a relationship that manifests devotion through candid, cutting correction rather than artificial, outward expressions of love (27:5–6). In conjunction with its corrective nature, true friendship is also depicted as a source of counsel and security. The discourse incorporates both odiferous and metallurgical images to describe the significance of reliable counsel (27:9) and constructive social interaction with a friend (27:17). Moreover, the composition highlights the indispensable value of friendship in times of distress (27:10; cf. 17:17; 18:24). In contrast to superficial relations based on material riches, in adversity a close neighbor or a tested family friend has genuine value (27:10). For Proverbs, relationships based on wealth are useless in times of distress, but familial ties and bona fide companions serve as a source of security.[120]

Together, the subsections within 27:1–22 reiterate previous material and develop particular themes to describe various matters related to interpersonal affairs. From the limitations of human wisdom and the inherent dangers of self-perception to economic dealings and the social significance of domestic solidarity, the composition assesses and advances familiar motifs from an anthropocentric frame of reference. However, among these motifs, the collection gives particular expression to the topic of friendship. The discourse elaborates on the positive and negative dimensions of genuine companionship and focuses on relationships that reach beyond the domestic sphere. In so doing, the composition supplements the previous poems; it moves from antisocial individuals who precipitate conflict (25:7c–10, 18, 19, 20, 23; 26:17–28) to interpersonal relations that offer correction, counsel, and security, especially in adverse situations. The composition's concern with friendship and general interpersonal affairs draws the addressee into a world in which the self is refracted through the other, and forces him to examine the nature of his personal relationships.

5.2.4 Proverbs 27:23–27

In contrast to the general, heterogeneous collection of aphorisms, Proverbs 27:23–27 represents a coherent, admonitory poem.[121] This piece performs a dual

---

119   Though Brown addresses the issue of frienship in the second Solomonic collection, his discussion is limited to a simple statement: "friendship is prized, a bond that is equal to, if not surpasses, that of kinship (27:6, 10; cf. 17:17)" ("The Pedagogy of Proverbs 10:1–31:9," 174). The present study will elaborate on this general conclusion.

120   Sandoval, *The Discourse of Wealth and Poverty*, 197.

121   Van Leeuwen, *Context and Meaning*, 131.

function. On the one hand, it serves as the conclusion to Solomon 2A.[122] This redactional notion is reinforced by the verbal links between the piece and the discourses (9:1–6), poems (24:30–34), and panegyrics (31:10–31) that close individual sections within the document.[123] On the other hand, the poem functions as an introduction to Solomon 2B (28:1–29:27).[124] The piece incorporates the fundamental symbol of kingship (נֵזֶר) and introduces the addressee to particular themes that pervade the final chapters of the second Solomonic collection, viz., the nature of the royal institution and the proper use of power (28:15, 16; 29:4, 12, 14, 26). This royal emblem has given rise to several objections, since the term appears to be incompatible with the general tenor of the poem.[125] The bucolic tone and the concern with domestic economy suggest the piece serves as a manual for simple, rustic farmers.[126] In view of the pastoral flavor of the poem, נֵזֶר may function as a metonymy for wealth, which is transitory in comparison to the perennial resources of the natural order. However, if the reference to נֵזֶר serves as a symbol for the royal institution,[127] the poem may reflect the wise, shepherd-king's care for his subjects. This reading is reinforced by the prevalence of the shepherd-sheep metaphor for king and people in both the ancient oriental world and the Old Testament.[128] If kings

---

122 Plöger, *Sprüche Salomos*, 293; Whybray, *The Composition of the Book of Proverbs*, 126; Waltke, *Proverbs: Chapters 15–31*, 390.

123 The bucolic poem contains several terms that link it with the concluding discourses within the document: שָׂדֶה ("field," 24:30; 27:26; 31:16), שִׁית לֵב ("to pay attention," 24:32; 27:23), לְבוּשׁ ("clothing," 27:26; 31:22, 25), and נַעֲרָה ("female attendant," 9:3; 27:27; 31:15). See Barucq, *Le livre des Proverbes*, 193; Van Leeuwen, *Context and Meaning*, 140–42; Murphy, *Proverbs*, 210; Waltke, *Proverbs: Chapters 15–31*, 390; Wilke, *Kronerben der Weisheit*, 241–42.

124 Malchow, "A Manual for Future Monarchs," 358–59; Van Leeuwen, "The Book of Proverbs," *NIB* 5:233; Waltke, *Proverbs: Chapters 15–31*, 390.

125 Many emend נֵזֶר to אוֹצָר ("treasures") or עֹשֶׁר ("wealth"), since these readings form a stronger parallel with חֹסֶן ("wealth") in 27:24a (McKane, *Proverbs*, 618; Plöger, *Sprüche Salomos*, 327; Clifford, *Proverbs*, 236–37). These emendations offer a possible solution to the obscure reference to royalty in the present context. Nonetheless, this is unnecessary, for the reference to נֵזֶר corresponds with both the discourse setting of the book and the royal provenance of the collection (25:1). See Van Leeuwen, *Context and Meaning*, 136–37; Waltke, *Proverbs: Chapters 15–31*, 389 n. 78.

126 Skladny, *Die ältesten Spruchsammlungen in Israel*, 55–56; von Rad, *Weisheit in Israel*, 185 n. 5; Murphy, *Proverbs*, 209–10; Clifford, *Proverbs*, 241.

127 See Van Leeuwen, *Context and Meaning*, 134–43; A. Salvesen, "The Trappings of Royalty in Ancient Hebrew," in *King and Messiah in Israel and the Ancient Near East: Proceedings of the Oxford Old Testament Seminar* (JSOTSup 270; Sheffield: Sheffield Academic, 1998), 125–26; L. G. Perdue, *Proverbs* (IBC; Louisville: John Knox, 2000), 228; Waltke, *Proverbs: Chapters 15–31*, 390–92.

128 See "The Epic of Gilgamesh," §1 lines 70–71 (B. R. Foster, *The Epic of Gilgamesh: A New Translation, Analogues, Criticism* [New York: Norton, 2001], 5); "Laws of Lipit-Ishtar," §1:20–55 (A I 20–III 8) (M. T. Roth, *Law Collections from Mesopotamia and Asia Minor* [2nd ed.; ed. P. Michalowski; SBLWAW 6; Atlanta: Scholars Press, 1997], 25), "Laws of Hammurabi," §1:50–62 (Roth, *Law Collections from Mesopotamia and Asia Minor*, 77); 2 Sam 5:2; 7:7; 12:2, 4; Jer 10:21; 22:22; 23:1–6; Ezek 34:23; Ps 23. Also see Malchow, "A Manual for Future Monarchs," 358–59;

attend to the needs of the people and promote their well-being, then the kingdom will be established and the crown will endure (27:23–27; cf. 14:28). The bucolic and royal images indicate that the poem may be read on two different levels: on the literal level, the discourse provides economic guidance for the farmer; on the metaphorical level, the poem admonishes members of the royal institution to care for their subjects. Each reading accounts for the fundamental features of the piece. For many, these readings are mutually exclusive. However, in light of the discourse setting of the book, the compositional setting of the second Solomonic collection (25:1), and the internal details of the poem, it seems that these distinct readings address the same type of individual.

In general, the admonitory poem describes the value of the "flock" (צֹאן). When the farmer tends to his livestock or members of the royal institution care for their subjects, they prosper, providing material resources and sustenance for the "house." Rather than focusing on the acquisition of transitory commodities (27:24), attention to the natural resources under one's charge produces a perpetual means of wealth that may be transferred to succeeding generations (27:25–27). Whether or not the poem has an application beyond its pastoral reference, several features suggest that it is more than a husbandry code for rustic farmers. In its literal sense, the poem assumes the addressee is a wealthy landowner, who possesses flocks (צֹאן), herds (עֲדָרִים), and a household staff (נְעָרוֹת). The reference to נַעֲרוֹתֶיךָ is especially significant, since anyone who possesses a retinue of נְעָרוֹת is considered a person of substance (cf. 9:3; 31:15).[129] The noble status of the poem's addressee suggests the piece is more than a simple manual for poor farmers; at minimum, it serves as a primer for aristocratic ranchers.

The aristocratic tenor of the poem is consistent with the discourse setting of the book and the compositional setting of the second Solomonic collection. The piece incorporates domestic resources and royal trappings that coincide with the noble status of the addressee and the royal provenance of the compendium (25:1). As the conclusion to Solomon 2A (25:1–27:27), the poem forms an implicit link with the introductory segment. While the opening verses of the compilation explicitly refer to the bureaucracy (25:2–7), the closing poem implicitly refers to the royal institution through its emblem, the נֵזֶר (27:24).[130] Moreover, the poem plays a formative role in the thematic development of the

Van Leeuwen, *Context and Meaning*, 136–38; D. Franke, "The Middle Kingdom in Egypt," *CANE* 744.

129 Perdue, *Wisdom and Creation*, 96; Leeb, *Away from the Father's House*, 43; Fontaine, *Smooth Words*, 38.

130 Meinhold, *Die Sprüche*, 2:461–62.

material.[131] On the literal level, the poem provides the addressee with indispensable advice concerning animal husbandry. On the metaphorical level, the poem elaborates on the communal orientation of the royal institution (cf. 14:28–35) and highlights the social responsibilities of the court. The piece emphasizes the importance of stewardship and seeks to rein in potential exploitation of power; it admonishes the addressee to act in the interests of those creatures and persons entrusted to their care, rather than exercising their authority in self-interest.

5.2.5 Section Conclusion

To summarize, Solomon 2A addresses particular themes that enhance the identity of the addressee. The compilation conveys an advanced moral vision through its focus on propriety, social conflict, the limitations of human wisdom, the value of genuine friendship, and the importance of stewardship, among others. While these themes pertain to various people in a variety of situations, a distinct, courtly flavor pervades the material. The individual discourses assume an affluent, distinguished addressee who has access to the court (25:2–15), the capacity to confer social honor on others (26:1, 8), the means to employ members of the community (26:6, 10), and the resources to sustain a large household (26:6, 10; 27:23–27). These features strengthen the aristocratic nature of the material and illuminate the status of the addressee. The same is true with regard to Solomon 2B (28:1–29:27). This composition advances particular themes and emphasizes certain motifs that bring the character of the addressee into sharper focus.

5.3 The Sapiential Vision of Solomon 2B (28:1–29:27)

In contrast to the sophisticated forms and artistic rhetoric of Proverbs 25:2–27:27, Solomon 2B consists largely of antithetical sayings. The compositional unit returns to the opposition between the righteous and the wicked (28:1, 12, 28; 29:2, 16, 27) and the general, antithetical style of Proverbs 10–15, bringing the sentence literature full circle. While many scholars maintain that the righteous-wicked sayings function as formal discourse markers within the composition,[132]

---

131 Though Brown mentions the poem in his discussion of the formal texture of the second Solomonic collection ("The Pedagogy of Proverbs 10:1–31:9," 170), he does not examine its content or its contribution to the thematic development of the sapiential material.

132 See Malchow, "A Manual for Future Monarchs," 352–60; Meinhold, *Die Sprüche*, 2:464–65; Waltke, *Proverbs: Chapters 15–31*, 403–06; Tavares, *Eine königliche Weisheitslehre?*, 13–52. Malchow highlights the literary and thematic links between the righteous-wicked sayings within the composition in order to identify a deliberate, structural pattern (28:1, 12, 28; 29:2, 16, 27). For

the structure of Proverbs 28:1–29:27 is comparable to the early collections. The composition does not examine specific topics within a clear, systematic structure; rather, these chapters incorporate common forms and emphasize certain motifs to form a loose instruction.[133] This instruction addresses various matters, ranging from the prerogatives of the royal institution to the function of the domestic unit. However, among the issues presented in the composition, the body politic, wealth and poverty, and the תּוֹרָה are given particular expression. The attention given to these themes suggests they represent the fundamental concerns of the composition. The thematic development of each motif deserves a brief comment.

The body politic receives considerable attention in Proverbs 28:1–29:27. Similar to the previous *Königssprüche*, the royal bureaucracy is presented as a vehicle for communal order. Through perception (28:2b),[134] the execution of justice (29:4a), and the protection of the disenfranchised (29:14), the king establishes socio-moral stability throughout the land. The compendium reiterates the responsibilities of the body politic and advocates conventional ancient Near Eastern royal ideology, which legitimized the exercise of political power for the benefit of the community. However, in contrast to the parochial portrayal of the royal institution in the preceding collections (14:28–35; 16:10–15; 19:12; 20:2; 21:1; 24:21–22; 25:2–5), several aphorisms evaluate the body politic from a critical perspective.[135] The monarch is depicted as a corrupt, autocratic ruler who abuses his political power. Rather than defending the rights of the poor, the tyrannical

---

Malchow, these links mark the poetic parameters of particular subunits and focus on the topic of righteous rule. The integral connection between these sayings leads him to conclude that the principal addressee of the collection is the future ruler ("A Manual for Future Monarchs," 358). Meinhold independently identified the structural significance of the righteous-wicked sayings (28:1, 12, 28; 29:16, 27) within the collection and classified the respective sections as descriptions of one's relationship to Torah, God, rearing, and rulership (*Die Sprüche*, 2:464–65). While the literary and thematic links between the righteous-wicked sayings are striking, the diverse nature of the material within the purported subsections undermines the notion that these compositional units address a fixed topic or theme.

133 Whybray, *The Composition of the Book of Proverbs*, 126–27; Fox, *Proverbs 10–31*, 817.

134 The imprecise parallelism, coupled with the obscure sense of כֵּן, has given rise to several emendations of 28:2. While the second colon is difficult, the sense of the initial verset is rather clear; socio-moral anarchy produces revolts that either necessitate a large bureaucracy or ensure a succession of leaders in volatile times. Within the second colon, it seems that מֵבִין יֹדֵעַ serves as an asyndeton ("a discerning person who knows") and כֵּן functions as an adjective indicating "right" or "order" (cf. 11:19; 15:7). In this case, the second colon may be rendered "but because of a discerning person who knows, right endures." The polyvalent nature of the verset suggests that the enduring "right" or "order" refers to both the land and the perceptive leader. Although this interpretation does not form a precise parallel with the initial verset, it implies that a discerning person has an advantage over many princes in securing order within society. For a discussion of the textual issues, see Driver, "Problems in the Hebrew Text of Proverbs," 191–92; Gemser, *Sprüche Salomos*, 98; Murphy, *Proverbs*, 213; Clifford, *Proverbs*, 243; Waltke, *Proverbs: Chapters 15–31*, 408.

135 Brown, "The Pedagogy of Proverbs 10:1–31:9," 171–72.

king exploits his authority by assaulting the weak (28:15). The wicked ruler is comparable to a אֲרִי־נֹהֵם וְדֹב שׁוֹקֵק; he is a ravenous beast who satisfies his irrepressible drives by feeding on the marginalized.[136] These vivid images introduce a striking development in the book of Proverbs.[137] Whereas earlier aphorisms incorporated the image of a roaring lion to describe the manner in which the king employs his power to inspire awe and rein in insubordinate subjects (19:12; 20:2), the present aphorism exploits the image to highlight institutional abuses of power. This exploitation is accentuated throughout the remainder of the collection. The king is portrayed as a venal despot who practices extortion (28:16a),[138] accepts kickbacks from lobbyists (29:4b),[139] and breeds corruption in his officials through his indifference to truth and his adherence to deceptive testimony (29:12). These cynical aphorisms not only serve as social observations regarding the nature of the *"real politik,"* but they also function rhetorically to rein in potential abuses of power.[140] In contrast to the preceding compendia, the latter half of the second Solomonic collection presents the human monarch as fundamentally flawed.[141] The composition widens the moral purview of the sentence literature through its emphasis on the potential institutional exploitation of royal power; it qualifies the sentence literature's idyllic portrait of the body politic and introduces a profound development in the book of Proverbs.

A similar development is presented in the collection's treatment of the righteous and the wicked. This familiar antithesis forms an envelope around the collection (28:1; 29:27), marking the poetic parameters of the piece.[142] The aphorisms placed at the composition's seams provide general observations concerning the ethical posture of the righteous and the wicked: the initial saying compares the psychological disposition of these antithetical groups (28:1), while

---

136   See Forti, *Animal Imagery in the Book of Proverbs*, 63–65.

137   Brown, "The Pedagogy of Proverbs 10:1–31:9," 172.

138   The MT reads נָגִיד חֲסַר תְּבוּנוֹת וְרַב מַעֲשַׁקּוֹת. The construction is difficult, since the compound subject has no predicate. While the colon may be read as a vocative (Delitzsch, *Proverbs of Solomon*, 418–19), it does not include the expected pronoun for the exclamation. The best solution is to emend וְרַב to יִרְבֶּה ("multiplies, increases"), which assumes the common scribal confusion between *waw* and *yodh* (Waltke, *Proverbs: Chapters 15–31*, 396 n. 14).

139   The term תְּרוּמוֹת ("offerings, contributions") is ambiguous. The noun may refer to the king's reception of contributions (Plöger, *Sprüche Salomos*, 343) or another's (Meinhold, *Die Sprüche*, 2:483). However, these options are not mutually exclusive. The ambiguity connects both the giver and the recipient of contributions in the corruption of justice and the downfall of the community (Waltke, *Proverbs: Chapters 15–31*, 399 n. 39). Elsewhere in the Old Testament, תְּרוּמָה is a cultic term referring to contributions to the temple or to the priests (Lev 7:14; Num 18:24; 31:29; 41, 52). In light of the injustice and communal destruction produced by these contributions, the term may denote bribes, blackmail, or extortion in the present saying. See Waltke, *Proverbs: Chapters 15–31*, 433.

140   Sandoval, *The Discourse of Wealth and Poverty*, 150.

141   Brown, "The Pedagogy of Proverbs 10:1–31:9," 171.

142   Malchow, "A Manual for Future Monarchs," 354.

the closing aphorism highlights their mutual abhorrence toward one another
(29:27). Within this general framework, the remainder of the composition situates
the conflict between the righteous and the wicked in the political and judicial
spheres.[143] In terms of the political realm, the compendium addresses the
significance of responsible, political leadership by describing the community's
response to those in positions of power. When the wicked assume control, they
dehumanize society and force people into hiding (28:12b, 28a; 29:2b, 16a).
However, when the righteous rule, they provoke communal celebration (28:12a;
29:2a) and promote legitimate jurisdiction (28:28b). With regard to the judicial
sphere, the composition describes the ethical disposition of these antithetical
groups through their concern for the marginalized. While the righteous exhibit
concern (יֹדֵעַ) for the legal rights of the poor, the wicked demonstrate their lack of
concern for the disenfranchised through ignorance and cruelty (29:7). In contrast
to the preceding collections, the composition profiles character through the
political sphere.[144] The compilation moves from general categories of virtue
(10:1–15:33) to the concrete, judicial (17:23, 26; 18:5; 21:7; 29:7) and political
(28:12, 28; 29:2, 16) values of these antithetical character types. In so doing, it
heightens the political flavor of the material and expands the dimensions of
character within the book of Proverbs.

In addition to the aphorisms concerning the royal institution and the
righteous and the wicked, several sayings within the composition contribute to
the discourse on wealth and poverty. The compendium employs economic
rhetoric to underscore the value of virtue and the odious nature of vice (28:6, 11,
19, 20, 22; cf. 12:11; 16:19; 19:1, 22; 22:1).[145] Moreover, the compilation
incorporates the character-consequence nexus to advocate generosity and inspire
benevolence toward the poor (28:8, 20, 22, 27). Similar to the previous
collections, the composition separates poverty from sloth and undermines the
value of wealth.[146] It creates an ideational world within which virtue and concern
for the weak transcend socio-economic boundaries and shape ethical decisions.

This ideational world is developed further through two significant themes:
the Torah and the YHWH sayings. Similar to the introductory lectures, the term
תּוֹרָה is a fundamental theme in the composition (28:4, 7, 9; 29:18). However, in
contrast to the prologue and the early collections, the term is dissociated from
domestic instruction (1:8; 3:1; 4:2; 6:20, 23; 7:2) and the teaching of the sages
(13:14). Within the compilation, the absolute form suggests תּוֹרָה refers to some

---

143 Brown, "The Pedagogy of Proverbs 10:1–31:9," 172.
144 Malchow, "A Manual for Future Monarchs," 354; Brown, "The Pedagogy of Proverbs 10:1–
      31:9," 175.
145 See Sandoval, *The Discourse of Wealth and Poverty*, 133.
146 Brown, "The Pedagogy of Proverbs 10:1–31:9," 174.

form of Israel's constitutional tradition.[147] This notion is reinforced by the juxtaposition of several Torah sayings with those that either mention or assume YHWH's involvement (28:4–5, 9). The composition separates humanity into two groups: those who observe the Torah and understand the tenets of justice, and those who reject the Torah and undermine righteous equity. Adherence to Torah and relationship with YHWH has both personal and communal implications. On the one hand, Torah observance is intimately associated with personal piety, as those who disregard the divine will find their own words to YHWH rejected (28:9). On the other hand, adherence to Torah and relationship with YHWH has implications that extend beyond the individual to the socio-political realm, for to keep Torah and seek YHWH is to strive against the wicked and establish justice (28:4, 5).[148] This personal-political orientation is escalated in the final Torah saying (29:18). Here the collocation of חָזוֹן and תּוֹרָה links the principal forms of divine revelation: the prophetic and the constitutional.[149] The aphorism incorporates the fundamental sources of personal and communal guidance to highlight the significance of Torah (29:18). In a world populated by tyrannical rulers, wicked oppressors, and avaricious loan sharks, the Torah serves as a bastion of communal order and the socio-religious guide to communal solidarity (cf. 11:14; 29:26).[150] Together, the Torah and YHWH sayings heighten the theocentric orientation of the sentence literature and introduce a basic theological principle into the sapiential material that sets the trajectory for Ben Sira's identification of wisdom with Torah (Sir 15:1; 19:20; 21:11).[151]

5.3.1 Section Conclusion

To summarize, Solomon 2B reinforces familiar motifs and assesses particular topics from a fresh, innovative perspective. Together with the topics discussed

---

147 McKane, *Proverbs*, 623–24; Garrett, *Proverbs*, 223; Van Leeuwen, "The Book of Proverbs," *NIB* 5:234; Murphy, *Proverbs*, 214; Perdue, *Proverbs*, 229; Waltke, *Proverbs: Chapters 15–31*, 408.

148 See Clifford, *Proverbs*, 244.

149 The term חָזוֹן occurs only here in the book of Proverbs. Elsewhere in the Old Testament, חָזוֹן designates the vision of the prophet, which is directed toward the nation in general or the king in particular. Many argue that the prophetic term takes on a different nuance in wisdom tradition and render חָזוֹן as either some form of the sage's revelation or a general designation for communal guidance (Meinhold, *Die Sprüche*, 2:489; Waltke, *Proverbs: Chapters 15–31*, 445–46). These proposals are possible, but unconvincing, since the terms חָזוֹן and תּוֹרָה are used in Ezekiel 7:26 and Lamentations 2:9 as designations for the community's authoritative means of divine guidance. When חָזוֹן is read in conjunction with תּוֹרָה, it seems the term represents the prophetic form of communal guidance. See Van Leeuwen, "The Book of Proverbs," *NIB* 5:244; Murphy, *Proverbs*, 222–23; Clifford, *Proverbs*, 253–54.

150 Brown, "The Pedagogy of Proverbs 10:1–31:9," 172.

151 Perdue, *Proverbs*, 230.

above, the composition contains a variety of ethical considerations, ranging from matters of correction (28:14, 23; 29:1) and adulation (28:23; 29:5) to domestic issues (28:7, 24; 29:3, 15, 17, 21) and interpersonal affairs (29:8, 9, 11, 20). However, these traditional themes are cast within a larger moral discourse that focuses on the correct exercise or illegitimate use of power, whether political, judicial, or economic. The compendium includes several explicit references to the royal institution (28:2, 15, 16, 29:2, 4, 12, 14, 26) as well as inferential references to governance (28:5, 12, 21, 28; 29:7, 13, 18; cf. Deut 1:16–18, 16:18–20). Moreover, the collection situates character in the political and judicial spheres. These features, coupled with the composition's concern with justice, wealth, and the marginalized, suggest the compilation is directed expressly to those in positions of power and influence within society.[152] The collection modulates particular themes and emphasizes certain motifs to provide a more graphic, realistic portrait of the socio-moral world. In so doing, it supplies the addressee with a comprehensive moral vision that accounts for the fundamental conflict between the righteous and the wicked, justice and exploitation, political reliability and bureaucratic corruption.

5.4 Conclusion

As the conclusion to the sentence literature, Proverbs 25:1–29:27 develops particular themes that bring the identity of the addressee into sharper focus. The composition moves from general, abstract virtues (10:1–15:33) to concrete, political expressions of character, from a simple, bipolar world to a complex, contentious world, and from the correct exercise of power to the abuse of power. As an independent collection, it seems the composition is addressed to prospective leaders within society. The compendium gives particular attention to relations with superiors, the body politic, propriety, social conflict, and justice, to name a few. The collection is not only set in the court or among individuals in close association with the court (25:1), but it also assumes an aristocratic addressee who has access to the court (25:2–15), the capacity to confer social honor on others (26:1, 8), the means to employ members of the community (26:6, 10), the resources to sustain a large household (26:6, 10; 27:23–27), and the power to promote political stability or communal aversion (28:2, 5, 12, 15, 16, 21, 28; 29:2, 4, 7, 12, 13, 14, 18, 26). The courtly nature of the second Solomonic collection is not surprising; rather it appears to be a natural progression in the

---

152 Skladny, *Die ältesten Spruchsammlungen in Israel*, 66; Alonso Schöckel and Vilchez, *Proverbios*, 482; Malchow, "A Manual for Future Monarchs," 355; Habel, "Wisdom, Wealth, and Poverty Paradigms in the Book of Proverbs," 45–46; Meinhold, *Die Sprüche*, 2:415, 464; Van Leeuwen, "The Book of Proverbs," *NIB* 5:245–46; Waltke, *Proverbs: Chapters 15–31*, 405–06; Wilke, *Kronerben der Weisheit*, 243–65; Perdue, *The Sword and the Stylus*, 95–96.

material consistent with the discourse setting of the book and the compositional setting of the second Solomonic collection.

Chapter 6

Applied Wisdom: Proverbs 30–31

The concluding compositions in the book of Proverbs bring the document's pedagogical program to a climax. Together with the prologue (1:1–9:18), the words of Agur (30:1–33) and the words of Lemuel (31:1–31) re-contextualize the litany of sayings in the sentence literature and form a hermeneutical envelope around the book.[1] These variegated compendia enhance the ideational world of the sapiential material and give particular expression to the application of wisdom. The words of Agur provide a theological framework through which to view the quest for wisdom (30:1–9) and present a series of numerical sayings pertaining to the proscribed parameters of the socio-moral order (30:10–33). The words of Lemuel delineate the responsibilities of wisdom (31:1–9) and filter the book's principal themes through a single, exceptional woman to describe the life of wisdom (31:10–31). The formal introductions and the parallel structures of these two sections suggest they are to be interpreted as a complex diptych. Their relationship may be highlighted as follows:[2]

---

1   Camp, *Wisdom and the Feminine*, 179; McCreesh, "Wisdom as Wife: Proverbs 31:10–31," 391–410; Meinhold, *Die Sprüche*, 1:26; Hausmann, "Beobachtungen zu Spr 31,10–31," 266; Whybray, *The Composition of the Book of Proverbs*, 159; R. D. Moore, "A Home for the Alien: Worldly Wisdom and Covenantal Confession in Proverbs 30,1–9," *ZAW* 106 (1994): 104; Van Leeuwen, "The Book of Proverbs," *NIB* 5:24; Fuhs, *Das Buch der Sprichwörter*, 15; Yoder, *Wisdom as a Woman of Substance*, 2; Brown, "The Pedagogy of Proverbs 10:1–31:9," 153. However, for some Proverbs 30:1–33 does not play a decisive role in the re-contextualization of the sentence literature (Camp, *Wisdom and the Feminine*, 151; Brown, "The Pedagogy of Proverbs 10:1–31:9," 175–78).

2   The basic contours of this interpretation derive from D. I. Block, communicated in personal conversation.

The Words of Agur (30:1–33)	The Words of Lemuel (31:1–31)
Narrative Introduction (30:1a)	Narrative Introduction (31:1)
Reflections [on the life of wisdom] (30:1b–9)	Reflections [on the responsibilities of kingship] (31:2–9)
Numerical Reflections on Recognizing a Noble Life (30:10–33)	Alphabetic Reflections on Finding a Noble Wife (31:10–31)

Table 6.1: A Structural Proposal for the Words of Agur and the Words of Lemuel

Together, these compositions form a bi-coda for the book: the words of Agur begin with a reflective monologue and close with a sequence of numerical sayings; the words of Lemuel open with a series of admonitions and conclude with an alphabetic acrostic. Agur moves from a soliloquy to numbers; Lemuel moves from a disquisition to letters. In concert, these pieces function as two panels of a diptych that examine particular topics from a dynamic frame of reference and mark the conclusion of the addressee's quest for wisdom. The hermeneutical significance and courtly character of these diverse compositions deserves specific comment.

6.1 The Words of Agur (30:1–33)

The Words of Agur (30:1–33) play an important role in the re-contextualization of the material in the book of Proverbs. This idiosyncratic collection has given rise to several questions, ranging from the nature of the piece to the extent of Agur's words. While many argue that 30:1–9 combines the authentic discourse of a non-Israelite cynic (1–4) with an orthodox response to the protagonist's nihilistic manifesto (5–9),[3] it appears the initial subsection represents a coherent, humble expression of the epistemological limits of human wisdom.[4] The formal

---

3   Scott, *Proverbs, Ecclesiastes*, 176; idem, *The Way of Wisdom in the Old Testament*, 165; McKane, *Proverbs: A New Approach*, 643; J. L. Crenshaw, "Clanging Symbols," in *Justice and the Holy* (ed. D. A. Knight and P. J. Paris; Philadelphia: Fortress, 1989), 51–64; repr. in *Urgent Advice and Probing Questions: Collected Writings on Old Testament Wisdom* (ed. J. L. Crenshaw; Macon: Mercer University Press, 1995), 371–82; Perdue, *Proverbs*, 252–53.
4   P. Franklyn, "The Sayings of Agur in Proverbs 30: Piety or Scepticism?" *ZAW* 95 (1983): 238–52; A. H. J. Gunneweg, "Weisheit, Prophetie und Kanonformel," in *Alttestamentlicher Glaube und Biblische Theologie: Festschrift für Horst Dietrich Preuß zum 65. Geburtstag* (ed. J. Hausmann and H.-J.

and thematic similarities between the monologue and several texts that compare divine wisdom with human ignorance (Isa 49:1–4; Ps 73; 90; Job 28:12–28; Bar 3:29–4:1) suggests 30:1–9 represents a logical, autobiographical discourse, delivered by Agur to highlight the preeminence of divine wisdom over human investigation. Nonetheless, this monologue does not function as an independent unit; rather it serves as an introduction to the remainder of the chapter. Though the central section of the composition is punctuated by numerical proverbs and independent sayings, several features suggest that Agur is responsible for 30:1–33. The composition is framed by material cast in direct address (30:1–9, 32–33), and it lacks internal titles to indicate a separate section within the collection.[5] In spite of the diverse forms and the oscillatory mode of address, the entire chapter falls under the formal superscription attributed to Agur (30:1a).[6] Whether the discourse originated with Agur or a creative redactor, the editorial heading invites us to read the entire piece as the words of a single speaker.

Though the Septuagint attributes the collection to Solomon, the Masoretic text assigns the composition to a new speaker, viz., אָגוּר בִּן־יָקֶה.[7] The superscription provides several indications that the composition functions as an oracle. This is evident in the use of the noun הַמַּשָׂא,[8] as well as the phrase נְאֻם הַגֶּבֶר.

---

5   Zobel; Stuttgart: Kohlhammer, 1992), 253–60; Moore, "A Home for the Alien," 96–107; Van
     Leeuwen, "The Book of Proverbs," *NIB* 5:250–51. Also see Clifford, *Proverbs*, 256–57.

5   G. Sauer, *Die Sprüche Agurs: Untersuchungen zur Herkunft, Verbreitung und Bedeutung einer biblischen
     Stilform unter besonderer Berücksichtigung von Proverbia c. 30* (BWANT 84; Stuttgart: Kohlhammer,
     1963), 112; A. E. Steinmann, "Three Things...Four Things...Seven Things: The Coherence of
     Proverbs 30:11–33 and the Unity of Proverbs 30," *HS* 42 (2001): 60, 65; Waltke, *Proverbs:
     Chapters 1–15*, 464. Many scholars follow the LXX and divide the chapter into two distinct units:
     vv. 1–14 and vv. 15–33 (Plöger, *Sprüche Salomos*, 356; Meinhold, *Die Sprüche*, 2:495–96; Whybray,
     The Composition of the Book of Proverbs, 149; Murphy, *Proverbs*, 226–27; Fox, *Proverbs 1–9*, 5).
     However, the Greek division does not demonstrate that the discourse consists of two separate
     parts, since the LXX represents a secondary arrangement of the document. See Washington,
     Wealth and Poverty, 125–26; Tov, "Recensional Differences Between the Masoretic Text and the
     Septuagint of the Book of Proverbs," 419–32; Clifford, *Proverbs*, 257.

6   Sauer, *Die Sprüche Agurs*, 112; Garrett, *Proverbs*, 235; Steinmann, "Three Things," 65–66; Waltke,
     Proverbs: Chapters 15–31, 463–64.

7   Skehan interpreted אָגוּר בִּן־יָקֶה as a riddle, arguing that אָגוּר means "I am a sojourner" and יָקֶה
     serves an acronym for YHWH. In so doing, he concluded that the collocation functions as a
     designation for Israel, YHWH's son ("Wisdom's House," in *Studies in Israelite Poetry and Wisdom*
     [CBQMS 1; Washington, D.C.: The Catholic Biblical Association of America, 1971], 42–43).
     This reading is possible, but the construction suggests the phrase denotes a proper name. The
     construction, proper noun + "son of" + proper noun, occurs over one thousand times in the
     Old Testament as a nominal designation (Waltke, *Proverbs: Chapters 15–31*, 465 n. 89).

8   Many scholars emend the noun to include a generic ending (הַמַּשָׂאִי, "the Massaite") or a
     preposition (מִמַּשָׂא, "from Massa") in order to establish the ethnic or locative origin of Agur
     (Sauer, *Die Sprüche Agurs*, 97; McKane, *Proverbs: A New Approach*, 644; Meinhold, *Die Sprüche*,
     2:494; Murphy, *Proverbs*, 227; Clifford, *Proverbs*, 260; Perdue, *Proverbs*, 253). These emendations
     are unnecessary, since the personal name אָגוּר indicates the foreign origin of the speaker and the

The former is a technical term for prophetic oracles (cf. Hab 1:1), while the latter is a "signatory formula" that highlights the divine origin and authority of the message (cf. 30:5–6).[9] In conjunction with דִּבְרֵי, the terms identify the oracular mode of the discourse and signal the confluence of sapiential and prophetic traditions.[10] This generic classification is significant, for it pertains to the chapter in general and the autobiographical confession in particular.

The generic designation gives way to the most notorious crux in the discourse. While the expression לְאִיתִיאֵל לְאִיתִיאֵל וְאֻכָל may refer to addressees of the piece,[11] or function as an agnostic, even atheistic confession ("There is no God, there is no God. How can I prevail?"),[12] it appears the expression represents an assertion concerning the futility of human efforts to attain knowledge of God ("I am weary, O God, I am weary, O God, but I can prevail").[13] This proposal is consistent with the remainder of the monologue. The

---

noun הַמַּשָּׂא stands in apposition to both דִּבְרֵי and נְאֻם, which are standard designations for prophetic speech.

9   With the exception of Proverbs 30:1, the expression נְאֻם הַגֶּבֶר occurs only three times in the Old Testament (Num 24:3, 15; 2 Sam 23:1). In general, the noun נְאֻם is associated with Yahweh to indicate the divine sanction and authority of the discourse that follows. The same is true with regard to the expression נְאֻם הַגֶּבֶר. Though נְאֻם is used in conjunction with a human spokesman, both Balaam and David assert that their expressions derive from the אִמְרֵי־אֵל and the רוּחַ יְהוָה, respectively (Num 24:4; 2 Sam 23:2). Since Agur incorporates the covenantal tradition to substantiate his argument (30:5–6), it seems נְאֻם הַגֶּבֶר also conveys the notion of divine origin and authority. See Franklyn, "The Sayings of Agur," 240–41; Garrett, *Proverbs*, 236; Moore, "A Home for the Alien," 97; E. S. Krantz, "'A Man Not Supported by God': On Some Crucial Words in Proverbs XXX 1," *VT* 46 (1996): 549; Fox, *Proverbs 10–31*, 852–53. For a discussion of the "signatory formula," see Block, *The Book of Ezekiel: Chapters 1–24*, 33–34.

10   Moore, "A Home for the Alien," 97.

11   See E. Lipinski, "Peninna, Iti'el et l'Athlète," *VT* 17 (1967): 68–75; Franklyn, "The Sayings of Agur," 241–42 n. 14. This proposal is less than convincing, since the repetition of לְאִיתִיאֵל is abnormal and אֻכָל is never used as a proper name in any Semitic language (Waltke, *Proverbs: Chapters 15–31*, 467 n. 101).

12   This interpretation reads לְאִיתִיאֵל אֵל לָאִיתִי אֵל וָאֹכֵל as an Aramaic expression and is incompatible with the moral vision of the sapiential material. For this proposal and comparable readings, see C. Torrey, "Proverbs, Chapter 30," *JBL* 73 (1954): 93–103; Scott, *Proverbs*, 175–76; idem, *The Way of Wisdom*, 169; McKane, *Proverbs: A New Approach*, 644–45; Crenshaw, "Clanging Symbols," 371–82; Murphy, *Proverbs*, 226.

13   This proposal emends לְאִיתִיאֵל to לָאִיתִי אֶל ("I am weary, O God") and reads אֻכָל as a defective form from the root יכל ("to be able, prevail"). Many argue that אֻכָל derives from the root כלה ("to be used up, spent") rather than יכל (Franklyn, "The Sayings of Agur," 243–44; Garrett, *Proverbs*, 210; Clifford, *Proverbs*, 260; Fox, *Proverbs 10–31*, 854). However, the former reading is preferred, since the defective form of the root יכל occurs several times in the Old Testament (Josh 7:12; Ps 18:39; Jer 20:11) and the verb is used without an object (Exod 1:23) or a complementary verb (Ps 101:5; Isa 1:13) in several instances (cf. Isa 16:12; Job 4:2). See Plöger, *Sprüche Salomos*, 354; Murphy, *Proverbs*, 226; Waltke, *Proverbs: Chapters 15–31*, 468 n. 102; *BHQ*; D. Barthélemy, ed., *Proverbia* (vol. 5 of *Critique textuelle de l'Ancien Testament*, Göttingen: Vandenhoeck & Ruprecht, forthcoming).

enigmatic confession summarizes Agur's argument in verses 2–6, which moves from the epistemological limits of human wisdom (30:2–4) to the divine solution to human ignorance (30:5–6). Agur expresses the tension between human competence and incompetence to illuminate the locus of true wisdom.[14] In so doing, he supplements the search for wisdom with a profound theological statement; he modulates the promise of wisdom by describing its limits (30:2–4) and links the acquisition of wisdom with Israel's covenantal tradition (30:5–6).[15] Within the larger context, the obscure expression seems to combine human exhaustion with confidence in the divine. This combination serves as a distillation of Agur's address, which balances human weakness (30:2–4) with divine enablement (30:5–6) and sets the trajectory for the rhetorical flourish that follows.

The discourse proper (30:2–9) develops the fundamental tension between human wisdom and divine revelation. Agur elaborates on the statement presented in the superscription (30:1bβ) through an ironic, hyperbolic confession of the limits of human wisdom (30:2–3; cf. Job 28; Qoh 7:23–24; Bar 3:9–37).[16] In a series of striking statements, the foreign sage acknowledges his epistemological limitations through a sequence of intellectual expressions: בִּינָה, חָכְמָה, and קְדֹשִׁים דַּעַת. These expressions are significant, for they are used both to introduce the book and to conclude the prologue (1:2; 9:10). Whereas the imperious injunctions and terse aphorisms in the book have attempted to inculcate these values, Agur has failed to grasp them. From basic intellectual virtues to wisdom based on the knowledge of God, Agur derides any pretense of apprehending comprehensive socio-religious knowledge by mere human genius or ingenuity.[17] In so doing, he identifies the fundamental human dilemma: the transcendence of divine wisdom and the problem of human ignorance.

This epistemological gulf is heightened in the series of rhetorical questions (30:4). This rhetorical barrage incorporates the conventional motif of heavenly ascent/descent to highlight the cosmic scope of investigative knowledge and the problem of limits.[18] Since the heavens are beyond human reach and the privileges

---

14   Waltke, *Proverbs: Chapters 15–31*, 467.

15   Moore, "A Home for the Alien," 104.

16   For a discussion of Semitic hyperbole, see Van Leeuwen, "The Book of Proverbs," *NIB* 5:252; Clifford, *Proverbs*, 261; Perdue, *Proverbs*, 255; H.-F. Richter, "Hielt Agur sich für den Dümmsten aller Menschen? (Zu Prov 30,1–4)," *ZAW* 113 (2001): 419–21.

17   G. T. Sheppard, *Wisdom as a Hermeneutical Construct: A Study in the Sapientializing of the Old Testament* (BZAW 151; Berlin: de Gruyter, 1981), 91.

18   Van Leeuwen, "The Background to Proverbs 30:4aα," in *Wisdom, You Are My Sister: Studies in Honor of Roland E. Murphy, O. Carm., on the Occasion of His Eightieth Birthday* (CBQMS 29; Washington, D.C.: The Catholic Biblical Association of America, 1997), 102–21. For the motif, see W. G. Lambert, *Babylonian Wisdom Literature* (Oxford: Oxford University Press, 1960; repr., Winona Lake: Eisenbrauns, 1996), 327; "The Dialogue of Pessimism" (*BWL* 149); Alster, *Studies*

of the divine are inaccessible to mortals, the limitations of corporeal existence preclude the acquisition of divine wisdom or immortality (cf. Deut 30:12; Job 28:12–28; Bar 3:29–37). Agur reflects on the unbridgeable gulf between human jurisdiction and divine territory, and moves from the epistemological limits of humans to their restricted faculties. Inasmuch as humans lack the capacity to gather the wind (cf. Amos 4:13; Ps 104:29), restrain the waters (cf. Isa 40:12; Job 26:8; 28:26; 38:25–27), and establish the boundaries of the earth (cf. Job 28:23–24), they are also unable to employ wisdom in the management of the cosmos. The rhetorical barrage covers the vertical and horizontal dimensions of the cosmic realm to demonstrate that no human has the wisdom or power to scale the heavens and rule the cosmos; only God is able to create and sustain the cosmic realm.

This conclusion forms a rhetorical foundation for final questions (30:4bβ).[19] Here Agur incorporates common traditions associated with God's creative power and reiterates Israel's foundational question, מַה־שְּׁמוֹ (Exod 3:13), to which there is but one answer—YHWH is his name.[20] This rhetorical question gives way to the final inquiry, מַה־שֶּׁם־בְּנוֹ. The identity of the son has been interpreted in several ways, ranging from members of the divine council (cf. Ps 29:1; 89:6) to Israel as the collective, covenant people of God (cf. Exod 4:22; Deut 14:1; Isa 43:6; Jer 3:4; Hos 11:1).[21] However, since בֵּן always refers to an individual in Proverbs, it seems a particular person is in view, viz., the king. As YHWH's adopted son (2 Sam 7:14; Ps 2:6–7; 89:27–28), the king mediated God's transcendent wisdom and served as the bridge between the hidden and the known (cf. 25:2–3). The sequence of rhetorical questions suggests that Agur incorporates these mysterious inquiries to highlight the extent of human finitude and provide a resolution to the human dilemma. The foreign sage moves from the inaccessible (30:1–2) to the accessible (30:4bβ) by challenging his addressee to declare what is known, viz., that YHWH is the sovereign over creation who mediates his inscrutable wisdom and transcendent power through his official agent, the king (cf. Job 38:3–5). Agur reorients the crisis in relational rather than epistemological categories and transforms the human crisis of knowing to a crisis of knowing YHWH, the sole possessor of wisdom.[22]

This relational solution is given particular expression in verses 5–6. Here Agur alludes to specific texts to demonstrate that true wisdom depends not on human investigation but a responsive relationship with YHWH through his

---

in *Sumerian Proverbs*, 88; F. E. Greenspahn, "A Mesopotamian Proverb and Its Biblical Reverberations," *JAOS* 114 (1994): 33–38.

19   Perdue, *Wisdom Literature: A Theological History*, 71–72.

20   Waltke, *Proverbs: Chapters 15–31*, 473.

21   See LXX; Franklyn, "The Sayings of Agur," 247–48; Meinhold, *Die Sprüche*, 2:498; Murphy, *Proverbs*, 228–29; Waltke, *Proverbs: Chapters 15–31*, 473–74.

22   Waltke, *Proverbs: Chapters 15–31*, 475.

revealed will.[23] Similar to Job and Baruch (Job 28:12–28; Bar 3:29–4:1), Agur moves from rhetorical questions that affirm God's possession of wisdom to the divine disclosure of wisdom to human beings. He incorporates a composite quotation from David's victory song (2 Sam 22:31 = Ps 18:31)[24] and Moses' sermons in Deuteronomy (Deut 4:2; 13:1)[25] to assert that divine revelation is the authentic source of wisdom. Agur's use of these quotations introduces a striking development in the book of Proverbs. In elevating divine revelation over human wisdom, Agur reshapes the quest for wisdom. He moves from the wisdom tradition to the covenantal tradition, from empirical investigation to divine revelation, and from conceptual knowledge to relational/covenantal knowledge.[26] In so doing, Agur modifies the search for wisdom with a profound theological statement: human wisdom cannot achieve comprehensive knowledge; rather it must rely on divine revelation preserved in the covenantal tradition. Ironically, a foreigner makes this conclusion.

The relational solution to Agur's epistemological dilemma is escalated in the closing prayer (30:7–9), as Agur moves beyond an acknowledgment of dependence on the divine word to an explicit confession of his dependence on YHWH. Similar to the numerical sayings that follow, Agur introduces his appeal with two requests (30:7).[27] In the first, Agur demands that deceitful lies (וּדְבַר־כָּזָב שָׁוְא)[28] be removed far from him (30:8a).[29] The second petition is formulated

---

23   Moore, "A Home for the Alien," 100–101.

24   Agur modifies David's victory song in several ways: (1) he omits the introductory phrase דֶּרֶכוֹ הָאֵל תָּמִים ("As for God, his way is perfect") in order to focus on God's revelation; (2) he transposes כָּל from verset B to verset A to emphasize the reliability of divine revelation; and (3) he replaces the Tetragrammaton with אֱלוֹהַּ. This variation represents a rhetorical attempt to delay the use of the divine name until the end of the monologue (Moore, "A Home for the Alien," 100 n. 12).

25   The notion of adding or subtracting from established documents follows a common ancient Near Eastern tradition, according to which warnings or curses were incorporated into the text to proscribe the alteration of the piece. This tradition is evident in Mesopotamian, Assyrian, Hittite, Greek and Roman texts. For the motif and a discussion of its significance, see "Laws of Hammurabi," §47:79–51:91 (Roth, *Law Collections from Mesopotamia and Asia Minor*, 134–40); S. Parpola and K. Watanabe, *Neo–Assyrian Treaties and Loyalty Oaths* (SAA 2; Helsinki: Helsinki University Press, 1988), 44–45; G. Beckman, *Hittite Diplomatic Texts* (2nd ed.; SBLWAW 7; Atlanta: Scholars Press, 1999), 86, 112, 167, 175; M. Weinfeld, *Deuteronomy and the Deuteronomic School* (Oxford: Clarendon, 1972), 262.

26   See Gunneweg, "Weisheit, Prophetie und Kanonformel," 257; Moore, "A Home for the Alien," 100–101.

27   For the relationship between the prayer and numerical sayings, see Sauer, *Die Sprüche Agurs*, 101–102; W. M. W. Roth, *Numerical Sayings in the Old Testament: A Form-Critical Study* (VTSup 13; Leiden: Brill, 1965), 69–70.

28   In its literal sense, the expression שָׁוְא וּדְבַר־כָּזָב reads "falsehood and a word of deceit." The rendering "deceitful lies" assumes that the expression is a hendiadys.

through both a negative and a positive appeal (30:8ba, 8bβ). Negatively, Agur asks for a life of moderation, burdened by neither wealth nor poverty. Positively, he requests victuals necessary for survival. This *in medio* perspective is developed in the closing explanation, which focuses exclusively on the second petition (30:9). Agur grounds his plea for moderation in the potential consequences associated with wealth and poverty. He presents a *via media* paradigm that is unique to the book of Proverbs. The wealth and poverty sayings in Proverbs form a complex socio-economic vision that balances the value of wealth with the hardship of poverty, the social effects of excessive wealth with the adverse effects of excessive lack, and the importance of character with social status.[30] To this complex web, Agur supplies a new element;[31] he underscores the corrupting influence of both wealth and poverty to promote a middle way. This notion of the golden mean marks a significant contribution to the economic discourse and forms an appropriate conclusion to Agur's monologue;[32] it elevates virtue over material resources and relationship with YHWH over economic status.

To summarize, Agur's autobiographical monologue plays an important role in the re-contextualization of the proverbial discourse. The foreign sage responds to the epistemological problem of human ignorance and the moral problem of avarice through dependence on divine revelation, relationship with YHWH, and concern for the divine reputation. In so doing, he provides a theological framework through which to view the quest for wisdom. Together with the aphorisms concerning the dangers of self-valuation (3:5–7; 26:12, 16), the limitations of human wisdom (16:9; 21:31; 25:3), and the fear of YHWH (1:7, 9; 9:10; 10:27; 14:27; 15:33; 19:23; 23:17), Agur affirms that human investigation alone cannot achieve comprehensive knowledge; rather it must be accompanied by divine disclosure.[33] The foreign sage supplements the sapiential tradition with the covenantal tradition, empirical investigation with covenantal knowledge, to demonstrate that divine revelation answers the questions that human wisdom cannot. The monologue places human investigation within its proper boundaries and highlights the divine dimension of proverbial wisdom.[34]

---

29   Together with verse 10, Brown identifies the theological orientation of lying/slander within the compositional unit and its thematic relationship with the previous collections ("The Pedagogy of Proverbs 10:1–31:9," 177).

30   See Sandoval, *The Discourse of Wealth and Poverty*, 112–13, *et passim*.

31   Whybray, *Wealth and Poverty in the Book of Proverbs*, 79–81.

32   Brown, "The Pedagogy of Proverbs 10:1–31:9," 178.

33   Moore, "A Home for the Alien," 104.

34   In addition to the theological perspective of Agur's words, Brown emphasizes the cosmic purview of the discourse, which is "unmatched in the previous collections except in a few isolated cases" ("The Pedagogy of Proverbs 10:1–31:9," 178). However, in contrast to the present study, Brown does not identify the role of Agur's words in the re-contextualization of the sapiential discourse or the way in which Agur modifies the quest for wisdom.

The concern with proper boundaries continues in the central section of the collection. These numerical sayings are divided into two sub-sections by independent, non-numerical aphorisms (30:10, 17).[35] The former functions as a transition from the autobiography to the series of numerical sayings (30:10);[36] the latter contains a series of catchwords that link the second unit of numerical sayings with the first (אָב, 30:11, 17; אֵם, 30:11, 17; אכל, 30:14, 17).[37] Together, these independent aphorisms proscribe actions that subvert the socio-moral order—a motif that pervades the numerical sayings throughout the chapter. The first seeks to rein in potential abuse of slaves/officials (עֶבֶד)[38] by describing God's implicit requital of the verbal oppressor (30:10), while the second provides a graphic portrait of ravenous birds plucking out and devouring the eyes of an arrogant child (30:17). These aphorisms focus on actions that undermine the hierarchical arrangement of the socio-religious order and identify particular, divine punishments that are absent from the numerical sayings that follow.[39] They promote virtues that establish socio-moral stability and present the fundamental theme that permeates the constituent numerical sayings within the collection.

The numerical sayings that make up the central section of the collection are cast in either graded or simple form. These sayings systematize various phenomena that share a common denominator to achieve a particular purpose.[40] Numerical sayings were employed throughout the ancient world to entertain, to reflect on the arrangement of the cosmos, to inculcate desirable human behavior, and to stimulate reflection.[41] These rhetorical functions are not mutually exclusive, since numerical sayings can operate on several different levels. However, within Proverbs 30, it seems the sayings appeal to the activities and mysteries of the human, animal, and natural world as a means for investigating

---

35   Waltke, *Proverbs: Chapters 15–31*, 464.

36   See Van Leeuwen, "The Book of Proverbs," *NIB* 5:253; Murphy, *Proverbs*, 230; Clifford, *Proverbs*, 256–57; Steinmann, "Three Things," 61, 65; Waltke, *Proverbs: Chapters 15–31*, 483.

37   Garrett, *Proverbs*, 240; Van Leeuwen, "The Book of Proverbs," *NIB* 5:254; Murphy, *Proverbs*, 235; Waltke, *Proverbs: Chapters 15–31*, 489.

38   The noun עֶבֶד is ambiguous in the present context. Based on the identity of the אָדוֹן, עֶבֶד may refer to a common slave or an official. See Meinhold, *Die Sprüche*, 2:501.

39   Waltke, *Proverbs: Chapters 15–31*, 482.

40   Forti, *Animal Imagery in the Book of Proverbs*, 120.

41   For the form and function of numerical sayings in both the ancient Near East and the Old Testament, see A. Bea, "Der Zahlenspruch im Hebräischen und Ugaritischen," *Bib* 21 (1940): 196–98; A. Alt, "Die Weisheit Salomos," *Theologische Literaturzeitung* 76 (1951): 139–44; repr. "Solomonic Wisdom" in *Studies in Ancient Israelite Religion* (ed. and trans. J. L. Crenshaw; New York: Ktav, 1976), 102–12; Sauer, *Die Sprüche Agurs*, 7–91; W. M. W. Roth, "The Numerical Sequence x/x + 1 in the Old Testament," *VT* 12 (1962): 300–11; idem, *Numerical Sayings in the Old Testament*, 5–9, *et passim*; H. P. Rüger, "Die gestaffelten Zahlensprüche des Alten Testaments und Aram. Achikar 92," *VT* 31 (1981): 229–34; P. J. Nel, *The Structure and Ethos of the Wisdom Admonitions in Proverbs* (BZAW 158; Berlin: Walter de Gruyter, 1982), 11–12; R. A. Kassis, *The Book of Proverbs and Arabic Proverbial Works* (Leiden: Brill, 1999), 234–41.

human behavior and social organization.[42] Each unit consists of a series of elements in which the final saying functions as the climactic element, integrating the diverse components around a specific theme.[43] In the main, these themes pertain to aspects of the socio-moral order. The extended numerical sayings elaborate on the independent, non-numerical aphorisms (30:10, 17) through two primary sub-sections (30:11–16, 18–31). The nature of each subunit deserves specific comment.

The first subunit (30:11–16) consists of three numerical sayings (30:11–14, 15a, 15b–16). These numerical units seek to preserve social order by reining in degenerate appetites. The initial segment catalogues the characteristics of the perverse דוֹר, that is, a particular class or breed of individuals (30:11–14).[44] This unit moves from the rejection of parental authority (30:11) to the arrogant, deluded logic of the wicked generation (30:12–13). These qualities form the foundation for the violent images in the final aphorism (30:14). Similar to 28:15, the saying incorporates arresting images to underscore the perverse generation's exploitation of the weak. This concluding aphorism heightens the sense of the unit, escalating the domestic and epistemological impropriety of the generation through their abuse of power. On the whole, the unit identifies the fundamental qualities of the perverse generation and promotes social order by proscribing greed, the dominant vice of the wicked generation.

The initial segment's concern with greed is given particular expression in the final numerical sayings of the subunit (30:15a, 15b–16). These sayings incorporate observations from the human, animal, and natural world to highlight the insatiable appetite of avarice. The first numerical saying serves as an introduction to the formal catalogue of insatiables in verses 15b–16 (30:15a). Here the bloodsucking leech is depicted as the mother of two voracious daughters (הַב הַב), who symbolize the unquenchable appetite of parasitic people. This notion is reinforced by the final numerical saying in the initial subunit, which enumerates a series of insatiable elements from the cosmic and human world (30:15b–16). These personified elements never say הוֹן ("enough," 30:15c, 16c). This declaration is significant, for it represents the only instance in which the common designation for wealth is used in an adverbial sense within the book.[45] By including the term, the poet produces a rhetorical pun. The unquenchable desires of Sheol, the barren womb, a parched land, and fire never achieve their desired

---

42 Meinhold, *Die Sprüche*, 2:506; Forti, *Animal Imagery in the Book of Proverbs*, 131.

43 M. Haran, "The Graded Numerical Sequence and the Phenomenon of 'Automatism' in Biblical Poetry," *VT* 22 (1972): 261–67; Steinmann, "Three Things," 63–65.

44 Though the title is absent, the initial anaphora of דוֹר unifies the diverse characteristics around a single subject. See Whybray, *The Composition of the Book of Proverbs*, 151; Van Leeuwen, "The Book of Proverbs," *NIB* 5:253; Murphy, *Proverbs*, 230–31.

45 Sandoval, *The Discourse of Wealth and Poverty*, 60.

"wealth."[46] In the same way, the parasitic or greedy person will never find satisfaction. The aphorism provides a graphic illustration of Agur's petition for a *via media* existence and develops the implicit concern with greed in the initial numerical unit (30:11–14).

The second subunit builds on the concerns of the first through four numerical sayings (30:18–20, 21–23, 24–28, 29–31), each of which begins with a formal title. The first unit expresses astonishment at the inexplicable wonder occasioned by the דֶּרֶךְ of four creatures within the created order (30:18–20). The poet's amazement is not necessarily directed toward the enigmatic movement of these creatures, but toward their irrecoverable course of action.[47] Just as one cannot trace the trajectory of a soaring eagle, plot the motion of the gliding serpent, or chart the passage of a ship slicing through the seas, so one cannot explain the magnetic attraction of erotic love. This enigmatic phenomenon forms the basis for the contrast in verse 20. Though verse 20 moves beyond the concerns of the numerical saying, it is linked to the sequence by the *Leitwort* דֶּרֶךְ and the sexual activities commensurate with the climactic element. In contrast to the enigmatic wonder of romantic love, the behavior of the adulteress not only evokes horror; it is also perfectly understandable. She gratifies her sexual palate as one appeases one's gastronomic appetite. Similar to the prologue, the vignette presents a דֶּרֶךְ that undermines the socio-moral order and replaces the legitimate expression of love with a blatant violation of the boundaries.

The concern with the proscribed parameters of the socio-moral order is heightened in the second numerical unit (30:21–23), which moves from the boundaries of the marital relationship to the public sphere. While the subunit contains elements of humor, the relational vignettes form a sober social commentary on an inverted world.[48] Within the ancient oriental world, this "world upside down" topos assumes a royal, hierarchical view of society and attempts to legitimate the status quo.[49] The same is true in the present numerical unit, which presents a series of inverted social relations to provide a socio-

---

46   Sandoval, *The Discourse of Wealth and Poverty*, 60; Fox, *Proverbs 10–31*, 868.

47   Murphy, *Proverbs*, 235. For a discussion of several other proposals concerning the enigmatic way of these phenomena, see Fox, *Proverbs 10–31*, 870–72.

48   Many read the numerical unit as a social satire, a comical caricature of apparent threats to the established order (McKane, *Proverbs: A New Approach*, 659–60; Whybray, *The Composition of the Book of Proverbs*, 152). However, the focus on inverted social relations, rather than individual character types, suggests the subunit is intended as a serious socio-political statement. See W. M. W. Roth, "NBL," *VT* 10 (1960): 403–04; R. C. Van Leeuwen, "Proverbs 30:21–23 and the Biblical World Upside Down," *JBL* 105 (1986): 599–610; Waltke, *Proverbs: Chapters 15–31*, 493.

49   For the "world upside down" topos, see "The Prophecies of Neferti" (*AEL* 1:140–45); "The Complaints of Khakheperre-Sonb" (*AEL* 1:146–49); "The Admonitions of Ipuwer" (*AEL* 1:150–63); Kitchen, "Studies in Egyptian Wisdom Literature: I. The Instruction by a Man for His Son," 189–208; Van Leeuwen, "Proverbs 30:21–23 and the Biblical World Upside Down," 599–610.

political vision of propriety. This vision is formulated by a description of four character types: a עֶבֶד,[50] a נָבָל,[51] a שְׂנוּאָה, and a שִׁפְחָה. These personages represent individuals of low standing who violate traditional social boundaries and secure a higher status in the community. In so doing, they invert conventional parameters of the social order and cause the world "to quake." The combination of the political and domestic spheres not only highlights the two fundamental social structures within society, but it also unites them. This confluence is particularly apparent in the climactic saying, which employs the designation גְּבִירָה, an honorific epithet for the queen mother (30:23; cf. 1 Kgs 11:19; 15:13; 2 Kgs 10:13; Isa 47:5, 7; Jer 13:18; 29:2; 2 Chron 15:16).[52] Together with the initial aphorisms concerning the socio-political realm, this epithet enhances the political agenda of the piece. The numerical unit promotes a hierarchical view of society, a royal vision of the status quo.[53] It underscores the importance of social propriety and seeks to establish appropriate boundaries at all levels of society.

In contrast to the preceding focus on humans who overturn the social order, the third subunit introduces four creatures from the natural realm that employ wisdom to secure order (30:24–28). In each case, the physical limitations of these creatures are counterbalanced by their intelligence—ants demonstrate industry and foresight to secure provisions, badgers incorporate technical ingenuity to construct an impenetrable fortress, and locusts overcome social disorganization to form a cohesive, integrated group.[54] In contrast to these vignettes, the final saying is unique. The aphorism does not employ a virtue to compensate for the vulnerability of the lizard; rather it presents an implicit reward for integrating wisdom: access to the royal residence. The saying moves beyond provision, protection, and communal order to social promotion—elevation to the circle of the court.[55]

---

50   Though עֶבֶד is a fluid term used in a domestic sense elsewhere in the book (11:29; 12:9; 17:2; 19:10; 22:7), it seems to function as a designation for a royal official in the present context. This is reinforced by the notion that a government official could more readily usurp the throne than a domestic servant. See Van Leeuwen, "The Book of Proverbs," *NIB* 5:254–55; Waltke, *Proverbs: Chapters 15–31*, 493.

51   The adjective נָבָל is typically rendered "fool." However, the term is associated with actions contrary to law and order and may be rendered "outlaw" or social outcast (cf. 12:9; 17:7). See Roth, "NBL," 401–04; Van Leeuwen, "Proverbs 30:21–23 and the Biblical World Upside Down," 607.

52   For the function of the queen in ancient Israel, see N.-E. A. Andreasen, "The Role of the Queen Mother in Israelite Society," *CBQ* 45 (1983): 179–94; C. Smith, "'Queenship' in Israel? The Cases of Bathsheba, Jezebel and Athaliah," in *King and Messiah in Israel and the Ancient Near East: Proceedings of the Oxford Old Testament Seminar* (JSOTSup 270; Sheffield: Sheffield Academic Press, 1998), 142–62, esp. 143–45.

53   Van Leeuwen, "Proverbs 30:21–23 and the Biblical World Upside Down," 609–10.

54   Forti, *Animal Imagery in the Book of Proverbs*, 117.

55   McKane, *Proverbs: A New Approach*, 662; Garrett, *Proverbs*, 242.

The royal color implicit in the preceding sections is given explicit expression in the fourth numerical subunit (30:29–31). This segment introduces figures from the animal and human world who stride in regal dignity over their respective communities: the לַיִשׁ, the זַרְזִיר מָתְנַיִם,[56] the תַּיִשׁ, and the מֶלֶךְ. These paragons of power and courage rule over their diverse communities with confidence and regal dignity. Just as these stately creatures establish orderly rule in their respective spheres, so the king inspires awe through his appearance and leadership over those under his charge.[57] The depiction of these figures may be interpreted as a social critique of royal arrogance, for several segments within the collection censure misplaced pride, expressed through injustice (30:11–14), greed (30:15–16), and the refusal to accept one's place in the social order (30:18–20, 21–23, 24–28). However, the final numerical unit situates dignity in its rightful place, viz., among chosen agents through whom divine rule is established.[58] The catalogue underscores the grandeur of the king and promotes royal respect by positioning prestige in its legitimate domain.

The majestic dignity of the monarch gives way to the closing admonition concerning legitimate authority and the maintenance of the social order (30:32–33). As noted above, the conclusion resumes the direct address of the autobiography (30:1b–10) and summarizes the fundamental message of the composition.[59] The opening admonition censures pride expressed in self-exultation and devious schemes that subvert the social order (30:32). This pointed command is grounded in the final aphorism, which catalogs three consequences of applying pressure (מִיץ). Just as the churning of cream produces butter and the pinching of the nose produces blood, so anger produces provocation when it is pressed beyond proper limits (30:33). Together with the admonition, the

---

56 In its literal sense, the phrase זַרְזִיר מָתְנַיִם means "girt of loins." The rendering "strutting rooster" follows the LXX (cf. Vulg.), which reads ἀλέκτωρ ἐμπεριπατῶν θηλείαις εὔψυχος ("a rooster walking about bravely among the female [hens]"). The *hapax legomenon* זַרְזִיר has been rendered in several ways, ranging from a greyhound and a war-horse to a specific bird within the raven family—a starling, crow, or magpie (*b. B. Qam.* 92b; *b. Ḥul.* 65a; *Gen. Rab.* 65:75). See McKane, *Proverbs: A New Approach*, 663–64; Forti, *Animal Imagery in the Book of Proverbs*, 119.

57 The term אַלְקוּם is uncertain and has been interpreted in several different ways. Many translations render the term in light of the Arabic definite article *'al* and the Arabic verb *qwm* ("levy") to read "calling his army with him" (cf. NASB, NIV). However, this reading mixes Hebrew and Arabic. Others emend the phrase אַלְקוּם עִמּוֹ to either עַמּוֹ לֹא־קָם ("against whom there is no rising up") or קָם אֶל עַמּוֹ ("standing over his people"). As the text stands, אַלְקוּם may be separated and rendered etymologically: אַל, "not," and קוּם, "rise up," with עִמּוֹ in an oppositional sense, "against him." In this case, the phrase may be rendered "no one dares to rise up against him" (cf. JPS). It conveys the king's majestic authority and appearance before the people. See Driver, "Problems in the Hebrew Text of Proverbs," 194; McKane, *Proverbs: A New Approach*, 664; Plöger, *Sprüche Salomos*, 355; Meinhold, *Die Sprüche*, 2:505 n. 170; Garrett, *Proverbs*, 243 n. 27; Waltke, *Proverbs: Chapters 15–31*, 462 n. 79.

58 Perdue, *Proverbs*, 266.

59 See Sauer, *Die Sprüche Agurs*, 111; Perdue, *Proverbs*, 267; Steinmann, "Three Things," 65.

concluding motivation recapitulates the principal themes of the collection. The aphorism promotes humility, respect, and social order in the place of hubris and self-exultation.

6.1.1 Section Conclusion

In sum, the final section of Agur's discourse elaborates on the fundamental themes presented in the monologue (30:1–9). The independent aphorisms and numerical units move from epistemological limitations (30:1–6) to social limitations (30:10, 17, 18–20, 21–23, 32–33) and from the corrupting influence of both wealth and poverty (30:7–9) to social exploitation and the insatiable nature of avarice (30:11–14, 15–16). In general, the composition seeks to censure hubris and greed by promoting subordination to divine revelation and conventional social boundaries, whether economic, domestic, or political.[60] The compilation presents a royal, hierarchical vision of the world that is maintained through submission to legitimate authority and the king within the proscribed parameters of the cosmic and social realm. This royal vision reinforces the sapiential concern with social propriety and provides the addressee with a worldview he must adopt, a hierarchy he must maintain.

6.2 The Words of Lemuel (31:1–31)

Together with the words of Agur (30:1–33), the words of Lemuel (31:1–31) coalesce with the introductory lectures and interludes to form an interpretive envelope around the book.[61] This framework is formulated through the use of common images, themes, and literary devices, each of which will be examined in the subsequent discussion. The concluding composition represents the culmination of the book's pedagogical program and the consummation of the addressee's moral formation; it marks the completion of the quest for wisdom, a journey of character that finds its concrete expression in the world of the court.

The concluding composition is marked off from the previous collection by a formal superscription (31:1). In light of the generic differences between the instruction (31:2–9) and the hymnic encomium (31:10–31), many limit the sense

---

60   See Brown, "The Pedagogy of Proverbs 10:1–31:9," 177. Brown observes that the composition's conception of self-exultation and hubris corresponds with the moral vision of the Hezekian collection (26:12; cf. 26:16; 27:2, 21).

61   See note 1 above.

of the heading to the former collection.[62] However, if the panegyric constitutes an independent composition, then it is the only discourse in the book without a formal title (cf. 1:1; 10:1; 22:17; 24:23; 25:1; 30:1).[63] Whether the encomium is an extension of the royal instruction or a discrete composition, the juxtaposition of the pieces appears to be intentional, for the collections contain several verbal and thematic links.[64] Both incorporate female imagery, the noun חַיִל (31:3, 10, 29), and express a particular concern for the marginalized (31:5–8, 20). These features suggest the poems have been deliberately collated. Though the instruction and the panegyric may have existed as independent documents, in their present location they function as part of a larger literary unit. The thematic emphases and hermeneutical significance of each unit deserves a brief comment.

The initial unit represents a royal instruction (31:1–9), delivered by the queen mother to her royal son. This instruction is comparable to several royal testaments in the ancient world.[65] However, in contrast to these royal testaments, the words of Lemuel are attributed to the king's mother (31:1). This designation preserves the familial flavor of the sapiential material and gives particular expression to the regal, maternal voice of the prologue (cf. 1:8; 6:20).[66] Lemuel memorializes the courtly counsel of his mother by enumerating three issues related to competent leadership.[67] In the first, the queen warns the young monarch against unrestrained sexual relations (31:3). By expending his royal power on the pursuit of sexual liaisons, the king anesthetizes his judgment, undermines his personal authority, and subverts the foundations of sound government (cf. 2 Sam 11–12; 1 Kgs 11–12). A similar point is made in the second appeal, which moves from obsession with women to obsession with wine (31:4–5). This prohibition does not function as a categorical proscription against the consumption of liquor; rather it is an admonition against intoxication,[68] for

---

62 This division follows the recensional scheme of the Septuagint and accounts for the disparate mode of address in the compositions. However, as noted above, the LXX represents a secondary arrangement of the document. See Washington, *Wealth and Poverty*, 125–26; Tov, "Recensional Differences," 419–32.

63 See Kitchen, "Proverbs and Wisdom Books of the Ancient Near East," 101; Waltke, *Proverbs: Chapters 15–31*, 502. Both Kitchen and Waltke attribute the heroic panegyric to Lemuel's mother.

64 See M. H. Lichtenstein, "Chiasm and Symmetry in Proverbs 31," *CBQ* 44 (1982): 202–11; repr. in *Learning from the Sages: Selected Studies on the Book of Proverbs* (ed. R. B. Zuck; Grand Rapids: Baker, 1995), 381–90; V. A. Hurowitz, "The Seventh Pillar—Reconsidering the Literary Structure and Unity of Proverbs 31," *ZAW* 113 (2001): 209–18.

65 See "The Instruction Addressed to King Merikare" (*AEL* 1:97–109); "The Instruction of King Amenhemet I for His Son Sesostris I" (*AEL* 1:135–39); "Advice to a Prince" (Foster, *Before the Muses*, 2:745–47).

66 Camp, *Wisdom and the Feminine*, 188–89; Fontaine, "Wisdom in Proverbs," 102; Brown, "The Pedagogy of Proverbs 10:1–31:9," 178.

67 Brown, "The Pedagogy of Proverbs 10:1–31:9," 179.

68 Meinhold, *Die Sprüche*, 2:518; Waltke, *Proverbs: Chapters 15–31*, 507–08; Fox, *Proverbs 10–31*, 886.

royal dissipation interferes with the cognitive faculties needed for the administration of justice in general and the protection of the oppressed in particular. This negative appeal is reinforced though a sarcastic, positive command that underscores the ineffectual nature of intoxicants (31:6–7).[69] Intoxicants may serve a positive purpose for the destitute,[70] but they do not palliate the plight of the poor. Rather, they simply desensitize the marginalized. This ironic, rhetorical command highlights the futility of intoxicants and encourages the king to acknowledge his fundamental responsibility: the institution of justice for the poor.[71] This implicit plea is made explicit in the third appeal (31:8–9), as the queen advises her son to be the voice of the defenseless, the exponent of justice, and the champion of the oppressed. The queen moves from the private behavior of the king to his public conduct to delineate the fundamental features of effective leadership and just governance.

As an independent instruction, the composition provides a socio-moral standard by which the royal institution may be assessed. In the main, the queen seeks to rein in the potential abuse of power for personal privilege. However, within the larger moral discourse of the book of Proverbs, the instruction contributes to the thematic development of the material. As noted above, the composition preserves the familial flavor of the document's pedagogical setting and gives particular expression to the regal, maternal voice of the prologue. Moreover, in contrast to the previous collections, the addressee is given specific reference.[72] The noble, silent "son" moves from the subject position of a liminal adolescent to the seat of royal power.[73] The journey of character culminates in the occupation of the throne by a king, who represents the embodiment of the community's ethos and the barometer of the nation's character. Within the context of the book as a whole, the royal instruction re-contextualizes the sapiential material. The piece reinforces the discourse setting of the prologue, heightens the thematic movement of the material, and strengthens the courtly flavor of the book.

In conjunction with the royal instruction, the heroic panegyric (31:10–31) also plays an important role in the re-contextualization of Proverbs. This paean is

---

69   Waltke, *Proverbs: Chapters 15–31*, 508.

70   See McKane, *Proverbs: A New Approach*, 410; J. L. Crenshaw, "A Mother's Instruction to Her Son (Proverbs 31:1–9)," in *Perspectives on the Hebrew Bible* (ed. J. L. Crenshaw; Macon: Mercer University Press, 1988), 9–22; repr. in *Urgent Advice and Probing Questions: Collected Writings on Old Testament Wisdom*, 391; Murphy, *Proverbs*, 241; Clifford, *Proverbs*, 270–71; Perdue, *Proverbs*, 273.

71   Garrett, *Proverbs*, 246; Waltke, *Proverbs: Chapters 15–31*, 508–09.

72   Brown, "The Pedagogy of Proverbs 10:1–31:9," 178–79.

73   Brown, "The Pedagogy of Proverbs 10:1–31:9," 181. Also see Perdue, *Proverbs*, 270–71. With regard to thematic development, Brown observes that the royal instruction moves from the king as mediator of divine wrath and the embodiment of divine power to the object of admonishment, held accountable for his public and private actions ("The Pedagogy of Proverbs 10:1–31:9," 179).

a sophisticated alphabetic acrostic that contains several verbal and thematic features that link the encomium with the prologue. In addition to the dominant female imagery, the אֵשֶׁת־חַיִל shares a number of characteristics with Woman Wisdom. Similar to Woman Wisdom, the אֵשֶׁת־חַיִל is difficult to obtain (מָצָא, 31:10, 1:28; 8:17), more precious than corals (פְּנִינִים, 31:10; 3:15 [Q]; 8:11), the proprietress of a substantial household (בַּיִת, 31:15, 21, 27; 9:1; נַעֲרָה, 31:15; 9:3), a source of security (בֶּטַח, 31:11; 1:33), and a paragon of the fear of YHWH (31:30; 1:29; 8:13).[74] However, this woman does not function as a simple, allegorical counterpart to Woman Wisdom;[75] she also represents the concrete embodiment of wisdom in an ideal, upper-class wife.[76] Together with several aphorisms in the sentence literature (11:16; 12:4; 14:1; 18:22; 19:14), the paean moves from the symbolic register to the historical register, providing an impressionistic portrait of an exemplary wife from a specific, narrow angle.[77] Though the portrait is composed through fantastic images, several features suggest the אֵשֶׁת־חַיִל may represent an actual woman. In contrast to Woman Wisdom, the valiant wife is characterized as an אִשָּׁה, which always denotes a real woman in Proverbs (e.g., 12:4; 14:1; 18:22; 19:13; 25:24; 27:15; cf. Ruth 3:11).[78] Moreover, the אֵשֶׁת־חַיִל participates in socio-economic ventures that are comparable to the activities of real women.[79] Whether the poem is read on the metaphorical level or the literal level, the paean coalesces with the introductory discourses to form a framework around the book. This framework transforms the fictional into the palpable, the

---

74 For a catalogue of the similarities between the אֵשֶׁת־חַיִל and Woman Wisdom, see Barucq, *Le livre des Proverbes*, 231; J. N. Aletti, "Seduction et parole, 129–44; McCreesh, "Wisdom as Wife: Proverbs 31:10–31," 391–410; Camp, *Wisdom and the Feminine*, 186–208; Whybray, *The Composition of the Book of Proverbs*, 153–62; Yoder, *Wisdom as a Woman of Substance*, 91–93; Fox, *Proverbs 10–31*, 908–09.

75 For an allegorical interpretation of the אֵשֶׁת־חַיִל, see E. Jacob, "Sagesse et alphabet. A propos de Proverbes 31.10–31," in *Hommages à André Dupont-Sommer* (Paris: Librairie d'Amérique er d'Orient Adrien Maisonneuve, 1971), 287–95; McCreesh, "Wisdom as Wife: Proverbs 31:10–31," 391–410; Hausmann, "Beobachtungen zu Spr 31,10–31," 265–66; Blenkinsopp, *Sage, Priest, Prophet*, 34–35.

76 See Plöger, *Sprüche Salomos*, 376; E. L. Lyons, "A Note on Proverbs 31:10–31," in *The Listening Heart: Essays in Wisdom and the Psalms in Honor of Roland E. Murphy, O. Carm.* (ed. K. G. Hoglund et al., Sheffield: Sheffield Academic Press, 1987), 237–45; A. Bonora, "La donna eccellente, la sapienza, il sapiente," *RevistB* 36 (1988): 137–64; Meinhold, *Die Sprüche*, 2:521; Van Leeuwen, "The Book of Proverbs," *NIB* 5:264; B. K. Waltke, "The Role of the 'Valiant Wife' in the Marketplace," *Crux* 35 (1999): 23–34; M. Beth Szlos, "A Portrait of Power: A Literary-Critical Study of the Depiction of the Woman in Proverbs 31:10–31," *USQR* 54 (2000): 97–103; Yoder, *Wisdom as a Woman of Substance*, 90, *et passim*; V. A. Hurowitz, "The Woman of Valor and a Woman Large of Head: Matchmaking in the Ancient Near East," in *Seeking out the Wisdom of the Ancients: Essays Offered to Honor Michael V. Fox on the Occasion of His Sixty-Fifth Birthday* (ed. K. G. Friebel et al.; Winona Lake: Eisenbrauns, 2005), 221 n. 1.

77 Yoder, *Wisdom as a Woman of Substance*, 75–76.

78 Waltke, "The Role of the 'Valiant Wife'," 30.

79 See Yoder, *Wisdom as a Woman of Substance*, 39–110.

figurative into the physical, to provide a captivating image of wisdom's inherent value.

The poet catalogs the activities of the אֵשֶׁת־חַיִל within an alphabetic acrostic to provide a comprehensive treatment of the subject.[80] Though the acrostic lacks a clear structure, its thematic unity is obvious.[81] As a whole, the poem is a heroic panegyric that integrates features from hymnic and heroic compositions.[82] However, in contrast to heroic poetry (1 Sam 18:7; 21:11; 2 Sam 1:17–27), the encomium replaces the intrepid, military exploits of aristocratic men with a woman's *vita activa* in the home and community (cf. Judg 5:1–31).[83] These domestic and communal activities are stunning, for many of the valiant wife's pursuits are delineated through royal military imagery.[84] The אֵשֶׁת־חַיִל exhibits endurance, prowess, and ingenuity to secure שָׁלָל (31:11) and טֶרֶף (31:15) for her household. She girds her loins with strength (31:17; 1 Kgs 18:46; 2 Kgs 4:29; Jer 1:17) and wraps herself in garments of honor (31:25). This portrait of power is not surprising, for the designation אֵשֶׁת־חַיִל evokes military connotations. In the main, חַיִל denotes power or prowess. The term is associated with military personnel (e.g., Josh 1:14; Judg 6:12; 11:1; 2 Sam 11:16; 2 Kgs 24:14), property owners (Gen 47:6), or community leaders (Exod 18:21, 25; Ruth 2:1)—prominent people of substance.[85] Though the idiom אֵשֶׁת־חַיִל has been translated in a variety of ways,[86] the images and activities attributed to the woman suggest that she is a noble, valiant figure. These activities illuminate her physical and socio-economic power, as well as her noble, courtly character.

The aristocratic character of the אֵשֶׁת־חַיִל is given particular expression throughout the poem. The panegyric highlights the social status of the valiant

---

80   W. G. E. Watson, *Classical Hebrew Poetry: A Guide to Its Techniques* (JSOTSup 26; Sheffield: JSOT, 1984), 190–200; Meinhold, *Die Sprüche*, 2:521; J. F. Brug, "Biblical Acrostics and Their Relationship to Other Ancient Near Eastern Acrostics," in *The Bible in the Light of Cuneiform Literature: Scripture in Context III* (ed. W. W. Hallo, B. W. Jones, and G. L. Mattingly; Lewiston: Mellen, 1990), 283–304.

81   Despite the thematic unity of the poem, there is no consensus concerning the structure of the piece. This is not surprising, since alphabetic acrostics are artificially arranged to meet the needs of the external factors. For some structural proposals, see Barucq, *Le livre des Proverbes*, 231; Lichtenstein, "Chiasm and Symmetry," 381–90; Watson, *Classical Hebrew Poetry*, 194; McCreesh, "Wisdom as Wife: Proverbs 31:10–31," 391–410; Wolters, "Proverbs XXXI 10–31 as Heroic Hymn," 449; Meinhold, *Die Sprüche*, 2:521–22; Garrett, *Proverbs*, 248; Waltke, *Proverbs: Chapters 15–31*, 515.

82   Wolters, "Proverbs XXXI 10–31 as Heroic Hymn," 446–57.

83   Wolters, "Proverbs XXXI 10–31 as Heroic Hymn," 457.

84   For a survey of the military imagery in the poem, see Wolters, "Proverbs XXXI 10–31 as Heroic Hymn," 452–55; Waltke, "The Role of the 'Valiant Wife'," 24–25; Szlos, "A Portrait of Power," 97–103.

85   Yoder, *Wisdom as a Woman of Substance*, 76–77.

86   For a list of various proposals, see Szlos, "A Portrait of Power," 98 n. 4; Yoder, *Wisdom as a Woman of Substance*, 76–77.

wife through her specific activity within the household and the community. The valiant wife is depicted as the proprietress of a large estate that enjoys the trappings of privilege and wealth. Similar to a merchant fleet, the אֵשֶׁת־חַיִל imports extravagant delicacies "from afar" (מִמֶּרְחָק, 31:14). Her household is not subjected to a hand-to-mouth existence; rather it enjoys choice, royal fare.[87] The table delicacies of the household are consistent with the expensive garments that clothe its members (31:21–22). The valiant wife does not fear the snow, for her family is dressed in "scarlet" (שָׁנִים, 31:21)—a palatial, dyed fabric that represents wealth and royalty (2 Sam 1:24; Jer 4:30).[88] These elegant garments correspond with the clothing of the woman (31:22). The אֵשֶׁת־חַיִל wears imported Egyptian linen (שֵׁשׁ; cf. Isa 3:23) and purple dyed wool (אַרְגָּמָן; cf. Judg 8:36; Esth 1:6; 8:15).[89] She is depicted as a noble matriarch who provides fine clothing for her family, dresses in royal apparel, and lines her bed with imperial covers (מַרְבַדִּים, 31:22; 7:16).[90]

In addition, the אֵשֶׁת־חַיִל supervises a retinue of נַעֲרֹת ("servants girls") and supplies her staff with their daily needs (31:15). Her management of the household mirrors her husband's management of the community (31:23). The woman's prominence in the home forms the foundation for her husband's respected position among the leaders at the gate. She is the crown that adorns her husband's head (12:4) and the subject of praise in her husband's office (31:31). This portrait of the domestic activities of the אֵשֶׁת־חַיִל suggests that she is far more than a supervisor of a simple, pedestrian domicile. The nature of her commodities, the scope of her household, and the prominence of her husband suggest an exceptional proprietress, a noble, aristocratic matriarch.[91]

The aristocratic status of the אֵשֶׁת־חַיִל is also evident in her commercial ventures and contributions to the community. As a perceptive purveyor, the אֵשֶׁת־חַיִל procures imported raw materials (31:13), weaves fine textiles with a spindle (31:19),[92] and produces precious garments that are sold in the marketplace

---

87　Yoder, *Wisdom as a Woman of Substance*, 83–84.

88　Many scholars follow the LXX and read שְׁנַיִם ("double") rather than שָׁנִים ("scarlet"), since the latter term is a rare plural (Gemser, *Sprüche Salomos*, 110; Murphy, *Proverbs*, 244; Clifford, *Proverbs*, 276). However, the rendering of the MT should be retained for two reasons: (1) the plural form שָׁנִים is attested in Isaiah 1:18, where it is parallel to שֶׁלֶג; (2) based on the parallel אַרְגָּמָן in verse 22, it seems the issue in the present text is the quality rather than the quantity of garments. See Yoder, *Wisdom as a Woman of Substance*, 84 n. 55; Waltke, *Proverbs: Chapters 15–31*, 512 n. 85.

89　Yoder, *Wisdom as a Woman of Substance*, 85. Also see McCreesh, "Wisdom as Wife: Proverbs 31:10–31," 393.

90　See D. R. Edwards, "Dress and Ornamentation," *ABD* 2:235; Yoder, *Wisdom as a Woman of Substance*, 85.

91　Wolters, "Proverbs XXXI 10–31 as Heroic Hymn," 455; Van Leeuwen, "The Book of Proverbs," *NIB* 5:264; Waltke, "The Role of the 'Valiant Wife'," 25; Szlos, "A Portrait of Power," 103.

92　For a detailed discussion of the relationship between the כִּישׁוֹר and the פֶּלֶךְ as well as their role in the art of spinning, see A. Wolters, "The Meaning of *Kîsôr* (Prov. 31:19)," *HUCA* 65 (1994): 91–104.

(31:24; cf. Judg 14:12–13; Isa 3:23). Rather than squandering her revenues on vain pursuits, the valiant wife acquires property suitable for agronomic returns (31:16) and distributes her wealth to the marginalized (31:20).[93] Her commercial exploits extend beyond the marketplace to include the destitute within the community. These communal contributions enhance her noble image and reinforce her aristocratic status. While the king defends the rights of the weak (31:8–9), the אֵשֶׁת־חַיִל provides for their practical needs (31:20). She incarnates the deuteronomic ideal (Deut 10:12–22; 15:7–8) and gives concrete expression to what it means to be wise.

In view of the exemplary character of the אֵשֶׁת־חַיִל, it is not surprising that the discourse moves from her mundane activities to her moral nobility. The paean offers a profound corrective to traditional ancient valuations of women.[94] Rather than focusing on the woman's physical charms or sexual appeal, the encomium highlights her internal beauty: she opens her mouth in wisdom (31:26) and fears YHWH (31:30).[95] The rhetorical flourish culminates in the fundamental sapiential virtue and grounds the mundane, practical activities of the אֵשֶׁת־חַיִל in the fear of YHWH (cf. Deut 10:12–13). In so doing, it creates a literary envelope around the book (1:7; 31:30), and illustrates the concrete embodiment of theoretical wisdom. The poem portrays wisdom incarnate, wisdom applied to every dimension of life.

The impressionistic portrait of the אֵשֶׁת־חַיִל forms an appropriate conclusion to the book of Proverbs. The paean combines with the introductory lectures and interludes to provide a coda for the book, filtering the document's principal themes through a single, exceptional woman.[96] As the conclusion to Proverbs, the encomium functions in two principal ways. First, the valiant wife serves as a counterpart to both Woman Wisdom and the Strange Woman. In contrast to the אִשָּׁה זָרָה, the אֵשֶׁת־חַיִל labors during the לַיְלָה (7:9; 31:15, 18), possesses a permanent form of יְפִי (6:25; 31:30), and drapes her bed with מַרְבַדִּים (7:16; 31:22) in order to enhance her household rather than entice prospective sexual partners. She represents the embodiment of Woman Wisdom's ideals and the concrete expression of Wisdom's value. Second, the panegyric provides a graphic description of a real woman who incarnates the fundamental principles of the sapiential material. Her domestic, commercial, and communal activities, coupled with her moral beauty, make her an ideal wife for any noble householder. She

---

93 For the chiasm in verses 19–20, see Lichtenstein, "Chiasm and Symmetry," 384–86.

94 See Wolters, "Proverbs XXXI 10–31 as Heroic Hymn," 456–57.

95 Some argue that the introduction of יְרְאַת־יְהוָה at this stage in the poem represents a redactional attempt to redeem the mundane activities of the woman by baptizing them in piety (Toy, *Proverbs* 548–49; Meinhold, *Die Sprüche*, 2:529–30). Based on the Septuagint's expanded translation, some argue the original text read "an intelligent woman" rather than "a woman who fears the Lord." However, this emendation is unconvincing, for the LXX also contains the phrase φόβον δὲ κυρίου. See Whybray, *The Composition of the Book of Proverbs*, 154–56; Waltke, *Proverbs: Chapters 15–31*, 535 n. 204.

96 McCreesh, "Wisdom as Wife: Proverbs 31:10–31," 391.

represents the feminine embodiment of wisdom, nobility, and the fear of YHWH. While this priceless, almost-unattainable woman exists, the poem emphasizes that she is a rare find (31:10).

The diverse achievements and exemplary character of the noble woman provide an answer to the introductory question: אֵשֶׁת־חַיִל מִי יִמְצָא. This rhetorical inquiry may be read in several different ways. On the one hand, it may highlight the unique character and exceptional energy of the אֵשֶׁת־חַיִל. On the other hand, the question may suggest the portrait is an impossible ideal, an unattainable mirage that eludes concrete representation.[97] However, within the context of Proverbs, the rhetorical device provokes an additional question, viz., who is looking for this noble wife? In light of the discourse setting of the book and the thematic movement of the material, the heroic panegyric presents the addressee with a paradigmatic portrait of an ideal wife, who corresponds with his aristocratic status and embodies his values. The poem elaborates on earlier aphorisms concerning marriage preparation (11:16; 12:4; 14:1; 18:22; 19:14) to provide a veritable mosaic that delineates the fundamental features of a virtuous wife. As an artificial construct, the alphabetic acrostic may serve as a mnemonic device that provides the young addressee with a comprehensive catalog that he can memorize and store in his mind as he searches for a suitable wife.[98]

6.2.1 Section Conclusion

In conjunction with the prologue and the words of Agur, the words of Lemuel (31:1–31) create a hermeneutical framework through which to read the terse aphorisms in the sentence literature and mark the culmination of the book's pedagogical program. These pieces plot the development of the addressee; they chart a journey of character that moves from hearth (1:8–9:18) to throne (31:1–9) to noble home (31:10–31).[99] The poems bring the quest for wisdom full circle. Whereas the book opens with a liminal, silent son, instructed in basic socio-moral values, it ends with a married, noble adult who has incorporated the moral vision of the book of Proverbs.[100]

---

97   Hausmann, "Beobachtungen zu Spr 31,10–31," 262.
98   See Hurowitz, "The Woman of Valor and a Woman Large of Head," 227.
99   See Brown, *Character in Crisis*, 47–49.
100   Brown, *Character in Crisis*, 48. In addition, for a discussion of the confluence of the domestic and royal settings within the concluding compositions of the book, see Brown, "The Pedagogy of Proverbs 10:1–31:9," 181.

6.3 Conclusion

The final collections in the book of Proverbs strengthen its courtly agenda (30:1–33; 31:1–31). These discrete compositions represent the culmination of the document's pedagogical program, as they develop particular motifs and emphasize certain themes to shape a specific moral vision for the addressee. This vision not only highlights the significance of certain virtues, but it also brings the identity of the addressee into sharper focus.

Together with the previous collections, the words of Agur (30:1–33) and the words of Lemuel (31:1–31) enhance the courtly ethos of the document. Agur provides a theological framework through which to view the quest for wisdom and presents a royal, hierarchical vision of the world, constructed through submission to legitimate authority within the proscribed parameters of the social-religious realm. The words of Lemuel then give concrete expression to the identity of the addressee. The royal instruction catalogues the moral and judicial responsibilities of the young king, while the heroic panegyric enumerates the multifaceted activities of an aristocratic wife—a woman who embodies the ideals of wisdom and reinforces the image of her noble husband. In conjunction with the prologue, these concluding pieces form a hermeneutical framework through which to read the aphorisms in the sentence literature. This framework, coupled with the thematic movement of the material, suggests that the noble addressee who cultivates the moral vision presented in the book emerges from his liminal state to assume either the throne or a seat among the elders at the gate. In view of the discourse setting of the book, the thematic development of the material, and the courtly flavor of the individual collections, this conclusion is not surprising.

Chapter 7

The Courtly Nature of the Book of Proverbs

Happy the generation where the great listen to the small,
for it follows that in such a generation the small will listen to the great.
—Hebrew Proverb

The preceding chapters have focused on the aristocratic elements within the constituent literary units of the book of Proverbs in order to explore the nature of the work. We have discovered that the book of Proverbs possesses a distinct, courtly flavor. Our recognition of the courtly vintage of the book is not novel, for many scholars have identified the royal character of individual collections as well as the aristocratic perspective of the material. However, rather than investigating the constituent collections as independent, isolated entities, this study has explored how these compendia function within the larger moral discourse of the book of Proverbs. In so doing, we have discovered a development in the book that accounts for the role of each collection.

As the introduction to the book of Proverbs, chapters 1–9 provide a hermeneutical framework within which to read the document. The extended lectures and interludes form a dialogical context that gives particular expression to the value of wisdom and the setting in which the material is conveyed. Together, these discourses present the material as a series of instructions delivered by a royal voice to a young, noble addressee within a domestic context. They delineate the principal features of the document's discursive setting and seek to transform the naïve predilection of the addressee. In so doing, the lectures and interludes shape the disposition of the moral subject and develop the requisite moral posture necessary for the apprehension of the moral vision delineated in the sentence literature. They persuade the addressee to acquire wisdom and provide a concrete context through which to explore the meaning and pragmatic significance of the individual sayings within the sentence literature.

In view of the value of wisdom and the discourse setting of the material, the sentence literature develops the inchoate ethical vision of the prologue through several distinct literary units. Together, these subunits provide a kaleidoscopic and paradigmatic portrait of the wise life. They move from elementary wisdom (10:1–15:33) to intermediate wisdom (16:1–22:16) to vocational wisdom (22:17–

24:34) to advanced wisdom (25:1–29:27). Solomon 1A presents an elementary paradigm of the wise life through a general, bifurcated world and a facile description of the character-consequence nexus (*Haltung-Schicksal Zusammenhang*). This collection highlights the distinctive features of the wise, the fool, the righteous, and the wicked and examines character and comportment through the traditional social structures of the monarchy, the community, the family, and the religious sphere. In so doing, it forms a rudimentary paradigm that serves as a foundation for the development that takes place in Proverbs 16:1–22:16.

Solomon 1B (16:1–22:16) widens the socio-religious purview of the sapiential world through its nuanced development of particular themes and its interest in subjects that receive only a brief treatment in the initial sub-collection. This compilation situates character within the judicial sphere (17:15, 23, 26; 18:5; 19:28; 21:7, 15), and devotes considerable attention to the royal institution (16:10–15; 19:12; 20:2, 8, 26, 28). In addition, the collection elaborates on the fiscal and domestic sayings within the initial compilation to enhance the moral vision of economic ethics (16:19; 19:1, 22; 22:1) as well as marriage preparation (18:22; 19:13–14; 21:9, 19). The compendium assumes an addressee familiar with the court, liable to judicial exploitation, and in need of a framework through which to assess the worth of particular values. On the whole, the compilation expands upon the general, ethical vision delineated in Solomon 1A and moves from the general to the specific, the conceptual to the concrete.

The terse aphorisms of the first Solomonic collection give way to a series of instructions devoted to vocational wisdom (22:17–24:34). These instructions resume the direct, pedagogical address of the prologue and emphasize specific, practical matters related to royal service to inculcate prudence in prospective courtiers, diplomats, or ambassadors (22:17–21). The attention given to royal affairs and matters of justice suggests the material is directed toward those in positions of power and influence within society. In the main, the admonitions assume an addressee who has access to the court (22:29; 24:5–6), judicial authority (22:22–23, 28; 23:10–11; 24:10–12; 24:23b–25), sufficient social standing to dine at a ruler's table (23:1–3), and the means to consume luxurious commodities (23:20–21, 29–35).

The aristocratic character of the instructional material is heightened in the second Solomonic collection (25:1–29:27). This eloquent compendium reinforces familiar motifs and assesses particular topics from a fresh, innovative perspective. The collection delineates the hierarchical structure of the socio-religious world (25:2–27), the principal contours of a conflicted community (26:1–12, 13–16, 17–28), the significance of friendship (27:1–22), and the correct exercise or illegitimate use of power, whether political, judicial, or economic (27:23–27; 28:1–29:27). In addition, the compilation gives particular expression to relations with superiors, the body politic, propriety, social conflict, and justice, among others. The extent to which these themes are discussed suggests that they constitute the

fundamental concerns of the collection. These thematic emphases, coupled with
the poetic sophistication of the material and the courtly provenance of the
composition (25:1), suggest the collection is directed expressly toward influential
individuals within society. The material assumes an affluent addressee who has
access to the court (25:2–15), the capacity to confer social honor on others (26:1,
8), the means to employ members of the community (26:6, 10), the resources to
sustain a large household (26:6, 10; 27:23–27), and the power to produce political
stability or communal aversion (28:2, 5, 12, 15, 16, 21, 28; 29:2, 4, 7, 12, 13, 14,
18, 26). In light of the formal and thematic development of the sentence
literature, the courtly nature of the second Solomonic collection is not surprising.
This is a natural progression in the document, a progression that coincides with
both the discourse setting of the book and compositional setting of the second
Solomonic collection.

The moral vision presented in the sentence literature culminates in the
concluding compositions (30:1–33; 31:1–31). Together with the prologue, these
variegated compendia re-contextualize the litany of sayings in the sentence
literature and form an interpretive envelope around the book. They enhance the
ideational world of the sapiential material and give particular expression to the
application of wisdom. The words of Agur (30:1–33) address the epistemological
limitations of human wisdom (30:1–9) and the proscribed parameters of the
socio-moral order (30:10–33). The foreign sage moves from cognitive limitations
(30:1–6) to social limitations (30:10, 17, 18–20, 21–23, 32–33), and from the
corrupting influence of both wealth and poverty (30:7–9) to social exploitation
and the insatiable appetite of avarice (30:11–14, 15–16). He links the acquisition
of wisdom with Israel's covenantal tradition (30:5–6) and presents a royal,
hierarchical vision of the world, constructed through submission to legitimate
authority within the proscribed parameters of the cosmic and social realm (30:10–
33).

The words of Lemuel delineate the responsibilities of wisdom and the life of
wisdom through the royal instruction and the heroic panegyric. The royal
instruction moves from the search for wisdom to the duties of wisdom, as
Lemuel presents the fundamental responsibilities of the royal institution (31:1–9).
This instruction preserves the domestic flavor of the book's discourse setting and
gives particular expression to the maternal voice (1:8; 6:20; 31:1). Moreover, in
contrast to the previous collections, the implied addressee is given specific
reference, as the book concludes in the royal home, with the installation of a
young king. The noble addressee moves from the subject position of a liminal
adolescent to the locus of royal power, as the journey of character culminates in
the person of the king.

The heroic panegyric (31:10–31) filters the book's principal themes through a
single, exceptional woman. In so doing, the encomium provides an
impressionistic portrait of the life of wisdom. The paean catalogs the domestic,

commercial, and communal ventures of a noble woman to delineate the materialization of wisdom in the diverse dimensions of human life. Within the context of the book, the heroic panegyric presents the noble addressee with a paradigmatic portrait of an ideal wife—a woman who corresponds with his aristocratic status and embodies his values. Together with the royal instruction, the encomium provides a concrete portrait of wisdom manifested in daily life. These constituent literary pieces mark the completion of the quest for wisdom, a journey of character that finds its concrete expression in the world of the court.

In view of the discourse setting of the work, the development of the material, and the thematic emphases of the constituent collections, the book of Proverbs may be considered a courtly document. The book integrates various topics and traditions to form an inclusive moral vision, an ethical perspective on the world that captures the diverse dimensions of social existence. As a literary whole, the work serves as a cultural primer that seeks to inculcate proper ethical values into its recipients; it highlights the value of wisdom and cultivates a sense of what is fitting in the socio-religious realm. In the main, the book of Proverbs is not a theoretical *Lehrbuch* or a vocational manual that describes the specific tricks of the bureaucratic trade; rather it serves as a codification of social competence that seeks to provide the noble, naïve youth with the *sensus communis* in order to transform his moral disposition, introduce him to the basic values of the socio-religious world, and present him with a sagacious vision of life in its various dimensions. The sapiential material orients the addressee to the fundamental values of the world and provides him with an ethical vision he is to embody.

The embodiment of the community's values was the fundamental responsibility of any leader within Israelite society. According to the deuteronomic torah, societal institutions of leadership—local courts (Deut 16:18; 17:2–7), the central court (17:8–13), the royal establishment (17:14–20), the levitical priesthood (18:1–8), and the prophetic office (18:15–22)—were to promote the covenantal values of the community.[1] In contrast to other polities within the ancient world, the deuteronomic program distributes power among a variety of civil institutions, each of which was to be dedicated to the cause of righteousness (Deut 16:20).[2] This precondition is most apparent in the restrictions placed on the royal establishment. The notion that the royal institution is to use its hegemonic power to secure cultic order or protect the people from external and internal threats is of no interest to the deuteronomic program. Instead of focusing on the administrative duties of the king, the deuteronomic torah places a series of constraints on the royal institution in order

---

[1] P. T. Vogt, *Deuteronomic Theology and the Significance of Torah: A Reappraisal* (Winona Lake: Eisenbrauns, 2006), 204–26; D. I. Block, *Deuteronomy* (NIVAC; Grand Rapids: Zondervan, forthcoming), s.v. 16:18–18:22.

[2] See G. N. Knoppers, "The Deuteronomist and the Deuteronomic Law of the King: A Reexamination of a Relationship," *ZAW* 108 (1996): 329–32.

to rein in the potential exploitation of power for personal privilege.[3] In so doing, Deuteronomy provides a paradigm for leadership. Though the ideals of health, security, proficient rule, prosperity, and justice may be inherent in this paradigmatic model of righteous governance, Deuteronomy's principal concern is the inculcation of the torah (Deut 17:18–20), that is, the cultivation and embodiment of the community's covenantal values in its ruler.

The same is true with regard to other societal institutions in Israel. Civic, judicial, military, economic, religious, and intellectual leaders were to model the values of the community and promote righteousness through their self-sacrificing service (Deut 16:20).[4] This vision may represent "the height of impractical idealism,"[5] for the Deuteronomist and the prophets often paint a different picture of these institutions, characterized by monarchic absolutism and political exploitation. Nonetheless, the deuteronomic program provides the ideal of just governance, the normative paradigm of righteous leadership. This paradigm involves the embodiment of the community's values and the promotion of righteousness; it perceives leadership as a call to responsibility, rather than an invitation to power. Though this commitment to righteousness and the interests of the community transcends specific offices to form the foundation of responsible leadership in its various dimensions, it represents the socio-religious crux of just governance.

The moral vision of the book of Proverbs seeks to reinforce the deuteronomic paradigm of leadership. Similar to the deuteronomic program, the sapiential material provides the noble, naïve youth with the fundamental values and formative attitudes of social existence; it delineates the traditional ethos that they are to embody in order to lead those entrusted to their care. The individual collections incorporate conventional concerns with courtly material to inculcate established values and practical advice in the addressee. In so doing, the book not only cultivates virtues that coincide with the interests of the community, but it also identifies certain values that correspond with the interests, aspirations, and temptations of its noble addressee. This ethical program complements the paradigmatic model of leadership presented in Deuteronomy. Within the deuteronomic vision, leaders within societal institutions were to embody the values of the community and promote righteousness within their respective social

---

3   See D. I. Block, "The Burden of Leadership: The Mosaic Paradigm of Kingship (Deut. 17:14-20)," *BSac* 162 (2005): 259–78.

4   For a discussion of the significance of Deuteronomy 16:20, see Block, *Deuteronomy*, s.v 16:20. Block argues that the emphatic repetition צֶדֶק צֶדֶק functions as a heading for the deuteronomic vision of societal institutions (16:18–18:22). As the heading of the sub-section, Deuteronomy 16:20 identifies the fundamental prerequisite of any socio-religious leader: righteousness. Also see Vogt, *Deuteronomic Theology and the Significance of Torah*, 212–13.

5   M. L. Segal, *The Pentateuch: Its Composition and its Authorship and other Biblical Studies* (Jerusalem: Magnes, 1967), 79.

spheres. The deuteronomic torah is not concerned primarily with the administrative duties of leaders; rather it focuses on character and righteousness demonstrated through a concern for the interests of those who are led.[6] In light of this normative paradigm of leadership, it seems the book of Proverbs supplements the deuteronomic program. While the deuteronomic torah catalogs the covenantal values of the community and delineates the principle function of leaders within societal institutions, the book of Proverbs enumerates the traditional values of the community and seeks to inculcate these virtues in prospective leaders. Together, these corpora promote the principal values and formative attitudes of Israelite life; they represent a comprehensive ethical vision that provides a guide to individual character, knowledge, and the multifaceted dimensions of the socio-religious world.

The discursive, thematic, and conceptual features of the book of Proverbs suggest the work is a courtly piece, intended to produce a view of the world necessary for those in positions of leadership. Though the collections convey a general, moral vision accessible to every member of the community, within the document, this vision is directed toward the noble youth. As a literary whole, the anthology incorporates material from a variety of social settings and periods within a distinct, discourse setting. When the diverse material in the document is read within this social and dialogical setting, the compendium functions as a repository of traditional values designed to cultivate a sagacious vision of life and a proper disposition toward fellow members of the Israelite community. The book incorporates the voice of the *hoi polloi* with specific matters pertaining to those in positions of power to shape a vision of life that is governed by the interests of the community as well as the responsibilities inherent in societal institutions of leadership. In light of this heterogeneous ethical vision, the democratization of the sapiential material is not surprising. The book of Proverbs promotes a moral vision that transcends social boundaries. However, when the material is read within the discourse setting of the book, it appears to be a work of the court, by the court, and for the court, but in the interests of the people.

With this conclusion the book of Proverbs may be incorporated more readily into the disciplines of Old Testament theology and biblical theology. Once viewed as an "errant child"[7] and "an orphan in the biblical household,"[8] recent studies place Israelite wisdom literature in general and the book of Proverbs in

6   Block, "The Burden of Leadership," 277.

7   R. E. Clements, "Wisdom and Old Testament Theology," in *Wisdom in Ancient Israel: Essays in Honour of J. A. Emerton* (ed. J. Day et al.; Cambridge: Cambridge University Press, 1995), 271.

8   J. L. Crenshaw, "Prolegomenon," in *Studies in Ancient Israelite Wisdom* (ed. J. L. Crenshaw; New York: Ktav, 1976), 1.

particular within the framework of creation theology.[9] This framework plays a significant role in modern theological syntheses, for it provides a heuristic grid through which to link the anthropocentric and theocentric dimensions of wisdom literature. However, while creation is the overarching horizon of wisdom, sapiential themes extend far beyond a parochial concern with creation. We have discovered that Proverbs integrates particular features from the anthropocentric and theocentric dimensions of the cosmos to create a picture of the world in which the addressee must exercise leadership. The book of Proverbs presents a portrait of concrete Israelite piety; it plays a vital role in describing what the fear of YHWH and practical righteousness look like, especially in the lives of those who govern the people of YHWH.

---

9   For discussion of creation theology as the framework of Israelite wisdom, see W. Zimmerli, "The Place and Limit of the Wisdom in the Framework of the Old Testament Theology," *SJT* 17 (1964): 146–58; repr. in *Studies in Ancient Israelite Wisdom*, 314–26; idem, *Old Testament Theology in Outline* (Atlanta: John Knox, 1978), 155–66; von Rad, *Wisdom in Israel*, 74–96, *et passim*; P. Doll, *Menschenschöpfung und Weltschöpfung in der alttestamentlichen Weisheit* (SBS 117; Stuttgart: Verlag Katholisches Bibelwerk, 1985); Perdue, *Wisdom and Creation*; idem, *Wisdom Literature: A Theological History*; Dell, *The Book of Proverbs*, 125–54.

Bibliography

Ahlström, G. W. "The House of Wisdom." Pages 74–76 in *Svensk Exegetisk Årsbok*. Edited by H. Ringgren. Uppsala: Gleerup-Lund, 1979.

Albright, W. F. "Some Canaanite-Phoenician Sources of Hebrew Wisdom." Pages 1–15 in *Wisdom in Ancient Israel and in the Ancient Near East: Presented to Professor Harold Henry Rowley*. Supplements to Vetus Testamentum 3. Leiden: Brill, 1955.

Aletti, J. N. "Proverbes 8:22–31: Étude et structure." *Biblica* 57 (1976): 25–37.

_____. "Seduction et parole en Proverbes I–IX." *Vetus Testamentum* 27 (1977): 129–44.

Alster, B. *The Instructions of Suruppak: A Sumerian Proverb Collection*. Mesopotamia: Copenhagen Studies in Assyriology 2. Copenhagen: Akademisk Forlag, 1974.

_____. *Studies in Sumerian Proverbs*. Mesopotamia: Copenhagen Studies in Assyriology 3. Copenhagen: Akademisk Forlag, 1975.

_____. "Proverbs from Ancient Mesopotamia: Their History and Social Implications." *Proverbium* 10 (1993): 1–20.

_____. "Literary Aspects of Sumerian and Akkadian Proverbs." Pages 1–21 in *Mesopotamian Poetic Language: Sumerian and Akkadian*. Edited by M. E. Vogelzang and H. L. J. Vanstiphout. Groningen: Styx, 1996.

_____. *Proverbs of Ancient Sumer: The World's Earliest Proverb Collections*. 2 vols. Bethesda: CDL Press, 1997.

Amsler, S. "La sagesse de la femme." Pages 112–16 in *La Sagesse de l'Ancien Testament*. Edited by M. Gilbert. Bibliotheca ephemeridum theologicarum lovaniensium 51. Gembloux: Duculot, 1979. Repr., Leuven: Leuven University Press, 1990.

Andreasen, N-E. A. "The Role of the Queen Mother in Israelite Society." *Catholic Biblical Quarterly* 45 (1983): 179–94.

Assmann, J. "Das Bild des Vaters im Alten Ägypten." Pages 12–49 in *Das Vaterbild in Mythos und Geschichte*. Edited by H. Tellenbach. Berlin: Kohlhammer, 1976.

_____. "Weisheit, Loyalismus und Frömmigkeit." Pages 12–72 in *Studien zu altägyptischen Lebenslehren*. Orbis biblicus et orientalis 28. Göttingen: Vandenhoeck & Ruprecht, 1979.

_____. "Schrift, Tod und Identität: Das Grab als Vorschule der Literatur im alten Ägypten." Pages 64–93 in *Schrift und Gedächtnis: Beiträge zur Archäologie der literarischen Kommunikation*. Edited by J. Assmann, A. Assmann, and C. Hardmeier. München: Fink, 1983.

_____. *Maât, l'Egypte pharaonique et l'idée de justice sociale*. Conférences, essais et Leçons du Collége de France. Paris: Julliard, 1989.

_____. *Ma'at: Gerechtigkeit und Unsterblichkeit im alten Aegypten*. Munich: Beck, 1990.

_____. "Weisheit, Schrift und Literatur in alten Ägypten." Pages 475–500 in *Weisheit*. Edited by A. Assmann. Münich: Fink, 1991.

_____. "Kulturelle und literarische Texte." Pages 60–82 in *Ancient Egyptian Literature: History and Forms*. Edited by A. Loprieno. Leiden: Brill, 1996.

_____. *Herrschaft und Heil: Politische Theologie in Altägypten, Israel und Europa*. München: Hanser, 2000.

_____. *The Search for God in Ancient Egypt.* Translated by D. Lorton. Ithaca: Cornell University Press, 2001.

_____. *The Mind of Egypt: History and Meaning in the Time of the Pharaohs.* Translated by A. Jenkins. New York: Holt, 2002.

Audet, J.-P. "Origines comparés de la double tradition de la loi et de la Sagesse dans le Proche-Orient ancien." Pages 352–57 in *International Congress of Orientalists.* Vol 1. Moscow: Actes du Congrès, 1964.

Avigad, N. *Corpus of West Semitic Stamp Seals.* Rev. and comp. by B. Sass. Jerusalem: The Institute of Archaeology, The Hebrew University of Jerusalem, 1997.

Baines, J. "Literacy and Ancient Egyptian Society." *Man* 18 (1983): 572–99.

_____. "Society, Morality, and Religious Practice." Pages 123–200 in *Religion in Ancient Egypt: Gods, Myths, and Personal Practice.* Edited by B. E. Shafer. Ithaca: Cornell University Press, 1991.

_____. "Kingship, Definition of Culture, and Legitimation." Pages 3–47 in *Ancient Egyptian Kingship.* Edited by D. O'Connor and D. P. Silverman. Leiden: E. J. Brill, 1995.

Baines, J. and C. Eyre. "Four Notes on Literacy." *Göttinger Miszellen* 61 (1983): 65–96.

Barker, M. *The Great Angel: A Study of Israel's Second God.* Louisville: Westminster John Knox, 1992.

Barré, M. L. "'Fear of God' and the World View of Wisdom." *Biblical Theology Bulletin* 11 (1981): 41–43.

Barthélemy, Dominique, ed. *Proverbia.* Vol. 5 of *Critique textuelle de l'Ancien Testament.* Göttingen: Vandenhoeck & Ruprecht, forthcoming.

Barucq, A. *Le livre des Proverbes.* Sources Bibliques. Paris: Librairie Lecoffre, 1964.

Baumann, G. *Die Weisheitsgestalt in Proverbien 1–9.* Forschungen zum Alten Testament 16. Tübingen: Mohr, 1996.

Bea, A. "Der Zahlenspruch im Hebräischen und Ugaritischen." *Biblica* 21 (1940): 196–98.

Beaulieu, P.-A. "The Social and Intellectual Setting of Babylonian Wisdom Literature." Pages 3–19 in *Wisdom Literature in Mesopotamia and Israel.* Society of Biblical Literature Symposium Series 36. Atlanta: Society of Biblical Literature, 2007.

Becker, J. *Gottesfurcht im Alten Testament.* Analecta biblica 25. Rome: Pontifical Biblical Institute, 1965.

Beckman, G. *Hittite Diplomatic Texts.* 2nd ed. Society of Biblical Literature Writings from the Ancient World 7. Atlanta: Scholars Press, 1999.

Bergant, D. *Israel's Wisdom Literature: A Liberation-Critical Reading.* Minneapolis: Fortress, 1997.

Bergman, J. "Discourse d'Adieu—Testament—Discours Posthume: Testaments juifs et enseignements égyptiens." Pages 21–50 in *Sagesse et Religion.* Paris: Presses Universitaires de France, 1979.

Berlin, A. *Poetics and Interpretation of Biblical Narrative.* Bible and Literature Series 9. Sheffield: Almond, 1983.

Birch, B. C. *Let Justice Roll Down: The Old Testament, Ethics, and Christian Life.* Louisville: Westminster John Knox, 1991.

Blenkinsopp, J. *Wisdom and Law in the Old Testament: The Ordering of Life in Israel and Early Judaism.* Oxford Bible Series. New York: Oxford University Press, 1983.

_____. *Sage, Priest, Prophet: Religious and Intellectual Leadership in Ancient Israel.* Library of Ancient Israel. Louisville: Westminster John Knox, 1995.

_____. "The Family in First Temple Israel." Pages 48–103 in *Families in Ancient Israel.* Louisville: Westminster John Knox, 1997.

Block, D. I. *The Foundations of National Identity: A Study in Ancient Northwest Semitic Perceptions.* Ann Arbor: UMI, 1982.

_____. *The Book of Ezekiel: Chapters 1-24.* New International Commentary on the Old Testament. Grand Rapids: Eerdmans, 1997.

_____. "Marriage and Family in Ancient Israel." Pages 33–102 in *Marriage and Family in the Biblical World.* Edited by K. M. Campbell. Downers Grove: InterVarsity, 2003.

_____. "The Burden of Leadership: The Mosaic Paradigm of Kingship (Deut. 17:14-20)." *Bibliotheca sacra* 162 (2005): 259–78.

_____. *Deuteronomy.* The NIV Application Commentary. Grand Rapids: Zondervan, forthcoming.

Blumenthal, E. "Die Lehre für König Merikare." *Zeitschrift für ägyptische Sprache und Altertumskunde* 107 (1980): 5–41.

_____. "Lehre Amenemhets I." Pages 968–71 in *Lexikon der Ägyptologie.* Edited by W. Helck and E. Otto. Wiesbaden: Harrassowitz, 1980.

_____. "Die Lehre des Königs Amenemhet (Teil II)." *Zeitschrift für ägyptische Sprache und Altertumskunde* 112 (1985): 104–15.

Boecker, H.-J. *Redeformen des Rechtslebens im Alten Testament.* Wissenschaftliche Monographien zum Alten und Neuen Testament 14. Neukirchen: Neukirchener, 1964.

_____. *Law and the Administration of Justice in the Old Testament and Near East.* Translated by J. Moiser. Minneapolis: Augsburg, 1980.

Bonora, A. "La donna eccellente, la sapienza, il sapiente." *Revista bíblica* 36 (1988): 137–64.

Boström, G. *Paronomasi i den äldre hebraiska maschalliteraturen.* Lunds universitets årsskrift 23. Lund: Gleerup, 1928.

_____. *Proverbiastudien: Die Weisheit und das fremde Weib in Sprüche 1–9.* Lunds universitets årsskrift 3. Lund: Gleerup, 1935.

Boström, L. *The God of the Sages: The Portrayal of God in the Book of Proverbs.* Coniectanea biblica: Old Testament Series 29. Stockholm: Almqvist & Wiksell International, 1990.

Brenner, A. "Some Observations on the Figuration of Woman in Wisdom Literature." Pages 50–66 in *A Feminist Companion to Wisdom Literature.* Edited by A. Brenner. Sheffield: Sheffield Academic Press, 1995.

Brongers, H. A. "Die Partikel *kma'an* in der biblisch-hebräischen Sprache." *Oudtestamentische Studiën* 18 (1973): 84-96.

Brown, J. "Proverb-Book, Gold-Economy, Alphabet." *Journal of Biblical Literature* 100 (1981): 169–91.

Brown, W. P. *Character in Crisis: A Fresh Approach to the Wisdom Literature of the Old Testament.* Grand Rapids: Eerdmans, 1996.

_____. "The Pedagogy of Proverbs 10:1–31:9." Pages 150–82 in *Character and Scripture: Moral Formation, Community, and Biblical Interpretation.* Edited by W. P. Brown. Grand Rapids: Eerdmans, 2002.

Brueggemann, W. A. "The Social Significance of Solomon as a Patron of Wisdom." Pages 117–32 in *The Sage in Israel and the Ancient Near East.* Edited by J. G. Gammie and L. G. Perdue. Winona Lake: Eisenbrauns, 1990.

Brug, J. F. "Biblical Acrostics and Their Relationship to Other Ancient Near Eastern Acrostics." Pages 283–304 in *The Bible in the Light of Cuneiform Literature: Scripture in Context III.* Edited by W. W. Hallo, B. W. Jones, and G. L. Mattingly. Lewiston: Mellen, 1990.

Brunner, H. "Die Weisheitliteratur." Pages 90–110 in *Handbuch der Orientalistik.* Leiden: Brill, 1952.

————. *Altägyptische Erziehung.* Wiesbaden: Harrassowitz, 1957.

————. "Gerechtigkeit als Fundament des Thrones." *Vetus Testamentum* 8 (1958): 426–28.

————. "Zitate aus Lebenslehren." Pages 105–71 in *Studien zu altägyptischen Lebenslehren.* Orbis biblicus et orientalis 28. Göttingen: Vandenhoeck & Ruprecht, 1979.

————. *Altägyptische Weisheit: Lehren für das Leben.* München: Artemis Verlag, 1988.

————. *Die Weisheitsbücher der Ägypter: Lehren für das Leben.* 2nd ed. München: Artemis Verlag, 1991.

Bryce, G. E. "Another Wisdom-'Book' in Proverbs." *Journal of Biblical Literature* 91 (1972): 145–57.

————. "'Better'-Proverbs: An Historical and Structural Study." Pages 343–54 in *The Society of Biblical Literature One Hundred Eighth Annual Meeting: Book of Seminar Papers.* Edited by L. C. McGaughy. Missoula: Society of Biblical Literature, 1972.

————. "The Structural Analysis of Didactic Texts." Pages 107–21 in *Biblical and Near Eastern Studies.* Edited by G. A. Tuttle. Grand Rapids: Eerdmans, 1978.

————. *A Legacy of Wisdom: The Egyptian Contribution to the Wisdom of Israel.* Lewisburg: Bucknell University Press, 1979.

Bühlmann, W. *Vom Rechten Reden und Schweigen: Studien zu Proverbien 10–31.* Orbis biblicus et orientalis 12. Göttingen: Vandenhoeck & Ruprecht, 1976.

Buccellati, G. "Wisdom and Not: The Case of Mesopotamia." *Journal of the American Oriental Society* 101 (1981): 35–47.

Burkard, G. "'Als Gott erschienen spricht er' Die Lehre des Amenemhet als postumes Vermächtnis." Pages 153–73 in *Literatur und Politik im pharaonischen und ptolemäischen Ägypten: Vorträge der Tagung zum Gedenken an Georges Posener 5.–10. September 1996 in Leipzig.* Edited by J. Assmann and E. Blumenthal. Cairo: Institut Français d'Archéologie Orientale, 1999.

Camp, C. V. *Wisdom and the Feminine in the Book of Proverbs.* Bible and Literature Series 11. Sheffield: Almond, 1985.

————. "Woman Wisdom as Root Metaphor: A Theological Consideration." Pages 45–76 in *The Listening Heart: Essays in Wisdom and the Psalms in Honor of Roland E. Murphy, O. Carm.* Edited by K. G. Hoglund, E. F. Huwiler, J. T. Glass, and R. W. Lee. Sheffield: Sheffield Academic Press, 1987.

————. "The Female Sage in Ancient Israel and in the Biblical Wisdom Literature." Pages 185–203 in *The Sage in Israel and the Ancient Near East.* Edited by J. G. Gammie and L. G. Perdue. Winona Lake: Eisenbrauns, 1990.

————. "What's So Strange About the Strange Woman?" Pages 17–31 in *The Bible and the Politics of Exegesis: Essays in Honor of Norman K. Gottwald on His Sixty-Fifth Birthday.* Edited by D. Jobling, P. L. Day, and G. T. Sheppard. Cleveland: Pilgrim Press, 1991.

_____. "Wise and Strange: An Interpretation of the Female Imagery in Proverbs in Light of Trickster Mythology." Pages 131–56 in *A Feminist Companion to Wisdom Literature*. Edited by A. Brenner. Sheffield: Sheffield Academic Press, 1995.

_____. "Woman Wisdom and the Strange Woman: Where Is Power to Be Found?" Pages 85–112 in *Reading Bibles, Writing Bodies: Identity and the Book*. Edited by T. K. Beal and D. M. Gunn. London: Routledge, 1997.

Carasik, M. "Who Were the 'Men of Hezekiah' (Proverbs XXV 1)?" *Vetus Testamentum* 44 (1994): 289–300.

Carr, D. M. *Writing on the Tablet of the Heart: Origins of Scripture and Literature*. Oxford: Oxford University Press, 2005.

Childs, B. S. *Introduction to the Old Testament as Scripture*. Philadelphia: Fortress, 1979.

Clements, R. E. "Wisdom and Old Testament Theology." Pages 269–86 in *Wisdom in Ancient Israel: Essays in Honour of J. A. Emerton*. Edited by J. Day, R. P. Gordon, and H. G. M. Williamson. Cambridge: Cambridge University Press, 1995.

Civil, M. "Notes on the 'Instructions of Suruppak'." *Journal of Near Eastern Studies* 43 (1984): 281–98.

Clifford, R. J. "Proverbs IX: A Suggested Ugaritic Parallel." *Vetus Testamentum* 25 (1975): 298–306.

_____. "Woman Wisdom in the Book of Proverbs." Pages 61–72 in *Biblische Theologie und gesellschaftlicher Wandel. Für Norbert Lohfink*. Edited by G. Braulik, W. Großgerman, and S. MacEvenue. Freiburg: Herder, 1993.

_____. *The Wisdom Literature*. Interpreting Biblical Texts. Nashville: Abingdon, 1998.

_____. *Proverbs*. Old Testament Library. Louisville: Westminster John Knox, 1999.

_____. "The Community of the Book of Proverbs." Pages 281–93 in *Constituting the Community: Studies on the Polity of Ancient Israel in Honor of S. Dean McBride Jr.* Edited by J. T. Strong and S. S. Tuell. Winona Lake: Eisenbrauns, 2005.

Cody, A. "Notes on Proverbs 22,21 and 22,23b." *Biblica* 61 (1980): 418–26.

Coggins, R. J. "The Old Testament and the Poor." *Expository Times* 99 (1987–88): 11–14.

Cole, S. W. "The Crimes and Sacrileges of Nabu-Suma-Iskun." *Zeitschrift für Assyriologie* 84 (1994): 220–52.

Conybeare, F. C., J. R. Harris, and A. S. Lewis. *The Story of Ahiqar from the Aramaic, Syriac, Arabic, Armenian, Ethiopic, Old Turkish, Greek and Slavonic Versions*. 2nd ed. Cambridge: Cambridge University Press, 1913.

Coogan, M. D. "The Goddess Wisdom—'Where Can She Be Found?' Literary Reflexes of Popular Religion." Pages 203–209 in *Ki Baruch Hu: Ancient Near Eastern, Biblical, and Judaic Studies in Honor of Baruch A. Levine*. Edited by R. Chazan, W. W. Hallo, and L. H. Schiffman. Winona Lake: Eisenbrauns, 1999.

Cook, J. "אשה זרה (Proverbs 1–9 Septuagint): A Metaphor for Foreign Wisdom?" *Zeitschrift für die alttestamentliche Wissenschaft* 106 (1994): 458–76.

_____. *The Septuagint of Proverbs: Jewish and/or Hellenistic Colouring of the LXX Proverbs*. Supplements to Vetus Testamentum 69. Leiden: Brill, 1997.

Cooper, A. "'The Lord Grants Wisdom': The World View of Proverbs 1–9." Pages 29–43 in *Bringing the Hidden to Light: The Process of Interpretation. Studies in Honor of Stephen A. Geller*. Edited by K. F. Kravitz and D. M. Sharon. Winona Lake: Eisenbrauns, 2007.

Cotterell, P. and M. Turner. *Linguistics and Biblical Interpretation*. London: SPCK, 1979.

Crenshaw, J. L. "Wisdom." Pages 225–64 in *Old Testament Form Criticism*. Edited by J. H. Hayes. San Antonio: Trinity University, 1974.

_____. "Prolegomenon." Pages 1–60 in *Studies in Ancient Israelite Wisdom*. Edited by J. L. Crenshaw. New York: Ktav, 1976.

_____. "Education in Ancient Israel." *Journal of Biblical Literature* 104 (1985): 601–15.

_____. "The Functions of the Sage in the Egyptian Royal Court." Pages 205–16 in *The Sage in Israel and the Ancient Near East*. Edited by J. G. Gammie and L. G. Perdue. Winona Lake: Eisenbrauns, 1990.

_____. "The Sage in Proverbs." Pages 205–16 in *The Sage in Israel and the Ancient Near East*. Edited by J. G. Gammie and L. G. Perdue. Winona Lake: Eisenbrauns, 1990.

_____. "Clanging Symbols." Pages 51–64 in *Justice and the Holy*. Edited by D. A. Knight and P. J. Paris. Philadelphia: Fortress, 1989. Repr. pages 371–82 in *Urgent Advice and Probing Questions: Collected Writings on Old Testament Wisdom*. Edited by J. L. Crenshaw. Macon: Mercer University Press, 1995.

_____. "A Mother's Instruction to Her Son (Proverbs 31:1–9)." Pages 9–22 in *Perspectives on the Hebrew Bible*. Edited by J. L. Crenshaw. Macon: Mercer University Press, 1988. Repr. pages 383–95 in *Urgent Advice and Probing Questions: Collected Writings on Old Testament Wisdom*. Edited by J. L. Crenshaw. Macon: Mercer University Press, 1995.

_____. "Poverty and Punishment in the Book of Proverbs." *Quarterly Review* 9 (1989): 30–43. Repr. pages 396–405 in *Urgent Advice and Probing Questions: Collected Writings on Old Testament Wisdom*. Edited by J. L. Crenshaw. Macon: Mercer University Press, 1995.

_____. "Prohibitions in Proverbs and Qoheleth." Pages 115–24 in *Priests, Prophets and Scribes: Essays on the Formation and Heritage of Second Temple Judaism in Honour of Joseph Blenkinsopp*. Edited by E. Ulrich, J. W. Wright, R. P. Carroll, and P. R. Davies. Sheffield: Sheffield Academic Press, 1992. Repr. pages 417–25 in *Urgent Advice and Probing Questions: Collected Writings on Old Testament Wisdom*. Edited by J. L. Crenshaw. Macon: Mercer University Press, 1995.

_____. *Education in Ancient Israel: Across the Deadening Silence*. The Anchor Bible Reference Library. New York: Doubleday, 1998.

_____. *Old Testament Wisdom: An Introduction*. Rev. and enl. ed. Louisville: Westminster John Knox, 1998.

_____. "The Contemplative Life in the Ancient Near East." Pages 2445–57 in *Civilizations of the Ancient Near East*. Edited by J. M. Sasson. Peabody: Hendrickson, 2006.

Crown, A. D. "Messengers and Scribes: The סֹפֵר and מַלְאָךְ in the Old Testament." *Vetus Testamentum* 24 (1974): 366–70.

Dahood, M. *Proverbs and Northwest Semitic Philology*. Scripta Pontificii Instituti Biblici 113. Roma: Pontificim Institutum Biblicum, 1963.

Davies, E. W. "The Meaning of *Qesem* in Prv 16,10." *Biblica* 61 (1980): 554–56.

Davies, G. I. *Ancient Hebrew Inscriptions: Corpus and Concordance*. Cambridge: Cambridge University Press, 1991.

_____. "Were There Schools in Ancient Israel?" In *Wisdom in Ancient Israel: Essays in Honour of J. A. Emerton*. Edited by J. Day, H. G. M. Williamson, and R. P. Gordon. Cambridge: Cambridge University Press, 1995.

_____. "Hebrew Inscriptions." Pages 270–86 in *The Biblical World*. Edited by J. Barton. London: Routledge, 2002.

_____. "Some Uses of Writing in Ancient Israel in the Light of Recently Published Inscriptions." Pages 155–74 in *Writing and Ancient Near Eastern Society: Papers in Honour of Alan R. Millard*. Edited by P. Bienkowski, C. Mee, and E. Slater. New York: T&T Clark, 2005.

Day, J. "Foreign Semitic Influence on the Wisdom of Israel and Its Appropriation in the Book of Proverbs." Pages 55–70 in *Wisdom in Ancient Israel: Essays in Honour of J. A. Emerton*. Edited by J. Day, H. G. M. Williamson, and R. P. Gordon. Cambridge: Cambridge University Press, 1995.

_____. "Does the Old Testament Refer to Sacred Prostitution and Did It Actually Exist in Ancient Israel?" Pages 2–21 in *Biblical and Near Eastern Essays: Studies in Honour of Kevin J. Cathcart*. Edited by C. McCarthy and J. F. Healey. London: T&T Clark International, 2004.

de Vaux, R. *Ancient Israel: Its Life and Institutions*. Translated by J. McHugh. Vol. 1. New York: McGraw-Hill, 1961.

Delitzsch, F. *Biblical Commentary on the Proverbs of Solomon*. Translated by M. G. Easton. Repr., Grand Rapids: Eerdmans, 1983.

Dell, K. J. "How Much Wisdom Literature Has Its Roots in the Pre-Exilic Period?" Pages 251–67 in *In Search of Pre-Exilic Israel: Proceedings of the Oxford Old Testament Seminar*. Edited by J. Day. London: T&T Clark International, 2004.

_____. *The Book of Proverbs in Social and Theological Context*. Cambridge: Cambridge University Press, 2006.

Denning-Bolle, S. *Wisdom in Akkadian Literature: Expression, Instruction, Dialogue*. Mededelingen en verhandelingen van het Vooraziatisch-Egyptisch Genootschap "Ex Oriente Lux" 28. Leiden: Ex Oriente Lux, 1992.

Dietrich, M., O. Loretz, and J. Sanmartin. "Die angebliche Ug.-He. Parallele SPSG // SPS(J)G(JM)." *Ugarit-Forschungen* 8 (1976): 37–40.

Doll, P. *Menschenschöpfung und Weltschöpfung in der alttestamentlichen Weisheit*. Stuttgarter Bibelstudien 117. Stuttgart: Verlag Katholisches Bibelwerk, 1985.

Doxey, D. M. *Egyptian Non-Royal Epithets in the Middle Kingdom: A Social and Historical Analysis*. Probleme der Ägyptologie 12. Leiden: Brill, 1998.

Dressler, H. H. P. "The Lesson of Proverbs 26:23." Pages 117–25 in *Ascribe to the Lord: Biblical and Other Studies in Memory of Peter C. Craigie*. Edited by L. Esinger and G. Taylor. Sheffield: JSOT, 1988.

Driver, G. R. "Problems in 'Proverbs'." *Zeitschrift für die alttestamentliche Wissenschaft* 50 (1932): 141–48.

_____. "Problems in the Hebrew Text of Proverbs." *Biblica* 32 (1951): 173–97.

_____. "Problems and Solutions." *Vetus Testamentum* 4 (1954): 223–45.

Driver, S. R. *An Introduction to the Literature of the Old Testament*. Gloucester: Peter Smith, 1972.

Duesberg, H. and I. Franzen. *Les scribes inspires*. 2nd ed. Paris: Maredsous, 1966.

Dunand, F. and C. Zivie-Coche. *Gods and Men in Egypt: 3000 BCE to 395 CE*. Translated by D. Lorton. Ithaca: Cornell University Press, 2004.

Dundes, A. "Who Are the Folk?" Pages 17–35 in *Frontiers in Folklore*. Edited by W. R. Bascom. Boulder: Westview, 1977.

Dürr, J. B. *Das Erziehungswesen im Alten Testament und im antiken Orient*. Leipzig: J.C. Hinrichs, 1932.

Eichler, E. "Zur Datierung und Interpretation der Lehre des Ptahhotep." *Zeitschrift für ägyptische Sprache und Altertumskunde* 128 (2001): 97–107.

Eissfeldt, O. *Der Maschal im Alten Testament.* Beihefte zur Zeitschrift für die alttestamentliche Wissenschaft 24. Giessen: Töpelmann, 1913.

————. *Einleitung in das Alte Testament.* 3rd ed. Tübingen: Mohr, 1964.

————. *The Old Testament: An Introduction.* Repr. ed. Translated by P. Ackroyd. New York: Harper and Row, 1976.

Emerton, J. A. "A Note on Proverbs XII.26." *Zeitschrift für die alttestamentliche Wissenschaft* 76 (1964): 191–93.

Eyre, C. "The Semna Stelae: Quotation, Genre, and Functions of Literature." Pages 134–65 in *Studies in Egyptology Presented to Miriam Lichtheim.* Edited by S. Israelit-Groll. Jerusalem: Magnes, 1990.

Falk, M. *Love Lyrics from the Bible: A Translation and Literary Study of the Song of Songs.* Sheffield: Almond, 1982.

Fensham, F. C. "Widow, Orphan, and the Poor in Ancient Near Eastern Legal and Wisdom Literature." *Journal of Near Eastern Studies* 21 (1962): 129–39. Repr. pages 161–71 in *Studies in Ancient Israelite Wisdom.* Edited by J. L. Crenshaw. New York: Ktav, 1976.

Fichtner, J. *Die altorientalische Weisheit in ihrer israelitisch-jüdischen Ausprägung: Eine Studie zur Nationalisierung der Weisheit in Israel.* Beihefte zur Zeitschrift für die alttestamentliche Wissenschaft 42. Giessen: Töpelmann, 1933.

Firth, R. "Proverbs in Native Life, with Particular Reference to Those of the Maori." *Folk-Lore* 37 (1926): 134–53.

Fischer-Elfert, H.-W. *Die Lehre eines Mannes für seinen Sohn: eine Etappe aud dem 'Gottesweg' des loyalen und solidarischen Beamten des Mittleren Reiches.* Ägyptologische Abhandlungen 60. Wiesbaden: Harrassowitz, 1999.

Fishbane, M. *Biblical Interpretation in Ancient Israel.* Oxford: Clarendon, 1985.

Fontaine, C. R. *Traditional Sayings in the Old Testament.* Edited by D. M. Gunn. Bible and Literature Series 5. Sheffield: Almond Press, 1982.

————. "Proverb Performance in the Hebrew Bible." *Journal for the Study of the Old Testament* 32 (1985): 87–103.

————. "The Sage in the Family and Tribe." Pages 155–64 in *The Sage in Israel and the Ancient Near East.* Edited by J. G. Gammie and L. G. Perdue. Winona Lake: Eisenbrauns, 1990.

————. "Wisdom in Proverbs." Pages 99–114 in *In Search of Wisdom: Essays in Memory of John G. Gammie.* Edited by L. G. Perdue, B. B. Scott, and W. J. Wiseman. Louisville: Westminster John Knox, 1993.

————. "The Social Role of Women in the World of Wisdom." Pages 24–49 in *A Feminist Companion to Wisdom Literature.* Edited by A. Brenner. Sheffield: Sheffield Academic Press, 1995.

————. *Smooth Words: Women, Proverbs and Performance in Biblical Wisdom.* Journal for the Study of the Old Testament: Supplement Series 356. Sheffield: Sheffield Academic Press, 2002.

Forti, T. L. "Animal Images in the Didactic Rhetoric of the Book of Proverbs." *Biblica* 77 (1996): 48–63.

————. *Animal Imagery in the Book of Proverbs.* Supplements to Vetus Testamentum 118. Leiden: Brill, 2008.

Foster, B. "Wisdom and the Gods in Ancient Mesopotamia." *Orientalia (NS)* 43 (1976): 344–54.

Foster, B. R. *Before the Muses: An Anthology of Akkadian Literature.* 2nd ed. Bethesda: CDL Press, 1996.

————. *The Epic of Gilgamesh: A New Translation, Analogues, Criticism.* New York: Norton, 2001.

Foster, J. L. "The Conclusion to *the Testament of Ammenemes, King of Egypt.*" *Journal of Egyptian Archaeology* 67 (1981): 36–47.

————. "Some Comments on Khety's Instruction for Little Pepi on His Way to School (Satire on the Trades)." Pages 121–29 in *Gold of Praise: Studies on Ancient Egypt in Honor of Edward F. Wente.* Edited by E. Teeter and J. A. Larson. Chicago: The Oriental Institute of the University of Chicago, 1999.

Fox, M. V. "Two Decades of Research in Egyptian Wisdom Literature." *Zeitschrift für ägyptische Sprache und Altertumskunde* 107 (1980): 120–35.

————. *The Song of Songs and Ancient Egyptian Love Songs.* Madison: University of Wisconsin Press, 1985.

————. "World Order and Maʿat: A Crooked Parallel." *Journal of the Ancient Near Eastern Society* 23 (1995): 37–48.

————. "The Social Location of the Book of Proverbs." Pages 227–39 in *Texts, Temples, and Traditions: A Tribute to Menahem Haran.* Edited by M. V. Fox. Winona Lake: Eisenbrauns, 1996.

————. "The Strange Woman in Septuagint Proverbs." *Journal of Northwest Semitic Languages* 22 (1996): 31–44.

————. "What the Book of Proverbs Is About." Pages 153–67 in *Congress Volume: Cambridge 1995.* Edited by J. A. Emerton. Leiden: Brill, 1997.

————. "Who Can Learn? A Dispute in Ancient Pedagogy." Pages 62–77 in *Wisdom, You Are My Sister: Studies in Honor of Roland E. Murphy, O. Carm., on the Occasion of His Eightieth Birthday.* Edited by M. L. Barré. Catholic Biblical Quarterly Monograph Series 29. Washington, D.C.: The Catholic Biblical Association of America, 1997.

————. *Proverbs 1–9: A New Translation with Introduction and Commentary.* Anchor Bible 18A. New York: Doubleday, 2000.

————. "Wisdom and the Self-Presentation of Wisdom Literature." Pages 153–72 in *Reading from Right to Left: Essays on the Hebrew Bible in Honour of David J. A. Clines.* Edited by J. C. Exum and H. G. M. Williamson. Sheffield: Sheffield Academic, 2003.

————. "The Epistemology of the Book of Proverbs." *Journal of Biblical Literature* 126 (2007): 669–84.

————. "Ethics and Wisdom in the Book of Proverbs." *Hebrew Studies* 48 (2007): 75–88.

————. "The Formation of Proverbs 22:17–23:11." *Die Welt des Orients* 38 (2008): 22–37.

————. *Proverbs 10–31: A New Translation with Introduction and Commentary.* Anchor Bible 18B. New Haven: Yale University Press, 2009.

Franke, D. "The Middle Kingdom in Egypt." Pages 735–48 in *Civilizations of the Ancient Near East.* Edited by J. M. Sasson. Peabody: Hendrickson, 1996.

————. "Kleiner Mann (*nḏs*) – was bist Du?" *Göttinger Miszellen* 167 (1998): 33–48.

Franklyn, P. "The Sayings of Agur in Proverbs 30: Piety or Scepticism?" *Zeitschrift für die alttestamentliche Wissenschaft* 95 (1983): 238–52.

Frick, F. S. *The City in Ancient Israel*. Society of Biblical Literature Dissertation Series 36. Missoula: Scholars Press, 1977.

Frydrych, T. *Living under the Sun: Examination of Proverbs and Qoheleth*. Supplements to Vetus Testamentum 90. Leiden: Brill, 2002.

Fuhs, H. F. *Das Buch der Sprichwörter: Ein Kommentar*. Forschung zur Bibel 95. Würzburg: Echter Verlag, 2001.

Gadd, C. J. *Teachers and Students in the Oldest Schools*. London: University of London, 1956.

Garrett, D. A. "Votive Prostitution Again: A Comparison of Proverbs 7:13–14 and 21:28–29." *Journal of Biblical Literature* 109 (1990): 681–82.

—————. *Proverbs, Ecclesiastes, Song of Songs*. New American Commentary 14. Nashville: Broadman, 1993.

Gemser, B. *Sprüche Salomos*. Handbuch zum Alten Testament 16. Tübingen: Mohr, 1963.

—————. "The Instructions of 'Onchsheshonqy and Biblical Wisdom Literature." *Scottish Journal of Theology* 7 (1960): 102–28. Repr. pages 134–60 in *Studies in Ancient Israelite Religion*. Edited by J. L. Crenshaw. New York: Ktav, 1976.

Gerstenberger, E. *Wesen und Herkunft des 'apodiktischem Rechts'*. Wissenschaftliche Monographien zum Alten und Neuen Testament 20. Neukirchen-Vluyn: Neukirchener, 1965.

Gesche, P. D. *Schulunterricht in Babylonien im ersten Jahrtausend v. Chr.* Alter Orient und Altes Testament 275. Münster: Ugarit-Verlag, 2000.

Gilbert, M. "Le discours de la sagesse en Proverbes 8." Pages 202–18 in *La Sagesse de l'Ancien Testament*. Edited by M. Gilbert. Bibliotheca ephemeridum theologicarum lovaniensium 51. Gembloux: Duculot, 1979. Repr., Leuven: Leuven University Press, 1990.

—————. "Le discours menaçant de Sagesse en Proverbes 1,20–33." Pages 99–119 in *Storia e tradizioni di Israele: Scritti in onore di J. Alberto Soggin*. Edited by D. Garrone and F. Israel. Brescia: Paideia, 1991.

Ginsburg, H. L. "The North-Canaanite Myth of Anath and Aqhat." *Bulletin of the American Schools of Oriental Research* 98 (1945): 15–23.

Goedicke, H. *Studies in 'The Instruction of King Amenhemet I for His Son.'* Varia Aegyptiaca Supplement 2. San Antonio: van Siclen Books, 1988.

—————. "Merikare[c] E 106–115." *Zeitschrift für ägyptische Sprache und Altertumskunde* 129 (2002): 115–21.

Goldingay, J. "The Arrangement of Sayings in Proverbs 10–15." *Journal for the Study of the Old Testament* 61 (1994): 75–83.

Golka, F. W. "Die israelitische Weisheitsschule oder 'des Kaisers neue Kleider'." *Vetus Testamentum* 33 (1983): 257–70.

—————. *The Leopard's Spots: Biblical and African Wisdom in Proverbs*. Edinburgh: T&T Clark, 1993.

Gordis, R. "The Social Background of Wisdom Literature." *Hebrew Union College Annual* 18 (1943/44): 77–118.

Gordon, E. I. *Sumerian Proverbs*. New York: Greenwood, 1968.

Greenfield, J. C. "The Dialects of Early Aramaic." *Journal of Near Eastern Studies* 37 (1978): 93–99.

_____. "The Seven Pillars of Wisdom (Prov 9:1): A Mistranslation." *Jewish Quarterly Review* 76 (1985): 13–20.

_____. "The Wisdom of Ahiqar." Pages 43–52 in *Wisdom in Ancient Israel: Essays in Honour of J. A. Emerton.* Edited by J. Day, H. G. M. Williamson, and R. P. Gordon. Cambridge: Cambridge University Press, 1995.

Greenspahn, F. E. "A Mesopotamian Proverb and Its Biblical Reverberations." *Journal of the American Oriental Society* 114 (1994): 33–38.

Gressmann, H. "Die neugefundene Lehre des Amen-em-ope und die vorexilische Spruchdichtung Israels." *Zeitschrift für die alttestamentliche Wissenschaft* 42 (1924): 272–96.

_____. *Israels Spruchweisheit im Zusammenhang der Weltliteratur.* Berlin: C. Curtius, 1925.

Grumach, I. *Untersuchungen zur Lebenslehre des Amenemope.* Münchner Ägyptologische Studien 23. München: Deutscher Kunstverlag, 1972.

Gundlach, R. "Ägyptische Weisheit in der politischen 'Lebenslehre' König Amenhemet I." Pages 91–105 in *"Jedes Ding hat seine Zeit...": Studien zur israelitischen und altorientalischen Weisheit.* Edited by A. A. Diesel, R. G. Lehmann, E. Otto, and A. Wagner. Berlin: Walter de Gruyter, 1996.

Gunneweg, A. H. J. "Weisheit, Prophetie und Kanonformel." Pages 253–60 in *Alttestamentlicher Glaube und Biblische Theologie: Festschrift für Horst Dietrich Preuß zum 65. Geburtstag.* Edited by J. Hausmann and H.-J. Zobel. Stuttgart: Kohlhammer, 1992.

Habel, N. C. "The Symbolism of Wisdom in Proverbs 1–9." *Interpretation* 26 (1972): 131–57.

_____. "Wisdom, Wealth, and Poverty Paradigms in the Book of Proverbs." *Bible Bhashyam* 14 (1988): 26–49.

Hadley, J. M. "From Goddess to Literary Construct: The Transformation of Asherah into Hokmah." Pages 360–99 in *A Feminist Companion to Reading the Bible: Approaches, Methods and Strategies.* Edited by A. Brenner and C. Fontaine. London: Dearborn, 1997.

Hallo, W. W., ed. *Canonical Compositions from the Biblical World.* Vol. 1 of *The Context of Scripture.* Leiden: E. J. Brill, 2003.

Haran, M. "The Graded Numerical Sequence and the Phenomenon of 'Automatism' in Biblical Poetry." *Vetus Testamentum* 22 (1972): 238–67.

_____. "On the Diffusion of Literacy and Schools in Ancient Israel." Pages 81–95 in *Congress Volume: Jerusalem 1986.* Edited by J. A. Emerton. Leiden: E. J. Brill, 1988.

Harris, R. "The Female 'Sage' in Mesopotamian Literature (with an Appendix on Egypt)." Pages 3–17 in *The Sage in Israel and the Ancient Near East.* Edited by J. G. Gammie and L. G. Perdue. Winona Lake: Eisenbrauns, 1990.

Harris, S. L. *Proverbs 1–9: A Study of Inner-Biblical Interpretation.* Society of Biblical Literature Dissertation Series 150. Atlanta: Scholars Press, 1995.

Hausmann, J. "Beobachtungen zu Spr 31,10–31." Pages 261–66 in *Alttestamentlicher Glaube und Biblische Theologie: Festschrift für Horst Dietrich Preuß zum 65. Geburtstag.* Edited by J. Hausmann and H.-J. Zobel. Stuttgart: Kohlhammer, 1992.

_____. *Studien zum Menschenbild der älteren Weisheit (Spr 10ff.).* Forschungen zum Alten Testament 7. Tübingen: Mohr, 1995.

Heaton, E. W. *Solomon's New Men: The Emergence of Ancient Israel as a National State.* New York: Pica Press, 1974.

_____. *The School Tradition of the Old Testament: The Bampton Lectures for 1994.* Oxford: Oxford University Press, 1994.

Heim, K. M. *Like Grapes of Gold Set in Silver: An Interpretation of Proverbial Clusters in Proverbs 10:1–22:16.* Beihefte zur Zeitschrift für die alttestamentliche Wissenschaft 273. Berlin: Walter de Gruyter, 2001.

_____. "A Closer Look at the Pig in Proverbs xi 22." *Vetus Testamentum* 58 (2008): 13–27.

Helck, W. *Der Text der "Lehre Amenemhets I. für seinen Sohn."* Kleine Ägyptische Texte 1. Wiesbaden: Harrassowitz, 1969.

_____. *Die Lehres des Dw³-Htjj, Textzusammenstellung.* Kleine Ägyptische Texte 3. Wiesbaden: Harrassowitz, 1970.

_____. *Die Lehre für König Merikare.* Kleine Ägyptische Texte 5. Wiesbaden: Harrassowitz, 1977.

_____. *Die Lehre des Djedefhor und Die Lehre eines Vaters an seinen Sohn.* Kleine Ägyptische Texte 8. Wiesbaden: Harrassowitz, 1986.

Hermisson, H.-J. *Studien zur israelitischen Spruchweisheit.* Wissenschaftliche Monographien Alten und Neuen Testament 28. Neukirchen-Vluyn: Neukirchener Verlag, 1968.

Hess, R. S. "Literacy in Iron Age Israel." Pages 82–95 in *Windows into the Old Testament History: Evidence, Argument, and the Crisis of "Biblical Israel."* Edited by D. W. Baker, V. P. Long, and G. J. Wenham. Grand Rapids: Eerdmans, 2002.

Hildebrandt, T. "Proverbial Pairs: Compositional Units in Proverbs 10–29." *Journal of Biblical Literature* 107 (1988): 207–24.

_____. "Motivation and Antithetical Parallelism in Proverbs 10–15." *Journal of the Evangelical Theological Society* 35 (1992): 433–44. Repr. pages 253–65 in *Learning from the Sages: Selected Studies on the Book of Proverbs.* Edited by R. B. Zuck. Grand Rapids: Baker, 1995.

Hoglund, K. G. "The Fool and the Wise in Dialogue." Pages 161–80 in *The Listening Heart: Essays in Wisdom and the Psalms in Honor of Roland E. Murphy, O. Carm.* Edited by K. G. Hoglund, E. F. Huwiler, J. T. Glass, and R. W. Lee. Sheffield: Sheffield Academic Press, 1987.

Hornung, E. *Der Eine und die Vielen: Ägyptische Gottesvorstellungen.* Darmstadt: Wissenschaftliche Buchgesellschaft, 1971.

_____. *Idea into Image: Essays on Ancient Egyptian Thought.* Translated by E. Bredeck. New York: Timken Publishers, 1992.

_____. *Conceptions of God in Ancient Egypt: The One and the Many.* Translated by J. Baines. Ithaca: Cornell University Press, 1996.

Houston, W. J. "The Role of the Poor in Proverbs." Pages 229–40 in *Reading from Right to Left: Essays on the Hebrew Bible in Honour of David J. A. Clines.* Edited by J. C. Exum and H. G. M. Williamson. Sheffield: Sheffield Academic, 2003.

_____. *Contending for Justice: Ideologies and Theologies of Social Justice in the Old Testament.* Library of Hebrew Bible/Old Testament Studies 428. London: T & T Clark, 2006.

Hugenberger, G. P. *Marriage as a Covenant: A Study of Biblical Law and Ethics Governing Marriage Developed from the Perspective of Malachi.* Supplements to Vetus Testamentum 52. Leiden: Brill, 1994.

Humphreys, W. L. "The Motif of the Wise Courtier in the Book of Proverbs." Pages 177–
90 in *Israelite Wisdom: Theological and Literary Essays in Honor of Samuel Terrien.*
Edited by W. A. Brueggemann, J. G. Gammie, W. L. Humphreys, and J. M.
Ward. Missoula: Scholars Press, 1978.

Hurowitz, V. A. *I Have Built You an Exalted House: Temple Building in the Bible in Light of
Mesopotamian and Northwest Semitic Writings.* Journal for the Study of the Old
Testament Supplement Series 115. Sheffield: JSOT, 1992.

_____. "The Seventh Pillar—Reconsidering the Literary Structure and Unity of
Proverbs 31." *Zeitschrift für die alttestamentliche Wissenschaft* 113 (2001): 209–18.

_____. "The Woman of Valor and a Woman Large of Head: Matchmaking in the
Ancient Near East." Pages 221–34 in *Seeking out the Wisdom of the Ancients: Essays
Offered to Honor Michael V. Fox on the Occasion of His Sixty-Fifth Birthday.* Edited by
K. G. Friebel, R. L. Troxel, and D. R. Magary. Winona Lake: Eisenbrauns, 2005.

Irwin, W. H. "The Metaphor in Prov. 11,30." *Biblica* 65 (1984): 97–100.

Jacob, E. "Sagesse et Alphabet. A propos de Proverbes 31.10–31." Pages 287–95 in
Hommages á André Dupont-Sommer. Paris: Librairie d'Amérique er d'Orient Adrien
Maisonneuve, 1971.

Jacobsen, T. *The Treasures of Darkness.* New Haven: Yale University Press, 1976.

Jamieson-Drake, D. W. *Scribes and Schools in Monarchic Judah: A Socio-Archeological Approach.*
Journal for the Study of the Old Testament: Supplement Series 109. Sheffield:
Almond Press, 1991.

Jouön, P. *Grammaire de l'hébreu biblique.* Rome: Pontifical Biblical Institute, 1947.

Junge, F. *Die Lehre Ptahhoteps und die Tugenden der ägyptischen Welt.* Orbis biblicus et orientalis
193. Göttingen: Vandenhoeck & Ruprecht, 2003.

Kalugila, L. *The Wise King: Studies in Royal Wisdom as Divine Revelation in the Old Testament and
Its Environment.* Coniectanea biblica: Old Testament Series 15. Lund: CWK
Gleerup, 1980.

Kassis, R. A. *The Book of Proverbs and Arabic Proverbial Works.* Leiden: Brill, 1999.

Kayatz, C. *Studien zu Proverbien 1–9.* Wissenschaftliche Monographien zum Alten und
Neuen Testament 22. Neukirchen-Vluyn: Neukirchener Verlag, 1966.

_____. *Einführung in die alttestamentliche Weisheit.* Biblische Studien 55. Neukirchen-
Vluyn: Neukirchener, 1969.

Kimilike, L. P. *Poverty in the Book of Proverbs: An African Transformational Hermeneutic of Proverbs
on Poverty.* Bible and Theology in Africa 7. New York: Peter Lang, 2008.

King, P. J., and L. E. Stager. *Life in Biblical Israel.* Library of Ancient Israel. Louisville:
Westminster John Knox, 2001.

Kirshenblatt-Gimblett, B. "Toward a Theory of Proverb Meaning." *Proverbium* 22 (1973):
821–27. Repr. pages 111–21 in *The Wisdom of Many: Essays on the Proverb.* Edited
by W. Mieder and A. Dundes. New York: Garland, 1981.

Kitchen, K. A. "Studies in Egyptian Wisdom Literature: I. The Instruction by a Man for
His Son." *Oriens Antiquus* 8 (1969): 189–208.

_____. "Proverbs and Wisdom Books of the Ancient Near East: The Factual History
of a Literary Form." *Tyndale Bulletin* 28 (1977): 68–114.

_____. "The Basic Literary Forms and Formulations of Ancient Instructional Writings in Egypt and Western Asia." Pages 236–82 in *Studien zu altägyptischen Lebenslehren.* Orbis biblicus et orientalis 28. Göttingen: Vandenhoeck & Ruprecht, 1979.

Klein, J. "Building and Dedication Hymns in Sumerian Literature." *Acta Sumerologica* 11 (1989): 28–67.

Klopefnstein, M. A. "Auferstehung der Göttin in der spätisraelitischen Weisheit von Prov 1–9?" Pages 531–42 in *Ein Gott allein? Jhwh-Verehrung und biblischer Monotheismus im Kontext der israelitischen und altorientalischen Religionsgeschichte.* Edited by W. Dietrich and M. A. Klopfenstein. Fribourg: Fribourg University, 1994.

Kloppenborg, J. S. "Isis and Sophia in the Book of Wisdom." *Harvard Theological Review* 75 (1982): 57–84.

Klostermann, A. "Schulwesen im Alten Israel." Pages 193–232 in *Theologische Studien, Theodor Zahn.* Edited by N. Bonwetsch. Leipzig: Deichert, 1908.

Knoppers, G. N. "The Deuteronomist and the Deuteronomic Law of the King: A Reexamination of a Relationship." *Zeitschrift für die alttestamentliche Wissenschaft* 108 (1996): 329–32.

Kottsieper, I. *Die Sprache der Ahiqarsprüche.* Beihefte zur Zeitschrift für die alttestamentliche Wissenschaft 194. Berlin: de Gruyter, 1990.

Kovacs, B. W. "Is There a Class-Ethic in Proverbs?" Pages 173–89 in *Essays in Old Testament Ethics.* Edited by J. L. Crenshaw and J. T. Willis. New York: Ktav, 1974.

_____. "Sociological-Structural Constraints upon Wisdom: The Spatial and Temporal Matrix of Proverbs 15:28–22:16." PhD diss., Vanderbilt University, 1978.

Kraeling, C. H., and R. M. Adams, eds. *City Invincible: A Symposium on Urbanization and Cultural Development in the Ancient Near East Held at the Oriental Institute of the University of Chicago, December 4–7, 1958.* Chicago: The University of Chicago Press, 1960.

Kramer, S. N. *The Sumerians: Their History, Culture, and Character.* Chicago: The University of Chicago Press, 1971.

_____. "The Sage in Sumerian Literature: A Composite Portrait." Pages 31–44 in *The Sage in Israel and the Ancient Near East.* Edited by J. G. Gammie and L. G. Perdue. Winona Lake: Eisenbrauns, 1990.

Krantz, E. S. "'A Man Not Supported by God': On Some Crucial Words in Proverbs XXX 1." *Vetus Testamentum* 46 (1996): 548–52.

Krispenz, J. *Spruchkompositionen im Buch Proverbia.* Europäische Hochschulschriften 349. Frankfurt: Peter Lang, 1989.

Kuschke, A. "Arm und reich im Alten Testament mit besonderer Berücksichtigung der nachexilischen Zeit." *Zeitschrift für die alttestamentliche Wissenschaft* 57 (1939): 31–57.

Laisney, V. P.-M. *L'Enseignement d'Aménémopé.* Rome: Pontifical Biblical Institute, 2007.

Lambert, W. G., ed. *Babylonian Wisdom Literature.* Oxford: Oxford University Press, 1960. Repr. Winona Lake: Eisenbrauns, 1996.

_____. "Kingship in Ancient Mesopotamia." Pages 54–70 in *King and Messiah in Israel and the Ancient Near East: Proceedings of the Oxford Old Testament Seminar.* Edited by J. Day. Journal for the Study of the Old Testament: Supplement Series 270. Sheffield: Sheffield Academic Press, 1998.

Lang, B. *Die weisheitliche Lehrrede: Eine Untersuchung von Sprüche 1–7.* Stuttgarter Bibelstudien 54. Stuttgart: KBW Verlag, 1972.

_____. "Schule und Unterricht im Alten Israel." Pages 186–201 in *La Sagesse de l'Ancien Testament*. Edited by M. Gilbert. Bibliotheca ephemeridum theologicarum lovaniensium 51. Gembloux: Duculot, 1979. Repr., Leuven: Leuven University Press, 1990.

_____. *Wie wird man Prophet in Israel? Aufsätze*. Düsseldorf: Patmos, 1980.

_____. "Vorläufer von Speiseeis in Bibel und Orient. Eine Untersuchung von Spr 25,13." Pages 218–32 in *Mélanges bibliques et orientaux en l'honneur de M. Henri Cazelles*. Edited by A. Caquot and M. Delcor. Neukirchen-Vluyn: Neukirchener Verlag, 1981.

_____. *Wisdom and the Book of Proverbs: A Hebrew Goddess Redefined*. New York: The Pilgrim Press, 1986.

Leeb, C. S. *Away from the Father's House: The Social Location of Na'ar and Na'arah in Ancient Israel*. Journal for the Study of the Old Testament: Supplement Series 301. Sheffield: Sheffield Academic Press, 2000.

Leliévre, A., and A. Maillot. *Commentaire des Proverbes. Les Proverbes de Salomon chapitres 10–18*. Lectio divina 1. Paris: Éditions du Cerf, 1993.

_____. *Commentaire des Proverbes II: chapitres 19–31*. Lectio divina 4. Paris: Éditions du Cerf, 1996.

Lemaire, A. *Les écoles et la formation de la Bible dans l'ancien Israél*. Orbis biblicus et orientalis 39. Göttingen: Vandenhoeck & Ruprecht, 1981.

_____. "The Sage in School and Temple." Pages 165–81 in *The Sage in Israel and the Ancient Near East*. Edited by J. G. Gammie and L. G. Perdue. Winona Lake: Eisenbrauns, 1990.

Lesko, L. H. "Some Comments on Ancient Egyptian Literacy and Literati." Pages 656–67 in *Studies in Egyptology Presented to Miriam Lichtheim*. Edited by S. Israelit-Groll. Jerusalem: Magnes, 1990.

_____. "Literature, Literacy, and Literati." Pages 131–44 in *Pharaoh's Workers: The Villagers of Deir el Medina*. Edited by L. H. Lesko. London: Cornell University Press, 1994.

Lichtenstein, M. "The Banquet Motifs in Keret and in Proverbs 9." *Journal of Ancient Near Eastern Studies* 1 (1968/69): 19–31.

Lichtenstein, M. H. "Chiasm and Symmetry in Proverbs 31." *Catholic Biblical Quarterly* 44 (1982): 202–11. Repr. pages 381–90 in *Learning from the Sages: Selected Studies on the Book of Proverbs*. Edited by R. B. Zuck. Grand Rapids: Baker, 1995.

Lichtheim, M. "Observations on Papyrus Insinger." Pages 284–305 in *Studien zu altägyptischen Lebenslehren*. Orbis biblicus et orientalis 28. Göttingen: Vandenhoeck & Ruprecht, 1979.

_____. *Late Egyptian Wisdom Literature in the International Content: A Study of Demotic Instructions*. Orbis biblicus et orientalis 52. Göttingen: Vandenhoeck & Ruprecht, 1983.

_____. *Maat in Egyptian Autobiographies and Related Studies*. Orbis biblicus et orientalis 120. Göttingen: Vandenhoeck & Ruprecht, 1992.

_____. *Moral Values in Ancient Egypt*. Orbis biblicus et orientalis 155. Göttingen: Vandenhoeck & Ruprecht, 1997.

_____. *Ancient Egyptian Literature: A Book of Readings*. 2nd ed. 3 vols. Berkeley: University of California Press, 2006.

Lindenberger, J. M. *The Aramaic Proverbs of Ahiqar*. The Johns Hopkins Near Eastern Studies. Baltimore: Johns Hopkins University Press, 1983.

Lipinski, E. "Peninna, Iti'el et l'Athlète." *Vetus Testamentum* 17 (1967): 68–75.

————. "Royal and State Scribes in Ancient Jerusalem." Pages 157–64 in *Congress Volume: Jerusalem 1986.* Edited by J. A. Emerton. Leiden: E. J. Brill, 1988.

Loader, J. A. "Wisdom by (the) People for (the) People." *Zeitschrift für die alttestamentliche Wissenschaft* 111 (1999): 211–33.

Loewenstamm, S. E. "Remarks on Proverbs XVII 12 and XX 27." *Vetus Testamentum* 37 (1987): 121–24.

Longman III, T. *Proverbs.* Baker Commentary on the Old Testament Wisdom and Psalms. Grand Rapids: Baker Academic, 2006.

Loprieno, A. *Topos und Mimesis: zum Ausländer in der ägyptischen Literatur.* Ägyptologische Abhandlungen 48. Wiesbaden: Harrasowitz, 1988.

————. "Defining Egyptian Literature: Ancient Texts and Modern Literary Theory." Pages 209–32 in *The Study of the Ancient Near East in the Twenty-First Century: The William Foxwell Albright Centennial Conference.* Edited by J. S. Cooper and G. M. Schwartz. Winona Lake: Eisenbrauns, 1996.

————. "Loyalistic Instructions." Pages 403–14 in *Ancient Egyptian Literature: History and Forms.* Edited by A. Loprieno. Leiden: E. J. Brill, 1996.

Loretz, O. "Ugaritische und hebräische Lexikographie (IV)." *Ugarit-Forschungen* 15 (1983): 59–64.

Lorton, D. "Ethics and Law Codes: Egypt." Pages 514–16 in *Religions of the Ancient World: A Guide.* Edited by S. I. Johnston. Cambridge: Harvard University Press, 2004.

Luc, A. "The Titles and Structure of Proverbs." *Zeitschrift für die alttestamentliche Wissenschaft* 112 (2000): 252–55.

Lyons, E. L. "A Note on Proverbs 31:10–31." Pages 237–45 in *The Listening Heart: Essays in Wisdom and the Psalms in Honor of Roland E. Murphy, O. Carm.* Edited by K. G. Hoglund, E. F. Huwiler, J. T. Glass, and R. W. Lee. Sheffield: Sheffield Academic Press, 1987.

MacDonald, J. "The Status and Role of the *Na'ar* in Israelite Society." *Journal of Near Eastern Studies* 35 (1976): 147–70.

MacIntosch, A. A. "A Note on Proverbs XXV 27." *Vetus Testamentum* 20 (1970): 112–14.

Mack, B. L. "Wisdom Myth and Myth-ology: An Essay in Understanding a Theological Tradition." *Interpretation* 24 (1970): 46–60.

————. *Wisdom and the Hebrew Epic.* Chicago: University of Chicago Press, 1985.

Maier, C. *Die 'Fremde Frau' in Proverbien 1–9: Eine Exegetische und Sozialgeschichtliche Studie.* Orbis biblicus et orientalis 144. Göttingen: Vandenhoeck & Ruprecht, 1995.

Malchow, B. V. "Social Justice in the Wisdom Literature." *Biblical Theology Bulletin* 12 (1982): 120–24.

————. "A Manual for Future Monarchs: Proverbs 27:23–29:27." *Catholic Biblical Quarterly* 47 (1985): 238–45. Repr. pages 352–60 in *Learning from the Sages: Selected Studies on the Book of Proverbs.* Edited by R. B. Zuck. Grand Rapids: Baker, 1995.

Marcus, R. "On Biblical Hypostases of Wisdom." *Hebrew Union College Annual* 25 (1950): 157–71.

Maxwell-Hyslop, K. R. *Western Asiatic Jewelry C. 3000–612 B.C.* Methuen's Handbooks of Archaeology. London: Methuen & Co, 1971.

McCreesh, T. P. *Biblical Sound and Sense: Poetic Sound Patterns in Proverbs 10–29.* Journal for the Study of the Old Testament: Supplement Series 128. Sheffield: Sheffield Academic Press, 1991.

_____. "Wisdom as Wife: Proverbs 31:10–31." *Revue biblique* 92 (1985): 25–46. Repr. pages 391–410 in *Learning from the Sages: Selected Studies on the Book of Proverbs*. Edited by R. B. Zuck. Grand Rapids: Baker, 1995.

McKane, W. *Prophets and Wise Men*. Studies in Biblical Theology 44. Naperville: Allenson, 1965.

_____. *Proverbs: A New Approach*. Old Testament Library. Philadelphia: Westminster, 1970.

_____. "Functions of Language and Objections of Discourse According to Proverbs, 10–30." Pages 166–85 in *La Sagesse de l'Ancien Testament*. Edited by M. Gilbert. Bibliotheca ephemeridum theologicarum lovaniensium 51. Gembloux: Duculot, 1979. Repr., Leuven: Leuven University Press, 1990.

McKinlay, J. E. *Gendering Wisdom the Host*. Journal for the Study of the Old Testament: Supplement Series 216. Sheffield: JSOT, 1996.

Meier, S. A. *The Messenger in the Ancient Semitic World*. Harvard Semitic Monographs 45. Atlanta: Scholars Press, 1988.

Meinhold, A. *Die Sprüche, Teil 1: Sprüche Kapitel 1–15*. Zürcher Bibelkommentare 16.1. Zürich: Theologischer Verlag, 1991.

_____. *Die Sprüche, Teil 2: Sprüche Kapitel 16–31*. Zürcher Bibelkommentare 16.2. Zürich: Theologischer Verlag, 1991.

_____. "Der Umgang mit dem Feind nach Spr 25,21f. als Maßstab für das Menschein." Pages 244–52 in *Alttestamentlicher Glaube und Biblische Theologie: Festschrift für Horst Dietrich Preuß zum 65. Geburtstag*. Edited by J. Hausmann and H.-J. Zobel. Stuttgart: Kohlhammer, 1992.

_____. "Das Wortspiel רצין-רזין in Prov 14,28–35." *Zeitschrift für die alttestamentliche Wissenschaft* 110 (1998): 615–16.

Mettinger, T. N. D. *Solomonic State Officials: A Study of the Civil Government Officials of the Israelite Monarchy*. Coniectanea Biblica: Old Testament Series 5. Lund: Gleerup, 1971.

Meyers, C. "The Family in Early Israel." Pages 1–47 in *Families in Ancient Israel*. Louisville: Westminster John Knox, 1997.

Michalowski, P. "Charisma and Control: On Continuity and Change in Early Mesopotamian Bureaucratic Systems." Pages 55–68 in *The Organization of Power: Aspects of Bureaucracy in the Ancient Near East*. Edited by M. Gibson and R. D. Biggs. Chicago: The Oriental Institute of the University of Chicago, 1987.

Mieder, W. "The Essence of Literary Proverb Study." *Proverbium* 23 (1974): 888–94.

Mies, F. "'Dame Sagesse' en Proverbes 9 une personnification féminine?" *Revue biblique* 108 (2001): 161–83.

Miles, J. E. *Wise King — Royal Fool: Semiotics, Satire and Proverbs 1–9*. Journal for the Study of the Old Testament: Supplement Series 399. London: T&T Clark International, 2004.

Millard, A. "The Knowledge of Writing in Iron Age Palestine." *Tyndale Bulletin* 46 (1995): 207–17.

Monroe, C. M. "Money and Trade." Pages 155–68 in *A Companion to the Ancient Near East*. Edited by D. C. Snell. Malden: Blackwell, 2005.

Moore, R. D. "A Home for the Alien: Worldly Wisdom and Covenantal Confession in Proverbs 30,1–9." *Zeitschrift für alttestamentliche Wissenschaft* 106 (1994): 96–107.

Morenz, L. D. *Beiträge zur Schriftlichkeitskultur im Mittleren Reich und in der 2. Zwischenzeit*. Ägypten und Altes Testament. Wiesbaden: Harrassowitz, 1996.

Morenz, S. "Feurige Kohlen auf dem Haupt." *Theologische Literaturzeitung* 78 (1953): 187–92.

Murphy, R. E. "Assumptions and Problems in Old Testament Wisdom Research." *Catholic Biblical Quarterly* 29 (1967): 101–12.

————. "Form Criticism and Wisdom Literature." *Catholic Biblical Quarterly* 31 (1969): 475–83.

————. "Wisdom—Theses and Hypotheses." Pages 35–42 in *Israelite Wisdom: Theological and Literary Essays in Honor of Samuel Terrien.* Edited by W. A. Brueggemann, J. G. Gammie, W. L. Humphreys, and J. M. Ward. Missoula: Scholars Press, 1978.

————. *Wisdom Literature: Job, Proverbs, Ruth, Canticles, Ecclesiastes, and Esther.* Forms of the Old Testament Literature 13. Grand Rapids: Eerdmans, 1981.

————. *Proverbs.* Word Biblical Commentary 22. Nashville: Thomas Nelson, 1998.

————. *The Tree of Life: An Exploration of Biblical Wisdom Literature.* 3rd ed. Grand Rapids: Eerdmans, 2002.

Naré, L. *Proverbes salomoniens et proverbes mossi: etude comparative á partir d'une nouvelle analyse de Pr. 25–29.* Publications Universitaires Européennes 23. Frankfurt am Main: Peter Lang, 1986.

Nel, P. J. "The Concept 'Father' in the Wisdom Literature of the Ancient Near East." *Journal of Northwest Semitic Languages* 5 (1977): 53–66.

————. "A Proposed Method for Determining the Context of the Wisdom Admonitions." *Journal of Northwest Semitic Languages* 6 (1978): 33–39.

————. *The Structure and Ethos of the Wisdom Admonitions in Proverbs.* Beihefte zur Zeitschrift für die alttestamentliche Wissenschaft 158. Berlin: Walter de Gruyter, 1982.

Newsom, C. A. "Woman and the Discourse of Patriarchal Wisdom." Pages 142–60 in *Gender and Difference in Ancient Israel.* Edited by P. L. Day. Minneapolis: Fortress, 1989. Repr. pages 116–31 in *Reading Bibles, Writing Bodies: Identity and the Book.* Edited by T. K. Beal and D. M. Gunn. London: Routledge, 1997.

Nussbaum, M. C. *The Fragility of Goodness.* Cambridge: Cambridge University Press, 1986.

O'Connell, R. H. "Proverbs VII 16–17: A Case of Fatal Deception in a 'Women and the Window' Type-Scene." *Vetus Testamentum* 41 (1991): 235–41.

Ogden, G. S. "The 'Better'-Proverb (Tôb–Spruch), Rhetorical Criticism, and Qoheleth." *Journal of Biblical Literature* 96 (1977): 489–505.

Olivier, J. P. J. "Schools and Wisdom Literature." *Journal of Northwest Semitic Languages* 4 (1975): 49–60.

Oppenheim, A. L. *Ancient Mesopotamia: Portrait of a Dead Civilization.* Chicago: University of Chicago Press, 1964.

Otto, E. "Law and Ethics." Pages 84–97 in *Religions of the Ancient World: A Guide.* Edited by S. I. Johnston. Cambridge: Harvard University Press, 2004.

Otto, E. and W. Helck. *Lexicon der Ägyptologie.* 3 vols. Wiesbaden: Harrassowitz, 1975–1980.

Overland, P. "Structure in the Wisdom of Amenemope and Proverbs." Pages 275–91 in *"Go to the Land I Will Show You": Studies in Honor of Dwight W. Young.* Edited by J. Coleson and V. Matthews. Winona Lake: Eisenbrauns, 1996.

Pardee, D. *Ugaritic and Hebrew Poetic Parallelism: A Trial Cut ('nt I and Proverbs 2).* Supplements to Vetus Testamentum 39. Leiden: Brill, 1988.

Parker, S. B., ed. *Ugaritic Narrative Poetry*. Society of Biblical Literature Writings from the Ancient World 9. Atlanta: Scholars Press, 1997.

_____. "Graves, Caves and Refugees: A Study in Microhistory." *Journal for the Study of the Old Testament* 27 (2003): 259–88.

Parkinson, R. B. "Teachings, Discourses and Tales from the Middle Kingdom." Pages 91–122 in *Middle Kingdom Studies*. Edited by S. Quirke. New Malden: SIA Publishing, 1991.

_____. "Individual and Society in Middle Kingdom Literature." Pages 137–55 in *Ancient Egyptian Literature: History and Forms*. Edited by A. Loprieno. Leiden: E. J. Brill, 1996.

_____. *Poetry and Culture in Middle Kingdom Egypt: A Dark Side to Perfection*. London: Continuum, 2002.

Parpola, S. "The Man without a Scribe and the Question of Literacy in the Assyrian Empire." Pages 315–24 in *Beiträge zu altorientalischen und mittelmeerischen Kulturen: Festschrift für Wolfgang Röllig*. Edited by H. Kühne, B. Pongratz-Leisten, and P. Xella. Neukirchen-Vluyn: Neukirchener Verlag, 1997.

Parpola, S. and K. Watanabe. *Neo-Assyrian Treaties and Loyalty Oaths*. State Archives of Assyria 2. Helsinki: Helsinki University Press, 1988.

Pearce, L. E. "The Scribes and Scholars of Ancient Mesopotamia." Pages 2265–78 in *Civilizations of the Ancient Near East*. Edited by J. M. Sasson. New York: Charles Scribner's Sons, 1995.

Pemberton, G. D. "The Rhetoric of the Father: A Rhetorical Analysis of the Father/Son Lectures in Proverbs 1–9." PhD diss., The University of Denver, 1999.

_____. "The Rhetoric of the Father in Proverbs 1–9." *Journal for the Study of the Old Testament* 30 (2005): 63–82.

Penchansky, D. "Is Hokmah an Israelite Goddess, and What Should We Do About It?" Pages 81–92 in *Postmodern Interpretations of the Bible: A Reader*. Edited by A. K. M. Adam. St. Louis: Chalice, 2001.

Perdue, L. G. *Wisdom and the Cult: A Critical Analysis of the Views of Cult in the Wisdom Literatures of Israel and the Ancient Near East*. Society of Biblical Literature Dissertation Series 30. Missoula: Scholars Press, 1977.

_____. "Liminality as a Social Setting for Wisdom Instructions." *Zeitschrift für die alttestamentliche Wissenschaft* 93 (1981): 114–26.

_____. "Cosmology and the Social Order in the Wisdom Tradition." Pages 457–78 in *The Sage in Israel and the Ancient Near East*. Edited by J. G. Gammie and L. G. Perdue. Winona Lake: Eisenbrauns, 1990.

_____. *Wisdom and Creation: The Theology of Wisdom Literature*. Nashville: Abingdon, 1994.

_____. "Wisdom Theology and Social History in Proverbs 1–9." Pages 78–101 in *Wisdom, You Are My Sister: Studies in Honor of Roland E. Murphy, O. Carm., on the Occasion of His Eightieth Birthday*. Edited by M. L. Barré. Catholic Biblical Quarterly Monograph Series 29. Washington, D.C.: The Catholic Biblical Association of America, 1997.

_____. *Proverbs*. Interpretation: A Bible Commentary for Teaching and Preaching. Louisville: John Knox, 2000.

_____. *Wisdom Literature: A Theological History*. Louisville: Westminster John Knox, 2007.

_____. *The Sword and the Stylus: An Introduction to Wisdom in the Age of Empires.* Grand
        Rapids: Eerdmans, 2008.

Pleins, J. D. "Poverty in the Social World of the Wise." *Journal for the Study of the Old
        Testament* 37 (1987): 61–78.

_____. *The Social Visions of the Hebrew Bible: A Theological Introduction.* Louisville:
        Westminster John Knox, 2001.

Plöger, O. "Zur Auslegung der Sentenzensammlungen des Proverbienbuches." Pages 402–
        16 in *Probleme biblischer Theologie: Gerhard von Rad zum 70. Geburtstag.* Edited by H.
        W. Wolff. Münich: Kaiser Verlag, 1971.

_____. *Sprüche Salomos (Proverbia).* Biblischer Kommentar, Altes Testament 17.
        Neukirchen-Vluyn: Neukirchener Verlag, 1984.

Ploeg, J. van der. *Spreuken.* De Boeken van het Oude Testament 8. Roermond & Maaseik:
        Romen & Zonen, 1952.

_____. "Proverbs 25:23." *Vetus Testamentum* 3 (1953): 189–91.

Posener, G. *Littérature et politique dans l'Égypte de la XII Dynastie.* Bibliothéque de l'École des
        Hautes Études 307. Paris: Librairie Honoré Champion, 1969.

_____. *L'enseignement loyaliste: Sagesse égyptienne du Moyen Empire.* Centre de recherches
        d'historie et de philologie 2. Hautes études orientales 5. Geneva, 1976.

_____. "Lehre des Djedefhor." Pages 978–80 in *Lexikon der Ägyptologie.* Edited by
        E. Otto W. Helck. Wiesbaden: Harrassowitz, 1980.

Postgate, J. N. *Early Mesopotamia: Society and Economy at the Dawn of History.* London:
        Routledge, 1994.

Potts, D. T. *Mesopotamian Civilization: The Material Foundations.* Ithaca: Cornell University
        Press, 1997.

Quack, J. F. *Die Lehren des Ani: Ein neuägyptischer Weisheitstext in seinem kulturellen Umfeld.*
        Orbis biblicus et orientalis 141. Göttingen: Vandenhoeck & Ruprecht, 1994.

Quirke, S. *Egyptian Literature 1800 BC: Questions and Readings.* Egyptology 2. London:
        Golden House, 2004.

Rad, G. von. "Der Anfang der Geschichtsschreibung im alten Israel." Pages 148–88 in
        Gesammelte Studien zum Alten Testament. Theologische Bücherei: Neudrucke und
        Berichte aus dem 20. Jahrhundert 8. München: Chr. Kaiser, 1958.

_____. *Wisdom in Israel.* Translated by J. D. Martin. London: SCM Press, 1972.
        Translation of *Weisheit in Israel.* Neukirchen-Vluyn: Neukirchener Verlag, 1970.

Redford, D. B. *Egypt, Canaan, and Israel in Ancient Times.* Princeton: Princeton University
        Press, 1992.

_____, ed. *The Oxford Encyclopedia of Ancient Egypt.* 3 vols. Oxford: Oxford University
        Press, 2001.

_____. "Ancient Egyptian Literature: An Overview." Pages 2223–41 in *Civilizations of
        the Ancient Near East.* Edited by J. M. Sasson. Peabody: Hendrickson, 2006.

Renfroe, F. "The Effect of Redaction on the Structure of Prov 1,1–6." *Zeitschrift für die
        alttestamentliche Wissenschaft* 101 (1989): 290–93.

Richter, H.-F. "Hielt Agur sich für den Dümmsten aller Menschen? (Zu Prov 30,1–4)."
        Zeitschrift für alttestamentliche Wissenschaft 113 (2001): 419–21.

Richter, W. *Recht und Ethos: Versuch einer Ortung des weisheitlichen Mahnspruches.* Studien zum
        Alten und Neuen Testament 15. München: Kösel, 1966.

Ricoeur, P. *Interpretation Theory: Discourse and the Surplus of Meaning*. Fort Worth: The Texas Christian University Press, 1976.

——————. *The Rule of Metaphor*. Toronto: The University of Toronto Press, 1977.

Ringgren, H. *Word and Wisdom: Studies in the Hypostatization of Divine Qualities and Functions in the Ancient Near East*. Lund: H. Ohlson, 1947.

——————. *Sprüche*. Das Alte Testament Deutsch 16. Göttingen: Vandenhoeck & Ruprecht, 1981.

Römheld, K. D. F. *Wege der Weisheit: Die Lehren Amenemopes und Proverbien 22,17–24,22*. Beihefte zur Zeitschrift für die alttestamentliche Wissenschaft 184. Berlin: Walter de Gruyter, 1989.

——————. *Die Weisheitlehre im Alten Orient: Elemente einer Formgeschichte*. Biblische Notizen-Beiheft 4. München: Manfred Görg, 1989.

Roth, W. M. W. "NBL." *Vetus Testamentum* 10 (1960): 401–04.

——————. "The Numerical Sequence X/X + 1 in the Old Testament." *Vetus Testamentum* 12 (1962): 300–11.

——————. *Numerical Sayings in the Old Testament: A Form-Critical Study*. Supplements to Vetus Testamentum 13. Leiden: Brill, 1965.

Rüger, H. P. "Die gestaffelten Zahlensprüche des Alten Testaments und Aram. Achikar 92." *Vetus Testamentum* 31 (1981): 229–34.

Salvesen, A. "The Trappings of Royalty in Ancient Hebrew." Pages 119–41 in *King and Messiah in Israel and the Ancient Near East: Proceedings of the Oxford Old Testament Seminar*. Edited by J. Day. Journal for the Study of the Old Testament: Supplement Series 270. Sheffield: Sheffield Academic, 1998.

Sandoval, T. J. *The Discourse of Wealth and Poverty in the Book of Proverbs*. Biblical Interpretation Series 77. Leiden: Brill, 2006.

——————. "Revisiting the Prologue of Proverbs." *Journal of Biblical Literature* 126 (2007): 455–73.

Sauer, G. *Die Sprüche Agurs: Untersuchungen zur Herkunft, Verbreitung und Bedeutung einer biblischen Stilform unter besonderer Berücksichtigung von Proverbia c. 30*. Beiträge zur Wissenschaft vom Alten und Neuen Testament Fünfte Folge 84. Stuttgart: Kohlhammer, 1963.

Schäfer, R. *Die Poesie der Weisen: Dichotomie als Grundstruktur der Lehr– und Weisheitsgedichte in Proverbien 1–9*. Wissenschaftliche Monographien zum Alten und Neuen Testament 77. Neukirchen: Neukirchener Verlag, 1999.

Schenke, W. *Die Chokma (Sophia) in der jüdischen Hypostasen-Spekulation: Ein Beitrag zur Geschichte der religiösen Ideen im Zeitalter des Hellenismus*. Kristiana: Jacob Dybwad, 1913.

Scherer, A. "Is the Selfish Man Wise?: Considerations of Context in Proverbs 10.1–22.16 with Special Regard to Surety, Bribery and Friendship." *Journal for the Study of the Old Testament* 76 (1997): 59–70.

——————. *Das weise Wort und sein Wirkung: Eine Untersuchung zur Komposition und Redaktion von Proverbia 10,1–22,16*. Wissenschaftliche Monographien zum Alten und Neuen Testament 83. Neukirchen-Vluyn: Neukirchener Verlag, 1999.

Schmid, H. H. *Wesen und Geschichte der Weisheit: Eine Untersuchung zur altorientalischen und israelitischen Weisheitsliteratur*. Beihefte zur Zeitschrift für die alttestamentliche Wissenschaft 101. Berlin: A. Töpelmann, 1966.

_____. *Gerechtigkeit als Weltordnung: Hintergrund und Geschichte des alttestamentlichen Gerechtigkeitsbegriffs.* Beiträge zur historischen Theologie 40. Tübingen: Mohr, 1968.

_____. *Altorientalische Welt in der alttestamentliche Theologie.* Zürich: Theologischer Verlag, 1974.

Schmidt, J. *Studien zur Stilistik der alttestamentlichen Spruchliteratur.* Alttestamentliche Abhandlungen 13. Münster: Aschendorfer Verlag, 1936.

Schniedewind, W. M. *How the Bible Became a Book.* Cambridge: Cambridge University Press, 2004.

Schöckel, L. Alonso and J. Vilchez. *Proverbios.* Nueva Biblia Española. Sapienciales I. Madrid: Ediciones Cristiandad, 1984.

Schroer, S. "Wise and Counseling Women in Ancient Israel: Literary and Historical Ideals of the Personified Hokmâ." Pages 67–84 in *A Feminist Companion to Wisdom Literature.* Edited by A. Brenner. Sheffield: Sheffield Academic Press, 1995.

_____. *Die Weisheit hat ihr Haus gebaut: Studien zur Gestalt der Sophia in den biblischen Schriften.* Mainz: Matthias-Grünewald, 1996.

_____. *Wisdom Has Built Her House: Studies on the Figure of Sophia in the Bible.* Translated by L. M. Maloney and W. McDonough. Collegeville: Liturgical Press, 2000.

Scoralick, R. *Einzelspruch und Sammlung.* Beihefte zur Zeitschrift für die alttestamentliche Wissenschaft 232. Berlin: Walter de Gruyter, 1995.

Scott, R. B. Y. "Weights and Measures of the Bible." *Biblical Archaeologist* 22 (1959): 22–40.

_____. *Proverbs, Ecclesiastes: Introduction, Translation, and Notes.* Anchor Bible 18. Garden City: Doubleday, 1965.

_____. *The Way of Wisdom in the Old Testament.* New York: Macmillan, 1971.

_____. "Wise and Foolish, Righteous and Wicked." *Vetus Testamentum* 23 (1972): 146–65. Repr. pages 145–65 in *Studies in the Religion of Ancient Israel.* Edited by G. W. Anderson. Leiden: E. J. Brill, 1972.

_____. "Folk Proverbs of the Ancient Near East." *Transactions of the Royal Society of Canada* 55 (1961): 47–56. Repr. pages 417–26 in *Studies in Ancient Israelite Wisdom.* Edited by J. L. Crenshaw. New York: Ktav, 1976.

Seeligmann, I. L. "Zur Terminologie für das Gerichtsverfahren im Wortschatz des biblischen Hebräisch." Supplements to Vetus Testamentum 16 (1967): 251–78.

Segal, M. L. *The Pentateuch: Its Composition and its Authorship and other Biblical Studies.* Jerusalem: Magnes, 1967.

Seibert, P. *Die Charakteristik: Untersuchung zu einer altägyptischen Sprechsitte und ihren Ausprägungen in Folklore und Literatur.* Ägyptologische Abhandlungen 17. Wiesbaden: Harrassowitz, 1967.

Seitel, P. "Proverbs: A Social Use of Metaphor." Pages 125–43 in *Folklore Genres.* Edited by D. Ben-Amos. Austin: University of Texas Press, 1976.

Sheppard, G. T. *Wisdom as a Hermeneutical Construct: A Study in the Sapientializing of the Old Testament.* Beihefte zur Zeitschrift für die alttestamentliche Wissenschaft 151. Berlin: de Gruyter, 1981.

Shupak, N. "The 'Sitz Im Leben' of the Book of Proverbs in the Light of a Comparison of Biblical and Egyptian Wisdom Literature," *Revue biblique* 94 (1987): 98–119.

_____. *Where Can Wisdom Be Found? The Sage's Language in the Bible and in Ancient Egyptian Literature.* Orbis biblicus et orientalis 130. Göttingen: Vandenhoeck & Ruprecht, 1993.

_____. "The Instruction of Amenemope and Proverbs 22:17–24:22 from the Perspective of Contemporary Research." Pages 203–20 in *Seeking out the Wisdom of the Ancients: Essays Offered to Honor Michael V. Fox on the Occasion of His Sixty-Fifth Birthday*. Edited by R. L. Troxel, K. G. Friebel, and D. R. Magary. Winona Lake: Eisenbrauns, 2005.

Silverman, D. P. "Divinity and Deities in Ancient Egypt." Pages 7–87 in *Religion in Ancient Egypt: Gods, Myths, and Personal Practice*. Edited by B. E. Shafer. Ithaca: Cornell University Press, 1991.

Simpson, W. K. *The Literature of Ancient Egypt: An Anthology of Stories, Instructions, Stelae, Autobiographies, and Poetry*. 3rd ed. New Haven: Yale Press, 2003.

Singer, K. H. *Die Metalle Gold, Silber, Bronze, Kupfer und Eisen im Alten Testament und ihre Symbolik*. Forschung zur Bibel 43. Würzburg: Echter, 1980.

Sinnott, A. M. *The Personification of Wisdom*. Society for Old Testament Study Monographs. Burlington: Ashgate, 2005.

Sjöberg, Å. W. "The Old Babylonian Eduba." Pages 159–79 in *Sumerological Studies in Honor of Thorkild Jacobsen on His Seventieth Birthday*. Edited by S. J Lieberman. Chicago: The University of Chicago Press, 1976.

Skehan, P. *Studies in Israelite Poetry and Wisdom*. Catholic Biblical Quarterly Monograph Series 1. Washington, D.C.: The Catholic Biblical Association of America, 1971.

_____. "Structures in Poems on Wisdom: Proverbs 8 and Sirach 24." *Catholic Biblical Quartery* 41 (1979): 365–79.

Skladny, U. *Die ältesten Spruchsammlungen in Israel*. Göttingen: Vandenhoeck & Ruprecht, 1962.

Smith, C. "'Queenship' in Israel? The Cases of Bathsheba, Jezebel and Athaliah." Pages 142–62 in *King and Messiah in Israel and the Ancient Near East: Proceedings of the Oxford Old Testament Seminar*. Edited by J. Day. Journal for the Study of the Old Testament: Supplement Series 270. Sheffield: Sheffield Academic Press, 1998.

Sneed, M. "Wisdom and Class: A Review and Critique." *Journal of the American Academy of Religion* 62 (1994): 651–72.

_____. "The Class Culture of Proverbs: Eliminating Stereotypes." *Scandinavian Journal of the Old Testament* 10 (1996): 296–308.

_____. "A Middle Class in Ancient Israel." Pages 53–69 in *Concepts of Class in Ancient Israel*. Edited by M. Sneed. Atlanta: Scholars Press, 1999.

Snell, D. C. "'Taking Souls' in Proverbs 11:30." *Vetus Testamentum* 33 (1983): 362–65.

_____. "The Most Obscure Verse in Proverbs: Proverbs 26:10." *Vetus Testamentum* 41 (1991): 350–56.

_____. *Twice-Told Proverbs and the Composition of the Book of Proverbs*. Winona Lake: Eisenbrauns, 1993.

_____. *Life in the Ancient Near East: 3100–332 B.C.E.* New Haven: Yale University Press, 1997.

Snijders, L. A. *The Meaning of zar in The Old Testament*. Old Testament Studies 10. Leiden: Brill, 1954.

Stähli, H. P. *Knabe–Jüngling–Knecht: Untersuchungen zum Begriff Na'ar im Alten Testament*. Beiträge zur biblischen Exegese und Theologie 7. Frankfurt: Peter Lang, 1978.

Stager, L. E. "The Archaeology of the Family in Ancient Israel." *Bulletin of the American Schools of Oriental Research* 260 (1985): 1–35.

Steiert, F.-J. *Die Weisheit Israels—ein Fremdkörper im Alten Testament?: eine Untersuchung zum Buch der Sprüche auf dem Hintergrund der ägyptischen Weisheitslehren.* Freiburger Theologische Studien 143. Freiburg: Herder, 1990.

Steinmann, A. E. "Three Things...Four Things...Seven Things: The Coherence of Proverbs 30:11–33 and the Unity of Proverbs 30." *Hebrew Studies* 42 (2001): 59–66.

Sternberg, M. *The Poetics of Biblical Narrative.* Bloomington: Indiana University Press, 1987.

Storøy, S. "Why Does the Theme of Poverty Come into the Context of Prov 14:20?" Pages 298–318 in *Text and Theology: Studies in Honour of Professor Dr. Theol. Magne Saebø.* Edited by A. Tångberg. Oslo: Verbum, 1994.

Sweet, R. F. G. "The Sage in Akkadian Literature: A Philological Study." Pages 45–65 in *The Sage in Israel and the Ancient Near East.* Edited by J. G. Gammie and L. G. Perdue. Winona Lake: Eisenbrauns, 1990.

_____. "The Sage in Mesopotamian Palaces and Royal Courts." Pages 99–107 in *The Sage in Israel and the Ancient Near East.* Edited by J. G. Gammie and L. G. Perdue. Winona Lake: Eisenbrauns, 1990.

Szlos, M. B. "A Portrait of Power: A Literary-Critical Study of the Depiction of the Woman in Proverbs 31:10–31." *Union Seminary Quarterly Review* 54 (2000): 97–103.

_____. "Body Parts as Metaphor and the Value of a Cognitive Appraoch. A Study of the Female Figures in Proverbs via Metaphor." Pages 185–95 in *Metaphor in the Hebrew Bible.* Edited by P. van Hecke. Leuven: Leuven University Press, 2005.

Tan, N. Nam Hoon. *The 'Foreignness' of the Foreign Woman in Proverbs 1–9: A Study of the Origin and Development of a Biblical Motif.* Beihefte zur Zeitschrift für die alttestamentliche Wissenschaft 381. Berlin: Walter de Gruyter, 2008.

Tavares, R. *Eine königliche Weisheitslehre? Exegetische Analyse von Sprüche 28–29 und Vergleich mit den ägyptischen Lehren Merikaras und Amenemhats.* Orbis biblicus et orientalis 234. Göttingen: Vandenhoeck & Ruprecht, 2007.

Thériault, C. A. "The Instruction of Amenemhet as Propaganda." *Journal of the American Research Center in Egypt* 30 (1993): 151–60.

Thissen, H. J. *Die Lehre des Anchscheshonqi (p. BM 10508).* Papyrologische Texte und Anhandlungen 32. Bonn: Habelt, 1984.

Thomas, D. W. "The Root *snh = sny* in Hebrew, II." *Zeitschrift für die alttestamentliche Wissenschaft* 55 (1937): 174–76.

Thompson, J. M. *The Form and Function of Proverbs in Ancient Israel.* Paris: Mouton, 1974.

Torrey, C. "Proverbs, Chapter 30." *Journal of Biblical Literature* 73 (1954): 93–103.

Tov, E. "Recensional Differences Between the Masoretic Text and the Septuagint of the Book of Proverbs." Pages 419–32 in *The Greek and Hebrew Bible: Collected Essays on the Septuagint.* Leiden: Brill, 1999.

Townsend, T. P. "The Poor in Wisdom Literature." *Bible Bhashyam* 14 (1988): 5–25.

Toy, C. H. *The Book of Proverbs.* International Critical Commentary. Edinburgh: T&T Clark, 1899.

van den Boorn, G. P. F. *The Duties of the Vizier: Civil Administration in the Early New Kingdom.* Edited by W. V. Davies. Studies in Egyptology. London: Kegan Paul, 1988.

van Dijk-Hemmes, F. "The I Persona in Proverbs 7." Pages 57–61 in *On Gendering Texts: Female and Male Voices in the Hebrew Bible.* Edited by A. Brenner and F. van Dijk-Hemmes. Leiden: Brill, 1993.

van der Toorn, K. "Female Prostitution in Payment of Vows in Ancient Israel." *Journal of Biblical Literature* 108 (1989): 193–205.

_____. *Scribal Culture and the Making of the Hebrew Bible.* Cambridge: Harvard University Press, 2007.

Van Leeuwen, R. C. "Proverbs 30:21–23 and the Biblical World Upside Down." *Journal of Biblical Literature* 105 (1986): 599–610.

_____. "Proverbs XXV 27 Once Again." *Vetus Testamentum* 36 (1986): 105–14.

_____. "A Technical Metallurgical Usage of axy." *Zeitschrift für alttestamentliche Wissenschaft* 98 (1986): 112–13.

_____. *Context and Meaning in Proverbs 25–27.* Society of Biblical Literature Dissertation Series 96. Atlanta: Scholars Press, 1988.

_____. "Liminality and Worldview in Proverbs 1–9." *Semeia* 50 (1990): 111–44.

_____. "Wealth and Poverty: System and Contradiction in Proverbs." *Hebrew Studies* 33 (1992): 25–36.

_____. "The Background to Proverbs 30:4aα." Pages 102–21 in *Wisdom, You Are My Sister: Studies in Honor of Roland E. Murphy, O. Carm., on the Occasion of His Eightieth Birthday.* Edited by M. L. Barré. Catholic Biblical Quarterly Monograph Series 29. Washington, D.C.: The Catholic Biblical Association of America, 1997.

_____. "The Book of Proverbs: Introduction, Commentary, and Reflections." Pages 19–264 in *The New Interpreter's Bible.* Nashville: Abingdon, 1997.

_____. "Cosmos, Temple, House: Building and Wisdom in Mesopotamia and Israel." Pages 67–90 in *Wisdom Literature in Mesopotamia and Israel.* Society of Biblical Literature Symposium Series 36. Atlanta: Society of Biblical Literature, 2007.

Vawter, B. "Prov 8:22: Wisdom and Creation." *Journal of Biblical Literature* 9 (1980): 205–16.

Veenhof, K. R. *Aspects of Old Assyrian Trade and Its Terminology.* Studia et Documenta ad Iura Orientis Antiqui Pertinentia 10. Leiden: E. J. Brill, 1972.

te Velde, H. "Scribes and Literacy in Ancient Egypt." Pages 253–64 in *Scripta Signa Vocis: Studies about Scripts, Scriptures, Scribes and Languages in the Near East Presented to J. H. Hospers by His Pupils, Colleagues and Friends.* Edited by H. L. J. Vanstiphout, K. Jongeling, F. Leemhuis, and G. J. Reinink. Groningen: Egbert Forsten, 1986.

Vernus, P. "Le discours politique de l'*Enseignement de Ptahhotep.*" Pages 139–52 in *Literatur und Politik im pharaonischen und ptolemäischen Ägypten: Vorträge der Tagung zum Gedenken an Georges Posener 5.–10. September 1996 in Leipzig.* Edited by J. Assmann and E. Blumenthal. Cairo: Institut Français d'Archéologie Orientale, 1999.

Vogt, P. T. *Deuteronomic Theology and the Significance of Torah: A Reappraisal.* Winona Lake: Eisenbrauns, 2006.

Volk, K. "Edubba'a und Edubba'a—Literatur; Rätsel und Lösungen." *Zeitschrift für Assyriologie* 90 (2000): 1–30.

Waltke B. K., and M. O'Connor. *An Introduction to Biblical Hebrew Syntax.* Winona Lake: Eisenbrauns, 1990.

Waltke, B. K. "The Book of Proverbs and Ancient Wisdom Literature." *Bibliotheca sacra* 136 (1979): 221–38.

_____. "The Role of the 'Valiant Wife' in the Marketplace." *Crux* 35 (1999): 23–34.

_____. *The Book of Proverbs: Chapters 1–15.* New International Commentary on the Old Testament. Grand Rapids: Eerdmans, 2004.

_____. *The Book of Proverbs: Chapters 15–31.* New International Commentary on the Old Testament. Grand Rapids: Eerdmans, 2005.

Washington, H. C. "The Strange Woman (אִשָּׁה זָרָה/נָכְרִיָּה) of Proverbs 1–9 and Post-Exilic
     Judean Society." Pages 217–42 in *Second Temple Studies 2. Temple and Community in
     the Persian Period.* Edited by T. C. Eskenazi and K. H. Richards. Sheffield: JSOT,
     1994.

     ————. *Wealth and Poverty in the Instruction of Amenemope and the Hebrew Proverbs.* Society of
     Biblical Literature Dissertation Series 142. Atlanta: Scholars Press, 1994.

Watson, W. G. E. *Classical Hebrew Poetry: A Guide to Its Techniques.* Journal for the Study of
     the Old Testament: Supplement Series 26. Sheffield: JSOT, 1984.

Weeks, S. *Early Israelite Wisdom.* Oxford Monograph Series. Oxford: Oxford University
     Press, 1994.

     ————. *Instruction and Imagery in Proverbs 1–9.* Oxford: Oxford University Press, 2007.

Weinfeld, M. *Deuteronomy and the Deuteronomic School.* Oxford: Clarendon, 1972.

     ————. "The Counsel of 'Elders' to Rehoboam and Its Implications." *Maarav* 3 (1982):
     27–53.

     ————. "Justice and Righteousness—מִשְׁפָּט וּצְדָקָה—the Expression and Its Meaning."
     Pages 228–46 in *Justice and Righteousness: Biblical Themes and Their Influence.* Edited
     by H. G. Reventlow and Y. Hoffman. Sheffield: Sheffield Academic Press, 1992.

Wente, E. F. "The Scribes of Ancient Egypt." Pages 2211–21 in *Civilizations of the Ancient
     Near East.* Edited by J. M. Sasson. New York: Charles Scribner's Sons, 1995.

Westermann, C. "Weisheit im Sprichwort." Pages 73–85 in *Schalom: Studien zu Glaube und
     Geschichte Israels. Alfred Jepsen zum 70. Geburtstag.* Edited by K. H. Bernhardt.
     Stuttgart: Calwer, 1971.

     ————. *Forschungsgeschichte zur Weisheitsliteratur 1950–1990.* Arbeiten zur Theologie 71.
     Stuttgart: Calwer Verlag, 1991.

     ————. *Roots of Wisdom: The Oldest Proverbs of Israel and Other Peoples.* Translated by J. D.
     Charles. Louisville: Westminster John Knox, 1995.

Whitelam, K. W. *The Just King: Monarchical and Judicial Authority in Ancient Israel.* Journal for
     the Study of the Old Testament: Supplement Series 12. Sheffield: JSOT, 1979.

Whybray, R. N. *Wisdom in Proverbs: The Concept of Wisdom in Proverbs 1–9.* Studies in Biblical
     Theology 45. Naperville: Allenson, 1965.

     ————. *The Intellectual Tradition of the Old Testament.* Beihefte zur Zeitschrift für die
     alttestamentliche Wissenschaft 135. Berlin: de Gruyter, 1974.

     ————. "Poverty, Wealth and Point of View in Proverbs." *Expository Times* 100 (1988–
     89): 332–36.

     ————. "The Sage in the Israelite Royal Court." Pages 133–39 in *The Sage in Israel and
     the Ancient Near East.* Edited by J. G. Gammie and L. G. Perdue. Winona Lake:
     Eisenbrauns, 1990.

     ————. *Wealth and Poverty in the Book of Proverbs.* Journal for the Study of the Old
     Testament: Supplement Series 99. Sheffield: Sheffield Academic Press, 1990.

     ————. "Yahweh-Sayings and Their Contexts in Proverbs 10,1–22,16." Pages 153–65
     in *La Sagesse de l'Ancien Testament.* Edited by M. Gilbert. Bibliotheca ephemeridum
     theologicarum lovaniensium 51. Gembloux: Duculot, 1979. Repr., Leuven:
     Leuven University Press, 1990.

     ————. "Thoughts on the Composition of Proverbs 10–29." Pages 102–14 in *Priests,
     Prophets and Scribes: Essays on the Formation and Heritage of Second Temple Judaism in
     Honour of Joseph Blenkinsopp.* Edited by E. Ulrich, J. W. Wright, R. P. Carroll, and
     P. R. Davies. Sheffield: Sheffield Academic Press, 1992.

_____. "The Social World of the Wisdom Writers." Pages 227–50 in *The World of Ancient Israel: Sociological, Anthropological and Political Perspectives.* Edited by R. E. Clements. Cambridge: Cambridge University Press, 1989. Repr., 1993.

_____. "The Structure and Composition of Proverbs 22:17–24:22." Pages 83–96 in *Crossing the Boundaries: Essays in Biblical Interpretation in Honour of Michael D. Goulder.* Edited by S. E. Porter, P. Joyce, and D. E. Orton. Leiden: Brill, 1994.

_____. *Proverbs.* New Century Bible. Grand Rapids: Eerdmans, 1994.

_____. *The Composition of the Book of Proverbs.* Journal for the Study of the Old Testament: Supplement Series 168. Sheffield: Sheffield Academic Press, 1994.

_____. *The Book of Proverbs: A Survey of Modern Study.* History of Biblical Interpretation Series 1. Leiden: E. J. Brill, 1995.

_____. "City Life in Proverbs 1–9." Pages 243–50 in *"Jedes Ding hat seine Zeit...": Studien zur israelitischen und altorientalischen Weisheit.* Edited by O. Kaiser. New York: Walter de Gruyter, 1996.

Wilcke, C. "Philologische Bemerkungen zum *Rat des Suruppag* und Versuch einer neuen Übersetzung." *Zeitschrift für Assyriologie* 68 (1978): 196–232.

Wilke, A. F. *Kronerben der Weisheit: Gott, König und Frommer in der didaktischen Literatur Ägyptens und Israels.* Forschungen zum Alten Testament 20. Tübingen: Mohr, 2006.

Wilson, F. M. "Sacred and Profane? The Yahwistic Redaction of Proverbs Reconsidered." Pages 313–34 in *The Listening Heart: Essays in Wisdom and the Psalms in Honor of Roland E. Murphy, O. Carm.* Edited by K. G. Hoglund, E. F. Huwiler, J. T. Glass, and R. W. Lee. Sheffield: Sheffield Academic Press, 1989.

Winter, U. *Frau und Göttin: Exegetische und ikonographische Studien zum weiblichen Gottesbild im alten Israel und in dessen Umwelt.* Orbis biblicus et orientalis 53. Göttingen: Vandenhoeck & Ruprecht, 1987.

Wolters, A. "Proverbs XXXI 10–31 as Heroic Hymn: A Form-Critical Analysis." *Vetus Testamentum* 4 (1988): 446–57. Repr. pages 3–14 in *The Song of the Valiant Woman: Studies in the Interpretation of Proverbs 31:10–31.* Carlisle: Paternoster, 2001.

_____. "The Meaning of *Kîsôr* (Prov. 31:19)." *Hebrew Union College Annual* 65 (1994): 91–104.

_____. *The Song of the Valiant Woman: Studies in the Interpretation of Proverbs 31:10–31.* Carlisle: Paternoster, 2001.

Yardeni, A. and B. Porten. *Textbook of Aramaic Documents from Ancient Egypt: Volume 3: Literature, Accounts, Lists.* Hebrew University, Dept. of the History of the Jewish People, Texts and Studies for Students; Jerusalem: Hebrew University, 1993.

Yee, G. A. "An Analysis of Prov 8:22–31 According to Style and Structure." *Zeitschrift für die alttestamentliche Wissenschaft* 94 (1982): 58–66.

_____. "'I Have Perfumed My Bed with Myrrh': The Foreign Woman (*iššâ zārâ*) in Proverbs 1–9." *Journal for the Study of the Old Testament* 43 (1989): 53–68.

_____. "The Theology of Creation in Proverbs 8:22–31." Pages 85–96 in *Creation in Biblical Traditions.* Edited by R. J. Clifford and J. J. Collins. Washington, D.C.: The Catholic Biblical Association of America, 1992.

Yoder, C. R. *Wisdom as a Woman of Substance: A Socioeconomic Reading of Proverbs 1–9 and 31:10–31.* Beihefte zur Zeitschrift für die alttestamentliche Wissenschaft 304. Berlin: Walter de Gruyter, 2001.

_____. "Forming 'Fearers of Yahweh': Repetition and Contradiction as Pedagogy in Proverbs." Pages 167–83 in *Seeking out the Wisdom of the Ancients: Essays Offered to Honor Michael V. Fox on the Occasion of His Sixty-Fifth Birthday*. Edited by K. G. Friebel, R. L. Troxel, and D. R. Magary. Winona Lake: Eisenbrauns, 2005.

Zimmerli, W. "Concerning the Structure of Old Testament Wisdom." Pages 175–207 in *Studies in Ancient Israelite Wisdom*. Edited by J. L. Crenshaw. New York: Ktav, 1976.

_____. "The Place and Limit of the Wisdom in the Framework of the Old Testament Theology." *Scottish Journal of Theology* 17 (1964): 146–58. Repr. pages 314–26 in *Studies in Ancient Israelite Wisdom*. Edited by J. L. Crenshaw. New York: Ktav, 1976.

_____. *Old Testament Theology in Outline*. Atlanta: John Knox, 1978.

Zybnek, Z. *Les Maximes de Ptahhotep*. Prague: Editions de l'Académie Tchécoslovaque des Sciences, 1956.

Index of Ancient Sources

Index of Authors